Grantlee Kieza is a prize-winning writer for the *Courier-Mail* and *Sunday Mail* newspapers in Brisbane. He has previously written for Sydney's *Daily Telegraph*, *Sunday Telegraph*, *The Australian* and *Sun-Herald*, covering assignments as diverse as adventure races in the Adirondack Mountains of New York, anti-apartheid activism in Soweto and boxing matches everywhere from Melbourne and Mexico to Manchester and Manhattan — and many other places that don't start with M. He was a finalist in the 2011 Walkley Awards for Excellence in Journalism. This is his eighth book.

BERT HINKLER

*The Most Daring Man
in the World*

Grantlee Kieza

ABC
Books

The ABC 'Wave' device is a trademark of the
Australian Broadcasting Corporation and is used
under licence by HarperCollins*Publishers* Australia.

First published in Australia in 2012
This edition published in 2013
by HarperCollins*Publishers* Australia Pty Limited
ABN 36 009 913 517
harpercollins.com.au

HarperCollins*Publishers*
Level 13, 201 Elizabeth Street, Sydney NSW 2000, Australia
31 View Road, Glenfield, Auckland 0627, New Zealand
A 53, Sector 57, Noida, UP, India
77–85 Fulham Palace Road, London W6 8JB, United Kingdom
2 Bloor Street East, 20th floor, Toronto, Ontario M4W 1A8, Canada
10 East 53rd Street, New York NY 10022, USA

National Library of Australia Cataloguing-in-Publication entry:

Kieza, Grantlee.
  Bert Hinkler : the most daring man in the world / Grantlee Kieza.
  978 0 7333 3223 4 (pbk.)
  978 1 7430 9654 3 (ebook)
  Hinkler, Bert, 1892-1933.
  Air pilots – Australia – Biography.
  Aeronautics – Australia – History.
  Australian Broadcasting Commission.
629.13092

Cover design by Matt Stanton, HarperCollins Design Studio
Front cover images: Bert Hinkler in his World War I uniform, courtesy of the
  Courier-Mail; Bert with the Avro Baby in Gavin Street, Bundaberg, courtesy of
  Hinkler Hall of Aviation Memorabilia Trust
Back cover image of Bert with his Avro Avian in England before his epic solo flight
  to Australia, courtesy of Hinkler Hall of Aviation Memorabilia Trust
Printed and bound in Australia by Griffin Press
The papers used by HarperCollins in the manufacture of this book
are a natural, recyclable product made from wood grown in sustainable
plantation forests. The fibre source and manufacturing processes meet
recognised international environmental standards, and carry certification.

5 4 3 2 1   13 14 15 16

For Gloria Kieza,
who has always put the other person first.
With love and gratitude ...

Chapter 1

Flight ever fascinated me!
**The first words of Bert Hinkler's
unfinished autobiography, 1932**

*Please convey to Mr Hinkler the expression of my
warmest congratulations on his splendid achievement.
I have been following his flight with the keenest interest
and I am delighted that he has been successful.*
King George V, 22 February 1928

Benito Mussolini was a worried man as he ran his thick, stubby fingers over his freshly shaved skull. It had been three and a half months since his hero Bert Hinkler slipped away from the almost deserted clutch of sheds at the aerodrome beside the ancient village of Heath Row in London's west and disappeared; a silvery ghost vanishing into a dark and foggy void.

The world's press had spent every hour since his mysterious departure speculating over his fate, and the Fascist ruler of Italy paced restlessly across the marble floors of Rome's magnificent Villa Torlonia. For weeks, Il Duce had prowled the corridors and chambers of his ornate white palace, past the many portraits of himself, anxious over the disappearance of an adventurer he so admired, a man whose daring and talent summed up everything Mussolini envisaged a superman to be. The Italians had invented aerial conflict, after all, and Mussolini had a fascination with aircraft and the men who harnessed their power.[1]

Charles Lindbergh, Charles Kingsford Smith and his own Francesco de Pinedo — whom he called the Lord of the Distances — were among Mussolini's heroes,[2] but it was Hinkler's epic solo flights that had enthralled him ever since the plucky Australian made a world-record air journey from London to Turin in 1920 while Italy was still recovering from the bloodletting that had ensnared Europe. That flight came as Mussolini was about to train as a pilot and to the Fascists there was no more overt symbol of masculinity than a man riding a flying machine high into the heavens to taunt the gods.

'Nothing seduces women as flying does,' Mussolini's Air Ministry journal once proclaimed, and the dictator knew that few things highlighted his image of masculinity and passion more than taking the controls of an aircraft himself.[3]

In April 1933, however, with Bert Hinkler having disappeared somewhere over Italy, events on the world stage were moving too fast for Mussolini's liking. There were problems in Africa he'd have to stamp out, and Hitler — he didn't like the look of him, for a start — was becoming more of a threat than a nuisance, igniting firestorms everywhere.[4] The Hinkler mystery only heightened Il Duce's tension.

Few apart from the airman's widowed mother, Mrs Frances Hinkler back home in Bundaberg, Queensland, believed there was any hope of ever seeing Bert again, and even she was more stressed than her family could remember.

Behind the latticework of her humble weatherboard home, 16,000 kilometres from Mussolini's opulent headquarters, the formidable 'Old Lady' Hinkler, as the neighbours knew her, kept up a brave public face, but sleep was a stranger to her. Every morning since Bert had vanished she scanned the newspapers with tired, red eyes behind her wire-rimmed spectacles. There was precious little information about the search. Precious little that was encouraging, anyway. When Bert had first gone missing the papers in Queensland were also reporting on the national elections in Germany and the faint hopes of a somewhat eccentric housepainter with a Charlie Chaplin moustache. Now, just three months later, the same papers were informing readers of Herr Hitler's attacks on the Jews and Communists.

The press had been full of cricket news, too, all about Don Bradman's battles with that Douglas Jardine fellow and how the Englishman Harold Larwood was bowling what they called 'Bodyline'. To Frances, all that was a waste of paper and ink. She just wanted news of her son.

Somehow, somewhere, in some way she prayed her boy — for he was still her boy even though he was now forty — was still alive and finding his way back home.

She reminded herself that Bert was smart enough to do anything. As a boy he'd never even seen an aeroplane when he took her ironing board and some junk he'd scrounged and built his own flying machine, soaring high above the beautiful blue surf of Mon Repos beach. He broke world flying records while most of Bundaberg, including the rest of her family, still travelled by horse and buggy. Then he flew halfway round the world — twice — with no co-pilot, no radio, no navigator, no financial backing — just a compass, a page from an atlas perched on his lap and a pocket torch in case he had to land in the dark.

Frances had known exactly what her boy could do since the days she'd towed his first flying machine behind her buggy through Bundaberg's verdant cane fields and watched him experiment with flight until he finally soared like the birds that had inspired him. She knew all about his courage and resourcefulness as a World War I pilot and then as the greatest solo aviator the world had seen. She thought she knew him back to front. But as it would transpire, there was also much about Squadron Leader Herbert John Louis Hinkler AFC, DSM that she didn't know and that he had kept securely hidden from the rest of the world. He was a man full of secrets.

Bert's life had been a marriage of courage and enterprise but, as Frances would soon learn, not only did he have a 'wife' in England, he also had a wife in the USA. When he left Heath Row just after three o'clock on that winter's morning of 7 January 1933, with the runway illuminated by the headlights of a friend's Rolls-Royce, his whole life was swathed in shadows.

In the midst of the Great Depression, Bert was a sad and weary man. His clandestine life was beginning to unravel, the world around him spiralling out of control like the planes he'd shot down in aerial warfare. Forty, childless and with a heavy heart, he had seen the stock markets collapse and his brilliant inventions and business ideas wither. There were rumours that Mussolini was planning to invade Ethiopia, and who knew what Hitler had planned for Germany?

Ahead of Bert was his most daring journey yet: 32,000 kilometres — first from London to Australia and then on to Canada — a journey he believed would set the world of flight on its head yet again. To sustain him he carried six sandwiches — one egg, two cheese and three made from tongue. He had three Thermos flasks of sugarless black coffee, another Thermos of water and four bottles of stout. Inside his breast pocket he carried a love letter from one of the two women who claimed to be his wife and ten small photos of a young woman standing next to an aeroplane.

But as Bert said farewell to his three-legged cat and his cottage in the woods near Southampton and set off on that dark morning to conquer the world yet again, he believed his great odyssey could change his life. Like the Phoenix, he would rise once more, sort out his tangled love life and again be hailed as the man who revolutionised air transport. He had written the first chapter of his autobiography with the promise to his publishers of more thrilling instalments. He said his goodbyes to the two friends who met him at the aerodrome, and then flew for six hours and fifty-five minutes before marking his log as he saw the River Arno wind its way through the glorious undulations of the Tuscan hills he knew well. Then he headed towards Florence and the Pratomagno mountains nearby.

Bert wasn't worried by the spiteful weather. His faithful Puss Moth with its tiny, trusty engine had once carried him down the Atlantic coasts of North and South America and across the South Atlantic to Africa through vicious gales. At times on that epic journey, with only a little pet monkey to keep him company, he had flown just 1.5 metres above huge rolling ocean waves to dodge thunderstorms. He believed his plane could survive any raging fury these mountains hurled at him.

Then, as the foul weather above Italy closed in, something utterly bizarre occurred. Something so freakish that it still confounds aircraft experts to this day. The tiny plane that had served Bert so admirably in so many perilous situations suddenly fell out of the sky and onto an Italian mountain.

Somehow Bert survived the shuddering, bone-jarring impact that crushed his plane like a tin can. He dragged his battered body from the crumpled wreckage and, minus his left shoe and his flying helmet, which had had been torn off in the crash, he crawled and rolled 80 metres down a slope before collapsing from shock and the effects of a gaping head wound. Blood gushed from lacerations all over his body where he had been catapulted against jagged metal.

In the Great War, Bert had survived many machine-gun battles with the Germans — thousands of feet in the air — and ever since he'd come through unscathed from close shaves travelling the globe. But were his secrets about to die with him on this lonely mountain?

High up on the freezing, barren rock of Pratomagno, Bert crossed his left foot over his right shoe, turned onto his side and tried to rest. Waves of nausea made him dizzy. As unconsciousness crept upon him, the cold bit his bloody face. The warm blood dripping like a tap from his head wound felt thick and sticky against his icy skin.

As he lay there, wrecked, high up in the mountains, the only noise was his laboured breathing, the driving wind and the soft footsteps of a hungry wolf.

Chapter 2

Bert Hinkler was born on 8 December 1892 in an age
bursting with energy and enthusiasm. Across the globe
new ideas and mind-boggling inventions were emerging,
delivering a whole new world of scientific wonder. For
Bert it was a time ripe for adventure and discovery as
things that were fantasy to his parents' generation became
everyday reality.

It was also an age borne of pain. A generation earlier
Europe had been on the move, and on a crowded dock
beside the River Elbe in Hamburg, ten-year-old Johann
Wilhelm Hinkler huddled beside his heavily pregnant
mother and gazed with excitement and awe at the sailing
ship that would carry his family to the other side of the
world. Johann's mother Anna was holding on tightly to
everything she held dear: her four frightened, confused

children, the baby jumping restlessly in her belly and her husband Ludwig Volk. It was 5 August 1865 and, amid the noise and bustle, people all around this tight family group were weeping and choking on their final goodbyes to loved ones they would never see again.

The three-masted barque *La Rochelle* rocked listlessly as it waited to carry Johann's family and 466 other desperate passengers to a place called Moreton Bay far, far away in the new colony of Queensland on the east coast of Australia. It would be a world so very different from the village of Hornsheim they were leaving in war-ravaged Prussia. *La Rochelle* was owned by German shipping magnate Johann Cesar Godeffroy, whose boats were death traps. The goodbyes were understandably anguished. Men with Father Christmas beards cuddled pale, sweating children for one final time, whispering, '*Auf wiedersehen, meine liebe,*' between sobs.

Napoleon's savage thrusts through the heart of Europe had left millions dead from warfare and disease and caused deep wounds that festered decades later. Many impoverished Germans could do nothing but flee their parlous circumstances. Queensland had separated from the colony of New South Wales in 1859 and, by 1865, was home to about 2000 German settlers. The Queensland Government wanted many more because Germans had a reputation as hard toilers, their limited knowledge of English made it difficult for them to protest against work conditions and, most importantly, to the early leaders of the colony, they were both Christian and white.[2]

Anna and Ludwig had heard the stories of overcrowding and disease on the immigrant boats; of bad food, piracy and shipwreck, but they were willing to take a chance on this brave, new world. Anna prayed that her children would have a better life in Moreton Bay than in Hornsheim, where at twenty-three she had married Johann Hinkler only to bury him two years later. She and their son Johann junior struggled on alone for five years until Anna found a new husband in Ludwig Volk, a butcher eight years her junior.

Ludwig was twenty-seven, Anna thirty-five and Johann junior had been joined by three step-siblings Elisabeth Volk five, Maria, four and baby Ludwig junior a year old.

Pregnant women had been warned not to sail, but the voyage was even more harrowing than Anna imagined. Below deck there was not enough room to stand upright. Claustrophobia was rampant. Then the seas became rough. *La Rochelle* lurched violently. The water in the oak casks turned rancid, and fever spread like wildfire. Just eleven days into the trip the first passenger succumbed to death, and by the time the ship lurched into the British naval base of Simon's Town on South Africa's Cape of Good Hope on 15 October, forty-two of the 472 passengers were dead. Thirty-two of them were children.

Captain Junge kept *La Rochelle* in South Africa for five weeks and while there Anna gave birth to tiny William Volk, another stepbrother for Johann. Finally, with the Roaring Forties putting a powerful westerly wind into the sails, the ship made fast time towards the Southern Ocean, but the wild weather returned and before long so did the sickness. A few days before reaching the coast of Victoria, one-year-old Ludwig junior became feverish and nauseous. As Anna nursed her newborn William, Ludwig's stomach cramps and fever became worse. He died on 20 December. The crew put his little body into a potato sack, and cast him into a watery grave.

On Christmas Eve at 6 p.m., *La Rochelle* sailed into Moreton Bay towards the Brisbane River, but there was no celebration. Sixty-two passengers had died on the voyage.[3] *La Rochelle* was towed to the quarantine station at Dunwich on North Stradbroke Island, and it was weeks before Johann Hinkler and his family could finally step onto the Australian mainland. When they did, Ludwig found work as a teamster, carting supplies on horse-drawn wagons between the sheep and cattle properties around the Burnett River, 480 kilometres north of Brisbane. At the vast 256,000-hectare sheep property Rawbelle Station in 1868 Anna gave birth to her sixth child, Louis Volk. Four more children would follow over the next six years.

As a teenager Johann Hinkler, now known as John Hinkler, started looking for work himself, and there was plenty to be found around Bundaberg and 200 kilometres further south in Gympie where the discovery of two huge gold nuggets in 1867 sparked a rush of settlers and prospectors. As John tried his luck on the goldfields, he met a Gympie dressmaker named Frances Atkins Bonney, whose people called her Fanny.

The Australian branch of the Bonney family began with the high-spirited Suffolk shoemaker Joseph Bonney, who as a teenager had eloped with his sweetheart Frances Atkins and who at the Suffolk Assizes in Bury St Edmunds on 23 July 1812 was sentenced to hang for burglary. The death sentence was commuted, and instead Joe Bonney, then thirty-six, was transported to Botany Bay on the prison ship *General Hewitt*. Manacled along with him were two convicted forgers who later became well known as an architect and artist respectively, Francis Greenway and Joseph Lycett. Left behind in England was Joe's pregnant wife Frances and their eight children.

After surviving a horror voyage that killed thirty-four of the 300 convicts Joe Bonney became a servant at Vaucluse House, home of Captain John Piper, the richest man in Sydney. A smooth talker, Joe was given plenty of freedom and soon took off to Hobart, where he started a new life, marrying pregnant 22-year-old Irishwoman Rose Sheridan on 21 March 1816 at St David's Cathedral. He started farming at New Town on the outskirts of Hobart and was self-confident enough, despite having been a condemned criminal only a few years earlier, to petition Lieutenant Governor Davey to be reunited with Frances and his English children at the government's expense.

Joe, now the husband of two women, became a prominent farmer, shoemaker and merchant. He toasted his good fortune every day until 13 February 1827 when, having celebrated with one ale too many, he was charging along the road on horseback near the New Town Inn when he fell, dislocated his neck, fractured his skull and died.

Joe's son, John Bonney, built Bonney's Inn at Deloraine, which is still operating, and in 1862, one of Joe's grandsons, James Edmund Bonney, married brewer's daughter Mary Ann Noake at Longford,[4] near Launceston. James and Mary, his parents and some of his siblings then joined the thousands of southerners and overseas immigrants trying to cash in on opportunities in the warm sunshine of Queensland.

In 1864, James Bonney, grandson of a convict and the man who would become Bert Hinkler's grandfather, wrote to the newly formed Queensland Acclimatisation Society overseeing the introduction of new animals, birds, fish, insects and plants into the colony to say that among the thirty applicants for the position of their deer procurer he was the man for the job.[5]

If the acclimatisation society wanted rabbits, even better, he wrote, because he could get as many silver-grey rabbits from Tasmania as they wanted. The society moved to accept James' offer to bring in fallow deer but passed on the rabbits.

Before long James was leasing 2430 hectares near Bribie Island, north of Brisbane, when his daughter Frances Atkins Bonney was born on 28 August 1866. James's brothers, Joseph junior and Walter, also took up land around nearby Caboolture and Toorbul, and Joseph went on to develop a property called Belli Park north of Maroochy, where he bred horses, made cheese and provided prize beef for butchers in Gympie and Noosa. James poured more and more energy into the diggings at Gympie. Success was rare, as it was for the shy labourer John Hinkler, who at thirty-six had all sorts of jobs around southeastern Queensland, as a stockman, bush carpenter, handyman and labourer. He found there was plenty of work cutting and loading sugar cane on the lush volcanic fields of Bundaberg, nestled against the blue Pacific where the Burnett River meets the southern tip of the Great Barrier Reef.

The Gurang Gurang Aborigines had lived off the abundant wildlife and fish there for thousands of years, yet surveyor James Burnett had visited the area in 1847 and declared it thoroughly unsuitable for agriculture. How wrong he was. Twenty years later, a pair of Scottish brothers, John and Gavin Steuart, came down the river in search of timber. Sawmills and paddle-steamers followed.

Before long there would be good seasons for corn and then, wide fields of sugar cane would dominate the landscape and become the lifeblood of the town. Seasonal work was available at Samuel Johnston's Waterview sawmill and in the big Millaquin sugar refinery and the smaller mills dotted around the flat landscape. With the opening of the Bundaberg Foundry on the north side of the Burnett in 1888, there were permanent jobs making moulds for casting iron. The foundry soon employed a hundred workers making everything from pipes to locomotives.

Just as the foundry opened, John Hinkler bought a block of nearby land at 69 Gavan Street (later renamed Gavin Street) and erected a small cottage. He tried to find his fortune on the Gympie diggings but, although he never struck the mother lode, he did find a wife in James Bonney's feisty 25-year-old daughter. John Hinkler and Frances Atkins Bonney were married by a Methodist minister at the Bonney family home in Excelsior Road, Gympie on 2 February 1892. Frances quickly became pregnant, and the happy couple set up home in Gavin Street, giving John's small house the name Woodbine Cottage.

Periodically fires would rage through the cane fields at the end of their street, driving out the rats and snakes, clearing out all the rubbish for new growth. And just like the cane refuse, the old order of the world was also going up in smoke. Frances had already seen steam take over from sail and horsepower, more and more machines replace human muscle and the telegraph make worldwide communication a reality. During her pregnancy two events took place that would have a profound effect on her life and that of her unborn baby.

A pair of bachelor brothers named Orville and Wilbur Wright, who had started a printing business in Dayton, Ohio, using a damaged tombstone for part of their press, had been swept up in the new craze of bicycle-riding that was sweeping the USA. And a wealthy Sydney inventor named Lawrence Hargrave, obsessed with his strange flying toys, discovered that his inventions achieved more lift in the wind with curved surfaces than with they did with flat ones.

In 1892 Frances and John Hinkler had never heard of the Wright brothers or Lawrence Hargrave, yet, in their humble house in a small country town, they couldn't help but feel that their child was entering the world at a momentous time.

Chapter 3

Bear this all-important fact in mind. Flying — that is, heavier than air flying — may never have come about but for an Australian. I refer to Lawrence Hargrave. It is a melancholy fact that Australia is apt to forget this great pioneer. He proved that the heavier than air machine could fly.

Bert Hinkler in a radio address to Australia, 1928

In the few years either side of Bert Hinkler's birth, humanity also welcomed such marvels as radios, automobiles, motorcycles, tractors, vacuum cleaners, X-rays, dishwashers, cheap cameras, escalators and zippers. People were conquering everything they surveyed and, while they had not yet taken possession of the heavens, they were well on the way.

No area of life was left untouched by the hand of innovation, even if rural Bundaberg, caught between its frontier past and the world of science on its doorstep, was still fighting to break its colonial shackles. In 1892 Bundaberg had a population of about 3000 settlers of European heritage as well as 2000 Kanakas, indentured labourers from Vanuatu, the Solomon Islands and New Guinea who were recruited — sometimes tricked and sometimes kidnapped — and brought to Queensland as cheap labour. Under their wide-brimmed hats, chained and shirtless in the broiling subtropical sun, the Kanakas sweltered in the back-breaking work of clearing the land and cutting sugarcane with machetes. Aborigines, the first owners of the country, were treated even worse by whites, and even in the 1890s many Bundaberg farmers remembered firing their guns at the local natives.

At the time, Bundaberg was beset by economic depression and drought as Australia reeled from collapsing banks, falling prices for wheat and wool, and strikes on the wharves, shearing sheds and mines.

It was not an environment to encourage deep thought or technological genius, yet little Bert Hinkler, a tiny, delicate baby, became a small, bright child with a strong constitution and an ever-inquiring mind. His Prussian ties evaporated as soon as Frances named him Herbert John Louis Hinkler at his birth in Woodbine Cottage — and all links with Hornsheim were gone the following year when his grandmother Anna Volk died after a stroke 1700 kilometres away in Charters Towers.

Frances instantly formed a strong, nurturing bond with her firstborn. They were both stubborn, single-minded people with a deep mutual respect, and Frances told Bert that despite their modest circumstances, he could achieve great things. By 1897, the same year Charles Kingsford Smith was born in the salubrious Brisbane suburb of Hamilton, Frances and John had two more children under their iron roof, two-year-old Beatrice Mary, whom the family called May or Mayme, and Bert's newborn brother Jack. The kids called their father Papa.

Bert was an adventurous boy, always asking questions, always poking his nose into things, and he got into his fair share of scrapes. One of his earliest sparked the passion for aviation, which became the love of his life. 'It seems almost absurd to say so,' he wrote in his unfinished memoirs, 'but the first yearning for wings seemed to have burned itself into my memory when I was a tiny mite of four. It was a yearning born of [the] sudden realisation of extreme danger into which I had innocently wandered.'

In 1897 the Burnett was spanned only by a single-track railway bridge, and most of the people in North Bundaberg took the ferry if they needed to go to the main township across the water. Frances was one of them and, as Bert remembered, 'four years of mischief was not always welcome tugging at her skirts'. On one occasion Frances slipped out the front gate leaving the boy she called Bertie in the backyard under what she thought was the watchful eye of her husband when the plucky four-year-old, dressed in knickerbockers and his good shirt, decided to follow her. As he did throughout his life, he decided to improvise and find his own way across the river to where his mother was shopping. He headed towards the iron lattice railway bridge 20 metres above the water.

'I began the passage without a moment's hesitation or thought of oncoming express trains,' he recalled. Carefully he began to thread his little legs across the narrow continuous planking for the gangers and platelayers next to the rail track, ignoring the long deadly drop beneath him. Then came the terrible, unnerving moment that chilled him to his core. 'No, not the express train,' Bert remembered, 'but the gruff voice of the ganger, unseen among the girders.'

'You young devil, do you want to be killed?' the ganger bellowed. 'Get back to land as quick as your legs will carry you or I'll be after you with a rope.'

Bert froze with dread as the plank seemed to shrink to the width of a ribbon, but he noticed that 20 metres below him seagulls skimmed the surface of the Burnett without a care. If only he could fly like them, he thought. As he scuttled back to safety all he could think of was being free like the birds.

Frances would recall that when he was five Bert was also constantly studying the birds fluttering about in two trees at the front of their house. 'I'm watching those birds, Mummy,' Bert told her. 'Some day I'm going to fly like those birds.'[1]

On 17 January 1898, Bundaberg North State School enrolled Bertie Hinkler, aged five years and one month, as pupil No. 685. His best friends were Stuart Tallon, Mary McLucas and John Henry Beyer. He was the smallest boy at the school, and his personal details were religion: Church of England, father's occupation: labourer. He was a clever lad, but the best part of school for him was the walk to and from it every day when he could study the birds that flocked around a lagoon at the bottom of a gentle slope nearby. Before long, as well as reading, writing and 'rithmetic, Bert was absorbing everything he could about a new religion called 'Aviation' (which he always spelled with a capital A) that was attracting devotees around the world. Their messiah was the savage-eyed, heavily bearded Lawrence Hargrave, but each devotee was adding a piece to the great mystery and building on each other's knowledge in the hope that eventually the riddle of flying would be solved.

Since the account of Nimrod and his Tower of Babel in the very first book of the Bible, all manner of means and devices to touch the sky had been explored. More than 2000 years before Christ, the Chinese experimented with kites and flying lanterns. The story of Icarus flying too close to the sun with his wings of wax intrigued the Greeks and, in the Middle Ages, sorcerers, monks, physicians and scientists tried to fly using voluminous cloaks, feathered wings, spells and prayer. Leonardo da Vinci made detailed studies of birds and bats, designed aircraft with flapping wings and improved on the design of spinning tops to fashion something like a helicopter. 'A bird is an instrument working according to mathematical law,' Leonardo wrote. 'It lies within the power of man to make this instrument with all its motions.'[2]

In 1507, Italian alchemist John Damian de Falcuis took Da Vinci at his word and, having failed to transform lead into gold as he'd promised, launched himself from the ramparts of Scotland's Stirling Castle wearing wings made from chicken feathers.[3] He ended up with a broken leg and on the nose after he landed in a dung heap at the bottom of the castle wall. Toward the end of the eighteenth century, French brothers Joseph and Etienne Montgolfier, intrigued by the way sparks rose in a fireplace, found they could make small balloons of cloth and paper rise by filling them with heated air. Before long they put on a show at the Palace of Versailles for King Louis XVI and his wife Marie Antoinette at which they made a sheep, a cockerel and a duck ascend almost 460 metres under a huge sky-blue and gold balloon made from taffeta, paper and alum. In Australia, the indigenous people had been experimenting with flight for thousands of years, refining such weapons as the boomerang and woomera by studying the way curved surfaces moved through the air, but it wasn't until 1 February 1858 that Englishman William Dean became the first person to fly in Australia when he took off in the 18-metre-tall balloon *Australasian*, travelling from the northern bank of the Yarra River near Punt Road, Melbourne, and landed 11 kilometres away in Sydney Road, Brunswick. While the achievements of the early balloonists were breathtaking, steering those huge cumbersome craft was at the mercy of shifting winds.

In 1809 a Yorkshire engineer named Sir George Cayley published *On Aerial Navigation* in which he outlined the three elements required for powered flight: lift, propulsion and control. But as the nineteenth century began to wane, achieving the dream of powered, controlled flight seemed no closer.

Then Lawrence Hargrave took off on what would become a new path as the world leader in aviation research. Hargrave's father, an English barrister, had married his first cousin and emigrated to Australia in 1858, eventually becoming the New South Wales attorney general. In 1865, after finishing school in England at the age of fifteen, Lawrence followed his father to Sydney and spent years on quests of adventure, mining for gold, exploring the wilds of New Guinea and contemplating flight. At twenty-eight he became an assistant astronomical observer at Sydney Observatory and worked there for five years, his study of the sky only fuelling his dream to one day fly. In 1883, when Hargrave was thirty-three, he inherited enough money and land after his father's death to devote the rest of his life to the selfless study of aviation.

He saw his devotion to heavenly travel as a higher calling and did not take out patents on his inventions because he wanted his findings to be available for the betterment of everyone. He conducted experiments to prove George Cayley's theory that wind rushing over a curved wing provided greater lift than wind over a flat aero plane. Hargrave also designed and built the first rotary engines, light but powerful devices that ran on compressed air or petrol vapour. The cylinders were laid around a central axis like spokes in a wheel so that the pistons caused the whole engine to revolve at high speed. The revolving cylinders cooled the engine, which meant that a water cooling system was not needed, thus saving weight. The engines powered a propeller that Hargrave called a screw. He began experimenting with box or 'cellular' kites that looked like pieces of honeycomb and were a huge hit at the International Conference on Aerial Navigation in Chicago in 1893, organised by a local, Octave Chanute, a retired French-born American railway engineer, who shared Hargrave's passion for all flying things.

Chanute sang Hargrave's praises to the world, writing in his 1894 book *Progress in Flying Machines*: 'If there be one man, more than another, who deserves to succeed in flying through the air, that man is Mr Laurence [*sic*] Hargrave, of Sydney, New South Wales. He has now constructed with his own hands no less than eighteen flying machines of increasing size, all of which fly, and as a result of his many experiments ... he now says, in a private letter to the writer, that: "I know that success is dead sure to come".'

While Bert was still toddling around his parents' back garden on unsteady legs, Hargrave was realising his dream of ascending into the sky. On 12 November 1894 near his home, at Stanwell Park Beach, 80 kilometres south of Sydney, Hargrave and his assistant James Swain anchored four box kites to a pair of sandbags, and Hargrave tethered a trapeze to the honeycomb-shaped kites. As the breeze blew up and the kites rose so did he, soaring majestically on the trapeze to a height of almost five fantastic metres, although it felt like heaven with the box kites floating overhead, the blue Pacific Ocean on one side and Bald Hill behind him.

Australia was preoccupied with impending nationhood in the 1890s, and Hargrave's work remained largely unappreciated in his own land. However, his work was soon being celebrated by the press in New York, Chicago and London. Alexander Graham Bell, the Scottish-born genius behind the telephone, and president of the National Geographic Society, was an unabashed fan and England's *National Observer* noted in 1896: 'Curiously enough it is to Australia and not America that we now have to look for the latest developments in the aeroplane flying machine.'

Hargrave said controlling his flying craft was a matter of utilising the wind after the mode adopted by the 'albatross, turkey buzzard, vulture and other sailing and soaring birds'.

Back at Bundaberg North State School, young Bert Hinkler knew little of the albatross, turkey buzzard or vulture, but he was learning a lot about the fruit bats called flying foxes, about gulls and especially about a curious bird called the ibis. As he sat on his hard wooden seat day after day the diminutive boy's attention couldn't help but drift from the times tables and ink-smudged copybook to these strange-looking things gathering outside the school. They had white bodies and wings, bald, black skulls and long thin black legs, curved beaks in the shape of scimitars and when they spoke to each other, which was often, it was in a piercing shriek, as startling as fingernails running down the classroom blackboard. They were odd creatures, defying gravity and rising effortlessly towards the orange Queensland sun.

To most of his classmates, the children of farmers and labourers, the ibis was nothing more than a rat with wings, a scavenger and pest. But to Bert, whose young mind was constantly ticking over like one of Hargrave's rotary engines, they were creatures that would fascinate him for years. Bert would spend most of his boyhood in a quest to somehow replicate the way they spread their thick white plumage in a great wide arc and ascended gracefully through the sky, banking, turning, catching the wind and floating wherever they liked. Bert wanted to fly like them and remarked years later: 'I can remember trying to reason out the mysterious ease with which the gull, the flying fox and the ibis banked, volplaned and rose again with only an occasional and scarcely perceptible flick of the wings.'

Bert was small and light on his feet and, in the school rugby league and cricket games, a good runner and jumper, which probably contributed to his nickname of 'Sponny'[4] after Spondulix, a jumps horse of the time owned by Queensland meat baron Ernest Baynes, although the more unkind of Bert's friends remembered that Spondulix was also slang for 'money' and that Bert was unusually careful with the few pennies he had. About the only luxury his family could afford for him were the occasional newspaper and boys adventure magazines, which were always full of stories about daring young men and their quests to conquer the sky.

Bert was absorbed by the tale of another avid bird-watcher, Clement Ader, who built a flying machine called the *Eole* in 1886. It looked like a giant version of the flying foxes that were always into the fruit trees around Gavin Street. In 1890 Ader claimed the *Eole* had flown uncontrolled for 50 metres and reached a height of a whopping 20 centimetres, although few believed him.

One of the most inspiring tales for Bert was that of the 'Glider King' Otto Lilienthal, who like Papa Hinkler was also Prussian and built an artificial hill outside Berlin from which he could launch his hang gliders. Lilienthal's dream of becoming the first man to make a powered flight died with him when he crashed a glider in 1896 and suffered a broken spine, uttering his unforgettable last words: 'Small sacrifices must be made.'

Three years after Lilienthal crashed, his great admirer Percy Pilcher, from Bath, England, who had designed a three-winged triplane with a four-horsepower motor, plummeted to his death in another glider crash.

These early aviators were both martyrs and heroes to the young Bert, who had just celebrated his seventh birthday when a new century dawned. By 1900 Bundaberg had a shiny new bridge — the longest steel traffic bridge in Australia at 412 metres — which replaced the ferry service across the Burnett. It was opened by Queensland Governor Lord Lamington, who was about to reach sweet immortality with the cake named in his honour. The following year, as Australia mourned the death of

Queen Victoria and the birth of a unified federation of Australian states, the death of ten Kanakas from dysentery in Bundaberg brought the whole question of cheap foreign workers into question. However, the Bundaberg and District Manufacturers Union said it was simple economics that while a white man earned more than a pound a week, farmers could recruit Kanakas for half that to do the tough stuff, shifting the volcanic rock, clearing the scrub and cutting the cane.[5]

Bert had no desire to find out about that sort of work because he believed he had a higher calling. Just after his eighth birthday at Christmas 1900 his school presented him with a book called *Great Inventors* inscribed 'To Bertie Hinkler for his excellent attendance during the year.' Bert read it and re-read it and studied every publication he could about the European aeronauts.

In Paris a French lawyer named Ernest Archdeacon and Gustave Eiffel, the builder of a great tower, had founded the Aéro-Club de France and in 1901, a German meteorologist, Reinhard Süring, and his Polish colleague, Arthur Berson, ascended from Tempelhof outside Berlin to an astonishing 10,800 metres in a balloon named *Prussia*, to study the earth's atmosphere. Berson was a student of the renowned Berlin geography professor Ferdinand von Richthofen, who had a nine-year-old nephew named Manfred also interested in flying.

Although he didn't scale such stratospheric heights, a debonair Brazilian coffee heir named Alberto Santos-Dumont was becoming the world's most celebrated action adventure hero at the controls of his cigar-shaped airships, steerable balloons, in the skies above Paris. Newspapers around the world, even thousands of miles away in

Bundaberg, thrilled to his exploits in his fourteen giant gasbags made from silk and bamboo and described him as 'wonderfully cool'. The daredevil young dandy stood out from everyone in Paris, especially when he would cruise around the top of the Eiffel Tower in his compact airship the *Baladeuse*, waving to pedestrians from his small wicker basket before descending to his favourite café. Bert read the newspaper articles with jaw-dropping awe, especially the ones about Santos-Dumont's hydrogen-filled airship falling from 600 metres to crash into the Trocadero Hotel. As the *Brisbane Courier* reported,

> Men and women around the Eiffel Tower and the Trocadero cried like children when Santos-Dumont fell, and they cheered as folk cheer a homecoming conqueror when they found him hanging over a parapet smiling, safe, and debonair. The firemen dropped Santos-Dumont a rope, which he looped around his arms. Then, as they pulled, he walked up the wall, still perpendicular. He was laughing like a boy, unworried and enthusiastic. He was made to drink a cup of coffee brewed for him by the hotel chef himself, and then he descended hatless to the street. He was smothered with embraces, hugged and kissed by women, cheered and cheered again, until the whole quarter was mad with excitement.[6]

Superman had arrived ahead of schedule in a balloon. Millions of men around the world would soon be copying Santos-Dumont's new fashion item, the wristwatch, a small clock on a leather strap that his friend Louis Cartier had designed for him,[7] so that the young airman could time his flights while keeping both hands on the controls. There was now just one job that Bert and thousands of boys like him wanted. Santos-Dumont had not yet achieved flight in a powered aeroplane, but it was getting closer.

Then the Wright brothers arrived at a windswept area of sand dunes known as the Kill Devil Hills, about six kilometres from the town of Kitty Hawk, North Carolina.

Chapter 4

*For some years I have been afflicted with the belief
that flight is possible to man. The disease has
increased in severity and I feel it will soon cost me
an increased amount of money, if not my life.*

**Bicycle repairman Wilbur Wright, beginning
his first letter to Octave Chanute, 13 May
1900, asking for advice on aviation**

By the time he was ten, Bert was the youngest student in
the sixth class at Bundaberg North State School, but the
sight of birds in full flight was more important to him than
his studies. He lay on the grass for hours watching them,
reasoning that there must be a wealth of mathematical
secrets locked inside their tiny bodies. Some of the other
kids called him a loony until he planted a fist on their chins,
and he was caned more than once for fighting. He was
certain that people had the capacity to fly like the birds.
On 14 May 1904, a small single column item appeared
on page 28 of the *Queenslander* newspaper to agree. The
article related to events that had occurred on the east coast
of the USA half a year earlier.

'A Real Flying Machine at Last!' the headline proclaimed.[1] 'Various vague and sensational accounts have appeared in the Press during the past few weeks,' the report announced, 'of a most important experiment made in America by the brothers Wright. We are now able to give an authentic account, kindly sent by Mr Orville Wright himself, of what actually occurred.'

News of the brothers' achievement had travelled slowly, bogged down by scepticism. There had been reports of powered flight earlier but without proof, from Clement Ader, from a Welsh carpenter named Bill Frost; an American, Gustave Whitehead; a New Zealander, Richard Pearse; and a German, Karl Jatho; and the Wrights were the most unlikely candidates for turning the world on its head. Bert read everything he could about this odd pair, the sons of Bishop Milton Wright of the Church the United Brethren in Christ. Orville and Wilbur were shy, dour men in their thirties who still lived with their parents. Neither had a high school diploma — let alone training in aeronautical science — yet they had been intrigued by aviation since childhood, playing with a helicopter-like toy powered by a rubber band.

At about the same time that Bert was born the brothers cashed in on the popularity of the Rover safety bicycles coming out of England and opened the Wright Cycle Exchange in Dayton. Bicycles were unstable but perfectly controllable with the right balance, and the brothers believed the direction of an otherwise unstable flying machine could be controlled in the same way a bicycle rider leans into a turn. They began experimenting with wings that twisted slightly using Hargrave-style box kites and found they could make the kites bank left or right by twisting or warping the wings. They wrote to Octave Chanute asking him to recommend sites with wide open spaces and strong steady winds to test their manned glider experiments and settled on the small fishing hamlet of Kitty Hawk, North Carolina, 1100 kilometres from Dayton.

From 1900 Wilbur, Orville and Chanute became frequent visitors there with various contraptions that took to the sky above the pounding Atlantic waves. Late in 1903 the brothers arrived with the ambitiously titled *Wright Flyer I*, built from spruce and ash, with wire struts and unbleached muslin stretched over the wings to make it smoother through the air. The machine had a wingspan of 12 metres and weighed 275 kilograms and, most importantly, it had a four-cylinder, 12-horsepower engine. Connected to a pair of chains, the engine would drive a handcrafted pair of 2.5-metre propellers that sat facing backwards behind the pilot and spun in opposite directions to counter the craft's tendency to twist in the air. The Wrights had deduced that the propeller itself was a wing in rotation, a revolving wing, which had to be shaped and angled precisely to create lift.

The pilot would lie prone in the centre of the bottom wing facing forward and control the craft with an elevator lever that determined pitch and a hip cradle connected to pulleys that controlled wing warping and a vertical rudder. The Flyer I was too heavy to be launched by wind gusts like their previous gliders so the brothers built an 18-metre wooden monorail they called the Grand Junction Railroad.

On 14 December 1903, they enlisted the help of men from the nearby Kill Devil Hills Life-Saving Station and carted the Flyer and its rail track to the incline of a sand dune known as Big Kill Devil Hill. Orville and Wilbur tossed a coin to see who would be the first man in history to fly. Will won but, after the Flyer raced 12 metres down the Grand Junction Railroad, it stalled and finished nose deep in the sand three and a half seconds later.

The brothers spent three days fixing the plane and then decided to try again in front of five witnesses, one of whom, John T. Daniels, was given Orville's complicated Gundlach Korona box camera to record the moment, although he was so excited he almost forgot what to do. Because Will had already had a turn at the controls three days earlier, Orville was given his chance at 10.35 a.m. on 17 December. As the Wright engine roared to life, the propellers began to whirr, sounding for all the world like a threshing machine.

Back in Bundaberg, Bert had just turned eleven and was getting ready for a sweltering Christmas. But in the shadow of Big Kill Devil Hill, half a world away, it was a freezing winter's morning with a gale of more than 20 knots blowing salty mist off the grey Atlantic. As Orville prepared to climb on board the rickety machine, the brothers shook hands solemnly and held on to each other's hand for some while as if they hated to let go and, as John Daniels would recall, 'like two folks parting who weren't sure they'd ever see each other again'.[2]

Orville climbed onto the Flyer's lower wing and, lying face down, took a nervous hold of a wooden lever in his left hand that would control the elevator that made the front of the Flyer rise into the wind. With the engine roaring and the propellers spinning, the Flyer headed down on its wooden runway, Wilbur holding one wing to keep the Flyer stable, sprinting along beside it as fast as his thick coat and trousers would allow. Orville pulled back on the elevator, and the Flyer rose into the teeth of an icy gale. Shaking all over, John Daniels took the snapshot some people called the photo of the century as Orville Wright briefly left the surface of the earth.

The first powered flight lasted just 12 seconds before the *Wright Flyer I* came down into the soft sand on its wooden skids. Orville had reached an altitude of just three metres and flown a total distance of 37 metres, one short flight for a man but one giant leap for mankind. After a firm handshake of congratulations the brothers then took turns breaking each other's world record for long-distance flying. Bang on noon Wilbur had the fourth and final turn for the day, flying 260 metres in 59 seconds before the Flyer pitched nose first into the soft sand.

The brothers decided that a defining moment for humanity was enough for the day, and they were standing about discussing their efforts when a sudden gust of wind caught the wings of the Flyer and flipped it over. The brothers and their five assistants rushed to grab hold of the machine. John Daniels hung on to it from the inside and, as a result, was knocked down and turned over and over as the Flyer cart-wheeled. Somehow he got out of the wreckage in one piece, but the Flyer was smashed beyond repair and never flew again. For the rest of his life John Daniels related the story of how he took the photograph of the century and survived the very first aircraft disaster.

The brothers ate a brief dinner, brushing the billowing sand from their meals, then travelled the six kilometres to Kitty Hawk to send a telegram to their father with the request 'inform press'. But the *Dayton Daily News* didn't run Bishop Wright's report, with publisher James Cox, a future Ohio governor and US presidential nominee, remarking years later: 'Frankly, none of us believed it.'[3]

In Bundaberg, Bert's dreams of flying took on new wings, although the Wright achievement was given less attention in the local press than the news that Aborigines had been banned from taking part in professional foot races and that Bundaberg police had been called upon to report any competing among the white populace at the Easter sports gathering of 1904.[4]

Still some in Bundaberg were trying to shake off the old ways and embrace the modern world. Photography was booming in popularity thanks to the cheap Brownie cameras being made by Eastman Kodak, and Bert took to it with nearly as much enthusiasm as he did aviation. He even talked Papa into tacking a darkroom onto their cottage to develop his own prints. Every chance away from his schoolbooks or when he wasn't milking the two cows Frances kept in a lucerne paddock on nearby Gavegan Street or tending to his mother's impressive vegetable garden, Bert was snapping away, even posing his family for portraits before jumping in among them while a timer mechanism released the shutter. For 1904 in rural Queensland this was cutting-edge equipment, but the technology that really had Bundaberg agog came along its dusty streets with the arrival of the Rover Imperial — built by the makers of the safety bike that had propelled the Wright brothers' venture into flying. People called the new machine a 'motorcycle', and it had been imported from Coventry in England by Andrew Brasch. Its 3.5-horsepower petrol engine had him chugging through the city streets with what the *Bundaberg Mail* called 'great expedition'.[5]

A family of Methodist missionaries lived next door to Bert in Gavin Street, and he was the first through the door at the special children's service every Sunday evening, slipping into the church through a slide rail in the fence, which he had adjusted for easy access. To him and his younger siblings the sight of the goggled Mr Brasch as he made his noisy way down Gavin Street and across Australia's longest steel traffic bridge was something of a revelation.

In Dayton, Bishop Wright's boys knew that, if they were to market their invention, it had to be able to do more than fly for a few hundred metres. They built a new aeroplane made from pine and using a catapult system for launching that required a whopping 725-kilogram weight dropped five metres from a derrick. They conducted tests of the *Wright Flyer II* on a cow paddock named Huffman Prairie near Dayton, which they were allowed to use for free if they moved the livestock before take-off. On 20 September 1904 they made their longest flight yet of 1 minute and 36 seconds as Wilbur covered 1244 metres in a circle around Huffman Prairie. One observer, Amos Root, a Sunday school teacher who ran a beekeeper's supply store, sat down to write the first eyewitness account of powered flight, but the prestigious journal *Scientific American* rejected his report as bunkum so instead *Gleanings in Bee Culture* became the first journal to publish an independent report of a man flying. Alongside the articles 'How I Manage Swarming' and 'Judging Honey at Fairs', Amos Root detailed what he called the grandest sight of his life.

Dear friends … I have a wonderful story to tell you — a story that, in some respects, outrivals the Arabian Nights fables. God in his great mercy has permitted me to be, at least somewhat, instrumental in ushering in and introducing to the great wide world an invention that may outrank the electric cars, the automobiles, and all other methods of travel and one which may fairly take a place beside the telephone and wireless telegraphy... Imagine a locomotive that has left its track, and is climbing up in the air right toward you—a locomotive without any wheels, we will say, but with white wings instead ...[6]

He described Bishop Wright's boys as 'scientific explorers who were serving the world in much the same way that Columbus did when he discovered America'.

The adventure magazines eventually picked up the story, feeding what Bert called his 'fetish for flying' with their drawings of countless types of gliders. Bert had the seemingly laughable notion that he could build his own craft and already had ideas of his own from his years of bird-watching. He started making model aircraft from wood and wire. He announced to his bemused parents and astonished siblings that one day he would fly like those brothers in the USA and, in his copybook hand, wrote impressive letters to the aeronautical authorities in Britain, Germany and the USA asking for assistance. At the time Papa Hinkler was an ancient looking fifty-year-old still labouring in Bundaberg's foundry despite arthritis that severely deformed his hands. His family extended to five children with the addition of George in 1900 and Frances junior, called Queenie, on Bert's twelfth birthday in 1904. But it was hard even for the weary Hinkler patriarch not to be moved by Bert's zeal.

Bert's schooling finished in 1906 but his quest for knowledge was unquenchable, however, and he was constantly inventing gadgets. He started calling his humble home by the grandiose title 'Woodbine Villa' and installed electric lights in every room, long before electricity was common in Bundaberg.[7] He made the lights from home-made rechargeable batteries with chemicals he mixed and caught the train down to Brisbane to buy special globes.

At night, when he bunked down and switched off his electric light he could hear the ibis squawks and flying foxes as they raided the mulberry bush in the backyard. He would drift off to sleep and dream he was a dapper hero circling the Eiffel Tower as women fainted with excitement. But when daylight shook him awake and it was time to milk the cows he was still a thirteen-year-old country boy with few prospects.

His grandparents, James and Mary Bonney suggested he come stay with them in Gympie and try his hand at photography. Bert asked his old headmaster George Stanley if he could earn some pocket money taking photos of Stanley's family and some of his old schoolteachers. The results, Stanley recalled, were 'thoroughly professional'. So Bert left home and took up a job as an assistant for a Gympie photographer named Fred Murray. At their home in Excelsior Road, Bert listened to his grandmother's stories about old Isaac Noake's great brewery and James Bonney's tales of how the rabbits almost came to Queensland. Occasionally on weekends, Bert made fishing trips with his new friends to Tin Can Bay and sometimes even travelled north to Yeppoon to holiday with other relatives.

More than anything he wanted to build his own flying machine so he soon headed back to Bundaberg. By now the streets there were being traversed by motorcars — Rovers,

De Dion-Boutons and Humbers — and Alderman Michael Duffy called the invasion 'odiferous'.[8] The association representing the drivers of Bundaberg's horse-drawn cabs complained bitterly about reckless motor driving, which caused horses to bolt and in one case forced a cart being pulled by two ponies to slew into a water channel.

In Paris the Aéro-Club de France had dismissed the Wright brothers' claims of powered flight as bogus and offered prizes for the first heavier-than-air machines to fly both 25 metres and 100 metres in public, believing that France was the centre of the scientific world and that a Frenchman was bound to emerge triumphant. Octave Chanute wrote to the Wrights with a grim warning that the Europeans were winning the aerial war. On 23 October 1906, before a cheering crowd at the Bagatelle park in Paris, Santos-Dumont unveiled a biplane that owed much of its design to Hargrave's box kites. He called it the 14-*bis* after his fourteenth dirigible airship that he used testing it, but most Parisiennes knew the craft as the *Oiseau de Proie* (*Bird of Prey*). In the crowd was the British aviation enthusiast and self-made newspaper magnate Lord Northcliffe, who had already appointed Harry Harper as aviation writer for his *Daily Mail* with the declaration: 'Make no mistake, the future lies in the air.'

The *Bird of Prey* shook under the power of its 50-horsepower V8 Antoinette speedboat engine. The frail Santos-Dumont controlled the great beast while standing on a platform behind the two wings, with cables and pulleys attached to his flying suit, giving him the appearance of a Roman chariot rider perched behind two charging white ponies. Directly behind him was the pusher propeller acting like a giant fan. Santos-Dumont opened the throttle and catapulted the craft along the grass, then to a height of three metres. It came down 60 metres away. To wild cheering Santos-Dumont accepted his prize of 3000 francs in what was the first flight to be officially certified by the newly formed Fédération Aéronautique Internationale.

Santos-Dumont swooped on the Bagatelle again three weeks later, on 12 November, when in front of an even bigger crowd he tried for the 100-metre record, this time with competition from the biplane of Gabriel Voisin and Voisin's design partner Louis Blériot, a heavily moustachioed inventor who had amassed a fortune making acetylene headlamps for automobiles. Voisin couldn't get his craft off the ground as Santos-Dumont astonished everyone again. The *Bird of Prey* bounded up and down on short powered hops as the Brazilian's friend Henri Farman drove alongside the plane tossing out plates to mark where it took off and touched down. After several short hops Santos-Dumont finally made a flight of 21.4 seconds covering 220 metres buzzing over the heads of people scattered across the field.

The following day the *Daily Mail* published a brief report of the event, causing Lord Northcliffe to phone the editor in one of his regular rages. The flight of 220 metres was *not* the story, Northcliffe told his stammering editor; the story was that 'England is no longer an island ... it means the aerial chariots of a foe descending on British soil if war comes.'[9] The *Daily Mail* then told its millions of readers — and, via the Australian press, Bert Hinkler back in Bundaberg — that 'M. Santos-Dumont has made the aeroplane a practical machine and that following Santos-Dumont's flight "new difficulties" would arise, not the least serious being the military problem caused by the virtual annihilation of frontiers ... the isolation of the United Kingdom may disappear ... the time is at hand when air power will be an even more important thing than sea power.' Certainly H.G. Wells thought so, too, starting work on his prophetic novel, *The War in the Air*.

Convinced that England must embrace the new technology shown by the *Bird of Prey* or fall victim to foreign military predators, Northcliffe offered £10,000 — about fifty years' wages for the average working man — for the first person to fly from London to Manchester. The *Daily Mail* soon offered other prizes, too, including £1000 to the first man to fly the English Channel.

In Bundaberg, Bert continued to develop a reputation as a promising photographer. He used a rubber stamp to autograph the back of his portraits and postcards with the moniker B.J. Hinkler and used some of them for magic-lantern slide shows for family and friends. But his yearning to fly was constant. Papa and Frances knew the idea of a teenage boy building a flying machine was laughable, but Bert was a good lad and they loved him. So Papa, having finished tacking on an extra bedroom to the cottage with Queenie's arrival, set to work on building a workshop for his eldest boy behind the mulberry tree at the back of the vegetable garden. Bert would later remark that the workshop was a place of limited facilities but unlimited patience and enthusiasm. By his early teens he also had a part-time job delivering copies of the *Bundaberg Mail* from his bicycle, which allowed him to read every titbit about aviation free of charge.

He had plans to become a printer and compositor and, although he did not stay long at the trade, he quickly showed the *Bundaberg Mail* staff his aptitude for mechanics, pulling the *Mail*'s printing press apart and repairing it with Jack Halpin, a draughtsman and engineer at the Bundaberg Foundry.[10]

Bert began putting his earnings into a moneybox to fund the construction of his flying machine. He found all sorts of seasonal work to support himself and buy the latest magazines on flight with their drawings of the newest machines. He took photos when jobs came up, followed the Wright example and sold bicycles, then gained more regular income at the Qunaba sugar mill, the Millaquin refinery and beside his father at the foundry. During the sugar-crushing season from June to December he found work cutting and loading cane.

Manual labour made Bert physically strong, with a deep chest and powerful arms, and at the foundry he had the opportunity to watch qualified mechanics and tradesmen repairing and rejuvenating all sorts of machinery. He had a goal in mind, and every day that he walked with his father the 200 metres to the end of Gavin Street to sweat it out shaping metal for locomotives and farm machines he told himself that one day he would be flying over the Eiffel Tower, crossing the English Channel and skimming the waves off Kitty Hawk.

Bert took his study of flying creatures and their wings to the next level to see how they made lift-off and landing look so effortless. Soon he became what he called an amateur 'taxidermist' — trapping different birds with a snare made from horse tail hair and shooting other birds and flying foxes with his shanghai and sometimes a rifle 'not from a love of killing', he was quick to explain, 'but in the quest of knowledge':

It seemed to me the slower-flying Ibis possessed all the secrets I needed and offered the safest line of research. So poor Ibis was stripped of everything but his 'chassis' and wings and was carefully stretched out on a board to dry in the subtropical sun. From that point my career as an airman began in earnest. The frame of the Ibis was stiffened and embodied in an improvised glider and the lessons of wing lift began as one begins his alphabet. But there were poise and steering to be mastered and along came more [magazine] drawings to show me the rudiments of frontal and tail planes and rudders.[111]

Bert weighed each part of the dead creatures and measured everything, taking special note of the surface-to-weight ratio of the wings.

Before long the increasing number of motorcycles and cars on Gavin Street had to dodge the small wooden model aeroplanes Bert was testing on the roadway. In England other flying enthusiasts were of a similar mind, and reporter Harry Harper turned up at Alexandra Palace in North London, on 15 April 1907 for the awarding of the *Daily Mail*'s first aviation prize, a cheque for £150, to Alliott Verdon-Roe, for his design of a model aircraft. A.V. Roe, as history remembers him, was then a 29-year-old engineer from Salford corresponding with the Wright brothers in Dayton for advice on building his own aeroplane. By the time Verdon-Roe won the contest, Lord Northcliffe's New York correspondent was reporting that President Teddy Roosevelt was about to approve purchase of a Wright machine for an American military air force.

Balloons had been used to spy on Confederate troop movements during the American Civil War, which many Americans still vividly recalled, and Orville declared that the Wright Flyer would give any army an advantage. A New York banker, arms dealer and hustler named Charles Flint, who years later would start a company called IBM, was hawking the Wright machine to the governments of Russia, England, France, Germany, Belgium, Japan and China.

At about the same time, Lawrence Hargrave moved his family to a mansion at 8 Wunulla Road, Woollahra Point overlooking Sydney Harbour and he and his son Geoffrey worked together on flying machine design and rotary engines all without patent. The Wrights were fiercely protective of their designs and so fearful of competitors Glenn Curtiss and Alexander Graham Bell copying their work that they did not fly at all in 1906 or 1907, saying they would reveal one of their machines again only when they had government contracts in hand. In France the reports of their flights were still greeted with derision and the brothers were a source of scorn as a pair of *'bluffeurs'* — liars, not flyers. Ernest Archdeacon from the Aéro-Club de France sent a taunting letter to the Wrights, and Santos-Dumont's pal Henri Farman dared them to a fly-off for a $5000 prize. The mockery hurt and, fearing that the squadron of Gallic aviators was stealing potential markets, the Wrights finally emerged from their shell of secrecy with a double-pronged counter-attack. Wilbur would take on the sceptics in France while Orville would win over the politicians in Washington.

The first public flight of a Wright machine was set at the Hunaudières horseracing track at Le Mans, 200 kilometres south of Paris, where Wilbur's new machine, called the Model A, was being repaired after being damaged by customs officials. A derrick needed to drop the 725-kilogram weight for the plane's launch and a wooden railroad line were assembled. On the afternoon of Saturday, 8 August 1908, Wilbur arrived at the track for the biggest gamble of his life, dressed in a dark suit, high starched collar and large green cloth driving cap turned backwards. Two horses towed his Model A into position. Wilbur declared to the assembled crowd of thirty invited guests that he would give them a demonstration of flying. Some in the small crowd guffawed. There was a snigger or two. Two of Wilbur's assistants cranked the propellers, each dragging down a blade. The engine kicked over but quickly died when Wilbur's back collar stud caught on the control wires. There were more guffaws.

Wilbur tried a nervous smile. The assistants yanked on the propellers again. Wilbur pulled a trigger near the pilot's seat, and the huge weight on the derrick fell like a guillotine blade cutting off the last piece of French cynicism. The falling weight dragged the Model A along the wooden track with a sudden rush, and the momentum lifted it almost instantaneously. The jaws of the Frenchmen dropped as they perceived the obvious superiority of Wilbur's machine over theirs as he flew for 1 minute and 45 seconds, circling the track and banking effortlessly. The brothers were *bluffeurs* no more.

When Wilbur landed, some of the Frenchmen rushed up to give him celebratory kisses on the cheek, but the chauffeur for his European agent stepped in to save him the embarrassment of this strange un-American custom. Asked by a reporter what he thought about the astonishing spectacle, a shaken Blériot could only stutter that he was 'not sufficiently calm' to make a statement. Later he conceded: 'Monsieur Wright has us all in his hands.'

The plane and the planet had changed forever.

In Bundaberg, Bert stayed busy with his models and rudimentary experiments but remarked later that 'there was the unfulfilled dream of something larger — something that would carry diminutive me'. On his salary he figured it would take about 10,000 years to save for one of the new Wright, Curtiss or Voisin aeroplanes. But he'd heard about experiments in France in which a human could transform himself into a bird, and he was willing to give it a try.

Chapter 5

*I felt a sensation of wonderful lightness and
confidence, coupled with a delicious feeling of
freedom and being independent of space and time.*
**American magician and escapologist Harry Houdini on
his flight at Diggers Rest, near Melbourne, in 1910**[1]

*There were hazards and disappointments, the
wind would not blow from the right quarter, but
what were these when [a] vaunting youth of 19 was
at last able to dispense with manpower haulage
on the tow ropes and rise 30 feet, airborne, in the
face of the breeze as I had seen my Ibis do?*
**Bert Hinkler, unfinished memoirs, 1932, recalling
his first flight on his home-made glider**

The teenage Bert Hinkler's first endeavours at flight
were absurd, but no more so than those made by many
of the leading thinkers of the time; attempts that were
only good for use on silent movie comedy reels. One of
the Multiplanes of Englishman Horatio Phillips had 200
small wings and looked like a mobile venetian blind. One

made an uncontrolled hop of 150 metres at Streatham in London, but another was so heavy it collapsed in upon itself after moving just a few feet. Burke's Seagull, complete with flapping wings, was a lame duck and Cooley's Airship, looking more like a boat than an aircraft, sunk without trace. British arms magnate Hiram Maxin was so confident his aerial Mammoth would fly that he even had it fitted with bumper bars in case of a crash landing. It never left the ground.[2]

In France there was a growing craze for manpower alone to create flight. Wings were attached to bicycles, and natty French chaps could often be seen furiously flapping their arms with all manner of kite-like devices strapped to their bent backs. The fad fluttered to other parts of Europe and eventually came all the way to Gavin Street where Bert designed his own personal 'aviette', recalling it as 'a pair of wings with arm sockets which I slipped on as one does a coat'.

With his home-made wings Bert would run as hard as he could, stretch his arms wide and hope the breeze would carry him towards the sky. He ran and ran and ran. He jumped off fences, chicken coops and house roofs. He ran through cane fields, across paddocks and along beaches, flapping his arms and skipping skyward. 'My idea that the manpower generated by my two short legs, running at their hardest, would give the lift momentum was quickly falsified,' Bert explained. 'My aviette went to the scrapheap. Some of my backyard "staff" no doubt still laugh at my idea.'

The Wright brothers were having more success with their inventions — even if death and disaster were constant threats. Three weeks after Wilbur's triumph in Le Mans, Orville began demonstrations of a similar machine, the

Wright *Military Flyer*, for the United States Army at Fort Myer, Virginia. On 9 September 1908, Orville made the first hour-long flight and, eight days later, emboldened by his success, took a passenger up with him: army lieutenant and fellow aircraft designer Thomas Selfridge, who was acting as an official observer. They circled Fort Myer four times and were halfway through a fifth loop at an altitude of about 30 metres when the right propeller broke, damaging the rudder. The Flyer nosedived into the ground. Orville shattered his left thigh, and a few ribs but Selfridge sustained a fractured skull and died that night, the first aeroplane fatality. The brothers' sister Katharine, a spinster schoolmarm who taught Latin and Greek, left her position at Steele High School in Dayton and stayed by Orville's side in hospital as he took seven weeks to recover.

In Le Mans, the news of the fatal crash stunned Wilbur, who had reluctantly become the most celebrated man in France. No American had received such adulation there since Benjamin Franklin. So many aristocrats were vying for his attention that he wrote to Orville to declare that princes and millionaires were thick as fleas around him. Among the thousands flocking to see Wilbur fly was A.V. Roe, who had cycled all the way from London.

At Gavin Street, fifteen-year-old Bert took a school book entitled *The Grammar School Exercise Book, Bundaberg* and began pasting newspaper clippings about aviation into it, smothering the cover with the clipped-out headlines 'Aeronautics', 'The World of Flight' and 'Conquest of the Air'. Wilbur Wright's exploits kept filling the pages.

After establishing a French arm of the brothers' aviation company, Wilbur covered 124.7 kilometres in a flight at

Le Mans on 31 December that lasted 2 hours, 20 minutes and 23 and one-fifth seconds. The cold was Arctic, worse even than at Kitty Hawk in 1903, but the achievement was front-page news for a new British weekly called *Flight*, which soon had a rival, *The Aero*, edited by the monocled C.G. (Charles) Grey, who over the next forty years used The *Aero*, The *Aeroplane*, *Jane's All the World's Aircraft*, the *Yorkshire Evening Post* and the *Edinburgh Evening News* to voice not only his views on the development of aircraft but also his support for fascism and his disdain for Jews and Bolsheviks. Decades later he informed his readers that the German Government under Hitler was 'full of peace and good will towards men' and that French plans to have 'niggers and moors' police the Rhineland was an abomination.[3]

In Bundaberg, Bert was not interested in Grey's politics so much as in his articles and diagrams of the new advances in flying. Every week new clippings went into the old exercise book.

In Paris, Wilbur was joined by Katharine and the patched-up Orville, walking with the help of two canes. Together the three became the royal family of aviation in Europe.

In March 1909, in the French resort town of Pau, Wilbur began training French pilots, and a month later, before heading back to a tumultuous welcome in the USA, the brothers travelled to Rome to train a pair of Italians at the Centocelle Field. This was big news for the 26-year-old former school teacher and draft-dodger Benito Mussolini, then the firebrand editor of a socialist newspaper *L'Avvenire del Lavoratore* ('The Future of the Worker'), who saw the aeroplane as a tool for Italy's advancement.[4]

Mussolini would be even more impressed when Louis Blériot finally emerged from Wilbur's shadow. At 2.30 on the morning of 25 July 1909 Blériot was woken in a grumpy mood at a hotel in Calais by a balloonist friend, who told him there had been a break in the foul weather gripping the French coast. The time was right for him to attempt the crossing of the English Channel in his quest for the £1000 *Daily Mail* prize. Blériot was in no mood to fly having recently suffered two serious burns, one from a defective exhaust pipe and one from his backfiring engine. But he knew the importance of this moment, having been locked in a battle for the prize with Hubert Latham, another Frenchman.

Latham slept blissfully at his lodgings as Blériot hurried to a farm at nearby Les Baraques where the Blériot XI monoplane — looking like a big skeletal dragonfly — was being readied by two mechanics. The Blériot had what was being called a tractor propeller at the front of the machine to pull it along rather than the pusher fan many aircraft were still using.

Half an hour before dawn Blériot limped to his aircraft on crutches and climbed into the open cockpit, trying hard not to aggravate his burns. The mechanics already had the engine running; smoke was billowing in the dark and the smell of oil stung the nostrils of a growing group of onlookers, including a dog, which snapped at the noisy motor until it was decapitated by the whirling propeller. Ignoring the grisly scene, and trying to calm his own nerves, Blériot asked directions to Dover, then set off into the mist at 4.41 a.m. He barely made it over the nearby telegraph lines as the XI spluttered towards England.

Droning along at 38 knots (70 kilometres per hour), Blériot passed above his escort vessel *Escopette*, which was carrying his wife 75 metres below. He feared that his tiny three-cylinder engine would overheat and that he'd end up using the inflatable tyre tube he'd put in the plane to survive a splash. However, a sudden downpour cooled his motor, and he pushed on, exposed to the foul weather but making progress through the worst of it.

Then he saw an opening in the white chalk cliffs and spied a friend near Dover Castle frantically waving a tricolour flag. At the risk of smashing his plane he cut the ignition twenty metres above the ground. The XI dipped alarmingly and hit Northfall Meadow with a heavy thud, damaging the undercarriage, fracturing the propeller and sending agony through Blériot's burns. But 37 minutes after leaving France, a pilot had landed in England.

'It marks a new era in the world,' the *Daily Mail* proclaimed, while H.G. Wells thundered an alert to Britain: 'Never was a slacking dull people so liberally served with warnings of what is in store for them. In spite of our fleet this is no longer an inaccessible island.'[5]

Blériot's aircraft went on display at Selfridges department store in Oxford Street, London, and he was seated next to the Antarctic explorer Ernest Shackleton and the yachtsman Sir Thomas Lipton along with one hundred and fifty guests at a lunch at the Savoy Hotel, where he collected his £1000. When he arrived home at the Gare du Nord in Paris a crowd of one hundred thousand cheered him.

Mussolini, calling himself a fanatic for flight, would hail Blériot in print for his 'Latin genius and courage'[6] and, back in Bundaberg, Bert thrilled at the pages and pages of reports in *Flight* and *The Aero*, giving them pride of place in his scrapbook. *Flight* called it the 'greatest of all great events in the annals of modern history' and published every detail imaginable about the XI.

At the same time Bert read that the Australian Minister of Defence Joseph Cook was offering £5000 to the newly formed Australian Aerial League if it could come up with an aeroplane for military purposes. The Aerial League was the brainchild of a *Bulletin* cartoonist, aviation enthusiast and epileptic named George Taylor, whose mentor Lawrence Hargrave chaired the first meeting of the group in Sydney on 28 April 1909.

The published diagrams of the Blériot XI gave Bert the idea that he could build a similar craft, and he said later, 'the Blériot design seemed to tally better with the lines upon which I had worked in my bird experiments'. Every penny of his wages from the foundry and Millaquin went into buying timber and calico for the construction of his own aircraft.

While Blériot celebrated his Channel crossing, the Wright brothers had returned to a stupendous welcome in the USA and were finally rejoicing over success at Fort Myer. In July 1909 they sold their aircraft to the army's Aeronautical Division, US Signal Corps for $30,000, which included a $5000 bonus for exceeding the speed specification of 40 miles (65 kilometres) per hour.

Wilbur climaxed an extraordinary year for aviation when he circled the Statue of Liberty on 29 September 1909 and made a 33-minute flight up and down the Hudson River as an estimated one million New Yorkers watched in astonishment. Three days later in Potsdam, Germany, Orville took a Model A an unprecedented

500 metres, impressing even Graf Zeppelin, the former German army general who was declaring his huge airships to be safe and reliable transport.

Bert wondered how long it would be before flying machines descended on Australia. He was soon to find out.

In September 1909, George Taylor opened Australia's first aeroplane factory in Brumby Street, Surry Hills, in Sydney, and in October a wealthy aviation aficionado, Lawrence Adamson, headmaster of Wesley College in Melbourne, imported the first powered aircraft to appear in Australia, a Wright Model A from France, which cost him £1500. He also brought in a Blériot that cost £800.[7] The Wright Model A was named the *Stella* in honour of the wife of Colin Defries, a London pilot who was ready to fly it on the first powered flight in Australia. Defries had taken flying lessons in Cannes and Paris and was being backed to present 'A Flying Fortnight' by the theatrical firm of J. & N. Tait, whose recent family venture, *The Story of the Kelly Gang*, was the world's first feature film.

George Taylor knew he had to get cracking if he was to beat the Wright machine into the air, and on sand dunes at Narrabeen Heads, north of Sydney on 5 December, he became the first man to fly a heavier than air machine in Australia when his glider took wing before about a hundred spectators. Just four days later, Defries took to the air in the Model A at Victoria Park racecourse in the Sydney suburb of Zetland. A disappointing crowd of only about 250 people paying 2s 6d watched as Defries reached an altitude of five metres before crash-landing after 105 metres as he tried to retrieve his hat, which had blown off. Debate grew over whether it was a controlled flight or an uncontrolled hop.

In England John Moore-Brabazon was awarded the Royal Aero Club Aviator's Certificate No. 1 on 8 March 1910, two years after he had learned to fly in France on a Voisin biplane. Long before he received his aviator's certificate, however, he was credited with the first officially recognised flight in England and had collected a £1000 prize from Lord Northcliffe's *Daily Mail* on 30 October 1909 for flying a circular mile. Five days later he proved that pigs could fly when he took a piglet skyward in a waste-paper basket tied to a wing-strut in what might have been the very first cargo flight.

In Australia there was a race to catch up. On 17 March 1910 at Bolivar, north of Adelaide, a nineteen-year-old motor mechanic named Fred Custance, who had never flown before but was up for anything, flew for about 180 metres, reaching an altitude of fifteen metres in a Blériot XI belonging to Adelaide businessman Fred Jones. He came down so hard that the undercarriage was smashed and the propeller broken.

It needed a touch of magic to control an aircraft properly, and who better to demonstrate that the very next morning than the world's greatest conjurer, Erik Weisz, better known by his stage name, Harry Houdini, who was in Melbourne performing as the Handcuff King. The Hungarian-born son of a New York rabbi, Houdini was the world's most feted escape artist. While performing in Hamburg in 1909 he paid $5000 for an 80-horsepower Voisin biplane that owed its design to the Hargrave kites. Houdini accepted an offer from Australian impresario Harry Rickards to perform his magic act at the Tivoli in Sydney and at the Melbourne Opera House. George Taylor invited Houdini to bring the biplane with him to spread the word on aviation and Lord Northcliffe helped sponsor the trip to show Australia the importance of this new technology in safeguarding the British Empire.

Although Houdini and his wife Bess, who doubled as his stage assistant, mesmerised Melbourne audiences by day, the Handcuff King was preoccupied with what was happening under a huge tent at Diggers Rest, about 40 kilometres northwest on the road to Bendigo. A field there known as Plumpton's Paddock had been chosen as an ideal spot for flying, and under the tent Houdini's French mechanic and flying tutor, Antonio Brassac, cared for the Voisin like a doting mother. Houdini waited for weeks for the right conditions and, while he waited, American mechanic Ralph Banks attempted to fly Defries' Model A there on 1 March. Banks made an uncontrolled hop for about 275 metres at a height of five metres but came down so hard that the Wright aircraft was smashed beyond repair.

Meanwhile, Lawrence Adamson was shattered by his aviation venture. Not long after Ralph Banks crashed the Wright machine the spinning propeller of his Blériot lopped off the right hand of 16-year-old Ewart Lock, one of 2500 spectators hoping to see a flying machine at Adelaide's Cheltenham racecourse.[8] Adamson had the engine removed from the Model A and then dumped both his aircraft into Melbourne's Hobsons Bay to regain £798 of his customs import duty.

Houdini had better luck. On Friday morning, 18 March, he declared conditions perfect for his attempt and assembled newspaper reporters as well as a photographer and a cinematographer. The Voisin was rolled out from its tent shortly before 8 a.m. Houdini passionately kissed

Bess as Brassac counted '*Un, deux, trois,*' and spun the aluminium propeller behind Houdini's seat. The engine growled into life. A quick touch to the clutch at Houdini's side and the big machine was thundering across the grass. After about 45 metres Houdini raised the elevator and was airborne. Just as it left the ground the Voisin swerved towards a massive gum tree. The spectators gasped. Houdini pulled again sharply on the elevating lever, making yet another of his miraculous escapes. He skimmed over the leaves with inches to spare. The *Argus* reporter wrote that the Voisin looked like a huge white bird with the fore-wheels, tucked up for flight, resembling great talons.[9] While all other flyers in Australia had so far crashed back to earth after their brief ascents Houdini came in for a graceful landing to hearty congratulations from all assembled. Before the day was out he made two more flights, the longest about three and a half minutes in which he flew in a great loop for more than three kilometres over rocky outcrops and stone fences. He admitted that he'd been nervous at the start but 'the funny thing was that as soon as I was aloft all the tension and the strain left me. As soon as I was up all my muscles relaxed, and I sat back, feeling a sense of ease. Freedom and exhilaration, that's what it is.'

Official witnesses from the Aerial League signed a document declaring that they had seen Houdini fly, and two days later he did it all again before a crowd of about 120.

Among those who saw Houdini fly at Diggers Rest was Harry Hawker, the son of a Moorabbin blacksmith. Hawker had already packed a lot of living into his twenty-one years. He had attended four schools in his six years of education before joining the workforce at the age of eleven with Melbourne's Hall & Warden bicycle depot. By thirteen he was test driving Oldsmobiles and by fifteen was a mechanic for Tarrant Motor and Engineering Co. in Lygon Street, Carlton, which made one of Australia's first cars. By the time he was eighteen, Hawker was looking after five vehicles, including a Rolls-Royce owned by the wealthy grazier Ernest de Little, lord of Caramut House in western Victoria. The magical experience of seeing Houdini fly primed Hawker for bigger things.

Bert pasted a report into his scrapbook in which Houdini declared that aviation was 'the most wonderful thing in the world today'. He also read in the *Queenslander* that Glenn Curtiss and yet another French aviator, Louis Paulhan, had demonstrated the military might of aircraft at an aviation meeting in Los Angeles as a Lieutenant Paul Beck dropped sandbags as dummy bombs from their planes. The sandbags landed frighteningly close to their targets, prompting Paulhan to explain: 'A fleet of aeroplanes could attack the harbour defences, and destroy the city, too. You saw me carry two passengers ... suppose I took up an equivalent weight of dynamite and let it fall on the fortifications?'[10]

Just a few weeks later, Paulhan defeated the Englishman Claude Grahame-White for the *Daily Mail*'s £10,000 prize, flying the 314 kilometres from London to Manchester in 12 hours, making just two stops along the way. That was about the same distance as a flight from Bundaberg to Brisbane, and Bert imagined himself high above the cane fields of Bundy soaring through the breeze to the great river city to the south. But he had never yet seen a flying machine, let alone ridden in one, so how would such a thing be possible for a young factory worker in a Queensland country town?

Less than three weeks after reading of Paulhan's epic flight, Bert heard that among the attractions of the recent annual show in the Central Queensland town of Longreach was an exhibition of the gliders and model aircraft belonging to lean, spare 47-year-old Lindsay Campbell, who for more than a decade had been experimenting with Hargrave box kites and gliders in Western Australia. After the Longreach show Campbell came to Brisbane and formed the Queensland Aero Club and Glider School, for which he leased city premises in Turbot Street, Brisbane. Within a month the club had forty members, including the Prime Minister Andrew Fisher, a former Scottish pit boy turned Gympie newspaper proprietor. The Aero Club then formed a branch of Taylor's Aerial League, and Campbell championed the cause of aviation for defence purposes, declaring that for the price of one naval war vessel Australia could place a fleet of 1500 aeroplanes around her coasts capable of wiping out any modern Dreadnought.[11]

Bert was one of the first to join the Queensland Aero Club and began corresponding with other members. Campbell and Thomas Macleod, a Brisbane barrister and aviation enthusiast, unveiled their Antoinette-style monoplane — Queensland's first aeroplane — albeit an engineless one, made from canvas, wire and wood. They erected it on 15 June on the corner of Turbot Street and North Quay opposite the Aero Club building, and Campbell, Macleod and an assistant stood on the framework to hold it down as photos were taken in gusting winds.[12] Before long their creation was joined by a biplane glider that combined the best features of the Wright and Farman designs with a box-kite tail.

Other Australians were busy building aeroplanes, and on 16 July 1910 at his father's farm near Kyneton, north of Melbourne, John Duigan made a seven-metre hop in his home-made Farman-style biplane. Nine days later Lawrence Hargrave, the man who'd started it all, received a visit from Alexander Graham Bell at his Woollahra Point house after Bell had first visited Melbourne to advise the Federal Government's Postal Commission on a new telephone exchange.

In Brisbane Lindsay Campbell organised a major display at the Brisbane Agricultural Show for August 1910 and an Aviation Week at the new Olympia theatre at North Quay where, to the accompaniment of film and slides, he outlined his belief that the aeroplane would soon supersede the car just as the car had superseded the horse. Despite public fears, he argued that flying was safer than riding a bicycle, and the thrill of launching oneself into space was far more fascinating than any other sporting pursuit. His Aero Club also built a shed on a grassless knoll in the northern Brisbane suburb of Eildon Hill from where they could fly kites, thus advertising the future of aviation for much of Brisbane to see. Thomas Macleod, who taught himself to fly using a balancing machine like a rotating see-saw in the backyard of his West End home and who used students from Brisbane Grammar School as his ground crew, tested his bat-wing glider at Herston Heights near the present-day Royal Brisbane Hospital before making the first documented flight in Queensland there on 11 October 1910.[13] The bat-wing glider was so difficult to control that after two narrow escapes he gave up using it and flew his biplane glider instead three days before Christmas on a property belonging to the pioneering Sinnamon family of Oxley.[14]

Bert and dozens of other budding aviators paid a penny for the 11 January edition of *The Aero*, which featured a long article on man-carrying gliders complete with detailed drawings and technical information. Bert was inspired to begin work on his own glider, but Campbell and Macleod knew it was time for Queensland to see aeroplanes with engines. So in March 1911 they invited visiting Frenchman Gaston Cugnet to exhibit his Blériot at Canada Motor Company on the corner of Brisbane's Creek and Adelaide streets. The exhibition was limited to ground running, which might have been just as well after Cugnet's flights in Melbourne where he had crashed into a cow when landing at Altona and then crashed into tennis courts at the Jolimont end of the Melbourne Cricket Ground.

Bert was having his own flirtations with danger. Late on a Wednesday afternoon in May 1911 he was fishing in the Burnett with his English-born mates Charlie Laffan, a moulder from the foundry, and George Macklin, who worked on the railways. Their little dinghy capsized under the same railway bridge Bert had tried to cross as a toddler. As all three plunged into cold water, they suddenly realised that Charlie, who'd arrived in Australia from Liverpool only two years earlier, couldn't swim. Bert and George dragged Charlie to the upturned dinghy and told him to hold on for dear life and keep kicking his legs. The dinghy could scarcely hold Charlie's weight, and he was soon in difficulties. Bert and George, weighed down by their trousers and shirts, both took off against a powerful and treacherous current as they headed towards some small boats stored on the river's northern shore. Horrified, they found when they lurched on to land with Charlie calling to 'come quick, hurry' that every boat on the shore was secured by chain and padlock. Almost spent by the swim, they then ran into nearby Perry Street to find help. All the while Charlie was battling to stay afloat. Frantic, Bert and George at last found someone with a key, raced back to the river, launched one of the boats and, despite their breathlessness, rowed as hard as they could back to where Charlie was on his last gasp, having spent twenty minutes in the chilly water. All three breathed easier once he was dragged into the boat, and it only made their friendship stronger.

Charlie and George became regulars at the Hinkler house over the next few months as Bert outlined his plans for constructing what he later called his Glider No. 1. They wondered whether he'd had too much sun when he told them he was already well advanced and was going to build a craft like Blériot's with a few touches of his own from studying the ibis. The flying position would be different, with the pilot lying prone as in the first Wright machine. His mates agreed to help him, even if the whole thing seemed like a giggle. Every night as Frances cooked dinner, Bert would sketch plans and make calculations on pieces of butcher's paper. He bought more wood and calico and scrounged old bicycle wheels for the undercarriage from anyone who had spares.

Under the spreading leaves of the backyard mulberry tree, from which Frances made thick black jam with the fruit the flying foxes left her, Bert shaped the pine for his machine using a steamer he built from a primus stove, rubber tube, kettle and box. At the foundry, his bosses let him use their machines to fashion metal sockets for spar joints for the wings and fuselage. To the Hinkler neighbours the skeletal machine taking shape amid the sweet potatoes and tomato plants seemed as implausible as Noah's ark but, with the eye of an engineer and the brain of an aeronautical physicist, the shy, diminutive eighteen-year-old foundry labourer constructed the glider's wings and body and stitched calico for the covering. Frances and Papa wondered when he'd grow out of his flying obsession, but they humoured him because he was so enthusiastic.

When the glider was finished Bert decided to test it on the gentle breezes and soft cushioning sandhills of Mon Repos beach, about thirteen kilometres from Gavin Street.

Frances took charge of transporting the glider. She and Bert's siblings and friends from the surrounding streets were pressed into service to tow it behind the horse and buggy for the three-hour journey through the cane stalks towering over Bert's head. The wings were removed and strapped to the fuselage for towing so that the glider was transformed into its own trailer. Plenty of the neighbours laughed at the regular procession of this strange wooden bird on wheels going up Gavin Street, but Bert saw Mon Repos as his Kitty Hawk.

On a wide, smooth sweep of sand he mapped out an area for testing the glider, but for months he might as well have been using his old aviette. Occasionally old-timers watching shook their heads at the folly of the young mugs running across the sand with guy ropes trying to get the big crate airborne. Glider No. 1 eventually achieved lift-off and flew unmanned while Bert had it tethered with a rope, but it crashed too often. Bert terrified the dairy cows on a Mon Repos paddock owned by the Taylor family, and on one notable occasion his craft ploughed into a cane field. Much of the cane in the paddock had to be knocked down so that the glider could be retrieved. The farmer's threats and explosive views on 'flying cranks' had Bundaberg laughing for years. Bert realised his glider needed work.

With no chance at any of Queensland's major universities or colleges — he didn't have the means to leave his part-time jobs — Bert did the next best thing and with the few pounds he had left after buying materials for the glider on 13 September 1911 he enrolled in a course on aviation run by International Correspondence Schools. Studying the intricacies of lift, thrust and control beside the faint glow of his home-made electric light, he learned more about air displacement and ailerons, the hinged surfaces on a wing that controlled lateral balance.

The Italians were studying other things about aircraft. On 23 October 1911, while Bert was achieving an average of 98.4 per cent in the thirteen subjects of his correspondence course, including arithmetic, elementary mechanics and logarithms, Captain Carlo Piazza made the first reconnaissance flight in an aircraft, using a Blériot XI to spy on Turkish troops near Benghazi in Libya during the Italo–Turkish war. A week later on 1 November, another Italian pilot, Lieutenant Giulio Gavotti, flying a Taube monoplane at 180 metres over Turkish camps near Ain Zara in Libya, took four grenades and tossed them over the side. Although no one was hurt, he had given birth to aerial bombing. The Australian Government noted the way aviation, still in its infancy, was changing dramatically, and in December 1911 the Australian Defence Department placed advertisements in Britain for 'two competent mechanists and aviators' to establish a flying corps and school.

As Christmas 1911 arrived, Bert announced that he was going to remodel the glider and that he would require Frances's ironing board as the pilot's seat. She could press the clothes on the kitchen table for a while.

The design he envisaged was not unlike the flying machines of Da Vinci and in its own way was a masterpiece. Under the mulberry tree Bert made changes to Glider No. 1 using the diagrams of the Blériot to guide him. He borrowed two guineas from Frances for new wheels shipped up from Melbourne with the promise that once he made it big she could have half of every pound he earned.[15] She also bought him 55 metres of linen to cover the new machine. After several weeks of painstaking weighing, measuring, bending, shaping and restitching he pronounced himself pleased with his remodelled glider, a craft with a wingspan of almost 10 metres, a length of more than six metres and a weight of 59 kilograms, about the same as the 160-centimetre teenager ready to fly it. To stiffen the fabric on his craft he used a 'dope' (varnish made from flour and water) rather than the sophisticated and expensive chemical agents used in aircraft factories.

Bert planned to lie flat on the ironing board like the Wright brothers at the Kill Devil Hills, controlling the elevator with his hands and using his feet to work a rocking pedal lever attached to the rudder. Every chance he got he tried out the glider on Mon Repos with his friends and neighbours as air crew. His experiments might have met with derision in some quarters, but Bert found a lifelong friend in *Bundaberg Mail* reporter Joe Marks, who was three years Bert's senior and came from a long line of distinguished journalists. Joe was only too willing to help Bert fly and to report on his achievements. Under the headline 'A LOCAL FLYING MAN', Joe wrote in the *Mail* on 25 March 1912:

> The aero youth of North Bundaberg, Bert Hinkler, who has been studying the art of aviation for some time past, and has made several highly satisfactory flights in the first machine which he constructed last year, has designed and constructed another glider,

which has occupied his spare time since Christmas.
The machine is entirely one of his own models and
the flying portion of it was studied by himself from the
flight of an ibis. We might mention that the inventor
is only 19 years of age. The machine was taken to
Mon Repos yesterday for a trial flight but there was
scarcely a breath of wind blowing, and consequently
the machine would not rise above a couple of feet.
However, the aviator is confident that with a strong
wind it will rise and soar through the air like a bird.[16]

Bert's confidence was warranted. He was not yet as famous
as that other Bundaberg teenager Gladys Moncrieff, who
had wowed even Dame Nellie Melba with her singing,
but his career as an aeronaut was taking wing. On Easter
Saturday, 6 April Bert gathered his brother Jack; sister
May; Charlie Laffan; the Macklin brothers George and
Charlie; another mate from the foundry, Charlie Griffin,
who boarded at Bert's house; Joe Marks and Joe's dog
Scamp for some more experiments on the sand and in
the sky. They took the glider apart, attached the pieces
with ropes to the back of their pushbikes and pedalled off
towards Mon Repos for an Easter camping weekend.

On the sand they reassembled the glider and carried it
to the top of a small sandhill overlooking the bright blue
waters. The breeze was blowing the wrong way to lift so
Bert told his helpers to grab the guy ropes, run like the
racehorse Carbine and 'Don't let go'.

Bert then climbed onto the plank that had replaced the
ironing board after Frances took it back and, with May
watching, gave the signal for his mates to yank as hard
as they could on the ropes connected to the nose of his

machine. The glider rose a couple of feet and came down with a thud. So they tried again with a similar result. A third effort gave a bit more of a hop. The more they tried, the higher the glider rose, until finally Bert pulled back on the elevator and the breeze joined the celebration. Up, up he went to thirty fabulous, fantastic feet as he gave a shout of triumph and the lads running underneath with the ropes waved their hands above their heads in joy. Bert hovered and wobbled in the breeze for 100 metres or so, waving at Joe and Jack and the other boys below as the colours of his world seemed to become brighter, the sounds more precise and his eyesight sharper. His whole future was opening up before him. Then the moment passed. Bert and his glider came down to earth with a solid bump, rather less gracefully than the ibis circling nearby.

Joe Marks made sure there was another report in the *Mail* under the headline 'SUCCESSFUL AERO FLIGHT' and, while Joe wrote that 'the youth who is only nineteen years of age is to be congratulated', Bert knew there was a world of difference between hovering in a home-made glider and being a fully fledged aviator like Blériot, Farman or the Wrights. Still he kept practising, recalling years later his mother watching 'white faced' with worry and shouting, 'Come down, Bert, or you'll get killed.' Looking back on those early days, he recalled: 'My little glider was too tiny and frail to carry an engine.'

To fly as Houdini had done at Diggers Rest, Bert knew he needed some magic of his own, and he found just the man. He was off to see the Wizard, and what a wonderful wizard he was.

Chapter 6

*Bert and I were more like pals than mother
and son. Bert never had a penny of assistance
from anybody all his life. He won through with
his own hard work and determination.*

Frances Hinkler, 1928[1]

*My first thought was 'I'll bet I won't get home
to dinner this time.' Funny, isn't it, when one is
facing death, but that was my first thought.*

**'Wizard' Stone, after his monoplane
fell from 300 metres into the waters of
Chicago's Lake Michigan in 1911[2]**

The American aviator Arthur Burr 'Wizard' Stone was a
death-defying daredevil. If opposites attract then nineteen-
year-old Bert Hinkler, quiet and shy, was immediately
drawn to the flamboyant performances of this American
showman twice his age who lived by the creed of the early
flyers that no pilot was any good until he had broken wood.

In the six years after Lieutenant Selfridge had died at
Fort Myer in 1908 as many as a thousand aviators were

killed, and it was estimated that the death rate among early pilots was a staggering 87 per cent. Even Cal Rodgers died when he crashed after colliding with a flock of seagulls at Long Beach, California, soon after making the first flight right across the USA on 5 November 1911.[3]

Wizard Stone began his working life as an apprentice machinist and toolmaker, became a professional bicycle rider and then, starting in 1901 when he was twenty-seven, a touring motorcycle stuntman, partnering his wife Irene as they looped the loop in their 16-foot steel wire globe they called — drum roll, please — the Globe of Death. Stone was doing his show in Berlin in 1909 when Orville Wright took the Crown Prince aloft, and he learned to fly a single-seat Blériot monoplane the next year at Étampes on the outskirts of Paris before embarking on a journey of 800 kilometres with frequent stops, from Paris to the Wright school in Pau.

After a Globe of Death tour of South America, Stone took a job as a test pilot for Queen Aeroplane Company on the corner of Amsterdam Avenue and 197th Street, New York City, working alongside thirty-year-old Oklahoma car dealer Clyde Cessna. The Queen company was engaged in making knock-offs of the Blériot XI — replicas without a licence fee — and by the time Stone arrived in Australia in December 1911 as the star attraction of the Phillip Lytton travelling vaudeville tent show, he had survived a dozen crashes. The most spectacular came the previous August when he was racing at dusk over Chicago's Lake Michigan against the Englishman Tommy Sopwith just a day after the deaths there of fellow pilots William R. Badger and St Croix Johnstone. Stone's plane fell from 300 metres into the cold water. Somehow he survived after leaping from the plummeting plane just before impact, although one of his shoes was torn off by the propeller. He was rescued by a motorboat just as he was at the point of exhaustion after half an hour treading water. Stone's survival was put down to the fact that Irene Stone ran from their hangar just before the flight and tied an inflated automobile tyre around his shoulders.

The Wizard came to Australia with an American-built Metz-Blériot that was powered by a small seven-cylinder 50-horsepower French Gnome Omega engine based on Hargrave's rotary principle. The Metz Company, of Waltham, Massachusetts, made automobiles but was licensed by Blériot to build copies of the French aeroplanes in kit form.

Stone set about thrilling audiences as soon as he arrived in Sydney, performing the Globe of Death with Irene for promoter J.D. Williams at Sydney Cricket Ground from New Year's Day 1912. Stone also ballyhooed a match race against William Ewart Hart, a Parramatta dentist who had the Aerial League's Aviation Licence No. 1 dated 5 December 1911 as the first man to qualify as a pilot in Australia. Hart had just opened a flying school at Penrith but crashed with an overweight pupil onto the railway lines at nearby Mount Druitt three days later. He had paid £1333 to a New Zealander named Joe Hammond for a Bristol Boxkite that Hammond had been demonstrating around Australia on behalf of the British and Colonial Aeroplane Co. As he talked up the race against Hart, the Wizard's first flights in Australia were at country fairs west of the Blue Mountains at Bathurst, then Orange, where he panicked horses at the showground, and then Dubbo.

Hart was also having problems with livestock and was sued for £30 by a Sydney dairyman whose cows on Epsom Road, Waterloo, had stampeded after Hart flew over them. Two of the cows had died. It was all good publicity for the race against the American wizard.

Wherever he went Stone told his audiences that Australia, with its vast tracts of level country, wide, open spaces, comparatively few mountain chains and numerous excellent landing places, was an ideal land for the aviator. Aeroplanes, Stone said, would soon be as common as automobiles. That was the same line that Lindsay Campbell was preaching as he wrote to newspapers and lobbied the Federal Government to set up an Australian aviation corps based in Queensland and equipped with Blériots. Campbell wanted one of the key positions in Australia's proposed Central Flying School but knew he needed formal qualifications if he was to be accepted by the government. So by the time Stone arrived in Australia, Campbell had sailed for England with his young family to train at the Bristol school at Brooklands in Surrey in the hope of earning an Aviator's Certificate from the Royal Aero Club. He was in England as the Wizard prepared to make the first powered flight in Queensland as Phillip Lytton's troupe headed for the Rockhampton Showgrounds.

On the way Stone showed off his Blériot in Brisbane and on Wednesday, 29 May, as Bert scanned the advertisements in the *Bundaberg Mail* over breakfast, looking for news on his glider going on display at the Bundaberg show, one advertisement almost made him choke on his toast. It was right below the promotion for Cook's Pictures featuring a 'cinematogram' of the Brisbane Thousand horserace

and the 'unparalleled sensation' of the midget circus at
Bundaberg's Queen's Theatre. It read:

> Extraordinary Announcement.
> Exhibition of the Famous Blériot Monoplane
> To-day from 2.30 til 10 pm
> Location — Next Lytton's Theatre, Esplanade.
> Mr Phillip Lytton begs to announce that he has
> arranged with the famous American Aviator Wizard
> Stone from Europe to Rockhampton Carnival to
> put on view for one day and night only the famous
> BLÉRIOT MONOPLANE in which he will race in his
> race with the Australian aviator W.E. Hart in Sydney
> on June 15th.[4]

The rumours were true. Wizard Stone was really coming
to Bundaberg. Bert could hardly believe his good fortune.
He'd spent most of the last three years obsessed with Blériot
and his gallant flight across the Channel, and now, a Blériot
just like that famous machine — even if it was a Yank copy
from Massachusetts — was coming right to his hometown,
just across the river from Gavin Street. As he later
explained it, the mountain had come to the 'Mechanical
Mahomet' of Bundaberg. Bert tore across the longest steel
traffic bridge in Australia on his bike to the Esplanade for a
look at the machine before doors opened. He tried to sneak
in under the tent housing the Blériot to scrutinise the object
of his obsession but only got halfway under the tent flap
when he heard rude words being shouted in his direction
and promptly got back on his bike.[5] Bert wanted to hang
around until the doors officially opened, but he was on the
noon to 8 p.m. shift that day at Millaquin and jobs were

too hard to come by to risk a late start. Instead, he spent most of his eight-hour labouring shift — carrying crates and boxes and sweeping up — thinking of ways to become the Wizard's apprentice. As soon as knock-off time came he pedalled home as fast as he could, collected Frances, May and George and headed for the commotion that was Lytton's travelling tent show.

The Esplanade was enveloped in a festive atmosphere and, while the rest of his family found the whoops and hollers of the carnival goers, the hypnotic vitality of a brass band and the garish acetylene lamps intoxicating, Bert had eyes for only one thing. For a shilling show-goers could enter Wizard Stone's tent, meet the guru of aviation himself and gaze upon his magical machine, a craft that Bert had already learned was roughly the same size as the glider he had built, weighing just 71 kilograms. Unlike Bert's glider, this machine had an engine. It was the first time Bert had laid eyes on a real powered aeroplane, and he was transfixed, not just by the technology that could propel a man through the air but also with his own ingenuity in building a machine very similar in structure underneath the mulberry tree.

To Bert's family the workings of the Blériot were as baffling as nuclear physics to a latter age, but Bert was right at home. The Wizard, dressed in old rags and with oil smudges on his face, looked more like a Dickensian villain than a hero of the new scientific age, but he had the bearing of show business royalty as he stood regally answering questions from the farmers and mill workers gathering around, telling them he'd wanted to fly in Bundaberg but the showground had too many tree stumps. Having heard that, since arriving in Australia, the Wizard had been confounded by problems with the Blériot's wings, Bert decided to marry opportunity with preparation. He approached the great man. Clearing his throat and standing on tiptoes, Bert introduced himself to 'Mr Wizard', shaking the hand that had shaken the hand of Orville and Wilbur Wright. He then told Mr Wizard that, according to his research, he knew the very solution to the handling problems of the machine.

Stone looked at Bert as though the callow country bumpkin had cracked open a rotten egg. Everywhere he went in Australia, there was some aviation know-all, and this one had even brought his mother, brother and sister. 'Hey kid, have you ever flown an aeroplane?' Stone asked.

'No, Mr Wizard,' Bert replied nervously.

'Have you ever seen an aeroplane before?'

'No, Mr Wizard.'

'Then what the hell makes you think you know about aeroplanes?'

'Well, Mr Wizard,' Bert ventured tentatively, 'I built my own glider and just a few weeks ago I flew it at a beach near here.'

The Wizard's eyes widened.

'And just recently in an issue of the English journal *Flight* they were talking about this same problem you're having with your machine.' Bert was on a roll. 'You see, Mr Wizard, *Flight* said that in the Blériot XI and the Blériot copies like this one the wire stays on top of the monoplane's wing need nearly as much strength as the stays underneath the wing. I reckon if you strengthened those wires you'd have a lot more control of your machine.'

The Wizard was astonished. Goddam it, maybe the kid did know about aeroplanes. Stone promised Bert that he'd fix the wires before he travelled to Rockhampton the next day.

Bert wasn't finished. He told Stone that he knew all about different engines and machines, too, not only from his aviation correspondence course but also from his time working among the steam engines and other equipment taking shape at the Bundaberg Foundry. If Mr Wizard knew of anyone who needed a good mechanic to work on an aeroplane he was just the man. And he was a hard worker. And most of the time he just shut up and did the job.

The Wizard was impressed and said that later in the year, when he took his performances to Victoria, he might need the services of an eager kid who loved planes. The opportunity was, Bert recalled twenty years later, 'as if heaven had opened its gates'.

The day after meeting Bert, the Wizard visited the Bundaberg show to give Bert's glider the thumbs up. He then packed his Metz-Blériot onto the goods train bound for the Rockhampton Showgrounds almost 300 kilometres to the north. There on Friday, 31 May, in ideal weather, a crowd of several thousand, including Bert and his father, gathered to see what all this flying fuss was about.[6]

Stone kept his machine in the marquee he'd used at Bundaberg, and it was examined by spectators in the shade before being wheeled out in mid-afternoon. Among those coming in for a closer look was a strapping 188-centimetre, 102-kilogram miner, rugby player, amateur thespian and aviation student named Stan Dallas, a twenty-year-old Adonis whose interest in flying had been accelerated in 1911 when Lindsay Campbell had opened the Mount Morgan chapter of the Queensland Aero Club. Dallas was driving trucks in the Mount Morgan Company's quarries on Iron Island when he heard Wizard Stone was going to fly at Rockhampton. Just like Bert, he was fascinated by birds in flight — particularly hawks and eagles — and he had also built his own glider, although without the success of his diminutive peer.

Stone took Bert at his word and strengthened the top wires on the Blériot's wing before the machine was wheeled out and the engine warmed up. He climbed into the giant dragonfly, adjusted his helmet and goggles and then darted along the grass for about 45 metres before the wheels left the ground and cheering broke out among the crowd. Stone flew in wide circles until he had attained an altitude of about 180 metres. He descended in a series of swoops until he landed just a few feet from where he'd taken off to more thunderous cheering. Bert hollered so loud he went hoarse.

Stone's celebrations were muted, though. At the same time as Rockhampton marvelled at his triumph the Wizard was mourning his first flying hero Wilbur Wright, who had died from typhoid fever in Dayton a day earlier, aged just forty-five, bringing an end to all of Orville's ambitions as well. The Wizard told reporters that he knew Wilbur well and had learned many of his flying tricks from him.[7] He put some of those tricks to use just four days later on 4 June, the same day Lindsay Campbell was being issued with Aviator Certificate No. 220 from the Royal Aero Club in England. The Wizard flew again in Rockhampton before a crowd of 7000, racing a taxi driven by twenty-year-old Sydney Taylor over 24 kilometres in loops of the Callaghan Park horseracing track. By the time the car had covered six kilometres Stone's machine was leading but, with victory beckoning, Stone ploughed into a nearby cricket field. As was his custom, he jumped clear just at the point of impact and escaped without injury, although his machine would need its regular rebuild.

He walked back to Callaghan Park to sustained cheering, but the damage to the Blériot meant he was forced to cancel a flight over Brisbane planned for 8 June. Although Bert's advice hadn't solved all Stone's problems, as he bade farewell to his new mate, Stone told him the mechanic's job was still there for him at the end of the year.

In the USA at roughly the same time, a shy, gawky, overly polite ten-year-old named Charles Lindbergh, the son of a Minnesota congressman and grandson of a philandering Swedish farmer, sat beside his slightly loopy mother in a makeshift grandstand watching a similar race between an aeroplane and a motor car around an oval track at the 1912 Fort Myer Aeronautical Trials. Lindbergh would later recall the moment of awe, an experience so intense and fascinating that he made up his mind there and then to become a pilot, too. It was a dangerous game, yet he reasoned that if he spent just ten years flying before being killed in a crash, the excitement would be a worthwhile trade for an ordinary lifetime.[8]

Bert felt the same, and his ambition increased after Aerial League stalwart Thomas Macleod invited him to bring his glider south to display at the Brisbane Agricultural and Industrial Exhibition ('the Ekka'), which started on 12 August. Brisbane, with 140,000 people, was the biggest city in Australia north of Sydney, and it presented myriad opportunities. Bert figured he'd get a job to support himself in the Queensland capital while the move would also allow him to speak with other members of the Queensland Aero Club. Macleod introduced Bert to many other aviation enthusiasts and said while there were young people like Bert in Queensland the science of flight would flourish in the state.

In Sydney Wizard Stone prepared for his 32-kilometre race with W.E. Hart set down for 15 June and sponsored by Black & White Whisky. It would pit the two warring aviators on a course from the Ascot racecourse[9] in Mascot to Parramatta Park. A crowd of 15,000 assembled at the racecourse for the starter's gun, but the event had to be postponed because of gusting winds. Two weeks later, when the race was set again, this time from the Surrey Park football ground at Rosebery, heavy rain was not about to stop either pilot, even though neither had protection from the elements.

Deciding that the best course of safety was a staggered start, Hart was the first to take off, 10 minutes before the American. Both flyers were quickly drenched. Stone was closing the gap until Hart's Bristol Boxkite disappeared into the rain clouds. A stranger in the Sydney skies, Stone had no reference point to see where he was going except a winding river that he'd been told to keep on his right. Without realising it, he followed the wrong ribbon of water, the Georges River instead of the Parramatta, and ended up coming down miles away in the suburb of Lakemba. Hart landed on target at Parramatta Park after 23 minutes and 53 seconds. Undeterred, the Wizard headed back to Brisbane with Irene and their five-year-old daughter Edna on the steamer *Aramac* to perform the first powered flight in the Queensland capital.

With the help of an early benefactor, Boer War veteran Lieutenant Colonel Hubert Harris, president of the Queensland Rifle Association and an aviation enthusiast, Bert landed a temporary job in Brisbane. He became a plumber's assistant and meter reader with the Survey Department of the Metropolitan Water Supply and Sewerage Board. Not only did he learn how to unblock a toilet but also he had plenty of time to experiment with the Queensland Aero Club's kites from the precipice of Eildon Hill. At work he would tell his friend Jack Gibson of his grand plans to tour Victoria as Wizard Stone's mechanic and one day to qualify for his own aviation licence.

On Saturday, 6 July, Bert was among the 8000 spectators packed around the oval at the Brisbane Exhibition Ground. Irene and Edna huddled in the main grandstand against the cold of the approaching winter's evening when, at 4.10 p.m. under clear skies and a light breeze, the Wizard, billed as 'The world's greatest airman', wheeled out his machine. His face was covered in oil smears to protect it from the propeller blast, and he surveyed the difficult task in front of him. The oval was encircled by a grandstand and Machinery Hill, meaning that he would only have a short take-off area and would have to make an almost vertical lift-off to avoid crashing into the crowd. As Stone revved the engine and braced himself against the smoke and noise his assistants dug their heels into the ground and hung onto the wings, allowing the machine to build as much momentum as it could. The huge blast of wind from the propeller drove a mix of oil and petrol back onto the unprotected heads of all those around the plane. Then they let go, and Bert watched spellbound as the Blériot tore across the grass and whooshed into the air.

By the time he reached Machinery Hill, Stone was roaring just above the heads of thrilled spectators. Stone ascended in a corkscrew pattern, going higher and higher as he made loops of the oval until he reached 120 metres. He flew above the crowd for about 10 minutes before deciding he'd have to come down. Suddenly he realised that it was going to be tougher than he thought. He'd landed on plenty of sports grounds before but not ones encircled by grandstands and a steep hill. He saw the Albion Park racetrack about two kilometres away, but there was a race meeting on with people and horses everywhere.

Reluctantly the Wizard headed back towards the Exhibition Ground at a dangerously steep angle like a dive-bomber of a future time. As Bert, Irene and Edna braced themselves for disaster, the Metz-Blériot hit the ground with a crack. One of the wheels sheared off and flew across the ground. The propeller dug into the dirt and blew apart. The machine did a somersault and crashed onto its back, breaking in half. While the crowd gasped in horror the Wizard limped from the wreckage and signalled to the crowd that he was all right. A huge mass of people surged towards him, not to check on his welfare but to get pieces of the smashed plane as souvenirs.[10] Stone later said landing on the oval was like landing in a well.

He told Bert that, while the job as Stone's mechanic in Melbourne was still on offer, he could start work right away rebuilding the machine. Bert knew he'd be kept busy working for this human time-bomb. However, before he went to Melbourne with Stone, he decided to insure his future prospects with a fallback plan. Bert wrote an impressive application to join the proposed Australian Flying Corps and sent it to Colonel George L. Lee, a hero of the Boer War and commandant of the First Military District at Victoria Barracks in Brisbane.

> I have always taken a keen interest in Aviation
> [Bert wrote], and have constructed several models
> with very satisfactory results. About 18 months
> ago I commenced to experiment with gliders and
> have constructed two of them with which I gained
> complete success. I should have liked to have
> experimented further by installing an engine etc.
> but owing to my financial position I have had to
> content myself with gliders. I commenced a course
> of Aviation with the International Correspondence
> School during September 1911 and am still continuing
> it. I attach hereto six photos of my gliders.[11]

As well as the photos of his two gliders airborne at Mon Repos, Bert also included the newspaper reports by Joe Marks and some impressive references.

A manager at Millaquin said Bert had been an excellent employee working part-time for the previous four years, and Bundaberg's mayor, Lewis Maynard, wrote that Bert was a young man of many talents. Not only was Bert his own photographer on his glider experiments but also 'in conversation with him he tells me he did not work out his measurements from the glider he has already constructed from the data available in the scientific treatises on the matter but from the study and measurement of the various birds — the type chosen being the ibis as this is the heaviest bird with the greatest power of gliding amongst our local species'.[12]

In a reference dated 19 July 1912, North Bundaberg headmaster George Stanley explained to Colonel Lee that 'many people at the local agricultural show were highly delighted with The Machine [Bert's glider] he had on exhibition there. Mr Stone, an aviator who was present, highly commended the effort'. Stanley also wrote that shortly after leaving school Bert took up photography and 'took some good pictures of our teachers and my family'.

Colonel Lee was suitably impressed and forwarded the application to his superiors in Melbourne with a note saying that Mr Herbert Hinkler of Bundaberg, Queensland, was 'desirous of enlisting in the aviation corps when it is formed':

> He appears to be a bright, intelligent young man and has some good, practical ideas upon the art of Aviation and I consider that he would be a very suitable applicant for appointment. As will be seen from the attached correspondence and photos, he has devoted much of his spare time to the study of Aviation, and experiments with gliders and models. Considering that he is only 19 years of age and has no mechanical knowledge at all, being employed at a sugar mill in Bundaberg in a non-mechanical capacity, I consider he has done very well. I recommend this application.[13]

Bert had also made an impression with Cyril Brudenell Bingham White, a former Gympie bank clerk who had risen through the army ranks to become Australia's Director of Military Operations. White wrote back to Colonel Lee, saying that the formation of the flying corps was still under consideration but that Bert should reapply once it had been established.

In England Lindsay Campbell was not put off by the news that the Australian Defence Department had appointed two pilots as the cornerstones for the flying corps. One was Henry Petre, an English solicitor who had become chief instructor on the French SPAD machines at Brooklands, then an aircraft designer and test pilot with the Handley Page company. The other was Harry Busteed, a Melbourne mechanic who had come to England with Harry Hawker and become chief test pilot for Bristol. Busteed later withdrew, and his flying corps place was taken by another of Hawker's mates, Eric Harrison. On Saturday, 27 July, Campbell wrote to his wife, who was staying with their two small children in Maida Vale, West London, to say he was still having a marvellous time at the Brooklands aerodrome, was very proud of the skills he was developing and would soon put them to good use. The following Saturday, 3 August, Campbell took up a Bristol monoplane on a misty summer's morning. By 6.20 a.m. he had covered almost 14 kilometres in eight minutes when, making a turn at a height of about 90 metres, the engine cut out and the plane dropped to about 30 metres. The engine spluttered as Campbell tried to stay horizontal. Then the Bristol nosedived into the earth. Campbell's chest was crushed, and he died a few minutes later.[14]

Wizard Stone was having his usual spectacular bad luck as he tried to draw crowds with his Blériot in Queensland. At the Toowoomba Showgrounds a brawl broke out after it was announced that unpredictable winds meant his plane would be displayed only on the ground and not in the air. An eyewitness sixty years later recalled Stone copping a punch right on the nose and it gushing blood.

On 16 August he left 10,000 people, including Sir William MacGregor, Governor of Queensland and former

Governor of Lagos and Newfoundland, waiting for more than an hour and a half at Brisbane's Eagle Farm racecourse when a proposed race between the Blériot and a 1912 Cadillac driven by Mr Arthur Hobbs went laughably wrong.

While the race was due to start at 11.30 a.m., the Wizard finally took to the air at 1.08 p.m. after much looking at watches and toe-tapping among the big crowd. He and Hobbs then got their directions confused. The Cadillac and the Blériot went in opposite directions, and Wizard Stone had given his name to another fiasco.

Bert was making a much better impression with the Governor. Near the site where Stone had crashed at the Exhibition Ground, Thomas Macleod opened an aviation display for the Brisbane Ekka, and Bert's glider was the star exhibit inside the huge tent. Governor MacGregor was amazed that a teenager could build such a thing. The *Brisbane Courier* published a photograph of the glider airborne at Mon Repos and another of it packed for transport with Bert standing in front of it — a short, stocky young man with his sleeves rolled up and wearing sandshoes and a battered felt hat with its brim turned upwards.

With the Australian Flying Corps still not taking recruits, Bert farewelled his family, and his first sweetheart Sarrah Laffan, Charlie's sister, and headed south to join the Wizard in Melbourne. There they began rebuilding the machine, using Australian ash to strengthen the tail but making it heavier in the process. Stone told reporters that, depending on the wind, his Blériot had to reach between 40 and 50 kilometres per hour across the ground to achieve take-off. In trials at Royal Park on 3 October he achieved a speed of 120 kilometres per hour in the air and said he was impressed by Bert's work. He was ready to crash again.

A few days later Stone gave an exhibition at the Redan Racecourse in Ballarat, 115 kilometres west of Melbourne, but a cross-current of wind shook the machine so violently that it broke a bolt holding Stone's chair and he nearly fell out of the sky. Then at Ballarat Oval on 19 October Stone took off in front of the grandstand but, as he dodged a row of tall trees, the propeller hit the telephone wires and his machine flipped over. Stone fell out of the Blériot as it tumbled to the ground with a shattering crash. He landed unconscious three metres from his machine and spent a week in Ballarat Hospital suffering from concussion, a fractured shoulder and shock.[15] Bert later wrote:

> Aviation technique had not in those days reached its present pitch of perfection and my American idol had more than his share of ill luck. Smashes occurred and the frail little monoplane had to be entirely rebuilt. The experience I gained then with no specialised equipment was of immense value to me. How happy I was to find in stripping the disabled Blériot that my earlier ideas of construction and building my gliders had not been a serious departure from textbook rules.[16]

Once Stone staggered out of Ballarat Hospital he followed a similar path to Bert in chasing employment of a safer nature. He wanted Bert to join him in a job with the government, instructing pilots and maintaining aircraft.

From his digs at 104 Queen Street, Melbourne, Stone's business manager Gus Adami addressed a letter dated 20

November 1912 to George Pearce, Minister for Defence in Prime Minister Andrew Fisher's Labor Government. The letter read in part:

Re aviation

Sir

As manager for Mr Arthur B Stone (Wizard) American aviator, I beg to inform you that it his intention to form in Melbourne a school for aviators and the building of machines. He will have two machines at his disposal — a Blériot type monoplane and a Bristol type biplane, each fitted with a 50-horsepower Gnome engine. They are both up to date machines but he is making alterations so that they will be more suitable for pupils, as machines such as they were before alteration, or those which your respected department are importing are much too fast for such a purpose and wholly unsuitable on account of the great risk to the beginner and his machine. Mr Stone has had over three years experience in the management of aviators and the building of different types of aeroplanes. As an aviator he was the 15th man in America to gain his flying certificate. He is a first class Engineer, Mechanic and Flyer and has flown various types of machines in France and America. Since his residence in Australia he has given flying exhibitions in different parts of Queensland, New South Wales and Victoria, having made in all sixteen exhibition flights and numerous private ones. [Adami didn't mention all the crashes.] His engineer and chief mechanic [19-year-old Bert] is a man who thoroughly understands the building and care of aeroplanes and engines. Now with this combination, I would respectfully submit that we have a first-class staff for the purpose. We would be pleased to receive military pupils nominated by your respected department, at a reduced fee. As this venture will be the first of its kind in Australia, and seeing the great advantage it will be to the whole Commonwealth from a defence point of view I would respectfully submit that your respected government should subsidise the undertaking to a limited amount.[17]

George Pearce wasn't buying. So the Wizard decided to test his luck on different shores, across the Tasman in New Zealand under the backing of Percy Cornwall, a motor racing and speedboat enthusiast from Melbourne. Bert was ready for his first international aviation assignment.

At the same time Henry Petre embarked on a tour of Australia on his motorcycle to select a base for the Central Flying School. He decided the government's preferred choice near Duntroon, the military college near Canberra, was too dangerous for flying, given its altitude and lofty surrounds, and finally settled on a 300-hectare sheep farm at Point Cook, west of Melbourne.

Interest in aviation continued to grow around the world. The *Daily Mail* was offering £10,000 for a transatlantic flight less than a year after the *Titanic* had sunk to the bottom of it, and on 17 April 1913 Briton Gustav Hamel took four hours 18 minutes to fly from Dover to Cologne in his Blériot XI, the first flight from England to Germany. Two days later, on 19 April, 11,000 spectators paying a shilling each turned up at the Auckland Domain cricket ground to watch the Wizard fly. Another 30,000 were watching free of charge outside. Most had never seen an aeroplane before and, looking at the massive crowd, Bert swung the propeller with all his might to kick-start the Gnome engine.

No sooner had the Wizard's plane left the ground than it veered off course and crashed into a hill. The spectators had seen a flight of just 360 metres lasting a mere 35 seconds. They wanted more. Several hundred people rushed over to the damaged plane in a fury and, determined to get their money's worth, carried it with its busted tail back to the cricket ground and the tent where Bert was waiting, watching from a gap in the tent flap, fearful of a full-scale riot.

Bert's heart felt like it was going to explode, but Stone stayed cool. As he examined the damage, Stone gave no hint that he had just survived another aircraft crash and was about to be set upon by a hostile mob. He said he was going into the tent to get ready for another attempt at flight. Nervously Bert peered outside to see mounted policemen trying to drive back the crowd, which was whipping itself into a frenzy. In the furore one of the police horses tripped on a rope holding the tent and fell, crashing and heaving among the furious throng.

A red-faced police sergeant burst into the tent and told Stone that he had better do something fast because there was no way his men could hold back the mob much longer. So Bert stuck his head out and told the angry horde that as soon as the plane was fixed Stone would go up again, higher, further and faster than before. It wasn't a complete lie. Stone would be going up again but not on this day and not for this crowd. The Blériot's tail needed major repairs.

Bert managed to keep the crowd stalled by frequently sticking his head out of the tent to assure them that the Wizard was busy preparing. Finally after an hour or so, even the most belligerent spectators headed home.

The Wizard copped a bucketing from the Auckland press, and on 24 April, writing from Auckland's Alexandra Park racecourse, Bert sent some of the reports home to his mother asking her to keep all the ones with the photos. He explained that Stone's first flight in New Zealand 'did not come up to the public's expectations':

At any rate, [Stone] made two lovely flights at the racecourse where we are now only yesterday (Wed). Of course these were only trials.

I am having a lovely time but I have to sleep in the tent with the machine, but that's only a trifle. I am on a good wicket and am learning a lot, especially my way about the world. Hope your mind is easy as to the danger you have often thought was connected with flying as I'm still mechanic and Stone is doing all the flying on this tour.

Hope Papa is still doing well and is pleased with my progress even though I am not quite an aviator yet. I guess you know I can look after myself and at present I'm playing a saving game. So far I have got a fiver put by and tomorrow, Friday, is payday with another £3/8– for the week. So you see my Aeroplane business is not a bad paying venture.[18]

On the day Bert wrote the letter, Stone made one of his best flights for a long time, travelling for 20 kilometres after taking off from Alexandra Park. While Bert assured his parents that flying was extremely safe despite Stone's frequent flops, he didn't relate the news that Percy Cornwall had told him his role in their enterprise would be more hands on than ever. Not only was Bert going to maintain the Blériot but also he was going to become part of the act, partnering Cornwall in a racing car as it competed against the Blériot at Auckland racecourse.

'Data had to be worked out,' Bert related, 'at what speed, for instance, could we in the car take the bends at Auckland racecourse. Cornwall was at the wheel and it was my task to sit, stopwatch in hand, as he reeled off a little more than a mile a minute.' But not for long, it seems. The pair was racing around the course in their car rehearsing for a show when a tyre blew out with a huge booming roar as the car skidded into the railings. 'We took a swathe of them with us,' Bert recalled, 'and they took me, battered and unconscious to the hospital. How I escaped instant death was a miracle.' Bert's left arm was almost torn through at the shoulder, and for some time doctors thought the kindest thing would be to amputate. 'But splendid surgery and the fighting spirit of youth triumphed,' Bert said later.[19] He was laid up for a month, and Stone had to cancel two scheduled exhibition flights because of wet weather. The papers led a chorus of boos against Stone but, moving on to Hamilton, he made successful flights from the Claudelands Showgrounds on 10 and 14 May.

With Bert out of hospital, the Stone troupe boarded SS *Wimmera* on 27 May and travelled from Auckland to Napier with a short stop at Gisborne. In a letter home from Napier racecourse dated Sunday, 1 June 1913, Bert reassured his family that he was still having 'a lovely time' and was strong and healthy again following the accident. 'Only for the mark on my arm [I] would hardly feel anything had happened.' Bert reminded his mother that it was twelve months since he had taken her, May and George to Stone's tent in Bundaberg. He said working with the Wizard, despite all his crashes, proved that he was on the right track with his own glider designs and that 'if I had enough money I could have turned out an aeroplane as successful as any of the present day'. 'This town of Napier is rather a pretty place about Bundy size,' Bert wrote. 'Stone is to fly here on Tuesday and Hastings (about 10–12 miles away) on Saturday, after that I think we are going to Whanganui.' At least, that was the plan.

At 3.30 p.m. on 3 June, as winds gusted off the turquoise ocean near Napier and over the local racetrack, a team of Boy Scouts hauled the Blériot out of its tent to a paddock at the northern end of the course in preparation for a show before a thousand people. Bert didn't want him to fly with such strong winds, but the Wizard was sick of postponements and he didn't want any more Kiwis chasing him for a refund. Bert helped him into the cockpit. The Wizard adjusted his leather helmet and goggles, and Bert spun the propeller. The Blériot shook all over as the engine roared into life, but it was hard to say what was making the plane vibrate so violently, the wind or Stone throttling the Gnome. Suddenly the plane was off. It climbed to about 20 metres, unsteadily, then veered wildly as the wind toyed with it. The Wizard dived straight for a huge willow tree. He wrestled for control but the wind was too strong. The wing hit the willow's top branches as the plane nosed over and splintered on the ground, sending its pilot — well used to such outcomes — for a tailspin of his own on the ground. The Wizard staggered to his feet and gingerly felt his fractured collarbone before declaring to the onrushing crowd, 'I'm okay, I'm okay.'

But the Blériot wasn't. Bert knew immediately that the tour was over. Percy Cornwall lost £600 on the trip, and it ended with a smashed machine, a wounded pilot and a busted-up mechanic. The Blériot was too badly damaged to be repaired in New Zealand so Cornwall packed up the team, and on Friday, 6 June, they headed for Melbourne and then Sydney, travelling again on SS *Wimmera*. Cornwall, the Wizard, Irene and Edna Stone were all in 'Saloon' class; Bert was in steerage, the cheapest ticket available.

On 15 June, Bert wrote to his mother from his lodgings at 313 Crown Street, Sydney, saying he was 'stony-broke' but about to be paid four weeks wages and that, while the trip back to Australia had been extremely rough, it was all 'good experience'.

> They talk of rebuilding the machine in Melbourne and touring West Australia in about two months but, owing to the big loss on this last tour, I hardly fancy they will get going for a while so I am leaving Stone here as soon as they pay me. I will probably stay here for a week or so to give you time to send an answer and then I have a big idea of getting a boat to London to see the flying with my own eyes and see what the prospects of the game are over there, as I ought to stand a good chance now after this experience with Stone. In your return letter let me know your opinion and of course Papa's ... But if you think I ought to come home for the [sugar cane] crushing let me

know, but I hardly fancy it. Of course if I did not get on well in England I would very likely be back again before Christmas. From your ever loving Son, Bert.[20]

Frances and Papa weren't pleased. It was one thing to be a mechanic for an aviator, and Bert had almost got himself killed doing that. Now he was talking about going to the other side of the world.

Bert managed to wangle a job at W.E. Hart's Australian Flying School, which he had moved from Penrith to Ham Common at Richmond, NSW, on a site that would later become an RAAF base. The flying dentist had been grounded by a crash in September 1912 when his machine had become entangled in telegraph wires in the Sydney suburb of Burwood, and he broke nearly every bone in his body. He never flew again, but his aviation school was a magnet for budding pilots. Hart went back to pulling teeth, and he also liked to pull the leg of anyone who listened to his tales. Years later in the huge dentistry practice he built on an entire floor at Boomerang House, in King Street, Sydney, he would tell his captive patients about the days when his school was home to Bert Hinkler and the young aircraft designer Edgar Percival. Hart even claimed that after weeks of pestering him Bert finally persuaded him to give him a free flight on the Bristol Boxkite — they normally cost £10 — when Frances arrived on the scene, all the way from Bundaberg, told Hart that her boy had run away from home and dragged him back to Queensland.[21]

In truth, Bert did go home for a holiday on 3 August 1913, an event that was worthy of a Joe Marks article in the *Bundaberg Mail* as Bert outlined plans to tinker with his glider and eventually to construct a machine for commercial purposes. It all came down to financial backing, he told Marks, but there was big money to be made in aviation if only he could make a start. Bert recalled in his memoirs that he was happy enough working for Hart but 'never abandoned the hope that someone would finance my desire to build an aeroplane of [a] new type embodying the principles I had worked out in my glider, and others borne of experience with the Blériot and Stone'. Bert could only roll his eyes in October 1913 when Stone, after a series of postponements because of rain in Brisbane, crashed again at Eagle Farm. At the same time the Wizard was sued for £5/15/2 by the Postmaster General for the damage to the telephone wires in Ballarat a year earlier.

Frances and Papa tried to talk Bert out of his planned trip to England, but his mind was made up. He was nearly twenty-one, at an age when he could make such decisions for himself, and if things didn't work out he'd be back in a few weeks having experienced a piece of the world few of the labourers, cane cutters and railway navvies in Bundaberg would ever get to see. He'd been telling Charlie Laffan all about his grand plans, and Charlie was keen for adventure. They told Frances and Papa there was safety in numbers. In late October 1913 on the eve of their grand adventure Bert and Charlie posed for pictures in the backyard at Gavin Street, Bert in a new suit and straw boater and proudly wearing the Queensland Aero Club badge on his heart. May joined them on the steamer *Cooma* to see Sydney.

Papa knew all too well about the perils of an ocean voyage and of aviation. But he knew Bert had the brains to make something grand of his life and, as Bert said goodbye to his father on the porch of Woodbine Cottage, he promised the old man with the long white beard that the next time they shook hands he would be a 'fair dinkum' aviator.

Chapter 7

*The enduring safety of this country will not be
maintained by force of arms unless over the
whole sphere of aerial development we are
able to make ourselves the first nation.*[1]

**Winston Churchill, First Lord of the Admiralty,
at the Lord Mayor's Banquet in London in 1913,
advocating the building of more British warplanes**

*My word, this is truly a case of beating
the birds at their own game.*

**Bert Hinkler in a letter to his mother on 29 March
1914 after seeing an air show at Hendon**

Frances couldn't let Bert go without giving him a proper
dockside send-off. So she came down to Sydney at the
end of December to join May as Bert and Charlie — like
millions of backpackers from a latter generation — looked
around for a cheap way to see the world. Sydney was
the most splendid place Bert had ever seen, the massive
sparkling harbour crying out for a bridge like the one
across the Burnett and the flotilla of sailing boats bobbing

about and steamers ready to journey through the Heads to Europe and the USA, Africa, Siam, Shanghai and all the exotic ports between.

The pair of eager adventurers tried to obtain work on some England-bound passenger ships, but there was nothing doing. Instead they found a big, old German trader that needed experienced firemen to stoke the boilers. Charlie had worked as a fireman and was hired straight away, but the skipper turned up his nose at *'der kleine junge'* — the small boy — with him. Charlie said if Bert wasn't going he wasn't going either, and eventually Charlie's little mate was hired as a coal feeder to help three burly Germans, who showed no regard for Bert's German ancestry.[2]

With Frances and May waving from Circular Quay, the Bundy boys finally set sail to work their passage to Hamburg, where forty-nine years earlier Bert's father had set sail on *La Rochelle*. Bert's journey was almost as rough, given the clips over the ear he received from the German firemen for the first few days. Charlie told Bert to hit one of the Germans over the head with a coal shovel and the other two would get the message, but the torment didn't end until Charlie, perhaps with an eye to looming Anglo–Germanic tensions, stormed into the boiler room brandishing the shovel. The skipper had to break up the standoff.

By the time Bert and Charlie arrived in Hamburg they had just £2 in their pockets. They made it to the northern English port of Grimsby but, after four months of travelling, Charlie had seen enough of chilly old England almost as soon as his feet touched his home soil. He was broke and headed back to his family in Steuart Street, working his way back on another vessel. In the first of his long letters home, Bert wrote to his mother from Liverpool on 29 March 1914, explaining in his copybook hand that he and Charlie came as far as Grimsby together 'and then I left him to go about my business in London and he was to wait in Liverpool until I came up. As it was he only stayed here two and a half days and got a boat back to Australia'.

Looking for a chance to gain his wings on a powered aeroplane, Bert counted what was left of his money and journeyed south from Grimsby to London on the train. While the sights and sounds of this imperial city made him blink with amazement at almost every turn and had his camera clicking overtime, it was the buzz of England's booming aviation industry that enchanted him more than Nelson's Column or the church of St Martin-in-the-Fields. He spent six days knocking on doors, visiting the offices of the magazines he read as a boy, telling them timidly about the gliders he built as a teenager[3] and asking for work at all the aviation companies springing up around London. He was, in his words, 'brimful of hope and ambition, disproportionately supplied with cash', and counting as his most valuable possessions several letters of introduction supplied by Wizard Stone and William Hart.

He had arrived in England at the right time. Urged on by First Lord of the Admiralty Winston Churchill, Britain was racing to surpass France, Germany and the USA as the hub of world aviation.

John Moore-Brabazon, Britain's first licensed pilot whose car proudly bore the personalised number-plate FLY 1, had received Aviator's Certificate No. 1 but gave up flying four months later in 1910 to please his wife after the No. 2 Certificate holder, the carmaker Charles

Rolls, business partner of Henry Royce, became Britain's first aviation casualty. The 195 centimetre Rolls was just thirty-two when the tail of his Wright Flyer broke off at Hengistbury Airfield in Bournemouth and he crashed to his death. Sam Cody, who had received Aviator's Certificate No. 9, and whose hop of 424 metres on 16 October 1908 was regarded by many as preceding Moore-Brabazon's feat as England's first powered flight, crashed to his death in 1913. Those disasters didn't stop others taking off.

During 1912 and 1913 Churchill made many flights himself, saying that the risky business was a tonic for the mental stress of politics, even though his wife Clementine pleaded with him to keep his feet on the ground. At Eastchurch in Kent, on 29 November 1913, flying tutor Gilbert Wildman-Lushington had taken Churchill up for three lessons in a Short Brothers S.38 biplane, and Churchill had taken the controls for a time. Just three days later the instructor died in a crash at the same airfield. Nevertheless Churchill's faith in aircraft could not be shaken.[4]

Aircraft factories were springing up everywhere in England. Claude Grahame-White had built an aerodrome on 89 hectares of pasture in the north London suburb of Hendon. The aerial exhibitions and races from there were among London's top attractions.[5] The engineering firm Vickers, which had a flying school at Brooklands, had received a contract from the Admiralty to build a fighting biplane armed with the Vickers machine-gun,[6] Geoffrey de Havilland, who had designed the BE2 (Blériot Experimental) for the Royal Aircraft Factory, was now chief designer at Airco, and Frederick Handley Page was tooling up his factory at Cricklewood, with an eye to the darkening political climate in Europe. Noel Pemberton Billing was trying to make a go of his seaplane company, which would soon be known as Supermarine, and Harry Busteed had helped to design the Bristol Scout for the British and Colonial Aeroplane Company. By 1910 in Manchester, Alliott Verdon-Roe, who had made his claim for Britain's first powered flight before Cody and Moore-Brabazon in his home-made triplane, had built an aircraft manufacturing business from the cellar of a mill owned by his brother. By 1914 he was selling more Avro 504s than he and his designer Roy Chadwick could produce.

In London, Bert found a kindred spirit in the dashing Tommy Sopwith, who at twenty-six was just five years older than him and who was impressed by the endorsement from Wizard Stone, his old rival in the Chicago air race of 1911.

On 18 December 1910 Sopwith had earned a £4000 prize from Churchill's friend Baron de Forest for the longest flight from England to the continent in a British-built aeroplane, covering 270 kilometres from Eastchurch to Tirlemont in Belgium in a biplane built by Englishman Howard T. Wright under a railway arch in Battersea, London. The flight took 3 hours 40 minutes and made Blériot's Channel crossing of a year earlier look like an insignificant hop.

Still, Blériot remained the biggest name in aviation, his company Blériot Aéronautique building 800 Type XI monoplanes between July 1909 and August 1914. The Type XI became the basis for most of the fledgling air forces of the world. Sopwith believed he could do better and used his £4000 prize money to set up the Sopwith School of Flying at Brooklands and in 1912, with his yacht mechanic Fred Sigrist, formed Sopwith Aviation Company, opening his factory that December in a recently closed roller-skating rink in Canbury Park Road in southwest London.

Bert forced himself out of his shyness and, with his pockets bare and his belly empty, badgered the Sopwith company for a job day after day until they finally said yes. The Queensland country boy now had a job in London in what he regarded as the most innovative industry in the world. With a small advance in pay he decided to take a look at the north of England to celebrate and see what was happening in aviation up there. Bert's first long letter home, written from Liverpool, reflected his enthusiasm and optimism at finally getting a start in the pursuit of his dreams. 'My Darling Mother,' he began, 'I left London on Tuesday last by an express train slightly faster than Queensland trains and arrived here in a little over three and three-quarter hours. Liverpool is a lovely, big place and no end of shipping.'

Bert related that he had visited the Liverpool Aviation School in the Merseyside suburb of Waterloo, run by Henry Melly, an electrical engineer, who learned to fly at the Blériot school in Pau on his honeymoon. At forty-three Melly had made the first powered flight in Liverpool in 1911, flying a two-seater Blériot across the Mersey and circling New Brighton Tower, a lattice-steel observation tower like Eiffel's that, at 173 metres, was the tallest structure in Britain. Bert noted that Melly had three Blériot monoplanes at his flying school but 'up in these parts there is pretty well nothing doing and at present he is running the show at a loss and may give it up after the summer'.

Bert described being in the midst of 'the enormous crowd' at Liverpool's Aintree racecourse to see the rank outsider Sunloch storm home to win the 1914 Grand National.

> I suppose you know this is about the biggest steeplechase in the world and it was a lovely day (for England I mean). The sun shone bright and very little wind. Soon after you get this I suppose you will be able to see the moving pictures in Bundy. I've had no more snow since I was in London and lately the weather here is becoming Australian like. A big difference I notice is that it seems to rain whenever it likes — not like in the land of the kangaroo where it gets hot and thunders for a day or two ahead.[7]

Charlie Laffan's brother Johnny joined Bert in England, and the pair visited Liverpool's Olympia and Hippodrome music halls and went to look at New Brighton, amazed by the huge tower and the ballroom at its foot. 'There was nothing on while we were over,' Bert wrote, 'but I believe it is something grand in the summer.' He had put his camera to good use and said the photographs included in the letter would save him ink 'trying to explain the beauties etc'. But in his most important revelation, Bert told his mother:

> I was in London about six days. While in that city I got a fine job at the Sopwith Aeroplane Works to learn the trade thoroughly and I think for the best of my future it is a wise idea to accept. I may start next week and if I do I suppose that will mean living over here for some time. So when you read this and Papa hears it, I think you will both agree that it's about the

best plan. You will see that I will have a trade which in a few years will be prosperous in Australia. So that even if I don't learn to fly (although in a few months I will have the best of opportunities) I have bettered myself to some extent. Just now the aeroplane business is getting very busy, as coming on for summer it is the season. Of course you might have read the telegraphic news which I suppose the other day included the feats of about five aviators looping the loop at Hendon on all sorts of different machines. My word this is truly a case of beating the birds at their own game.[8]

Bert's gumption in sailing halfway around the world to learn all he could about flying reminded Sopwith of his test pilot Harry Hawker, another jockey-sized Australian with big ambitions. From the time Hawker had seen Houdini dodge the gum tree and the craggy rocks to soar at Diggers Rest, he had been determined to conquer the skies. Hawker was twenty-two when he left his job and the Rolls-Royce at Caramut House and, with three friends, Harry Busteed, Harry Kauper and Eric Harrison, arrived in London in May 1911, seeking the source of all knowledge on aviation.

But aviation was not about to give up its secrets readily to a small, softly spoken young man who looked for all the world like a schoolboy. Hawker knocked on doors for three months, at all the aircraft companies and then at the automobile workshops with no luck. By the end of July 1911 he was ready to head home a beaten man but finally landed a job with the Commer company in Luton building trucks and buses. His reputation as a mechanical genius quickly spread. Within a few months he had moved on to the British workshop of Mercedes for a modest pay rise and from there to Austro–Daimler, where the chief designer was a German named Ferdinand Porsche.

In the middle of 1912 a friend suggested that Hawker might find work with Sigrist and Sopwith and before long he became the company's employee No. 15 as a mechanic. From the money he'd saved he paid Sopwith £40 for flying lessons and after just three lessons flew solo for 50 minutes, Sopwith remarking that he was a 'beautiful pilot'.[9]

Hawker was awarded his Aviator's Certificate No. 297 on 17 September 1912 and within days had recovered the £40 by giving lessons to other budding pilots. Sopwith made Hawker his test pilot and gave him free rein as a designer. Hawker broke de Havilland's British altitude record for a solo flight in June 1913, climbing to almost 3500 metres until his carburettor froze. Later he took a passenger to 4000 metres.

Hawker and Sopwith tested their new machine, the Sopwith Tabloid, in November 1913 at Farnborough, about a 40-kilometre lorry drive from their old skating rink. The Tabloid, as the name suggested, was a compact short-winged biplane. Hawker had it up to almost 150 kilometres per hour while carrying a passenger, and it took only a minute to climb to almost 370 metres. Sopwith then put it on show at Hendon to great acclaim from the public and military, and it would soon be the fastest and most manoeuvrable aeroplane in the world. This was the machine Sopwith was busily building when he gave Bert his start in British aviation.

There was no talk yet of Bert learning to fly, but he was prepared to bide his time, writing later that he would be eternally grateful to Sopwith 'who gave me my first opportunity. It was only a position on the [assembly] bench but I was among airmen and aeroplanes — that was sufficient'.

Hawker was not in London when Bert first rolled up his sleeves at the Canbury Park Road factory. The Tabloid trials had gone so well that Hawker and his mechanic Harry Kauper took one to display in Australia arriving in Melbourne on the steamer SS *Maloja* on 13 January 1914. Hawker was an instant hit in Melbourne as he flew over cheering, waving children at Sandringham and Mordialloc and landed on the lawn at Government House. Hawker performed before 30,000 people at Caulfield racecourse and gave flying exhibitions in Sydney, Albury and Ballarat.

He was packing up ready to return to England when a 31-year-old Frenchman, Maurice Guillaux, arrived in Sydney on RMS *Orontes*, with a dodgy reputation and an impressive handlebar moustache as well as a Blériot XI 'Looper' stunt machine and a Farman hydroplane belonging to Lebbeus Hordern, of the wealthy family of Sydney merchants. Guillaux, who had looped the loop on Christmas Day, 1913, in Paris,[10] had been banned from competing in European air races for ten years because of claims that he cheated by overstating the distance he covered in the Pommery Cup.[11] He had been employed to assemble the Farman and test it for Hordern and, as he set about giving exhibitions in both planes, he would become another thorn in the side of Wizard Stone, still trying to make a quid in Australia even though his young 'Mechanical Mahomet' had gone.

Back at Canbury Park Road, Bert had thrown himself into his new job. He never tired of seeing plywood sheeting and glue turn into magnificent aircraft. The Tabloid was a sensation, and Sopwith had modified it into a seaplane called the Sopwith Schneider. On 20 April, just a couple of weeks after Bert first signed the Sopwith time book, Howard Pixton flew one at nearly 145 kilometres per hour in Monaco to win the Schneider Trophy, a seaplane race instituted by the French financier Jacques Schneider.

When he wasn't helping put together the forty Tabloids and 160 Schneiders Sopwith constructed or attending the regular air shows around London, Bert was writing home to the folks. On 24 April 1914, he wrote to his nine-year-old sister, showing that, although he dreamed of being a death-defying pilot, he remained a loving older brother. 'My Darling Queenie,' he started, 'I hope you are going to school everyday and learning your lessons. What are Jacky and George doing now? Tell them both if they write I will answer them. There are plenty of aeroplanes here and the other day an airship and an aeroplane flew right over the house. Love to all and write soon.'

There was also plenty of aviation action back in Australia, thanks to Guillaux and Wizard Stone. On 20 April, Guillaux, dressed in a hooded jersey like a polar explorer, had performed his loop the loop in a trial flight at Sydney's Victoria Park,[12] then repeated the feat a week later at the Newcastle Showground.[13] Then, back at Victoria Park before a crowd of 60,000 — half of them watching from the sandhills outside the stadium — he looped the loop ten times in succession as a bright silk tricolour tied to his rudder fluttered proudly. As he explained it, the French were lords of the skies and always would be, no matter how much military might was on display in other countries. 'France today is the greatest power in the air,' he told the

Sydney Morning Herald, 'and if she comes into conflict with any nation ... her aeroplanes will win the day.' Guillaux rated the world's air powers as (1) France, (2) Germany, (3) Russia, (4) England and (5) Italy. The USA was several lengths back in the field, he said, with most of its planes being chiefly for exhibition purposes. Australia wasn't even in the race.[14]

But as Guillaux talked up himself and his nation's air force and drew huge crowds to his aerial exhibitions, it was Wizard Stone, the perennial warhorse of the skies, who was to be given Australia's next aviation honour. Arthur Rickard, a Sydney property developer with land subdivisions from Woy Woy to Port Hacking, was promoting an aerial mail service and was backing the first ever flight from Melbourne to Sydney to prove its viability. Rickard's aeronaut was to carry 500 kilograms of postcard mail in what he claimed would be 'an epoch in Australian history'. Less than three years earlier Earle Ovington, one of Stone's colleagues at Queen Aeroplane Co. and a one-time lab assistant for Thomas Edison, had been sworn in as the USA's 'first Aeroplane Mail Carrier', flying one of Queen's Blériot knock-offs from Garden City on Long Island, New York, to Mineola, all of five kilometres away, with a sack containing 640 letters and 1280 postcards squeezed between his legs. From a height of 150 metres he dropped the sack over the side to waiting postal officials. The sack burst on impact and letters flew everywhere, but airmail had arrived in the USA.

Thanks to Rickard and Stone, it was about to arrive in Australia, too. The flight of almost 940 kilometres from Melbourne to Sydney showed just how far aviation had come in three years. Souvenir postcards were printed bearing the unsmiling faces of Stone and his new 'Organizer and Manager' P.V. Ryan, who would follow the flight in a motorcar with a team of mechanics. Rickard's proposal was approved by the Postmaster General on 12 May, but the PMG had been following Stone's career and had his doubts. He ordered that the postcards bear the inscription: 'This card is purchased on the distinct understanding that the Postmaster General accepts no responsibility in the event of non-delivery through accident or any other cause.'

Irene Stone was pregnant with their second daughter, and the Wizard had just recovered from yet another bad fall in Brisbane. The first postal flight had to be delayed, but the Wizard, ever the showman, insisted that he would leave Melbourne on the morning of 23 May, cover the distance in seven days and most likely land at one of the Sydney racecourses on the afternoon of 30 May. He would be flying a brand-new Blériot-designed aircraft. Fourteen fuel depots would be established en route.[15] On 23 May engine trouble ensured that Stone remained grounded. The mail run was postponed to 6 June.

In Bundaberg Frances kept her eye on the papers for reports on Stone making history to send to Bert, but the next batch of news had a familiar refrain. 'SENSATIONAL ACCIDENT. MONOPLANE FALLS 200FT. "WIZARD" STONE'S ESCAPE FROM DEATH,' screamed one headline. '"WIZARD" STONE INJURED. HIS MONOPLANE WRECKED', cried another. 'WIZARD STONE FALLS. LUCKY ESCAPE FROM DEATH'. Stone had crashed again while testing his new plane beside Maribyrnong Road at Sunshine on 1 June. All his teeth were knocked out, his top lip all but severed and his back, neck and jaw seriously damaged.[16]

As Stone lay in his sickbed battered and bruised, Guillaux took off from the Melbourne Showgrounds at 9.12 a.m. on Thursday, 16 July, heading for Sydney's Moore Park with a sack containing 1785 souvenir postcards and a few letters along with Australia's first air freight: some Lipton tea and O.T. lemon squash bound for Sydney's Commercial Travellers Club.

He was flying in an aircraft with an open cockpit over mountains he had never seen before and with only a compass and the railway line to guide him. The Blériot's fuel capacity meant that it could be in the air for only two hours at a time, and he had seven refuelling stops planned at towns that could provide a racecourse or a field to land on and a bonfire to point the way. Heading north he flew at just 90 metres as he passed over Wandong, scaring horses and cattle, startling chickens and causing no end of barking from the farm dogs. He stopped at Seymour and in freezing cold and fog he rose to 4500 metres over Wangaratta before refuelling there, landed for lunch with the French-born mayor of Albury despite arriving at the wrong racecourse just as the horses crossed the finish line, flew over Culcairn, refuelled again at Wagga Wagga, passed over Junee and then stopped at Harden because of driving rain and the roughest conditions he'd ever encountered. At times he said a cyclonic tail wind and rain had pushed his flimsy machine to 200 kilometres per hour.[17]

The next day the weather was even worse. He became violently ill trying to ride his bucking machine and feared that the wind would hurl him out of the sky. He was forced to return to Harden to spend another night. The next morning, Saturday 18 July, Guillaux landed at Goulburn racecourse to refuel and to nurse the aches in his wrists from wrestling the controls.

He stopped at Liverpool on Sydney's outskirts because he did not want to arrive at Moore Park too early for a planned civic reception and to fill in time he circled around Parramatta and Manly for an hour or so. Then just before three o'clock, in torrential rain, and with a crowd of 10,000 assembled at the Sydney Sports Ground to see a rugby union Test match between Australia and New Zealand, Guillaux began circling high above the arena looking for a bonfire in Moore Park that would mark his landing spot. He finally saw it as the storm passed and dived towards the ground at a furious speed. When he landed, looking like he'd flown in from Antarctica, he was met with massive cheering from the crowd pouring from the Sports Ground and then more cheering when he raised the sack containing Australia's first air mail high above his head, although the mail could have got there sooner on the train. He had covered the 940 kilometres in a total flying time of 9 hours 15 minutes. Pushing his way through the crowd to shake his hand was Australia's new Governor General, Sir Ronald Munro Ferguson. The crowd carried the beaming Frenchman into the arena to the sounds of thousands singing 'For He's a Jolly Good Fellow'. The longest airmail flight in the world to that time even managed to soften the blow of the All Blacks' 5–0 victory. Guillaux said he loved Australia but didn't know how the people put up with such lousy weather.[18]

The weather in London in the middle of 1914 wasn't much better, at least not on the foggy afternoon of 6 June when Bert took the train to Hendon and joined a crowd of 60,000 to watch the 1914 Aerial Derby, a race over a circuit around London, measuring 150 kilometres. Competing were two Blériots, the Sopwith Tabloid, a Sopwith Schneider, four biplanes built by the Farman brothers and three Morane-Saulnier monoplanes, similar to the one Frenchman Roland Garros had flown for the first non-stop crossing of the Mediterranean nine months earlier. The Derby got under way at 4.16 p.m. and finished an hour and 18 minutes later with victory going to the only American competing, William L. Brock, a flying instructor at Grahame-White's Hendon school, in an 80-horsepower Morane-Saulnier.[19]

As Bert watched the Derby fascinated, he wondered how long it would be before he had a chance to race against the best pilots in the world.

Delighted that Sopwith had hired another Australian — and a dead keen one at that — Harry Hawker's first task back in Britain was to correct a fatal flaw in aircraft even if it meant risking his own life. The problem of how to control an aeroplane in a spin, when one or both wings were stalled, had confounded just about everyone who had ever flown, often with deadly consequences. A pilot's natural instinct to pull back on the stick served only to aggravate the spin and make recovery all but hopeless. A few days after Brock had won the Aerial Derby, Hawker took up a Sopwith biplane over Brooklands and at 300 metres put his machine into a deliberate spin like those that had killed hundreds of aviators before him.

After dropping nose first, while spinning round its longitudinal axis, the machine appeared to flatten out when a couple of hundred feet from the ground, but then dived again and disappeared behind some trees. Onlookers rushed to the crash site expecting Hawker to be dead but instead they found him climbing into the sidecar of a motorcycle. His machine had flattened out just before reaching the ground, and had crashed into the top of a tree, where it hung for a few precious moments like a stuck parachute before dropping to the ground.[20] The tiny airman declared: 'I know what I should have done — if only I had the guts to do it.' Hawker was flying again the next day and, a few days later at Brooklands, he again risked death with another deliberate spin. This time, however, rather than pull the stick back to try to regain control he pushed the stick forward. Instead of exacerbating the problem the dive increased the airflow over the surfaces of the plane and allowed him to regain control. To celebrate Hawker looped the loop a dozen times. His daring experiment would save thousands of lives.[21]

Yet pilots around the globe were about to meet perils never before experienced, and Bert sensed that he would soon be facing a whole new world of danger and excitement. The buzzing beehive of activity throughout the aviation factories of England was being mirrored in similar factories, munitions warehouses, armament manufacturers and naval shipyards across Europe.

The political dynamite of 1914 was just waiting to explode. Conflicts like those in Prussia that had caused the exodus of Papa Hinkler's family had simmered for decades. Nationalistic fervour swept the continent as military men flexed their muscles and diplomats formed complex political alliances that heightened tension. Kaiser Wilhelm made it clear that Germany planned to surpass Britain's naval strength, and each major power was coming up with new weapons of mass destruction.

Bert remained desperate to fly but the £75 he needed for lessons was still beyond his means and, even if they wanted to teach him, Hawker, Sopwith and the others in the Canbury Park Road factory had no time to do so. There was a storm brewing, unlike any storm the world had ever seen, and the shackles holding Bert on the ground would soon be torn loose. 'I was at the very door of opportunity,' he wrote later, 'when and how it was to be opened to me mattered little, I knew that my chance would come. And when it did I had little choice of the time or method of it. The call to arms in August 1914 decided it.'[22]

Chapter 8

*I must tell you how disappointed I was not to get a
shot or two into that darned gasbag and made at
least one less to hand out death from the air.*

**Bert Hinkler in a letter to his parents after a German
Zeppelin bombed Newcastle on Tyne on 14 April 1915**

*When my brother and I built and flew the first
man-carrying flying machine, we thought we were
introducing into the world an invention which
would make future wars practically impossible.*[1]

**Orville Wright, on his disappointment at
how an invention designed to help mankind
had been turned into a killing machine**

A few days after Bert had watched Harry Hawker cheat
death in solving the riddle of the tailspin, six suicide
terrorists and their handler were loitering along Sarajevo's
Appelkai, a wide avenue in the Bosnian capital. They were
a motley gang of misfits. Five of them were teenagers,
three were dying of tuberculosis and all had told their
masters in the Black Hand terrorist cells that they were

ready to sacrifice themselves to free their people. Each had a cyanide tablet to end his life when the mission was accomplished. They mingled uneasily with the festive crowd cheering the fifty-year-old Archduke Franz Ferdinand, heir to the Austro–Hungarian throne, and his wife Sophie. Two decades earlier the Archduke had gone as far as Narromine in the colony of New South Wales shooting kangaroos, emus, pelicans, turkeys and ibis[2] — whatever crossed his path — but on this bright Sunday morning of 28 June 1914 he was the hunted.

Franz Ferdinand had accepted an invitation to look over army manoeuvres outside Sarajevo. After a brief review of the troops, the Archduke's motorcade of six cars headed along the Appelkai towards Sarajevo's Town Hall at 10 a.m. He and Sophie were seated in the back of an open-top 1910 Graf & Stift Double Phaeton limousine, and the Archduke was wearing the finery of an Austrian cavalry general. Sophie, radiant in her white silk dress, looked every inch the princess. Many of the buildings lining the route were festooned with flags and flowers, some displayed the Archduke's photograph, and there were cheers of 'Long may he live'.[3]

As the Archduke's car approached the first two assassins, they hesitated and kept their grenades in their pockets. Further along, the third assassin, Nedeljko Cabrinovic, drew his grenade from a long black coat, smashed the detonator against a lamppost, and tossed it at the Archduke.[4] The grenade bounced off the folded-back hood of the Double Phaeton and exploded underneath the car behind, injuring two of the Archduke's officers and more than a dozen bystanders. Cabrinovic swallowed his suicide pill and dived into the Miljacka River, but the cyanide mix only made him vomit and the water was only a few inches deep. He was dragged out, bashed and arrested. Franz Ferdinand's driver put his foot to the floor, and the Double Phaeton raced to the Sarajevo Town Hall as fast as its four-cylinder engine could go, passing three other assassins who either had second thoughts or were unsighted.[5]

One of them, Gavrilo Princip, dejected because the assassination attempt had been a disaster like the rest of his life, trudged off to console himself at Moritz Schiller's food store near Sarajevo's Latin Bridge. The Archduke's car screeched to halt at the Town Hall as local dignitaries, none of whom knew about the grenade explosion, prepared to honour him with a public reception. As Sarajevo's mayor began his well-rehearsed welcoming speech, a furious Franz Ferdinand leapt from his car and cut him off, shouting: 'Mr Mayor, I came here on a visit and I get bombs thrown at me. It is outrageous.' But, soothed by his wife's gentle hand, the Archduke allowed the mayor to carry on before asking to visit the garrison hospital to see the soldiers who had been wounded by the grenade. He and Sophie set off for the hospital, but the chauffeur took a wrong turn into the narrow Franz Joseph Street, stopped in front of Schiller's food store and, realising his mistake, began to slowly reverse. Gavrilo Princip, the sickly 19-year-old with TB and a death wish, was almost overwhelmed by the serendipity but managed to still his trembling heart for a moment, drew his pistol from his suit-coat and opened fire from five feet. Princip's first bullet struck the Archduke in the jugular and lodged in his spine. As Sophie dived to shield her husband Princip's second bullet went through the side of the car, Sophie's corset and her right side, lodging in her abdomen. Blood began to bubble from beneath her white dress.

Princip bit into his cyanide capsule, but a policeman swung a baton at his head and knocked it from his mouth and then, as the boy assassin placed the muzzle of his pistol against his own head, the gun was wrestled off him before he could pull the trigger. The Archduke's car sped across the Latin Bridge towards a nearby hospital as blood gushed from Franz Ferdinand's mouth. Seeing his wife's wounds, he managed to gasp, 'Sophie dear. Sophie dear. Don't die. Stay alive for our children', but within an hour they were both dead.

After a month of diplomatic threats and riots, Austria, with Germany's backing, declared war on Serbia on 28 July 1914, setting off a chain reaction around the globe. The Tsar mobilised Russia's massive forces to defend Serbia, and France agreed to support her. Germany declared war on Russia, France mobilised against Germany and Germany declared war on Belgium to get at France. Britain, having guaranteed Belgium's neutrality, declared war on Germany on 4 August. Just a few hours later Australia had joined what had become the first war involving the whole world, firing the Allies' first shot at Fort Nepean in Victoria and forcing the German cargo steamer SS *Pfalz* to surrender as it was leaving Port Phillip Bay. At Trafalgar Square and Whitehall thousands of Londoners gathered to sing patriotic songs and cheer, believing victory was only weeks away.[6] At the Sopwith factory, Bert knew differently, but he wrote to his parents and told them not to worry, and in a letter to little sister Queenie he softened the horror of what was happening.

'My Dear Queenie,' Bert wrote, 'You are right in saying that I ought to have been home for some coconut ice. I suppose Mum has told you of the big war over this side of the world. All England is ready and wherever you go you can see policemen and soldiers. A great number of aeroplanes are needed for the war and in our factory we are working from 6 o'clock in the morning till 10 o'clock at night.'

War spread like a virus, and soon the whole world seemed to be fighting. By the end of August the Austro–Hungarians were attacking the Serbs, and the Germans were in Belgium. French and British troops invaded the German protectorate of Togoland in Africa, and German troops were about to move on South Africa. New Zealand soldiers occupied German Samoa, and the Australians were preparing to take New Britain, part of German New Guinea.

Despite the build-up of warplanes in the months before the Archduke's assassination and the intense training of pilots in centres unfortunately named concentration camps,[7] the number of British planes available for the military was still low. The Royal Naval Air Service (RNAS) had ninety-three aircraft, six airships and two balloons. The Royal Flying Corps (RFC), founded in 1912 from the Balloon Section of the Royal Engineers, had eighty-four aircraft. Germany had 246 planes and five Zeppelin airships, France had 132 aircraft and fifteen airships and the Austrians thirty-six aircraft and one airship. Russia had just twenty-four planes and twelve airships but, in keeping with the vast size of his land, 25-year-old designer Igor Sikorsky was developing the first airliner, the Ilya Muromets biplane, which was powered by four V8 engines. It had a cabin with wicker chairs, dining tables with linen cloth and even a washroom. Its top wing measured nearly 30 metres across. It was quickly converted to a bomber.

Aircraft soon showed their importance in combat. On 22 August 1914, the same day the Germans shot down their first British aircraft, RFC Captain Lionel Charlton and his pilot Lieutenant Vivian Wadham reported to Field Marshal Sir John French that, from their observation flights, they had seen the Germans making moves to surround the British Expeditionary Force near Mons in Belgium. The British retreated, and Charlton's keen eye probably saved 100,000 British lives. A week later, the French used intelligence gathered from their planes to drive the Germans away from Paris in the First Battle of the Marne.

On the Eastern Front, field marshal Paul von Hindenburg scored Germany's first mighty blow of the war near Tannenberg in Prussia as 78,000 of the Tsar's troops were killed or injured and another 92,000 were captured. The old Field Marshal said there would have been no victory if not for the aerial reconnaissance provided by pilot Ernst Canter and his observer Gottfried Mertens flying an Austrian Rumpler Taube.[8] Its translucent linen wings made it virtually invisible above 400 metres. Lawrence Hargrave took no delight in comparisons between the Taube and his box kites.

Caught up in the stampede of young men rushing to serve King and Empire, Bert was hooked by what he called 'a glaring advertisement' for the RNAS and enlisted on 7 September as No. 318 on the list of accepted volunteers, destined, he said, 'to get more flying than I had ever thought possible'.[9] Bert wrote to his sister May that his RNAS induction was all so exciting and that the service was well prepared for war with 'a special set of aeroplanes solely for the purpose of pupils to learn on and ... different types of engines for practising' with both pusher and tractor aircraft.

His Royal Navy Certificate of Service listed his trade as aeroplane erector and described him as standing 5 feet 3.5 inches (161 centimetres), with a 35-inch (89-centimetre) chest, dark brown hair, grey eyes, dark complexion and with a pronounced scar on his left shoulder, a legacy of his car accident while working for Wizard Stone. He gave his religion as Church of England and confirmed that he could swim. He was hoping to become a trainee pilot but instead was given the grading of leading mechanic and went off to the Pembroke III base at Sheerness next to the Eastchurch airfield for basic training, drills and weapons practice with the Lee–Enfield rifle.

In the first few days of the fighting rival reconnaissance planes were said to throw nothing more savage at their foes than an upturned finger or brandished fist. But before long pilots and observers from the rival nations were throwing rocks at each other mid-air, then firing shotgun pellets, bullets, grenades and sometimes even rope and grappling hooks to jam propellers. On 8 September 1914, the day after Bert's enlistment, Russian pilot Pyotr Nesterov gave a glimpse of the future when he rammed his machine into an Austrian reconnaissance plane over Galicia on the Eastern Front, ending his own life and that of the crews on both aircraft.[10]

Then on 5 October 1914, over the village of Jonchery near Reims, came French pilot Joseph Frantz and his observer Louis Quenault, flying their Voisin LA pusher aircraft. They were on a mission to drop six artillery shells on German troops and intercepted a German Aviatik tractor bi-plane. Quenault, fighting the slipstream and half hanging out of the open cockpit, opened fire with his great lumbering Hotchkiss machine-gun on the German pilot Wilhelm Schlichting and his observer Fritz von Zangen. Quenault fired forty-eight rounds before the gun jammed, and the German observer fired back at them with his rifle. With the noise of the propeller behind him ringing in his ears, Quenault picked up his carbine and let off a round that hit the German pilot and sent Schlichting and von Zangen spinning out of control to a fiery death, the first plane destroyed in an aerial shootout.[11] The race would begin to quickly produce planes to shoot reconnaissance machines out of the air, and before long their combat was so fierce that they were called 'dogfights'. Aviators who shot down at least five of the enemy were called 'aces'.

On 9 October, after just a month into his service, Bert wrote to his mother from the Central Flying School in Upavon, Wiltshire, that he felt like he was a boy in Bundy again being lined up each morning and marched into school. But this time he was seated in a 'large aeroplane hangar with diagrams of engines, aeroplanes and all sorts of things connected with Aviation hung about the walls. On a little raised platform stands a blackboard, whereupon our teacher, one of the naval officers, will begin to explain the mysteries of the art of Aviation': 'Yes, I can tell you,' he wrote, 'it was one of the luckiest things that ever happened for my benefit, the day I left the sunny Australian shores. I little dreamed what was in store for me. There is one thing I have set my heart on and that is to fly for my aviator's certificate before I forsake merry England.'

As Bert was penning his letter, RNAS Wing Commander Charles Samson, who two years earlier had been the first pilot to take off from the deck of a ship, followed Churchill's orders and dispatched the first strategic air raid on Germany. Two Sopwith Tabloids left Antwerp, each with a pair of nine-kilogram bombs, to blow up Zeppelin sheds in Cologne and Dusseldorf 200 kilometres away. Squadron Commander D.A. Spenser Grey became lost in the fog and bombed the Cologne railway station instead, killing three civilians, but Flight Lieutenant Reggie Marix hit his bullseye, a Dusseldorf hangar containing the Zeppelin ZIX.[12]

In Australia, in the big cities and in the country towns, on the coast and in the Outback, men, fired up by propaganda and unemployment, were clamouring for a chance to drive back the Hun. Recruiting officers rejected boys in short pants and bare feet as young as thirteen and men as old as seventy-one. From the Federal Parliament in Melbourne, Prime Minister Andrew Fisher, back in office after toppling Joseph Cook, offered Britain 20,000 troops but, by the end of 1914, 52,561 Australian men had enlisted.[13] Among them was Geoffrey Lewis Hargrave, twenty-two years, described on his enlistment form at Sydney's Rosebery Park Camp on 12 September 1914 as 5 feet 8¾ inches (175 centimetres), 10 stone 5 pounds (66 kilograms), dark complexion, grey eyes, brown hair. He joined the 13th Battalion of the 4th Infantry Brigade and gave his occupation as junior draftsman and his next of kin as his father, Lawrence Hargrave of Wunulla Road, Woollahra Point. In Bundaberg on 19 October, Charlie Laffan, also twenty-two, brandishing tattoos of sailing ships on both arms, 5 feet 7 inches (170 centimetres) with fresh complexion, black eyes and dark brown hair, signed up for C Company of the 15th Battalion under Captain Hugh Quinn, two weeks before Russia, Britain and France declared war on the Turks.

Bert's family regularly kept him informed of their day-to-day dramas and comedies in Bundaberg. His mother wrote him incessantly, his father as often as his arthritic hands would allow, and Bert always got a kick out of the reports on pets, neighbours and school life from his younger brothers and sisters, how they sold old Ida the horse and about all the goings on of Mr Gladwell who lived next door to the foundry and the Chinese men who worked his market garden and how on Mondays and Fridays the Chinese strapped a pole across their necks and shoulders and walked over to Quay Street to sell their produce. How Mr Grace was selling watermelons and rockmelons from the back of his horse and cart and how every afternoon Papa would go to the Mulgrave Hotel or the Young Australian dressed in his checked woollen smoking cap and slippers for a drink and chat with the foundry boys and Mrs Naylor, the Young Australian licensee, Thelma Rawlings the barmaid and 'Cranky Alf'. Papa had been spared the internment camp fate endured by thousands of Australians of German birth or ancestry such as the brewery king Edmund Resch.

The letters from home gave Bert a brief respite from the horror unravelling around him. On 16 December, German battleships bombed the northern British cities of Hartlepool, Whitby and Scarborough, centres for the manufacture of arms and munitions, killing 112 civilians and nine soldiers and destroying 340 buildings. Bert's birthday letter to ten-year-old Queenie from the RNAS base at nearby Newcastle-on-Tyne three days later tried to keep her spirits up while still acknowledging that the world had gone mad. He even illustrated the letter with an intricate drawing of a monoplane and a Hendon air race marker pylon, memories of a more innocent time.

My Dear Queenie, I got your nice kind letter the other day and thank you very much [he started]. I hope you will write me many more like it. I hope you had a nice birthday. I must be a bad brother to you, not sending you any presents. I had a very quiet birthday, not even wetting it with a glass of wine. So let us look forward to next December when I shall be home and we will have a fine time. This machine I have drawn is a Morane Monoplane, the same as won The Aerial Derby this year, the London–Manchester–London race and the London–Paris–London race. The same aviator each time [William L. Brock] now don't you think this is wonderful? Tell Papa I'm very glad to know he is much better. I am sending you my picture and you must be a good girl and send me yours. Don't forget.[14]

His letter changes tone when he mentions the bombing of Hartlepool. 'I am sending the *Daily Mirror* and you will see that a lot of poor women and children were killed. Hartlepool is only about 40 miles from us here and our aeroplanes have flown over it many times.'

At the end of 1914, aircraft on all sides of the conflict were still primarily reconnaissance planes, and Bert worked on machines little different from civilian aircraft. It was not long, however, before all the aircraft began to carry weapons. The pushers, with the propeller behind the pilot, were slower than the tractor type but had the advantage of allowing an unobstructed path for the bullets from a forward-mounted machine-gun or rifle. In the tractor planes the weaponry early in the war was usually just a rifle and some hand grenades thrown by the observer. Safety was rudimentary. The normal safety harness was a simple leather strap, and parachutes were shunned to reduce weight and because some pilots saw them as symbols of cowardice. On rough flights or when a pilot engaged the enemy, it was not uncommon for observers to fall out of their machines as the plane rolled from side to side.

Things quickly became even more hazardous. On the night of 19 January 1915, two 150-metre shark-shaped Zeppelins, having cruised across the darkness high above the North Sea, dropped 50-kilogram bombs on Great Yarmouth, Sheringham, King's Lynn and surrounding Norfolk villages, killing four people and injuring sixteen.[15] Hatred for Germans throughout England intensified. Even dachshunds were stoned in the street. Anyone with a German-sounding name was the target of scorn but Bert, despite his Prussian background, was proving to be an outstanding asset for the RNAS as a brilliant mechanic and crack rifle shot.

By April 1915, Bert had moved to the RNAS coastal defence station in Whitley Bay. He was still working as a mechanic and aeroplane builder, but he was desperate to fly even if it was while dodging bullets and he was constantly volunteering to accompany pilots on their most hazardous missions. There were opportunities aplenty to be shot at, and Bert had his first taste of combat and of a real powered flight on 14 April. It was nothing like the experience of soaring over the waves at Mon Repos. At 8 p.m. the alert went up at Whitley Bay that one of the Zeppelins — later identified as L9 — was nearby over the North Sea's English coast. Bert and his commanding officer Reg Nicoll raced to their pre-war Gnome-powered Bristol two-seater parked on the base's rifle range and prepared to fight the 160-metre monster in the sky. As the fragile Bristol made a noisy, shaky ascent along the grass and into the night Bert's sheer delight at finally being in a powered aeroplane was tempered by the noise of bombs exploding nearby. Yet as the Bristol laboured into the night sky, the weightless freedom he experienced and the sense of mastery over gravity made him feel invincible. The flashes and fires from the bombing in the distance made him wonder how long he would enjoy that sensation.

Bert checked his Lee–Enfield and some of the new incendiary bullets that were supposed to ignite the hydrogen in the Zeppelin's huge gasbags. It wasn't much firepower against the machine-guns on the German giant 'but of course', Bert later explained, 'Fritz never knew that'. Bert and his pilot flew back and forth over Whitley Bay for an hour, Bert savouring every turn and bump of the machine as they saw the L9 drop twenty bombs far off. As whistles and bells below them warned of approaching doom, lights in Newcastle and surrounding towns as far away as Hull 225 kilometres to the south were extinguished, making it almost impossible for the airship to find its targets and for Bert to find the airship. He couldn't see a thing, hardly even a star in the sky.

The Zeppelin's incendiary bombs spared human life, but they did ignite a haystack at Choppington, an outhouse at Seaton and a home at Wallsend, where one bomb narrowly missed a train loaded with passengers. Another bomb crashed into a room where a woman was bathing a baby. Fortunately, she was only slightly injured by a piece of flying masonry, and the baby wondered what all the excitement was about.[16]

The Zeppelin proved impossible to find after a fruitless, frustrating, maddening search, and when Bert and Nicoll were finally 50 kilometres out over the North Sea, Nicoll turned back. There were no lights in any direction for 160 kilometres and not much moonlight so they had to fly by a compass illuminated by a pocket torch. When they guessed that they were pretty close to the airfield, the pilot gave the prearranged signal by cutting his engine and restarting it a few times. Petrol flares were lit below so that they could land safely. The L9 drifted back down the Tyne and headed for Germany.[17]

Bert had just risked his life against one of the most fearsome weapons yet launched on Britain, but the sense of being up in the air like the birds was so overwhelming that more than ever he wanted his chance to fly.

The hunt for the Zeppelin broke up the daily grind of life in the RNAS. With dawn patrols at 4.30 a.m. and evening patrols at sunset, Bert's night finished at 8 p.m. when the aircraft were refuelled with petrol and oil and cleaned ready to fly again the next morning. Starting on 29 April the Zeppelin raids became an almost weekly occurrence.

On 5 May 1915, eighteen days before Italy declared war on Austria–Hungary, Bert wrote to tell his mother that although he was still not in line for pilot training he had at least been promoted and gone through another terrifying experience.

Yes, I am official observer with one of the pilots and I generally go up each day for training. There is a soldiers' encampment not far from here and the other day he flew me over and I had to draw a map and positions of trenches etc. Fair dincum [sic] it's fairly difficult at first, sketching from 5000 feet or so, but I am gradually acquiring this new art and am beginning to fancy myself quite expert already. Today I had quite an exciting time, was up in the air for just on two hours, flew down the coast, past Hartlepool and not far from Whitby, although the air was rather misty. Returned alright and was just near the aerodrome when our motor failed us. We were gliding down alright but in trying to clear a hedge we lost flying speed and fell to the ground. My word, what a sensation. I have it all clear now. I knew we were falling and there I was — could do nothing but wait for the crash. Oh, those few moments were terrible and when the crash did come the sudden stoppage was awful. I can still see bits of broken propeller and wood flying about in all directions. I was thrown forward but as I was prepared for it I came off lucky, yes, very lucky indeed as only a few scratches on my nose serve as a souvenir of the event. The pilot came off alright but the poor machine, it was in a terrible mess and fearfully bent. Still, of course, in these days of war and strife that is only a mere detail and will not hinder yours truly in the least from his ambition in the art of Aviation. Now please, Mum, don't worry over the events I have chronicled this time or I'll be sorry I have written too much about trifles. With my best love to all at home and, on the quiet, wishing I were back again with you all.[18]

While Lawrence Hargrave's lightweight rotary engine concept made it possible for flimsy aircraft to achieve the power necessary for flight, the nature of the Gnome engines — a large spinning mass of metal with a propeller attached that powered most of the Allied machines — created massive forces at the front of the aircraft and made the early aeroplanes difficult to control. The problem was compounded exponentially by aerial combat, and Bert knew that the role of observer and gunner was one of the most hazardous jobs in the war. Still, he figured he was a lot better off in the air than many of the poor blighters on the ground, bogged down in the Somme or trying to get a foothold at Gallipoli.

Two weeks before the Australian and New Zealand troops launched their offensive on 25 April 1915 at Anzac Cove as a way of securing the Dardanelles shipping lanes, Bert's mate Charlie Laffan was wounded near there in a bomb blast.[19] He had been part of the advance that had started trying to soften up the Turks after the arrival of British and French battleships and the world's first true aircraft carrier, HMS *Ark Royal*. For three weeks RNAS Wing Commander Samson and his pilots photographed and bombed the southern half of the peninsula and provided some cover for the troops in the first wave of the invasion.[20] The dense scrub around Anzac Cove proved almost impenetrable to their eyes when the fighting began and many of the Turkish embattlements went undetected. The reconnaissance planes helped the Navy's prize battleship *Queen Elizabeth* sink a Turkish supply vessel and, on 17 May, Samson and Reggie Marix, flying a French Breguet, dropped a 45-kilogram bomb on a dock where Turkish troops were being unloaded. They killed fifty-seven men, then warned the Anzacs of an imminent Turkish attack. It was also in May over Gallipoli that the RNAS launched their eagle-eyed Australian Captain A.H. Keith Jopp, who became an expert at shooting German pilots and their Turkish observers.

Gallipoli had seen the first combination of a land invasion backed by air power and on 12 August, Flight Commander Charles Edmonds, flying a Short 184 folder seaplane, launched another first, a torpedo to finish off a 5000-tonne Turkish steamer that had already been damaged by a submarine strike. Edmonds had made the first successful aerial torpedo attack in history. While the sight of the warplanes overhead would inspire some Anzacs watching them, such as Charles Kingsford Smith, Charles Ulm and Ross Smith, to launch their own aviation careers, more than 130,000 men, 8709 of them Australians, lost their lives on the Turkish peninsula.

Lawrence Hargrave had in 1892 expressed his strident opposition to the idea of the 'connection of the flying machine with dynamite missiles' but the war at Gallipoli took his life, too. Geoffrey Hargrave, who worked side by side with his dad perfecting their kites and engines, wrote out his will the night before the April 25 invasion, leaving all his earthly estate to his father. Ten days later he was dead, and it was said that the bullet that killed the son killed the father as well. As soon as he heard the terrible news, the fire was extinguished from the old man's piercing eyes. The thinker who had inspired everyone from the Wright brothers to Bert Hinkler to take flight dropped his bundle. His health deteriorated. He underwent surgery for appendicitis at Lister Private Hospital in Darlinghurst but developed peritonitis and died at his Woollahra Point home on 6 July, aged sixty-five.

Nine weeks after Geoffrey was killed, Lawrence Hargrave was buried at Waverley Cemetery, overlooking the endless waves of the blue Pacific. Before long his wife Margaret auctioned all his furniture and household goods and took their youngest girl to England, to be with the Hargraves' two married daughters. The newspapers eulogised Hargrave as a prophet without honour in his own land, a man whose work was applauded around the world but largely ignored in his own country. Some of the obituary writers, though, quoted the pugnacious Sir Richard Threlfall, who had established the University of Sydney's School of Physics, as saying: 'Sydney will one day be noted, not for its famous harbour but as being the home of Hargrave, the man who invented the flying machine.'[21]

Chapter 9

Will you jump or will you burn?

**German reporters to Zeppelin commander Heinrich
Mathy on whether he would prefer to fall from a
stricken airship or stay on it and burn to death**

*Don't allow yourselves to be worried by any of the
adventures I am experiencing over this side because
even if the worst came to the worst at least we
have tried to do our little bit in this great war.*

Bert Hinkler in a letter home to his parents, 1915

Like a creature from a horror story the great monster
materialised from the dark just on midnight 31 May 1915
and was spotted heading silently, malevolently towards
London. Police were alerted, and they went about the
streets blowing warning whistles as searchlights strafed
the sky, but the giant airship LZ38 was beyond reach of
the anti-aircraft guns that began blasting from battlements
around the capital. Thousands of terrified residents ran
to hide in subways. A few minutes later small incendiary
bombs began to fall from the Zeppelin, the first hitting

a house in Stoke Newington, then the Shoreditch Empire Music Hall. Heavier bombs rained like fire on Spitalfields, Stepney, Stratford and Leytonstone. The RNAS sent up fifteen planes, but the Zeppelin was too high and too well concealed by the dark and the clouds. When the bombing finished at about 2.30 a.m. seven people had been killed, thirty-five were injured; forty-one fires had started, seven properties had been burnt to the ground and Londoners would not sleep soundly for a long time. The great airships flew too high for conventional aeroplanes and one estimate claimed that it took 8000 shots from the anti-aircraft guns to land a single blow and that blow seemed to have little effect. The anti-aircraft shells that missed sometimes came back to kill the people they were intended to protect.

Some British pilots managed to score fateful blows. Bert had missed his opportunity over the Tyne, but 23-year-old RNAS Flight Sublieutenant Reg Warneford wasn't going to miss his second chance after LZ39 soared out of his range on a bombing raid on 17 May. Three weeks later on 7 June, while based at Veurne on the Belgian coast, he spied LZ37 and chased it in his Morane-Saulnier from near Ostend for about 65 kilometres to Ghent, dodging the Zeppelin's machine-gun fire and in the process dropping six nine-kilogram bombs on the 180-metre giant. The Zeppelin burst into an enormous fire that lit up the sky for kilometres and then crashed into the convent school of St Amandsberg like a meteorite. One nun died and two were badly burned as they rushed into the street with children in their arms.[1]

For his extraordinary bravery Warneford was awarded the Victoria Cross and the Légion d'honneur, but he had no time to savour them as, just ten days later, while ferrying the American journalist Henry Beach Newman, the right wings of his biplane collapsed, and both men fell out of the aeroplane to their deaths.

The Zeppelins kept coming. Under the cover of darkness, the L10 loomed over Whitley Bay late at night on 15 June, crossing the coast at Blyth, and turning south towards Wallsend. Armed with his Lee–Enfield and some grenades, Bert climbed in behind his pilot as they again sped along the rifle range that was their makeshift airfield. The machine hit a small trench on the field but was travelling so fast that the violent collision, shaking Bert fiercely, propelled them into a dark night sky dotted with flashes from bombs falling onto Wallsend's Marine Engineering Works 10 kilometres away.

Bert's eyes darted left and right as he searched for the Germans, his pilot going full throttle at 760 metres. The Zeppelin continued south, drifting silently, for another few kilometres until it reached Palmer's Shipyard in Jarrow at about 11.40 p.m. It dropped seven heavy explosive and five incendiary bombs with devastating results. By the time it had finished its night's work sixteen men had been killed and seventy-two injured. An elderly lady died of shock.[2] 'Oh it was fairly hideous,' Bert later told his father. 'What a ghastly war this is.'

But as Bert and his pilot gave chase in their fragile machine the flashes from the bombs suddenly stopped. There seemed something dark and menacing in the thick storm clouds above, and Bert readied his rifle as the pilot ploughed into the void. It was so dark that Bert could see no further than the wingtips three metres on either side, and the only noise was the Bristol's whirring engine and the British anti-aircraft shells exploding uncomfortably close. For fifteen minutes the pair climbed through the billowing clouds, but all they could see was the trail of fire left by the bombing.

They decided to head home, disappointed that yet again the vast darkness of the sky had thwarted them.[3] 'Just check on the undercarriage, Bert?' the pilot asked. 'See what damage was done when we hit that bump taking off.'

Bert stuck his head over the side of the plane and leaned halfway out of the machine with nothing to stop him falling 600 metres. To his horror, most of the undercarriage was missing. The plane would be wrecked when they tried to land. Sitting there with his supply of grenades and incendiary bullets as they headed back to base, Bert waited for doom like a condemned man in his cell. He said his prayers and braced for the inevitable bang. The pair gingerly came into land. The machine hit the ground with an almighty thump, and Bert felt as if his back had been broken as the plane slithered along the rifle range grass on its belly to the sound of cracking struts, breaking wings and a splintering propeller. Somehow, they managed to survive. Having climbed out of the wreckage without so much as a scratch he had an even greater belief that a good pilot could handle any crisis. 'No doubt you will soon get as much confidence in Aviation as I have,' he wrote to his parents, 'and you will note that while the odds are sometimes against you, with careful flying you can nearly always get off at the expense of a wrecked machine.'

British aircraft were still not effective attack weapons by the middle of 1915. Two-seaters at least had an observer, usually with a machine-gun, but the single-seat scout aircraft were particularly vulnerable. The pilot not only had to fly but to shoot his machine-gun as well. Major Lanoe

Hawker of No. 6 Squadron RFC was one pilot who could multi-task. His motto was 'Attack everything' and on 25 July 1915, when flying a Bristol Scout C biplane, he attacked three German two-seaters over Passchendaele in Belgium, squeezing the trigger on the Lewis machine-gun mounted on the left side of his plane at an angle to avoid blowing the propeller to smithereens. His heroics in shooting down all three planes earned him a Victoria Cross.

Other solo pilots had machine-guns mounted above the propeller on their biplanes, but firing them and reloading the magazines was complicated and dangerous. That would soon change thanks to the Frenchman Roland Garros. In December 1914, while on reconnaissance with the French Escadrille (squadron) MS26, he had visited the Morane-Saulnier factory to persuade Raymond Saulnier to fit one of his planes with a Hotchkiss machine-gun that would shoot straight through the propeller as it rotated. Saulnier had been working on a synchroniser gear that would coordinate the bullet with the propeller rotation, but the unpredictable rate of fire from the Hotchkiss made the system unreliable. He fitted metal deflector plates to the propeller, so any bullets that did hit the propeller spun away from the pilot. Garros persuaded Saulnier to equip one of his Type L parasol wing planes with the metal propeller shields but without the added weight of the synchronising gear. He figured that the machine-gun's rate of fire was less than the propeller's speed of rotation so most of the bullets would get through. The deflector system worked well, and Garros shot down his first plane while aiming through the propeller on 1 April 1915.[4]

Just seventeen days later, however, Garros was forced down and captured by the Germans after his plane suffered engine failure, possibly because of the crankshaft overloading with the force of all the bullets deflecting off his propeller. The wreckage was taken to Anthony Fokker, a young Dutchman who was born to a coffee plantation owner in what is now Indonesia. Fokker was turning out machines for the Germans from his factory in Schwerin and inspected the Garros system. He decided that the 'interrupter gear' he'd been working on for six months was much better as it stopped the gun firing as the propeller blade passed in front of the barrel. When the interrupter gear was fitted to a range of Fokker monoplanes called the Eindecker, launched in July 1915, Germany had its 'Fokker Scourge', and the aeroplane had become a deadly accurate machine-gun on wings. Until early 1916 Allied planes, including the new single-seat Sopwith Baby — developed for the RNAS from the two-seater Schneider — would become known as 'Fokker Fodder'.[5]

Bert's bravery in constantly asking to accompany pilots on their missions resulted in a promotion to Petty Officer Mechanical on 1 August 1915. He told his commanding officers that, while he hadn't yet arrived at his destination with an Aviator's Certificate, he was patient and determined, prepared to do whatever it took to realise his ambition. He was appointed to the RNAS No. 3 Wing under the ubiquitous Wing Commander Samson. Bert underwent months of training at the RNAS Air Gunnery School at White City, in London, not far from Wormwood Scrubs where No. 20 Squadron RNAS Armoured Car Division were developing Churchill's concept of a land ship, a mobile fortress to break the deadlock in the trenches of the Somme. To keep these huge machines secret they were described in dispatches as water carriers — or tanks.

The Zeppelin attacks continued and throughout 1915 killed 181 people and injured 455. Among the 37 tonnes of bombs they dropped was one from the airship of Heinrich Mathy that weighed 300 kilograms and gouged a crater almost 2.5 metres deep at Bartholomew Close, not far from the newspaper offices of Fleet Street.[6]

Noel Pemberton Billing, the man who had started Supermarine and was now a politician, had a plan to stop the Zeppelin attacks. He had left school at fourteen to become a bricklayer, tram conductor, policeman, boxer, estate agent, law graduate, inventor, playwright, publisher, aviator and entrepreneur. Pemberton Billing had sold the Supermarine company and joined the RNAS only to leave in 1915 with the rank of squadron commander and enter parliament with the backing of Lord Northcliffe's *Daily Mail*. He demanded the RNAS and RFC merge into a single airforce and escalate the air war and, despite having a German wife, called for the bombing of enemy civilians. The Zeppelin raids on London of 1915 bolstered public support for his crusade even though many in government regarded him as a dangerous ratbag.

Troops poured in from all over the Empire to help Mother England, and on 2 March 1916, with the signatures of his parents John W. Hinkler and Frances A. Hinkler approving his decision, Bert's younger brother Jack William Hinkler, labourer aged nineteen, height 5 feet 6 inches (168 centimetres), weight 144 pounds (65 kilograms), swore that that he would well and truly serve his Sovereign Lord the King in the Australian Imperial Force until the end of the war, and a further period of four months thereafter and that he would resist His Majesty's enemies and cause His Majesty's peace to be kept and maintained. 'So help me God.' Now Frances would have two reasons to pray that the local clergyman would not pedal his bicycle down Gavin Street to Woodbine Cottage, with the sad face and the telegram that every wartime mother dreaded. Everyone who saw the clergyman coming through the front gate knew its content before trembling fingers tore open the envelope.

At about the same time as Jack enlisted, Petty Officer Bert Hinkler wrote from White City to tell his parents how privileged he felt to be a Queenslander, how much he missed home and how he had been given a recent afternoon off from practice flying and bomb instruction. He had used his time to visit the London office of the monocled C.G. Grey, now editor of *The Aeroplane*. 'It's about the best paper on Aviation,' he told Frances and Papa, 'and the Editor is rather a nice chap and a severe critic on flying matters.' Even though he was still short of having his own Aviator's Certificate, Bert could see that plenty of improvements were needed in 'the art', and he relayed some of them, about advancing night flying for repelling the Zeppelin raids, to Grey. 'I believe I made a very good impression and I don't want to blow about myself but he agreed that my suggestions were real good,' he wrote, before lecturing his parents on the subject:

As we all know in night flying the most dangerous and difficult procedure is the landing. This is facilitated to a large extent when the pilot has his own aerodrome lit up and is able to land there. But as I suggested this is the main reason during a Zep raid that a pilot is afraid to wander far for fear of getting lost and the consequent drastic finish-up. Well, by my method of preparation the pilot has no need to bother about the aerodrome after he leaves it but pursue the Zep in whatever direction it may go until, very optimistically speaking, it is brought down. During the chase and all these manoeuvres we will no doubt get absolutely lost and here is where my idea comes into play. By my procedure the observer leaves the aeroplane per parachute and on the way down fires special illuminated lights which lighten up the country for miles and so he can pick out the nearest and most suitable open field. On reaching Earth he makes for it with all possible speed and with the aid of a number of torches which we have in use he lights them and dots them round the border of the field and the pilot is able to judge and land in the middle. Now the next thing I want to do is put it before the authorities and then demonstrate the soundness of my proposition myself. I am sure you would be absolutely astounded with what aeroplanes are capable of today.[7]

Grey would recall years later that there was 'rather a row' at the time because so many British planes had crashed in the dark and Bert was complaining bitterly that his commanding officer wouldn't let him demonstrate his parachute plan for night landings. 'Bert could not be made to see that the job of being an observer in those circumstances would not be popular,' Grey wrote. 'He was quite game to do it and could not see why anybody else should not.'[8]

Though Grey once remarked that Bert was 'as brave as brave could be all through the war', Petty Officer Hinkler was constantly frustrated by his low rank in the service, trying to make himself heard. 'As I have often told you before,' Bert explained to his parents, 'such progressive improvements when worked out by those in such a humble position as myself generally receive no encouragement whatever. So don't think I have almost made my fortune just yet. [But] I do hope you are proud and happy with my latest ambitions and efforts to make good.' His ideas apparently went unheeded. Just two and a half weeks later he wrote home again, outlining another plan:

The idea I wrote and told you of in one previous I am sorry to say is no further advanced. I am waiting till I go to some air station where it would stand more chance of being tried than here. White City is not an air station. It is really a big depot or sort of headquarters. The instruction we get here is mostly theory. But I have not been idle. I had also worked up another idea for dual control. In some machines it is suggested to have dual control for both pilot and gunner. To disconnect and then reconnect the passenger's control is a very highly desirable feature. Then finally if the pilot were hit the gunner could take control and fly back. I have designed a very simple and effective device, so that the pilot can put the other control out of or in gear instantly. I applied to the necessary quarter here and have consequently been granted full run of the workshops and a free hand to demand whatever material I require for my job. The last couple of days I have been as happy as a dog with two tails, working away on my own little job just as I like. Almost like the old days under the old mulberry tree at home on my glider.[9]

Always desperate to prove himself, Bert saw the beginnings of a career in aviation design.

Of course don't be afraid I shall give my invention away for nothing. I don't suppose I shall get much, being in the Navy, but rest assured [I have] an eye to business as well as a heart for Aviation. Yet you might say, I have talked a lot about inventing things and still as hard up as ever. Well that's so but yet my designs have been copied in the service, which at least shows the soundness of my ideas. There is the little attachment I told you of when I was up at Whitley. I designed [it] to carry bomb-dropping gear on the aeroplane. The Navy way previously weighed about 7–9 lbs [3–4 kg] and, very clumsy and unsightly. I assured the officer I could greatly improve upon it, he let me, and my way weighed 1lb 1oz [482g], strong, neat and light. He was so pleased with it that he had drawings taken of it and sent it on to the Admiralty. Now I see the same principle used almost everywhere. Although I consider myself vastly ill rewarded, still it's all these little things that caused my promotion so that's something. Anyhow, if my latest device is all that I claim — and I have good reasons for claiming such — do not fear I shall do my utmost to get a fair deal. For the present I have yet to work hard to get it complete. And some day if I happen to get in the light where one's efforts are not without effect, you might still have reason to be proud of your son.[10]

The first detachment of No. 3 Wing began moving to France on 16 June 1916 to begin the construction of a base at Luxeuil-les-Bains about a hundred kilometres from Nancy, using Sopwith's new two-seat Strutter biplane to escort heavier bombers as they targeted Zeppelin hangars and German industry. Bert had completed a course as an aerial gunlayer by the time he arrived in France and was an expert on assembling, preparing and servicing machine-guns and anti-aircraft artillery. For the next couple of years he and his machine-gun would sit behind a pilot in a tandem cockpit accompanying bombers on their raids as protection against German counter-attacks. But while he was preoccupied with day-to-day combat against Germans and the constant stories of the Zeppelin's killing and maiming civilians in London and the thousands upon thousands dying in the trenches, a little piece of wattle sent to him by Queenie stopped him going completely mad. The smell and the familiar, comfortable waxy texture of the leaves from the backyard of Woodbine Cottage reminded him of happier times. 'Many, many thanks,' Bert wrote back to his sister.

I can tell you it has brought me back some very happy memories and I wonder how long before I shall see some growing again. I suppose you do not want me to write about this rotten war. The daily newspapers will supply you with all you want to know on that point — and a little bit more. Of course we are right out in the country and in comparison to Queensland one might say like Tambo or Longreach. Only when a country has a network of railways it makes all the difference. When we were leaving Paris at the same time as our train left the station [there] was another, an express to Nancy. The lines ran parallel for quite a distance.

My word they were close and the two trains rushing along at about sixty odd miles an hour. They were that close that you could quite easily kiss something nice in the other train, providing of course that something nice had no objections. At any rate some of us chaps had handshakes with the engine driver before our ways parted. The scenery was very pretty, although France is mostly a very flat country. This district is typically rural France, agriculture being predominant but you would be surprised to see the way people live. Stock, poultry, pigs, produce and the whole bally family under the one roof. Of course, that's not everybody, other residents better off have some very comfy and picturesque 'maisons'.[11]

Over the next few months Bert would get plenty of chances to see the countryside from the air. No. 3 Wing began its aerial bombardment campaign at 4.34 a.m. on 30 July 1916, when nine planes in a combined French and British patrol took off to destroy benzine stores and barracks at Mulheim.[12]

Back in the threatening summer night skies of England, Germany unleashed the first super Zeppelin, the 198-metre-long L31 under the command of Heinrich Mathy. It could climb as high as 5500 metres to avoid enemy planes, and its payload was four tonnes of bombs. Hull was subjected to intense bombing on 8–9 August, and on the night of 24–25 August Mathy's monster ship dropped thirty-six bombs on London, killing nine people and destroying several buildings around Greenwich.

England cried out for a saviour against what the press were calling the 'Hun death dealers'. On the night of 2–3

September 1916 more doom appeared overhead when the airship SL11, nearly 175 metres long and powered by four massive Maybach engines, started dropping bombs over London Colney and South Mimms, 30 kilometres north of London's centre. Just before 2 a.m. the great airship drifted into the beam of a searchlight over Hornsey, but the blasts and roars from the anti-aircraft guns ringing London had no effect and it started to drop bombs at Ponders End. Three aircraft went up to chase the massive enemy. One of the pilots from the RFC's No. 39 Home Defence Squadron, 21-year-old William Leefe Robinson, flying a BE2c with a Lewis gun mounted on the top wing, decided he was going to kill the beast even if it meant he died in the process. He had a mix of explosive-tipped and incendiary bullets: the explosive bullets to pierce the Zeppelin's tough outer skin and the incendiaries to ignite the leaking hydrogen.

The German airship climbed to 3500 metres, which should have been beyond the range of the flimsy British machine and beyond the range where Robinson could function without oxygen. But the young pilot pressed on, higher and higher, gasping for breath. Flying within 150 metres of the SL11 and somehow dodging the airship's machine-gun bullets tearing towards him like red-hot rocks, he emptied the 97-bullet magazine of his Lewis gun.

Robinson retreated to reload and passed the German machine again, so close that he could see the crew inside shooting at him from their gondola. He fired another ninety-seven bullets until the magazine was empty. Still no effect. He was trying to kill a giant whale with pebbles. Then he came again. Approaching from below the airship, he squeezed the trigger on the Lewis, the gun bucking and screaming in the freezing night air as he grew dizzy from the lack of air. Within seconds another magazine was empty. Another ninety-seven bullets wasted. Robinson began to turn away to prepare for a fourth try and, in that instant, the brightest light he had ever seen exploded before his eyes like the dawn of a new sun. All 175 metres of the SL11, all 21 tonnes of Germany's finest engineering, tumbled over and over out of the sky in a burning fireball until it crashed in a storm of cinders in a field behind the Plough Inn at Cuffley. Commander Wilhelm Schramm and his fifteen crew members had been incinerated.

Thousands of Londoners who watched the fire in the sky cheered, sang 'God Save the King' and danced with joy in their pyjamas to the sound of bagpipes outside their homes. Robinson became the first man to be awarded a Victoria Cross for action within Britain. Before long the airships were back. On the night of 24 September Heinrich Mathy commanded twelve airships on a raid over Britain. One of the ships, the L33, was forced down and its crew arrested by police, and at 1 a.m. Mathy and his crew in L31 watched in horror as their sister ship L32, flying at almost 4000 metres, was fired upon by another pilot from the Home Defence Squadron, Second Lieutenant Fred Sowrey, in another BE2c. Sowrey emptied three drums of incendiary ammunition into the belly of the ship before it exploded in flames. There were no survivors; most of the bodies recovered were burned, and the site of the crash near Billericay in Essex became a tourist attraction for weeks.

Back in Germany, reporters asked Mathy what he would do if his machine caught fire: would he prefer to burn to death or jump? 'I won't know until it happens,' he replied, glumly. On 1 October 1916 he found out. Mathy led eleven airships on a bombing raid over London and the Midlands. As three planes chased his L31, Mathy dropped fifty bombs on Cheshunt. But just before midnight Second Lieutenant Wulstan Tempest gave Mathy's L31 three bursts of incendiary bullets from his BE2c, and the giant craft became like a massive flaming tissue tossed by the breeze. As its crew was surrounded by flame it came crashing down at Potters Bar. A policeman running across a field barely dodged a three-metre propeller cartwheeling towards him. All nineteen of the crew died. Heinrich Mathy was discovered taking his last anguished breaths on his back with his arms outstretched, his body embedded 10 centimetres into the ground. He had jumped.

At Luxeuil-les-Bains, Bert closely studied the workings of the thirty or so RNAS planes and waited for the chance to fly one, buoyed by the news that his application for a patent on his dual-control system for aircraft was to be published by the Australian *Journal of Patents*.[13]

Bert's wing was boosted by the arrival of more Sopwith Strutters and a wave of new pilots, many of them Canadians such as Raymond Collishaw. One of the most admired pilots was the flamboyant ladies man Sidney Cotton, who like Bert hailed from rural Queensland (Proserpine) and who would become one of the inspirations for the fictional secret agent James Bond.

No. 3 Wing mostly flew Sopwith 1½ Strutters that were configured as either bombers or fighters. Both machines were fitted with extra fuel tanks that gave them an endurance of more than seven hours. The fighter was a two-seater, the first British plane with the Ross interrupter gear, which allowed the pilot to fire a fixed Vickers machine-gun through the propeller arc. Behind the pilot sat gunners such as Bert with a Lewis gun mounted on a Scarff-ring swivel bracket.

As well as Luxeuil-les-Bains, No. 3 Wing also used the nearby aerodrome at Ochey. By October 1916, three of No. 3 Wing's pilots had already been killed and Reggie Marix had lost a leg in a crash. Although the weather late in the year played havoc with bombing raids, in October and November there were missions to destroy the Mauser arms factory at Oberndorf and furnaces and iron works in Hagendingen, Völklingen, Dillingen and St Ingbert. Not only did they do considerable damage to German industry but also Canadian pilot G.S. Harrower from Montreal bowled over a highly regarded French racehorse, Mademoiselle de Machefein, which was about to foal, while making a forced landing near Dijon.

In the skies over London the airship menace had died down, but German air power was rising fast again on a new front. Major Lanoe Hawker VC was now with RFC Fighter Squadron No. 24 based at Bertangles, north of the Somme. His squadron of Airco's de Havilland-designed DH.2 pusher machines had been an antidote for the Fokker Scourge, shooting down seventy German planes for the loss of twelve British machines and twenty-one men.

At 1 p.m. on 23 November 1916 Hawker, dressed in his trademark 'fug-boots' (fur-lined boots that reached to the upper thigh to prevent frostbite at high altitude), took off in a DH.2 from Bertangles with two other machines. They became involved in a running battle with German fighters near Bapaume, almost 50 kilometres away. Hawker began a long dog-fight with a far superior aeroplane, a new German Albatros D.II biplane powered by a six-cylinder

Mercedes engine and being piloted by a 24-year-old Prussian nobleman, a cavalry officer who now rode aerial chargers and had who had already shot down ten Allied planes. The Albatros fired 900 bullets at Hawker from its two Maxim-style machine-guns operating in sync with the propeller. Hawker's antiquated machine couldn't compete with the German's turning and climbing ability or rate of fire. He was running low on fuel as it was, and broke off the fight to head back to Allied lines. Just as he did a bullet caught Hawker in the back of the head, killing him instantly.

His young German adversary claimed the Lewis gun from Hawker's smashed plane and hung it above the door of his room like the antlers of a mighty stag. And just as he had done with the first ten planes he shot down, he placed an order with a Berlin jeweller for a five centimetre high silver cup bearing the name of his victim and the date. The young pilot's name was Baron Manfred von Richthofen.[14]

The shooting down of a VC recipient was a blow to the heart of British morale. Nevertheless, as a gloomy mist descended over No. 3 Wing in France in December 1916, Bert's fellow servicemen tried to make the most of a rotten war. They looked for something nice to kiss or relaxed in the thermal springs around Luxeuil-les-Bains and tried to imagine a time without warfare.

Bert wrote home to say that he spent his twenty-fourth birthday cleaning his Lewis machine-gun, making sure it was in perfect order. He went out to the dark-green Sopwith Strutter he was assigned to, with its RNAS badge of blue, white and red concentric circles, and checked the forward-firing Vickers gun. He strapped his safety harness on in the rear tandem seat and spun his Lewis gun round and round on its Scarff ring, checking the ninety-seven rounds in each ammunition drum and aiming the gun past the tail and over the wing tips, imaging what he would do if Richthofen or his crazy brother Lothar or Ernst Udet or Joseph Jacobs or any of the other German top guns were suddenly upon him, machine-guns blazing. Bert wanted to make sure that he was ready to meet any emergency, and after an hour or so of shooting at imaginary adversaries from all angles he declared 'the whole show right as rain'. His machine-gun was about to be working overtime.

Chapter 10

*It's most unpleasant coming through shellfire
without the roar and pull of the motor ...*

**Bert Hinkler after his engine stopped during
a dogfight with German planes in 1917**

*I think of this war as it really is, not as the
people at home imagine, with a hoorah! and
a roar. It is very serious, very grim.*[1]

**German fighter ace Manfred von Richthofen,
having lost his appetite for killing after
sustaining a serious head wound in 1917**

Bert found the experience of aerial combat at high altitude
in the European winter to be like driving a car at breakneck
speed down a bumpy, potholed, undulating road, tearing
straight into an icy wind with his head out the window.
It was hard to breathe because the air so high was cold
and thin and at the same time his heart was racing as men
fired machine-guns at him while he sat atop more than
100 litres of petrol. The only thing keeping him bobbing
around thousands of feet above the icy ground was a small

motor prone to stalling in the cold and a flimsy machine made of wood and cloth being assailed by red-hot bullets. He and other gunner/observers often had to stand up in the open cockpit to use the Lewis machine-gun and had to discard their gloves to fire it properly. Frostbite was common, and the whole sensation was like trying to ride a beach ball in violent Arctic surf while being shot at. Often the machine-gun would jam and the pilot would roll to escape his attackers. If the gunner was still strapped in and hadn't fallen out of the machine he would find himself defenceless and flying upside down.

The observer was the first target for Richthofen, who told his comrades: 'If you are fighting a two-seater, get the observer first; until you have silenced the gun, don't bother about the pilot.'[2]

By January 1917 Richthofen had received Germany's highest military honour, the Blue Max, and was using British machines for target practice. He had also graduated to the fast and agile Albatros D.III biplane painted a vivid red, which gave rise to his nickname in later years of the 'Red Baron'.[3] Richthofen's mentor Oswald Boelcke had written a textbook on the art of dogfighting, the *Dicta Boelcke*, but by contrast, as the war ground on, some British pilots were being sent into the sky to fight the Baron with just three and a half hours flying experience. Bert was desperate to take on the German aces himself yet, despite his many requests for pilot training, his value as a mechanic and gunner were obvious, and he was told to concentrate on his job and let others do the flying.

Atrocious weather choked the skies around Ochey for the first three weeks of 1917. Finally, on the morning of 23 January, there was a break in the fog and clouds, enough for the restless airmen to be sent out on a bombing raid on the German blast furnaces at Burbach in the Saar Valley 160 kilometres away. Bert had grown up in the tropics and never could get used to all the snow and ice. With his teeth chattering from the cold, he smeared himself in whale fat before putting on the fur-lined flying suit that made him look like a baby grizzly bear. He then pulled on the thick gloves that would keep his fingers from freezing stiff, at least for the first three hours of a mission. He knew that every time he and his comrades took to the skies someone's father, son or brother, sometimes many of them, were going to die. Some of them on the Hun side might even be long lost relatives of that small boy Johann Hinkler. But Bert told himself that his survival and that of his comrades depended on him fighting to the death.

That morning, dawn sunbeams clawed holes in the clouds. The planes were pointed towards the icy wind, and their engines started up in turn, filling the frigid air with a mighty roar and the pungent odour of petrol and oil fumes. As a young man still in awe of aviation, the sight of the twenty-four fighters and bombers in formation in the foot-deep snow of Ochey was, in Bert's words, 'very pleasing to the eye … quite contrary to the deadly missions they were about to perform' and a slap in the face to all those in Bundaberg who had laughed at his devotion to flying just a few years earlier with their jibes that aeroplanes would always be glorified toys.

Each crew received good luck wishes from their comrades and, with the engines at full revs, each pilot in line pulled down his thick goggles and waved his hand for the crews to stand clear. Then one after the other the aeroplanes charged across the cold ground, spraying snow, and zoomed up, circling round and round the aerodrome to gain height, before heading towards Burbach in a V formation. The piercing cold played havoc with the engines, and eight of the machines stalled, spluttered, coughed and died before turning back. The noise and the excitement was a heady feeling for Bert, racing to battle behind the pilot in their two-seat Strutter. 'Come along into my cockpit,' he once wrote to his parents, 'and see the show from another aspect':

Very soon you're climbing fast. On the way we generally run a few shots through the guns, making sure that everything is absolutely okay. Gradually forming together we get into a position with the squadron and when X number of thousand feet altitude is attained we point towards our objective. It's quite easy going until we reach the lines. On my first occasion I wasn't really sure where we crossed into Germany but I soon found out! We soon see the results of the Boche [German] gunners. Those puffs suddenly appearing everywhere around look very interesting. But now and again when they become too familiar one feels rather uncomfortable, particularly when the 'old bus' would begin to rear up and buck about all over the show. I must say it does not seem as though there's any shortage of shells with the enemy. We are absolutely peppered all the way and they're pretty hot stuff with their guns, too. Of course, we resort to various dodging manoeuvres, still I think it's mostly luck when you get hit or not. After a time I soon got used to the experience which the first time as you might guess to me was a bit of a thriller.[4]

Ten of the bombers reached Burbach and, as the strong northeast wind pushed back the clouds like curtains, they rained almost 1200 kilograms of bombs from about 2500 metres onto the city's great furnaces. The German fighter force had come out for revenge, and nine of the British planes became involved in combat, although the only casualties from the dogfighting were a couple of German planes, including one of the outdated Halberstadt Scouts. All in all it was a successful operation for Bert's outfit, although Sublieutenant Leslie Pearkes, the observer for P.G. McNeil and a key figure in the Hinkler story in years to come, was one of five from the raiding party to suffer frostbite. He complained long and loud about the repeated jamming of his Lewis gun and the inadequate size of the ammunition drums, which required constant and cumbersome changes, unlike the belt-fed German weapons, which never let up.

It was a great comfort to the ground crew at Ochey when the distant hum of the Sopwith rotary engines grew louder and the specks in the sky became larger. All the machines that had taken off for Burbach were accounted for. A popular music hall song of the day was George Robey's 'Archibald, Certainly Not!', and it was common for the RNAS ground crews to ask pilots, 'Archibald give you any trouble today?' awaiting the response of 'Archibald? Certainly not!'. Archibald was shortened to 'Archie', which became the nickname for the German guns for the rest of the war.[5] But things took a tragic turn as the planes made their way to the Ochey hangars. Pilot Maurice Stephens, of Toronto, landed his bomber and shut his engine off, then realised he still had a bomb hanging out of the rear left-hand door. Stephens got out and tried to prise the bomb loose but, failing miserably, said it would need a crowbar to dislodge it. He restarted the engine and prepared to taxi to the hangar. Leading Mechanics Fraser and Sims went out to steady the plane, one on either wing tip, but as they got hold of the machine the bomb dropped from the door and a massive sheet of flame engulfed the whole area. Fraser suffered burns, a broken leg, a large wound over his heart and three broken ribs. Sims bled profusely from a severed artery in his right thigh. Both died within fifteen minutes. Maurice Stephens lost his right leg.[6]

Bert was mortified. Just six days after fighting deathly battles with the Germans and then seeing some of his comrades killed and maimed, he wrote home, sparing his family the goriest details and trying to stay upbeat. He told Queenie, who was now twelve:

I am glad to read in your letter that you had a good time in Brisbane and enjoyed yourself so much. And don't you think you would like to live in the big city? I notice that you are attending school regular, and in your letters too, I have watched the progress you are making. Good Kid, keep doing your best, and it's yourself [who] will reap the benefit later on. My word, I should like to come home and see your little Teddy Bear. It reminds me of the days at home, when I used to have no end of pets myself. But what a big change comes round with the times. At present my 'pet' is a large 100-horsepower fighter aeroplane, as I write, waiting patiently in the hangar for our next job on an air raid. The weather lately has been so very bad that we have had to stop on the ground. But the atmosphere was good enough last Tuesday and we did not miss the opportunity. Perhaps you may have read of our raid on Burbach, Saar Valley on the 23rd. We had a fine time, and so to speak the air seemed full of aircraft and exploding shells. Of aircraft, I must say Germany was well represented, even on our side of the lines, too. It was bitterly cold up top, more especially as we fly at 10,000 feet and often higher still. One of our chaps had both hands frostbitten. And perhaps you may not know, but the frostbitten part swells up the size of watermelons. The real pain is when you're getting warm again. And I suppose I'd better assure you all at home that for my part I am okay, having come off without a scratch. My only grumble — of course I must have one — was that our motor was inclined to be rather sulky and not doing its work properly at all. Therefore on occasions when we gave chase, we were left miles behind for as you might know it's all a question of speed. My luck, there is no doubting the fact that the Boche pilots are still some goers. They were over here the other day and it was blowing a bally hurricane. Oh well, I suppose the old saying 'fortune favours the brave.' Hoping you are all well and happy at home. And when you write tell me in detail how Papa, Mum, May, George and you all are doing. And now with my best love and kisses I am as B4 your loving brother Bert.[7]

The snow and the ice prevented any more bombing missions from Ochey until 25 February when thirteen bombers and five fighters took off for the Brebach iron works, 145 kilometres away. It was a day of carnage with two planes from either side shot down and Canadian pilot L.E. Smith and his gunlayer R.S. Portsmouth killed. Two Sopwiths also suffered severe damage when they collided landing back at base.

On 4 March, Bert and his Canadian pilot, twenty-year-old Sublieutenant Charlie Pattison from Winona, Ontario, were part of a formation of fourteen bombers and six fighters that set out for another burst on Brebach. The Germans were ready for them, and seven German fighters attacked Bert's plane together, like ravenous animals leaping onto prey. Bullets whizzed past Bert's head so fast that they melted the ice on his flying helmet, and he quickly jumped up and emptied the first pan of ninety-seven rounds from his Lewis gun, doing so — in his words — while shouting his side of the argument in 'fiery lingo'.

> The bullets were cracking all round [Bert recalled]. Oh, what a time! We were over our objective, about 60 miles into Boche land. We had just loosed our bombs, the anti-aircrafts were also busy and shells were exploding all over the place. When slap bang a squadron of no less than seven machines with iron crosses on the wings surrounded us and then followed about the busiest 10 minutes of my life. One time we were cut off, and every machine I saw had enemy marking.[8]

The planes came at him from all angles. Bert emptied another pan of ammo into the closest machine bearing German markings, and it spun away out of control. He had shot down his first plane as the British aircraft made their escape. Although no Allied planes were lost, Lieutenant J.E. Sharman, of Winnipeg, had to escape into a cloud at 850 metres when his Vickers gun and his observer's Lewis gun both jammed. 'Those Boches have powerful machines,' Bert told his parents in his next letter. 'Climb? They're great. Just point their nose up nearly 45 degrees and up they go like a rocket.' He recalled another mission when he and Pattison were attacked by a couple of LFG Roland fighter biplanes:

[They are] some buses and they look wicked too! But my luck was in, as after the first couple of bursts one changed his mind and sheered off. The other chose the popular position for attacking, beneath and behind, sheltered by [my] fuselage and elevators. But by some skilful manoeuvring my pilot made it clear for me to reply without shooting away our own tail. Then we settled down to it and he had come so close that we were at point-blank range. As soon as I had emptied one pan it was replaced by another and blazing away again. The bullets were cracking all-round at the rate of about 1000 per minute. That's pretty fast isn't it? But you must know they have two machine-guns in unison. Another pan of ammunition runs out and I quickly put a full one on again and let her rip. Yet all the time I could see my 'tracers' splashing on his machine. Why didn't he go down? Though naturally I suppose you're lucky to hit some vital part, ignition, petrol pipe or so, it wouldn't have much effect on the solid mass of motor. Also he was so well protected that while he's coming head on it's almost bullet proof. Well, just as I had used

about half the pan — hooray! Down, down he goes.
I'm so intently watching his descent when my joy is
cut short by the sudden realisation of intense pain in
my hands. The cold wind had its effect. During the
rest of the flight except for a little job now and again,
I kept rubbing and clapping my hands to keep the
circulation going. Anyhow I was soon alright again
and ready for more business.[9]

Cold was Bert's greatest enemy. On 22 March, he was
part of another raid on the Saar Valley during which the
Sopwiths managed to avoid enemy fighters but were beset
by frozen oil pumps, frostbite and lost bearings. The cold
was so vicious — 'it could penetrate anything', Bert said —
and somewhere over enemy territory all the compasses
froze. Bert and Pattison flew headlong into a snowstorm
and, enveloped in white, they lost all sense of direction.
Bert described it as the weirdest sensation possible and,
when he and Pattison remerged from the storm, they
steered by the sun along a course they reckoned to be a
beeline for France.

Being right off our map we could not very well pick up
our bearings so the best thing was to keep flying as
long as possible and hope for the best [Bert recalled].
Putting in the time in a half frozen condition you
may guess was simply awful but we had no desire
to become an inmate of one of the Kaiser's hostels.
After a time our motor conked out. There was no
choice, we had to land. My pilot feared we were still
on the wrong side of the lines, though I had different
ideas.[10]

Bert and Pattison had a two-franc wager on their position and, given Bert's care with his cash, he had to be confident before taking the bet.

> We landed in the most desolate spot we could find and while the pilot went to meet a couple of peasants in the distance and see in what part of the world we were I got ready in case it should be necessary to fire the machine. But you can guess my joy when according to our prearranged signals I saw we were alright. We had come down about seventy miles from our aerodrome and about forty from the frontier. Only one machine found the aerodrome that day and everybody was frostbitten about the face and hands.[11]

Despite the RNAS raids, by April 1917, German air power was at its zenith, and the British commander in France, Sir Douglas Haig, was questioning the worth of long-distance bombing, claiming that aerial missions were more effective in support of ground forces. In the skies over Arras and Valenciennes in northern France, Richthofen reigned supreme. He had taken over command of the fighter squadron Jasta 11, which would eventually include some of the most feared pilots of the war, including his brother Lothar, Ernst Udet, Karl Schäfer, Kurt Wolff and the dashing Hermann Göring.[12] It was said the life expectancy of a British pilot over Arras in April was about seventeen hours in the air.[13]

During that 'Bloody April' Richthofen and his red Albatros shot down twenty-two British aircraft, including a spree of four planes in one day. He dived from above like a bird of prey with the advantage of the sun behind him and with other German pilots protecting his rear and flanks.[14]

With the need for more reinforcements to bolster the RFC operating on the Western Front, Bert's No. 3 Wing was about to be disbanded. The new massive Handley Page 0/100 twin-engine bombers — one of the biggest aeroplanes in the world and the biggest being built in Britain — had just started to operate out of Ochey, armed with their five machine-guns and sixteen 50-kilogram bombs. Before long Bert and the rest of the Sopwith Strutters would be flying their last mission from there. On the night of 20 March near Avonmouth, in Bristol, a German U-boat had torpedoed His Majesty's Hospital Ship *Asturias*, which two years earlier had ferried some of the wounded from Gallipoli. Thirty-five British crewmen died.[15]

In retaliation, on 14 April, in a combined French and British operation from Luxeuil, twenty-one bombers and seventeen fighters wreaked mayhem on the town of Freiburg, just over the Rhine to the east, operating in two shifts like a slaughterhouse, one in the morning and one in the afternoon. They dropped two tonnes of bombs along with propaganda leaflets declaring that the attacks were justice for the *Asturias*. Many of the Allied bombs hit Freiburg houses rather than factories, and Bert's machine copped plenty from 'Archie'. Gunlayer R.G. Kimberly downed one Fokker despite being shot in the leg and wrist, and Bert and Pattison pounced on a German fighter attacking one of their planes, Pattison later recalling that before the German pilot could react Bert sprayed machine-gun bullets all along his fuselage 'whereupon [the German] immediately fell quickly towards the ground in a spinning nose dive'. But the Sopwith hadn't escaped unscathed.

Bert and Pattison were about 13 kilometres from the safety of the French lines when a German bullet severed their petrol pipe, causing the engine to fail as anti-aircraft shells exploded all around them. 'We managed to glide into our side of the lines to about three miles, crossing the trenches at about 3000 feet,' Bert wrote home. 'Oh I should tell you we were in the Vosges; the mountainous country is even worse than Gympie. But the worst was still to come. The clearest spot we had picked out in the distance, when we got nearer showed high electric standards and cables running across it. As we were too low to make further choice, we had nothing else but to make the best of a flop. The hills and trees loomed up all around and almost below us was just a small clearing not more than about a quarter of an acre. We managed to fall into this with a crash.' Both men were knocked cold by the impact. 'When we came to, we found the machine all smashed and upside down just on the edge of a gully. Well, I guess luck was with us. Both of us had bruises about the head but they're all gone now and my only souvenir is a walking stick made out of the remains of the broken propeller.' Bert said the bruising on one side of his nose was 'a beautiful colour'.

The pair hobbled to a French military base where the commanding officer plied them with champagne and baguettes and assigned a car to ferry them back to Luxeuil. 'We got back to the Aerodrome next day after a delightful car ride of about 60 miles. The most part of it, beautiful mountain scenery. On the way we called at a hospital and saw a gunlayer pal who had been wounded in the leg during the same raid. He had a tough time but bagged two Boches, so made a good deal. I do hope this bally war will soon come to an end.'

All the French bombers returned safely from the Freiburg mission, but three Sopwith gunners were killed and Canadian pilots George Fleming and Harold 'Gus' Edwards and British Wing Commander Charles Rathborne were taken prisoner. Fleming, who had the tail of his aircraft blown off, died three days later from his wounds.[16]

On 24 April, Bert was reassigned to the RNAS base at Dunkirk, where in his spare time he developed the Hinkler Double Lewis Gun, a dual machine-gun system, that won approval from the Australian commanding officer at No. 5 Squadron, Jimmy Goble, a Melbourne railway stationmaster turned fighter ace with ten victories over the Western Front. The exploits of two other Australians were already legendary around Dunkirk. One was a small, slightly built graduate of Melbourne's Scotch College named Robert Little, whose mates called him Rikki because he was as aggressive and as deadly as Rikki-Tikki-Tavi, the swift cobra-killing mongoose in Rudyard Kipling's *Jungle Book*. By the 'Bloody April' he was at the controls of the 188-kilometre-per-hour Sopwith Triplane painted in cardinal, gold and blue, the colours of his old school.

The other Australian pilot who'd made his name at Dunkirk was Stan Dallas, the outwardly gentle giant who had been with Bert and Papa Hinkler at Rockhampton five long years earlier when they'd seen Wizard Stone fly and wondered where the experience would lead them. In a Sopwith Triplane he named 'Brown Bread' as in 'dead', he was a fearless fighter, had risen to the rank of flight commander, set an altitude record of almost 8000 metres while enduring frostbite and oxygen intoxication and been awarded the Distinguished Service Cross and the French Croix de guerre.

By the time Bert arrived at Dunkirk, Dallas's No. 1 Squadron had moved to Chipilly in France. He had set the bar for Bert to follow even if, in the rank of petty officer with lofty but unrealised ambitions, Bert's frustration was palpable when he wrote home in August 1917.

Watching men who knew far less than he did about aeroplanes getting their wings and commissions was chafing, and his frustration spilled out after Frances wrote to him asking if there was any chance he could come home for a holiday.

> Oh Mum, you do write optimistic about getting
> leave and all that [he replied]. I must explain right
> now that such an idea of getting leave to go to
> Australia is absolutely impossible. If I had started
> life on a different plane and joined the service
> with a commission there's no telling what strings
> you can pull. But as it is on the lower deck, you're
> not supposed to have nerves, brains or anything
> requiring talent. Simply, so to speak, one horse in a
> team.[17]

He was desperate to prove himself to his parents, to his comrades and to himself, but then he remembered all those young men who wanted to prove themselves, too, but would never make it home, remarking that while his progress in the service was 'bally slow, I'm not so bad off after all'.

While in Dunkirk Bert also began to fly missions on the Handley Page machines, which were being designed in an even more potent form called the 0/400. 'I did a number of raids at night on the giant aeroplanes you may have heard about,' Bert relayed.

You can guess how big when I tell you they've carried about 22 persons up to 12,000 feet high at about 80 miles an hour. But of course we carry about the equivalent weight in bombs. It was quite an experience and the sight of the many enemy searchlights sweeping the sky trying to find us was very novel. And what a curious feeling as the beams would light up the machine then the consequent manoeuvring, side slipping, turning sharply right, left etc to dodge them. Around Ostend, Bruges and Ghent the searchlights there are so numerous that it's impossible to count them, they are tremendously powerful too. Naturally the guns work in conjunction with the lights and when they get on you up come the shells. They also have an idea which seemed to me rather pretty [and] consists of a train of magnesium lights on a line. We call them 'Bubbly' — these strings of lights — about 20 or so at a time. If a machine gets caught in them they are supposed to set it on fire, but luckily none have yet taken effect.[18]

Bert also began flying as a gunner behind a pilot on a two-seater de Havilland-designed Airco DH.4. He figured he knew as much as the man in front of him, Charles Beverley Sproatt, who had joined the RNAS after graduating from the Toronto Curtiss School of Aviation in 1915.[19] Sproatt let Bert test that theory.

The weather around Dunkirk in summer and autumn was much better than the winters around Ochey and Luxeuil, which meant that Bert was flying raids every other day, and when he wasn't exchanging bullets he was studying everything that Sproatt was doing on the other side of the fuel tank that separated them. In one fortnight Bert went on eleven raids in the DH.4, but the really exciting part was when Sproatt, using Bert's idea for dual controls, let his gunner have a turn 'flying the bus' on the way home from a raid.

Bert was ecstatic at finally getting his hands on the controls of the plane and its massive 250-horsepower motor, at last actually flying himself. He couldn't help but morph into the aviation instructor he'd aspired to be ever since the night at Lytton's show when he'd told Wizard Stone how to fix his machine. 'Of course flying is not a hard job,' he wrote home, 'but it's practice, so as to do all movements of the control to a nicety':

Now flying in a straight line I might compare to riding a bike. For the beginner he is all the time correcting his balance, for each little turn he over-corrects it so that he's got to correct the other way. In flying, when you move your ailerons for your lateral balance the tendency is also to swing the machine round also. Well, you've got to correct that with your rudder which, as I say, until you have practice you perhaps overdo it and then steer the other way. The result is that you fly in a very wobbly path. Well, even the first time I wasn't so bad and my pilot complimented me and now I'm going very strong and I'm beginning to fancy myself, dincum! [*sic*] See me doing banks right and left — oh, by the time I come home I shall be able to show you some stunts. I'll tell you what I was thinking of doing, that is get all the practice I can as I am and when on leave in England see if I cannot arrange to qualify for my pilot's ticket. I ought to

stand some chance of a pilot's job in the Australian
Flying Corps, what say you?[20]

The RNAS had other ideas and Bert and his machine-gun
were to spend a few more months working together. This
was despite a chronic shortage of pilots brought about
largely by von Richthofen and his comrades, who were
now known as the Flying Circus because of their brightly
coloured machines and the tents and trains they used to
swiftly move camp.

Over London, the twin-engined Gotha bombers were
proving even more deadly than the Zeppelins, and in the
first daylight raid on the capital on 13 June 1917 they
caused 162 deaths and 432 injuries. Among those killed
were forty-six children sheltering in a kindergarten in
Poplar.

To return fire, Harry Hawker and Tommy Sopwith
played Britain's trump card. Their new aeroplane, a single-
seat biplane fighter, was designed by their chief engineer
Herbert Smith and called the Camel because of a metal
hump over the breeches of the two forward-firing Vickers
machine-guns. Like a real Camel, the new Sopwith was
ornery and unpredictable, and could turn around and bite
you when you least expected it. It was fast, agile and highly
manoeuvrable in the hands of a skilled pilot, yet it killed
many inexperienced ones because of its unstable nature, a
short wingspan and the massive destabilising torque created
by its heavy, spinning rotary engine and propeller. It scared
pilots on both sides, offering them a choice, it was said,
between Victoria Cross, wooden cross and Red Cross.

The Camel entered service with the RNAS at Dunkirk
in June 1917 and, despite the fact that almost as many

crashed on landing and take-off as were being shot down by Germans, it was the most effective weapon the Allied flyers had. Bert was itching to try his luck as a Camel wrangler. While he waited he kept busy following orders, dropping bombs, shooting at enemy planes and coming up with ideas that he thought would benefit the British cause.

He worked on a navigation aid to correct drift in aeroplanes and a device to safeguard gunners like himself who often had to shoot while the pilot turned their plane upside down. Having experienced red-hot ejected shells spitting back onto his face and chest many times, Bert invented a system to make ejected shells fall away to one side and worked on an improved gun sight. He also developed new techniques for aerial photography, and would take photographs of enemy troop movements when he wasn't shooting the Lewis gun. Bert spent time making friends and talking to all the Canadians, absorbing everything he could about aviation. He whiled away his time playing cards and writing letters to his parents and sisters, reassuring them that Jack was bearing up well despite the mud and the blood of the Western Front. Jack had corresponded with his family as regularly as Bert, sending postcards and letters at weekly intervals, sometimes writing from the trenches, sometimes from tunnels. Once, on a short leave Bert had the chance to travel down the French coast from Dunkirk to visit him in Boulogne-sur-Mer, where Jack was helping to load wounded soldiers onto a hospital ship. It had been four years since Bert had seen his younger brother, and for a while he didn't recognise him, wondering who 'that big, burly fellow could be'.

Whenever he found himself back in England Bert pursued his first serious romantic relationship. He had met an elegant well-spoken nurse named Hannah Jervis, from a Yorkshire coal-mining family, who called her Nance. She and Bert had become an item despite the fact that she was sixteen years older than the 24-year-old petty officer and had given birth to a daughter named Maida Vivian Crossland nearly twenty years earlier, before Bertie Hinkler had even started school. Nance's husband back then was Herbert Crossland, a railway signalman from Barnsley, but by the time Bert met Nance he had gone from her life, or so she thought. Nance was among the new breed of British women; she had a job, would soon have a vote and loved art and painting and theatre and tennis and cafés. Bert's friends always found him shy in social settings, somewhat introverted whenever the subject deviated from aviation, and believed that in Nance he had found the loyal love and nurturing care he had experienced growing up at Woodbine Cottage. The relationship he developed with Nance was just the sort of comfort he craved while risking his life almost every other day in appalling, terrifying conditions.

Bert was always secretive about his personal life, even with his family, and while he wrote to them about his many adventures and harrowing moments in the sky, it was a long time before he told them he had a lady friend. As it was, in late 1917 passion, and not just flying machines, was in the air over London. At St Peter's Anglican Church in Ealing, Bert's old boss Harry Hawker married Muriel Alice Peaty, a 22-year-old woman he'd met two and a half years earlier when her car had broken down in London's Richmond Park. Soon they were going on long, romantic drives in Harry's new Austro–Daimler.

While Nance had entered Bert's life, his one true love was still aviation, and there was no hiding it. His sense of duty, enthusiasm for flying and obvious courage was at last being recognised by his commanding officers at Dunkirk. He took the next step to gaining his wings when he was transferred to the RNAS Officers Section on 30 September and the next day promoted to warrant officer, with a recommendation for pilot training. Still he kept flying missions over Germany, practising at the controls of the DH.4 every chance he got. In November he was awarded the Distinguished Service Medal, a decoration awarded to non commissioned officers for bravery and resourcefulness.

For his twenty-fourth birthday Bert had spent the time polishing and checking his machine-gun. For his twenty-fifth on 8 December 1917 he wrote to Queenie to say he'd spent part of the day 'up top at about 10,000 feet taking photographs and dropping bombs':

> Having a high old time wasn't I! The Huns sent me up some lovely presents which went off with a bang, and I wonder did they really know it was my birthday? I had a letter from Papa today and he says he has received no letter from me for some time. Well I think they must have got in the way of some U-boat because I wrote in reply to every one I received from him and occasionally an extra edition. And I will be writing him a few days after this.[21]

Despite the U-boat menace, the end of 1917 looked far more promising than the start of the year for the Allies. Air power had swung back in their favour thanks to the massive numbers of the Sopwith Camel, the Royal Aircraft factory's SE.5a and the French SPAD S.XIII, which were beginning to dominate the German Albatros fighters.

The Americans were pouring into France in numbers that would eventually pass two million.

By late December, Bert had flown 122 missions over enemy territory, thirty-six of them bombing raids. Officially he had shot down four enemy planes, although privately he always claimed it was six, and at long last the RNAS decided to send him back to London to make him a pilot. They transferred him to the Royal Naval College, Greenwich, on the south bank of the Thames for training. He and Nance decided to celebrate. On 29 December, they went to her local place of worship, the nearby St Giles Anglican church at Camberwell, and applied for their Banns of Matrimony, the public announcement of an impending marriage. The next day Bert was made a Temporary Probationary Flight Officer in the RNAS. Life was looking up.

Chapter 11

*This blessed war is making me a
cold-blooded murderer*

**Bert Hinkler, October 1918, after being ordered to
shoot retreating Austrian troops in northern Italy**

*By the end of the war you had aircraft with 200-plus
horsepower engines, you had aluminium frames on
the aircraft whereas everything before was wood,
you had supercharged engines and you had pilots
using parachutes and oxygen. Like it or not war
enhances technological growth out of necessity.*

J.R. Williams, League of WWI Aviation Historians

Noel Pemberton Billing was winning his battle with the
British Government over its aerial strength, yet as 1918
dawned he faced the fight of his life to avoid a nine-
year prison sentence. On 26 January, Pemberton Billing
published an article in his magazine *Imperialist* alleging
that the Germans had compiled a 'Black Book' with
the names of 47,000 British homosexuals and lesbians,
some of them even Cabinet ministers.[1] He said that

Germany was blackmailing all of England's 'perverts' into undermining the British war effort. Then on 16 February, in his magazine, now renamed *Vigilante*, he inferred that the Canadian-born belly dancer Maude Allan, who was about to open at London's Prince of Wales Theatre in Oscar Wilde's *Salome*, was one of the many lesbians in the grip of the Germans. Allan sued but Pemberton Billing, facing prison for criminal libel, came out swinging at the Old Bailey, using a mixture of persuasion and perjury. His lover, a female government agent he'd seduced, said she'd seen the Black Book and that it even contained the name of the trial judge, Mr Justice Darling. Pemberton Billing eventually won the case to thunderous applause.

An even bigger victory for the man who had started the Supermarine company came on 1 April that year when the British Government, after two years of agitation from him, formed the Royal Air Force by merging the Royal Flying Corps with the Royal Naval Air Service.

Bert had been transferred from Greenwich to Eastbourne in East Sussex on 9 March 1918, and on the day the RAF was formed he was made a Second Lieutenant (Technical) in the new force. A few weeks later he was a Second Lieutenant (Aeroplanes and Seaplanes) and was undergoing intense training as a pilot at No. 2 Fighting School in the village of Marske-by-the-Sea in Yorkshire. He seemed to show much more aptitude for aviation than the flying instructor there, Captain W.E. Johns, a Gallipoli veteran who destroyed three planes in three days and twice shot off his own propeller with his Vickers gun. Johns would have much more success in later years writing about Biggles, a dashing Camel pilot inspired by characters he met during the war.

As Bert trained in Yorkshire, Manfred von Richthofen was suffering nausea and constant headaches, the legacy of a serious head wound sustained when he was shot down the previous year. During his convalescence he completed his autobiography *Der Rote Kampfflieger* (*The Red Battle Flyer*) under instructions from the German propaganda machine. Despite the headaches and a growing disdain for killing, he refused to take a desk job, declaring that every German must do his utmost for the war effort. So Richthofen started shooting down RAF planes again, now flying a fast and agile Fokker Dr.1 triplane, the aircraft he is most famously associated with and in which he scored nineteen aerial victories.

At 6.40 p.m. on 20 April he shot down a Camel being piloted by a Londoner, Richard Raymond-Barker, the machine exploding in a ball of flame near Le Hamel in the Somme Valley. Just three minutes later Richthofen was diving, rolling and pulling the trigger again, scoring his eightieth aerial victory by blasting a Camel being flown by Rhodesian-born David Greswolde 'Tommy' Lewis northeast of Villers-Bretonneux. Richthofen's bullets hit Lewis's compass, goggles, the elbow of his coat, a trouser leg and, critically, the aircraft's 18-litre emergency petrol tank. The burning machine crashed into the ground, but Lewis was somehow thrown clear and, except for a few superficial burns and nicks from the Baron's bullets, was completely unharmed. As Lewis checked his body all over to make sure he was OK and pinched himself hard to make sure he wasn't dreaming, Richthofen flew by just 30 metres above the stunned pilot and gave him a good-natured wave.

The next morning at eleven o'clock, Richthofen was chasing a Camel being flown by rookie Canadian pilot

Wilfrid 'Wop' May when another Canadian, Arthur 'Roy' Brown, came to May's rescue. The young German turned to avoid Brown's attack and then, like a dog after a bone, went right back in pursuit of his original target. He flew low over enemy territory, into a part of France held by the Australian Imperial Force. Bullets from the Aussie troops shot skyward, and a single .303 shell burst through Richthofen's lungs and heart. Despite the injury he still had enough control to land in a field near the village of Vaux-sur-Somme but, as Sergeant Ted Smout[2] of the Australian Medical Corps reached him, the man whose name was synonymous with terror fluttered his glassy eyes a couple of times and uttered his last word: '*Kaput*.' He was twenty-five.

The RAF credited Roy Brown with the victory, but the fatal shot was almost certainly fired by one of the Australians: Cedric Popkin, Snowy Evans or Robert Buie.

The following day the baron was buried with full military honours in the cemetery at Bertangles, the village from where Lanoe Hawker had taken off for his fatal meeting with Richthofen two years earlier. Hermann Göring took over as the leader of the Flying Circus and the skies remained deadly, although in the next few weeks Stan Dallas and Rikki Little made life hell for the Germans every chance they got.

Little, who liked collecting French wildflowers for his young wife and son when he wasn't shooting it out in the sky, had built his reputation on fearless aggression, downing fourteen German planes in the month of July 1917 alone. By May 1918, he was a captain in Raymond Collishaw's RAF No. 203 Squadron and had been credited with shooting down forty-seven enemy planes. On the night of 27 May, he went hunting German Gotha bombers in his Camel when he was struck by a bullet that passed through both his thighs. He crash-landed in a field near Noeux-les-Mines and bled to death. He was twenty-two.

Just five days later over the nearby town of Lievin, Stan Dallas, about to be made a lieutenant colonel after being recommended for the Victoria Cross several times, was flying a solo mission in his SE.5a. He'd just sent a letter home pleading with his father to quit mining because it was too dangerous, promising him that he would be home soon to support his parents through aviation. But at high noon over the picturesque French village he elected to shoot it out with three Fokker triplanes. They got the jump on him, and Big Stan Dallas, who might have shot down more than fifty enemy aircraft, was dead at twenty-six.[3]

Every trainee pilot in Britain knew the risks. Even Bert's Canadian mate, good old Charlie Pattison, promoted to captain and awarded the Croix de guerre, had burned to death when his Camel crashed after hitting overhead wires near Redcar Racecourse in Yorkshire on 2 April. Yet air-minded youngsters from all over the British Empire were more eager than ever to drive the Huns from the heavens. At Marske and Eastbourne Bert had an assortment of machines on which to practice: the DH.4, the DH.9, the capricious Camel, the Sopwith Pup, the Bristol M.1C monoplane and the old faithful Avro 504. Bert just had to stay alive long enough to enjoy it. He'd passed the RAF's many and varied pilot tests, making turns right and left, forced landings, doing the spin, loop and half roll; he'd flown through the clouds for five minutes, stayed at 4500 metres for a quarter of an hour, made cross-country flights, done the sideslip right and left, landed off a sideslip and flown for 'not less than 25 hours aggregate'.

On Saturday, 6 July, at Eastbourne the time came for his final test as he was called upon to prove his mastery over a Camel combat machine. The Camel's engine was continually lubricated by castor oil that was blown out like exhaust fumes, soaking the pilot,[4] and, as Bert prepared himself for his final test, he made sure his helmet and goggles were firmly in place. Once again he had covered himself in whale grease before donning his thick fur suit because he'd be taking his 'little bus' up to 4500 metres. He climbed onto the Camel's hump, which covered the Vickers machine-gun breeches and the two belts containing 500 rounds of .303 ammunition, then slid into the narrow cockpit, slipping his toes under the straps on the rudder bar. His heart racing with nervousness, excitement and a sense of achievement, he checked the wings, flaps and rudder, moving the stick and rudder bar.

He made sure that both the magneto switches, which provided power to the spark plugs, were switched off and then he turned the petrol tap on. He used the hand air-pump to build the air pressure in the petrol tank and then pushed the short lever forward about half way to control the petrol/air mix. The mechanic stepped forward when all was in readiness and called out, 'Switches off, petrol on, suck in.' As the mechanic began to twist the propeller, Bert moved a long lever forward slightly to open the barrel throttle-valve and listened intently for the sucking noise as the petrol and air were drawn into the overhead inlet valves. He checked that his seat belt was secure around his waist, wrapped his scarf over his nose and mouth to make sure he didn't choke on the castor oil spray and made the scarf secure by pushing one end under the chin strap of his leather helmet. The mechanic revolved the propeller around a few times in readiness and then, when the blade reached a point of about ten o'clock, he shouted: 'Contact.' Bert put both the magneto switches on, pulled the petrol fine adjustment lever back, pulled the throttle to half open and yelled back: 'Contact.' The mechanic slammed the propeller towards the ground as hard as he could and jumped clear as the propeller and the nine cylinders began to whirr furiously.[5]

An aircraft rigger draped himself across the rear fuselage to keep the Camel's tail down as Bert built the revs to 1050 a minute and the chocks holding the wheels were pulled away. As he started to taxi along the Eastbourne grass Bert couldn't see over the machine-guns and the Aldis sight between them so he steered along the grass with his head stuck out the side of the cockpit. The rigger jumped off and, as the Camel lurched forward, Bert checked Eastbourne's windsock direction and turned the machine into the wind. He looked around to make sure there were no other machines nearby, pulled down his goggles; opened the throttle wide and moved the fine-adjustment lever just past half-way. He listened intently to make sure his petrol/oil mix was spot on and that the engine was firing evenly. Bert reminded himself that the take-off could be treacherous; young Camel pilots were dying every week. As his speed picked up across the grass Bert pushed the stick forward to get the tail skid off the ground and, as the nose came down a fraction, he could at last see over the guns and the engine cowling. He let the stick come back a touch until the wheels came off the grass, then felt the rushing wind lifting him and his machine towards the wild blue yonder.

Before long the Camel was doing 160 kilometres per hour and, knowing that he had to finesse every movement of the precocious controls, Bert pulled the stick back and started climbing faster than 300 metres a minute, reminding himself to keep working the fine adjustment lever every 300 metres so that the machine didn't stall.

It was a nightmare to fly at first and, once Bert had reached 4500 metres, the gyroscopic force of the spinning engine meant that he had to constantly apply forward pressure on the stick just to stay level. But the Camel could turn right like a top, and the scarf across Bert's face concealed a smile wider than the bridge across the Burnett. As he climbed and dived and rolled the Camel in his final test Bert could check off the last criteria for his pilot's certificate: have flown satisfactorily an active service machine — check, check and double check, underline and exclamation mark.

'I have graduated as a pilot,' Bert wrote in his next letter to his mum and dad. 'I know you will both be delighted.' He enclosed a photo of the Camel, describing it as a high-speed scout used all over the front. He raved about its 130-horsepower motor and its climbing ability and told them he'd had plenty of practice operating the two machine-guns, diving onto targets from on high and describing the whole experience as 'quite good sport'. 'Of course each machine has its own peculiarities and the Camel is quite a strange mount to handle until you're used to it,' he said, describing how he tried doing some rolls on one at 1200 metres on a windy day:

While flying along level you suddenly roll the machine over sideways till you are upside down and then round straight again. My first try, oh Lor', the machine spun round nearly twice before I realised what was happening. But before long I could manage the manoeuvre quite good, so good that I must have done it over a dozen times. When I landed instructors and fellow pupils thanked me for the exhibition. I also tried to loop but the Camel is well known as being most difficult, some of the experienced instructors say they cannot loop it properly. I tried several times but each time I would get half way over on my back and then would spin upside down. Yesterday ... I climbed to 6000 feet then shut off my motor and spiralled, first left then right, banking the machine until it was standing on the wingtips. To tell you the truth I am really beginning to enjoy flying properly now that I have learnt how to handle the machine.[6]

Bert told his parents he still had further tests to pass at the School of Aerial Gunnery before he was given his wings to wear as 'a badge of qualification' and sent into combat. He assured them he intended to get plenty of practice before 'I am turned out complete'. And then Bert gave the first indication of the dream that would one day define his life. 'I shall be terribly disappointed,' he declared, 'if I do not have a machine to fly back to Bundy as I am quite ready to give you a fair show overhead before I land. And I think it is after all this, the only way to return and justify my hopes and yours.' The letter was dated 11 July 1918, and an epic journey from England to Bundaberg was already taking wing in his mind.

Three weeks after passing his flying test at Eastbourne and having passed his gunnery tests, Bert received his orders. He said goodbye to Nance with a promise that he'd be back soon and was packed off to the Italian Front as a flight officer at the controls of a Sopwith Camel with RAF No. 28 Squadron. Two of England's most admired flyers, James McCudden and Edward Mannock, had both been killed in July, and Italy had only recently lost her leading ace, Francesco Barraca, who shot down thirty-four enemy aircraft before Austrian groundfire brought down his SPAD fighter, resplendent with its symbol of a prancing horse on its side, the very same symbol that would one day adorn all the cars made by his admirer Enzo Ferrari.

Two days after the Sopwith Camels arrived in Italy packed in crates, No. 28 Squadron was operational, boasting such aces as the Canadians Clifford McEwen and William Barker. Bert flew his first training flight on 6 August and his first scouting mission four days later as No. 28 Squadron prepared to set up its headquarters at the Sarcedo airfield near the city of Vicenza, in northern Italy.[7] For three years the many battles in the mountains around the turquoise Isonzo River on the Austro–Italian Front had claimed two million casualties from fighting, avalanches, frostbite, malaria, cholera and prisoner-of-war starvation.[8]

From the trenches dug into the thick snow thousands of metres up the Julian Alps, Sergeant Benito Mussolini had looked up in awe at the aircraft circling and weaving like prizefighters overhead on the days when they could get through the fierce wind and deadly snowstorms.[9] At first the Italians used Nieuports, Bleriots and Maurice Farmans to gather intelligence but, as the battles around the Isonzo wore on, the Austrians improved their airpower with German Rumplers and Aviatik C.1s and a whole fleet of Fokker monoplanes and biplanes. The Austrians had even dropped grenades into Mussolini's freezing trench two weeks before he was invalided out of combat with forty-four pieces of shrapnel from one of his own mortar shells in February 1917. His respect and admiration for aviators and air power grew even more as the war reached its final months.[10]

Following a cataclysmic defeat against the Germans at Caporetto in October 1917 the Italians won a decisive battle in June 1918 around the swollen Piave River as 20,000 Austro–Hungarian soldiers drowned while trying to retreat. By the time Bert and No. 28 Squadron arrived in Sarcedo, the Italians were planning a counter-offensive against the Austrians at Vittorio Veneto, and the British and French were at Germany's throat, driving the Kaiser's last hopes back to the Hindenburg Line in France. No. 28 Squadron's mission was to ensure the Italians snuffed out the last gasp of any remaining Austrian threat amid Italy's soaring peaks and plunging ravines. Bert flew scouting missions in his Camel, observing Austrian troop movements and becoming increasingly familiar with the unique characteristics of an aircraft that shot down more enemy planes than any other Allied fighter.[11]

Although there was a war going on and millions were dying, Bert tried to find happiness in the clouds. On 2 October 1918, he wrote to his sister May congratulating her on her forthcoming wedding and gushing with the joy of flying, saying that it was going along 'absolutely glorious' and that he was ready at any moment to 'burst into song over Aviation' despite the fact that conditions were very different from the day she'd watched him fly at Mon Repos. 'Practically each time we are out on patrol, Archie is as energetic as ever, but there are very few Huns to be seen around this way,' he wrote.

Generally each time one is sighted it's goodbye to
the luckless Fritz. The other day weather conditions
not being good enough for patrols we went up for
practice. The clouds, oh, they were glorious: those
big fleecy rock-like formations. Another machine
and I had a fine chase and hide and seek around
the clouds. I must tell you I found infinite joy in our
fooling. Sometime in the future, wars finished, home
again etc etc when the sky contains such glorious
clouds floating about, I must take you around.
Shooting past, just skimming over the top, and
then banking over to the vertical, rounding some
monstrous cloud pillar and then diving right through
the middle, oh it's fine sport. The clouds were so wet
that each time I dived through, it was like a shower
bath and I had to wipe the wet from my goggles so as
to see.[12]

Bert then told his sister that on the very same morning he
wrote his letter, he had a 'unique experience' flying his
Camel through thick clouds, an experience that totally
mystified and disoriented him and if not for sheer luck
could have killed him.

Flying in a formation through rain clouds that swirled
around 1800-metre mountains, Bert's goggles became so
wet that he couldn't see and he lost sight of the patrol's
leader. He could barely make out the wingtips of the
Camel, but he pulled hard on the stick to keep its nose up,
hoping to burst out above the clouds and rejoin his group.
At 2700 metres he saw a patch of blue sky and thought
he was right when, suddenly, he was swamped by another
thick rain cloud and felt worse than ever, 'hopelessly lost

and out of equilibrium'. Without him realising it Bert's plane had fallen 300 metres and he didn't know which way was up. He quit trying to climb above the clouds and switched off his engine. He couldn't stop the machine rocking.

'I was falling all roads,' he told May, 'and my big fear was the mountains. So I prayed that if I was to bump I would hit the ground when the speed was zero.' As Bert's altimeter showed 1800 metres he was sure he was about to plunge into the side of a mountain very soon but, instead, he caught sight of some white irregular lines over the top of his wings in the distance through the mist of the clouds. His machine twisted and soon the lines were below him. Using those lines as a marker he kept his Camel level, eventually steadied the machine and realised that the lines were roads around a nearby mountain. 'Gee, wasn't I glad when I got straight and found where I was.'

Just a couple of weeks later, though, Frances Hinkler received the knock on the door at Gavin Street she'd been dreading all through the war. With a shaking hand she took the message from the Australian Imperial Force, Victoria Barracks in Melbourne and dated 18 October 1918. It was written on a wonky typewriter. 'Dear Madam,' it began, 'I regret to advise you that Private J.W. Hinkler has been reported ...' Frances gripped the telegram as fear stabbed her nerves. Her eyes lost focus, and she dared not read any more. But she had to. She had to know. '... reported admitted 6/10/18 to Town Hall Hospital, Torquay, England gassed (classed as wounded) mild.' Thank God. Jack was crook, gassed by the Boche, but he was still alive and he'd be coming home. Now she just had one son to worry about.

And worry she did. The allies lost 560 planes in September 1918 even as their troops marched closer to a final victory. Even the luck of the intrepid Roland Garros ran out. He finally managed to escape from a German POW camp after repeated attempts and settled back into the cockpit of a SPAD fighter only to be shot out of the sky and killed near Vouziers, in France, on 5 October.

Bert had to keep his head down and his finger on the trigger if he was to survive.

Italy launched the battle of Vittorio Veneto on 24 October, the anniversary of its horrific defeat at Caporetto, and the following day Bert was in a three-Camel patrol when they encountered seven Albatros D.V biplane fighters at 4300 metres over the snow-covered town of Feltre and heading towards the Piave River. Rocking his wings to signal enemy aircraft, the leader of Bert's pack went in for the kill, shooting down one of the German aircraft. The fighting finished with the Camel's guns jamming but, as the RAF planes headed for home, only five of the seven Germans remained in the air.

Five days later, Bert was ordered to lead an attack by three planes on Austrian troops as they fled the fighting. Bert's posse was to fly low and cause as much death and destruction as possible. As well as the belts of ammunition for its Vickers gun each plane carried four nine-kilogram Cooper bombs. Bert also carried the weight of the world on his shoulders. Dogfighting with German aces and dropping bombs on armament factories from 2000 metres he could handle, but bombing and shooting at troops on the ground — troops retreating at that — was something altogether different. The Austrian army, which had marched into Serbia so proudly four years earlier and ruthlessly executed prisoners of war, was now a starving, freezing rabble riddled with malaria, cholera and influenza.[13] Bert was ordered to fly so low over the soldiers that he could see their faces as he dropped the bombs.

Just north of Sacile, his squad found a convoy of soldiers in trucks, with their weary, hungry Haflinger packhorses behind them pulling carts. Bert felt hollow, but he did what he was told even if it chilled his soul. From 30 metres he dropped three of the Cooper bombs. Carnage erupted. The convoy came to a dead stop, and the men and horses that hadn't been hit ran for cover in the bushes. Bert rode the Camel in even lower as he buzzed back the other way, pulling the trigger on the Vickers guns as he swept down. He emptied the ammunition belts and flew off to drop the one remaining bomb on another ragtag bunch he spotted closer to Sacile. The other two pilots targeted soldiers waiting in the village square and at a railway siding. It was one of the most horrific moments of Bert's life. Two days later he was part of a bombing raid around the Tagliamento River, dodging machine-gun fire from the ground that brought down one of the Camels and left another pilot with a bullet in the hand.

Bert wrote an emotional card to May:

This blessed war is making me a cold-blooded murderer — well that's how I feel since the last few days. We go over, low flying, say about 100 feet, bombing and machine-gunning the enemy's transport and whatever of him we can find. Most of the roads back to his lines are crowded as he is moving back, retreating as fast as he can go. And it is our bloody duty to shoot him down, not only in tens, but hundreds. I suppose if we did not do him first he would do the same and possibly worse for us.[14]

The only consolation for Bert was that everyone was saying the war couldn't last much longer. He told May that despite his revulsion at what was happening, on the way back from one of his bombing missions, he 'nearly went crazy with a peculiar, joyful feeling': 'Flying just over the tops of the small trees, over our newly regained ground — where before we used to get Archied hot if we came in sight — I waved to the troops still advancing and they waved and cheered back.'

He took his mind off the cruelty of war by composing intimate love letters to Nance, even writing one in Morse code, in case it fell into the wrong hands. They had not yet gone through a marriage ceremony, but Bert considered that just a formality. To him Nance was Mrs Hinkler even if they had no piece of paper to prove it. 'How soon now, before I can hold you tightly in my arms, in a long, loving embrace,' he asked her, 'and those glorious kisses, those wonderful kisses ... My beloved wife you are my constant thought by day, and companion in dreamland by night.'

On 3 November, the German fleet staged a mutiny in Kiel, and at 3 p.m. the next day the armistice sought by the Austro–Hungarians came into effect. A week later at 11 a.m. on the eleventh day of the eleventh month, with the Kaiser having abdicated, the Great War was officially over. More than 16 million lives had been lost and an even greater number wounded. Bert had escaped in one piece, but 16,623 airmen from the RAF, RFC and RNAS had not. The world would never be the same again and, while the politicians were calling it the war to end all wars, it had become painfully obvious to every military leader that air power would be a major factor in any future conflicts.

World War I had seen astonishing technical improvements to aircraft that might have taken fifteen to twenty years to achieve in peacetime. By November 1918, more than 250,000 Britons were employed making aircraft engines and parts, and Airco, Britain's biggest aircraft company, had a staff of 7000. Harry Hawker had been Sopwith employee No. 15 when he signed on in 1912, but by the end of 1918 Sopwith employed 5000 itself and perhaps 5000 more through its subcontractors such as Fairey Aviation Company.[15] Over the four years of war Sopwith had built 16,000 planes, and Fred Sigrist, who received £50 for every plane produced, was £800,000 richer or about £40 million in 2011 values.[16]

During his three months in Italy Bert flew fifty operations, totalling 93 hours and five minutes of airtime. He made his last flight with the squadron on a training exercise on 29 November 1918. His commanding officer, Major William Guilfoyle,[17] helped expedite his return to London so that he could be with Nance and plan his trip back to Bundaberg. In another letter, Bert told Queenie that with another English winter coming on he couldn't wait to get back to Woodbine Cottage to sink his teeth into one of those big fat juicy watermelons he'd been dreaming about for so long. He promised Queenie a ride in his aeroplane when he got there. He just needed to find a small machine of wood and fabric that would carry him cheaply for almost 20,000 kilometres to her front door, and there were plenty of second-hand aeroplanes all over England. How hard could it be?

Chapter 12

If I am able to acquire the machine I have great confidence in being able to annihilate the distance between the Thames and the Burnett.

Bert Hinkler, 22 March 1919, telling his parents of his plans to enter the England to Australia race for a £10,000 prize offered by Prime Minister, Billy Hughes

Take it from me, Hughes with his big, wide Welsh noisy mouth is feeding you people on the cheapest sort of claptrap possible. He has already got more than his share of advertisement out of the belated flight.

Hinkler, six months later, voicing his disgust at being bogged down by red tape surrounding the contest

An uneasy peace had descended over Britain when Bert returned to London from the war and waited to be officially demobilised. He and Nance lived together in a flat in Shepherds Bush but did not go through an official marriage ceremony. To the rest of the world Nance would always be known as Mrs Hinkler, and on all official forms Bert always described himself as married. Britain experienced collective relief that the brave boys in uniform had come home and the bombs had stopped falling from the sky, but social and political unrest gripped the nation. Factory workers, dockhands, shipyard labourers and railway navvies demanded a forty-hour week for more pay since they were on the winning side. Fear of bolshevism was rife. More than a quarter of the world came down with Spanish flu, and as many as 250,000 Britons died in the epidemic. Thousands of restless foreign troops were still garrisoned there, impatient to return home and Bert was one of them.

Ever since he'd written to his parents outlining his dream of flying back to their front door, a notion at first so fantastic became totally plausible. In Italy he'd flown through some of the most hazardous terrain in Europe for hours at a time. All he would have to do, he told himself, was replicate each day's flying for a couple of weeks or thereabouts and he'd be with his folks at Woodbine Cottage enjoying a cup of tea with toast and mulberry jam. And he wouldn't have Archie or some hotshot like Richthofen sitting on his tail. There were 22,000 unemployed pilots at the war's end and hundreds, probably thousands, of surplus Sopwith Camels all around Britain, and he knew he could snap one up cheaply and fit it with extra fuel tanks for the long legs of his journey.

Hell, the first flight between England and Australia would be such a good advertisement for Sopwith and Hawker that they might even let him have a Camel for free. While Bert worked out ways to make it home he developed another invention for patent, the 'Navigation Board' made from protractors and sliding arms to calculate changes in course caused by wind drift. It was 'bally simple' to use, he told his parents, promising them a practical demonstration as soon as he reached Gavin Street.

The development of aerial machines during the war was astonishing, and if anything good came out of the four years of madness it was that safe, reliable and regular international air transport was becoming a reality.

Just two days into 1919, Captain Andrew Lang, son of the Victoria Racing Club's handicapper and formerly a flight instructor for the Australian Flying Corps at Richmond Air Base, rocketed with an observer to a world record of 9300 metres at Martlesham, near Ipswich, England, in a DH.9. Two weeks later, the monstrous Handley Page V/1500 biplane bomber, with four huge Rolls-Royce engines and a wingspan of 38 metres, finally arrived in Delhi a month after leaving Britain. Handley Page announced that soon it would begin regular flights to Calcutta (now Kolkata) and then on to Australia with passengers enjoying the comfort they'd find in Pullman railway carriages, complete with armchairs and electric lights.[1]

The war had halted attempts on the £10,000 *Daily Mail* prize for a transatlantic flight but, with production at Sopwith stalled by the Armistice, Harry Hawker, who was now the father of a baby daughter named Pamela, made his move. Early in 1919 he began preparations with his navigator, Lieutenant Commander Kenneth Mackenzie Grieve, to tackle the vast ocean that had claimed the *Titanic* and so many other great ships. Sopwith's engineering whiz, thirty-year-old George Carter, designed what he saw as the perfect machine for the task, appropriately named the Sopwith Atlantic, a single-engine biplane powered by a twelve-cylinder Rolls-Royce engine.

Bert followed the development of Hawker's machine closely and figured that he could fly four or five times the distance of the Atlantic Ocean on his flight to Australia using a machine with much less power. And solo. He would be his own navigator and mechanic and, unlike Hawker, wouldn't need a wireless operator because he wouldn't be taking a wireless. It was unnecessary weight. As Bert mulled over ways to finance his trip and to tackle all the logistical problems of finding places to land in the remote areas between London and Bundaberg, Australia's pugnacious Prime Minister Billy Hughes was about to light the path for him. Bugger all those foreign pilots, Hughes said, Australia had the best airmen in the world even if the Hun had robbed his sunburnt country of Stan Dallas and Robert Little.

The PM they called the 'Little Digger' planned to show the world that Australian aviators were second to none, just like the country that raised them. He had met many Australian airmen in Britain after the war and, on 18 February 1919, cabled the Australian Government to advise that some were keen to beat Handley Page to Australia. In March, Hughes' government announced that it would offer £10,000 for the first flight from London to Darwin. And only dinki-di Australians flying British machines could apply.

At the time Hughes was in Paris punching far above his weight against the American President Woodrow Wilson. They were among the seventy delegates at the Paris Peace Conference, which concluded the Treaty of Versailles and eventually formed the League of Nations, yet there was nothing peaceful about Hughes. He was a small, tough man with prominent ears and a sandpaper voice who had grown up in Wales and emigrated to Australia at twenty-two. He had dragged himself up from his days as a bush cook and umbrella repairman, and no one was going to push him or Australia around. President Wilson, a professor of jurisprudence educated at Princeton, took a conciliatory approach to Germany as a valuable trading partner, but Hughes, who'd earned his law degree part time, wanted to hang the Kaiser and take German New Guinea as compensation for Australia's 60,000 war dead. The Australian terrier was such an irritant to Wilson and his Fourteen Points Peace Plan that the President referred to him as a 'pestiferous varmint'. Undettered, Hughes pressed on, showing the same persistence he expected from the aviators chasing his 10,000 quid.

To Bert, the £10,000 represented more money than dear old Papa had earned in a lifetime of hard toil, and he could hardly contain his excitement when he read news of the prize. He had no doubt that he'd win and become rich for doing something he had been planning to do for free. Even more important than the money, he would prove he was a first-class airman. Although the rules for the contest had not been formalised, Bert outlined his proposed itinerary in a letter home on 22 March 1919. He said he would start his flight from London at 2 a.m., fly by the compass and finish his first day's journey in the late afternoon, thus avoiding the perils of Italy's treacherous mountains in the dark. By landing in the afternoon each day he would have time to examine his engine and make any needed repairs before the next day's flying. Provided his machine didn't let him down, he reckoned he could make it from London to Gavin Street in just 10 days: day 1: London to Brindisi (Italy) 2000 kilometres; day 2: Damascus (Syria)

3700 kilometres; day 3: Shiraz (Persia) 5300 kilometres; day 4: Karachi (India) 7000 kilometres; day 5: Calcutta (India) 9000 kilometres; day 6: Tenasserim (Siam) 10,600 kilometres; day 7: Macassar (Celebes, East Indies) 12,230 kilometres; day 8: Darwin 13,800 kilometres; day 9: Hughenden (Qld) 15,500 kilometres; day 10: Bundaberg 16,700 kilometres.

Bert had spoken to a number of Indian pilots in Britain who told him that the journey from Karachi to Calcutta would be the toughest. Nevertheless he assured his parents he was up to the challenge and that he was working on a machine that wouldn't fail him. He'd received a ringing endorsement from C.G. Grey at *The Aeroplane*, and Grey told all the English aircraft manufacturers that Bert was the perfect pilot for such a journey. Bert even broached the subject of government funding with Queensland's Agent General, Lieutenant Colonel Sir Thomas Bilbe Robinson, at Australia House in London. Robinson wished him all the very best of luck but, as Bert recalled with some chagrin, he was 'politely referred to another department; in other words shown the door'.

Still he wasn't about to give up, estimating that with his timetable he 'ought to be able to make a noise over the city of Bundaberg quite early on the afternoon of the 10th day'. This was no flight of fancy, he assured his parents and yes, Mum, he was eating well and thinking straight. He told them he'd been carefully planning out his route for six months, even as he was flying into battle over Italy. 'So you will see I am living in great anticipation. These days I am quite busy running around London to various departments etc, finding out necessary information for the journey [and] I have secured assistance at the Air Ministry for charts and information on the position of aerodromes en route.'

Harry Hawker, meanwhile, was committed to adding to the many aviation records he'd already set. By March 1919, he had said goodbye to his wife Muriel and five-month-old Pamela, and arrived by steamer at St John's in Newfoundland with his Sopwith Atlantic ready for the greatest flight in history. Newfoundland offered favourable winds and was the closest part of the Americas to the Irish coast.

The actual crossing of the ocean would take nineteen and a half hours, but Hawker's aircraft could stay in the air for twenty-five hours at a speed of 160 kilometres per hour.[2] He told reporters from the world's major papers gathered in Newfoundland that the Sopwith's undercarriage would be dropped off after take-off to stop the drag of the wheels through the air and that the fuselage was shaped like a boat just in case. 'If our descent is forced,' Hawker said, 'we undoubtedly will be rescued. If we are not, someone will find our observations, which will greatly aid others in trying the passage.'[3]

Hawker and Mackenzie Grieve mapped out a runway on a straight stretch of grass on a 162-hectare farm belonging to Andrew Glendenning[4] in the Mount Pearl area next to H.M. Wireless, one of the Royal Navy's thirteen wireless stations around the globe, with three Marconi radio towers 93 metres high.[5]

Back in London Bert found his attempts to get a start in the great race like walking through quicksand. His plan to fly a Camel home changed when Sopwith offered to lend him the new Herbert Smith-designed Sopwith Dove, a small, fast two-seat civilian version of the single-seat Pup fighter. Bert sat down with Sopwith and Smith and made changes, replacing the second seat with more storage for petrol. Not everyone shared his confidence over the flight, however. As he tried to drum up support the 'Royal Aero Club, appointed by Billy Hughes to supervise the competition, kept a wary eye on the ambitious young aviator. They had granted him a Civil Pilot's Licence No. 48 but after all, he was still inexperienced and had been at the controls of a Camel for just three months before the Armistice. Although he knew all about aeroplanes and his war service suggested that he was a first-rate mechanic, his experience at intercontinental aerial navigation was nil. The whole route hadn't even been surveyed properly, and who knew what the airfields were like along the way? How could anyone, let alone a novice, be expected to fly, navigate and repair a machine solo in the great void that awaited?

Still, Bert told Sopwith he was ready to take off for Bundaberg at a moment's notice. Sopwith told him that rather than fly off at the handle, so to speak, he should attempt the longest flight in the short history of aviation only as an official entrant in the competition so that his progress could be properly monitored. There was also the enormous publicity value to them both. Bert finally wrote to his parents apologising for the long delay in his correspondence but explaining that he thought a letter would be 'superfluous' as he had planned to beat the mail home to Bundaberg. He was growing hot under the collar.

Ten to one you'll be wondering why no news of me of late [he wrote on 7 May 1919]. Perhaps I may be a little too optimistic as I had been expecting I should be talking to you before any letters could reach you. As a matter of fact I should have been on my way already, but for the amount of wangling going on. It's d ... rotten the time the authorities take to fix conditions. The latest is that entries for the flight must be accompanied by £100 and one must wait a clear fortnight and after that no one will be allowed to start until there are at least two competitors ready. I can tell you I'm just about fed up.

With Hawker, Sopwith's regular test pilot, in Newfoundland, Bert had taken the Dove for a thorough three-hour examination on 3 May and told his parents his 'dinky little bus' was 'a grand machine' with a capacity for ten hours' continuous flight.

I flew all over the country between London and the South Coast, passing over Brighton and Eastbourne. There was a fairly stiff cross-wind blowing and the clouds were pretty low, from 2500 feet to 5000 feet [he wrote]. Anyhow, in all I travelled about 220 miles. The test being satisfactory in every way I completed all my maps ready for Sunday and hoped to make a start on Wednesday (yesterday) morning and now I find obstacles on every side, as I have already spoken of. My luck, what a day when I land in Gavan Street! I am well looking forward to it. But, of course, if I am delayed much longer the weather conditions in India will make a continuous flight impossible.

Bert went into a long and detailed description of his Navigation Board for his parents to scratch their heads over during dinner, complete with diagrams of wind direction and flight paths between Bundaberg and Brisbane, and enclosed a couple of snaps of the Dove at Brooklands. He asked his mother to get his old room ready and to air his pyjamas.

But the delays continued. As Bert argued with officials at Australia House and at the Royal Aero Club about leaving immediately, London bookies were offering five to one on Hawker and Mackenzie Grieve making their flight from Newfoundland. A rival machine, Fred Raynham's Martinsyde biplane, being tested at Quidi Vidi in Newfoundland, was quoted at eight to one.[6] Raynham's plane was a curiosity for locals who had never seen such a thing. One woman put a hole in a wing walking across it while another asked the pilot to show her how the wings were inflated.

Other machines were also being prepared in Newfoundland to tackle the ocean. Handley Page was readying a huge bomber to take off from Harbour Grace and was dismantling houses to make sure the machine had enough runway. Vickers was entering the competition with a plane piloted by Captain John Alcock. Threatening to beat them all across the ocean was a team of three US Navy Curtiss NC seaplanes that looked like Hargrave box kites 38 metres wide.[7] One of the planes, NC1, had once carried a world-record fifty-one people. This time each had six crew members. The seaplanes left Newfoundland late in the afternoon of Friday, 16 May. The fog became so thick that two crews put down in the water and experienced such damage from the mountainous waves that taking off again was impossible. The third plane, NC4, flew for more than fifteen hours through the fog to land safely in the water 2000 kilometres away in the Azores, a group of nine volcanic islands almost 1500 kilometres from Lisbon. That news spurred Hawker into action. Even though the Americans weren't competing for the £10,000 prize for a non-stop flight, Hawker still wanted to be the first aviator across that great stretch of water.

So, at 1.55 p.m., 18 May, Hawker and Mackenzie Grieve, wearing thick woollen clothes under inflatable rubber suits, took off into a cloudless blue sky and a light breeze blowing east. They dropped their detachable undercarriage into the water, where it was retrieved by fishermen and given to the local museum. Then the Sopwith turned towards the horizon, roaring over the seemingly endless, featureless water underneath. About an hour later Fred Raynham went sloshing down the runway in Quidi Vidi, but the boggy ground slowed his take-off and he crashed the Martinsyde from a height of 60 metres.

Hawker figured he'd be in London the following afternoon but, as Mackenzie Grieve tried to keep the navy ships following their progress informed, he soon found his wireless wasn't working. The winds changed direction, and the sunshine surrendered to a mass of fog and thick clouds as the Sopwith was blown 240 kilometres off course. Darkness came upon them like death, and halfway into the journey the plane had used up much more than half its petrol. Knots of barbed wire twisted in Hawker's stomach. Ice formed on the wings as they ploughed through the dark cold to the noise of the huge motor. Steam poured out of the radiator like it was a locomotive.

At Brooklands Muriel Hawker waited with the same anxiety she felt all those times before when her Harry pushed the envelope to bursting point. He didn't arrive at

4 p.m. as he had promised. He didn't arrive at five or six or seven or eight. There was no sight and no word from him. She cuddled Pamela tightly.

'HAWKER MISSING. ALL NIGHT SEARCH AT SEA', said the next morning's headlines. 'HAWKER'S FATE — GLOOMIEST VIEW TAKEN', said another. 'HOPE ABANDONED'.

Gale-force winds lashed the Irish coast, and nine destroyers searched vainly for wreckage and bodies. Day after day there was no trace.

The *Daily Mail* told Muriel they were going to give her Harry's share of the £10,000 prize, but she wrote to Lord Northcliffe, thanking him, before adding that she didn't want the money because 'I cannot and will not believe that my husband is not alive'. The Sopwiths and Sigrists tried to keep her spirits up and, while Muriel put on a brave face, in Australia, Hawker's friends and admirers mourned his death and newspapers eulogised a magnificent career. Banjo Paterson was so moved by the tragedy that he penned 'Hawker, The Standard Bearer', with the last verse:

> *Though Hawker perished, he overcame*
> *The risks of the storm and the sea,*
> *And his name shall be written in stars of flame,*
> *On the topmost walls of the Temple of Fame,*
> *For the rest of the world to see.*

Bert was so caught up in the emotion that he declared an Aussie would make history after all and submitted a formal entry for the flight to Australia, telling the Royal Aero Club that he planned to leave the official starting point — England's first civil aerodrome at Hounslow Heath — and go beyond the official finish of the race at

Port Darwin, flying all the way to his mother's front door in Bundaberg.

On Monday, 26 May, as the vain search for Hawker was still being reported, Bert's name was in all the Australian papers as the first entrant for the great race. Race rules gave competitors thirty days to make the trip, and Bert amended his optimistic timetable of ten days to a more manageable seventeen. He told the Royal Aero Club yet again — and he was getting bally sick of telling them — that he wanted to make an immediate start because the monsoons in India would prevent flying for three months.

He assured the club that there was no chance he'd end up like Hawker yet, even as Bert argued his point, there was a shock in store for everyone. Especially Muriel Hawker, who had just received a telegram from Baron Stamfordham, King George V's private secretary, who informed her: 'The King, fearing the worst must now be realised regarding the fate of your husband, wishes to express his deep sympathy and that of the Queen in your sudden and tragic sorrow. His Majesty feels that the nation lost one of its most able and daring pilots to sacrifice his life for the fame and honour of British flying.'

Muriel had read in the morning papers that all hope was lost and went across the road from the Hawkers' Surrey home in Hook Road, Surbiton, to St Paul's Church where prayers were offered for the missing aviators.

About an hour later, with Muriel in the depths of depression, a reporter from the *Daily Mirror* rang.

Muriel picked up the phone despondently.

'Mrs Hawker, have you heard the news,' the reporter blurted, 'your husband is alive!"

Muriel almost fainted with joy and listened stunned as the reporter told her that a Danish ship without wireless had just signalled a message with flags to a lighthouse on a Scottish outcrop that the two aviators were safe. He then asked, since he'd broken the good news, whether he could have an exclusive interview. As Muriel kissed Pamela a hundred times and began to cry she left the reporter dangling at the other end of the phone, waiting in vain for his scoop.

Six days after they disappeared Hawker and Mackenzie Grieve were now in Scotland, laughing and joking with British sailors. They had flown for fourteen hours and travelled almost 1700 kilometres — only about halfway across the Atlantic — when Hawker finally admitted that, with their motor cooking like a pot full of potatoes, their mission was doomed. Although the buffeting winds made him seasick as he flew low to see under the dense fog, Hawker managed to keep his Sopwith airborne until he almost crashed into the deck of the Danish tramp steamer SS *Mary* on its way to Scotland from New Orleans. He brought the Sopwith down into the water about three kilometres away with a mighty splash among the heavy, rolling waves. The two airmen spent an hour and a half on top of their shattered craft, sick and shivering, before the crew of the *Mary* could drag them into a lifeboat as the sea raged all around. The *Mary* had no radio, and the world and Muriel Hawker had to wait nearly a week for the news of their rescue when the ship reached the Outer Hebrides. Off Loch Eriboll the two aviators were transferred to the destroyer *Woolston* and the news of their salvation was sent to London.

The Navy put the flyers on a train to London, and at every station on their journey home they were greeted by waving and cheering crowds. Women threw flowers and kisses, and men tried to climb into their railway carriage to shake their hands even as the train was moving.

When Hawker and Mackenzie Grieve reached King's Cross Station, hundreds of thousands of Londoners, including an ecstatic Muriel and 5000 Aussie soldiers, were there to cheer them on their route to the Royal Aero Club in Clifford Street.

The papers said that no such scenes of enthusiasm had ever before been witnessed in London, not even at the end of the 'war to end all wars' just six months earlier. Cries of 'Coo-ee' rang out like air raid sirens. The soldiers plonked Diggers' slouch hats on the two fliers, and Hawker was bounced along the shoulders of the massive throng like a human beach ball, all the time with a smile on his face as wide as the ocean that had defeated him.[8] Lord Northcliffe then gave Hawker and Mackenzie Grieve £5000 each for putting on such a jolly good show even if they only made it halfway. The Sopwith machine, the only Atlantic ever built, was eventually hauled out of the ocean like a dead whale and along with it the soggy mail that Hawker had carried. The aircraft finally crossed the Atlantic to Scotland in a crumpled heap aboard an American ship just as the American NC4 seaplane arrived in Lisbon from the Azores. Hawker and Mackenzie Grieve completed a remarkable week of plummeting lows and unprecedented highs when they fronted up to Buckingham Palace to receive the Air Force Cross from the King.[9]

It was almost an anti-climax when two weeks later pilot John Alcock and his navigator Arthur Whitten Brown, descended from the gloomy mist onto a bog on Derrygimlagh Moor near Clifden in Ireland, at 8.40 on the morning of 15 June. The pair was flying a twin-engine Vickers Vimy bomber, with a wingspan of 20 metres, which had left Newfoundland sixteen hours and twenty-seven minutes earlier. On their 3000-kilometre journey they had encountered the same poor visibility that had plagued Hawker's machine and, as snow fell into their cockpits, Brown had to keep climbing out onto the wing, sometimes at 3500 metres, to scrape ice from the engine's air intakes. Not only did they collect their £10,000 prize from Winston Churchill but the King knighted them as well.

Prizes for long-distance flights were suddenly all the rage, and in New York Frenchman Raymond Orteig, who'd risen from immigrant busboy to the owner of the Big Apple's grand Lafayette and Brevoort hotels, offered $25,000 to the first airman to fly non-stop between New York and Paris.

Back in Australia, newspapers around the country informed readers that Bert's Dove would carry 260 litres of petrol, enough for ten hours flying each day at a cruising speed of 145 kilometres per hour. All he now needed was an official starter to check him off from Hounslow Heath and for a monitor to check his arrival in Singapore. If he didn't make a start soon his little bus would be overtaken by bigger, more powerful machines. His fears were soon realised when Charles Kingsford Smith and his mate Cyril Maddocks, who'd been giving joy rides in war-surplus DH.6 planes, announced they would start for Australia in mid-June, flying a Blackburn Kangaroo anti-submarine biplane.[10]

By early August there were five entries for the great race and many more in the wings. Bert received his official discharge from the Royal Air Force Depot at Uxbridge on

18 August 1919 and was allowed to use the generic rank of lieutenant as a courtesy, even though he had only been a second lieutenant in the service. His happiness at finally being free to return home when he chose was kicked in the teeth, however, three days later when the Royal Aero Club announced additional regulations for the journey to Australia. Each crew would have to include a proven navigator, and it was hinted that each plane would have to have a range of 3000 kilometres because of the scarcity of airfields in India. Bert knew that if he could make a start he'd leave the rest behind, rules or no rules, but Tommy Sopwith, realising that Bert was not going to meet the race criteria no matter how much he protested, decided to take back the Dove. Although business had boomed during the Great War, the British Government had cancelled all orders with the company in 1919, and Sopwith faced financial ruin. He needed Bert's plane to make a sale.

On 23 September Bert wrote home saying he was busy running around London all the time, still hoping for a solution to what he called 'the wangle' over his entry. 'There are a few intending competitors of the Australian Flying Corps,' he wrote, 'but there are one or two others like myself demobilised from the RAF and from what I can see, are not counted as Australians in these matters. I've been wearing my boots out all this time and no prospects or resoling them yet either.' Years later Bert wrote: 'I get wild whenever I think of that time. I was all dressed up and no place to go.'[11]

At the same time as Bert was looking for another plane, Kingsford Smith and Maddocks were dumped from the Blackburn Kangaroo team because of a perceived lack of experience. Bert hunted around for a sponsor to help him buy the Dove, but backers did not match his enthusiasm. He couldn't even get a camera firm to lend him one to record all the bizarre and mysterious people and places he expected to see along his trek home. So he designed a camera of his own 'far better than I could buy', with a lens aperture of f3.5, small enough to carry in his coat pocket but with a film container good for a hundred frames and so sophisticated that parts of the film could be developed without spoiling the unexposed part. The frugal young airman told his family he was especially proud of the fact each photograph blown up to postcard size cost less than a penny to produce. Photography was his fallback career, he said, if the aviation door kept being slammed in his face. He was considering an offer from a Canadian pal he met in the RAF to form a photographic business in Halifax, Nova Scotia, but he felt more inclined to wait around in England, somehow raise some capital and buy his own machine in the hope, he wrote, that 'all the wangling over the Aus. Gov. prize' would be sorted out and there would be no more obstructions to his flight home. There was no way he was coming back by ship because he couldn't face that humiliation after everyone in Australia had read about him being the first entrant in the great race. There was also that promise to his father that when he returned to Australia it would be as a first-class aviator.

In the end there were six official entrants. After Bert's Dove was sold from underneath him, Sopwith entered another crew with a bigger, more powerful machine, the Sopwith Wallaby, a modified version of Hawker's Atlantic. It was the first aircraft to take off for Port Darwin, leaving Hounslow on 21 October with Sopwith employee and Gallipoli veteran Captain George 'Skipper' Matthews at the controls and Sergeant Tom Kay navigating. Both were in military uniform and carried a generous supply of Bovril and Wrigley's chewing gum. Five weeks later, on 29 November, following long delays in Germany after damage on landing, they arrived in Vienna. They were arrested as suspected Bolsheviks 160 kilometres north of Belgrade and thrown into prison, finally breaking out and making their escape in the Wallaby on 11 December. They pressed on towards Australia, encountering fuel shortages, a forced landing, an engine leak that was fixed with some of the chewing gum, a sandstorm in Persia, a forced landing on a desert beach and dengue fever in Bangkok before the Wallaby's run ended with a crash into a Bali banana plantation.

Given the success of Alcock and Brown, it was only natural that Vickers would have a crack at flying a Vimy to Darwin and, although the one they entered was built too late for war service, it was just the machine for a long, arduous campaign over hostile territory. The aircraft was registered as G-EAOU, which the crew said stood for 'God 'Elp All Of Us'. The pilot was the fearless 26-year-old South Australian Captain Ross Smith, the navigator his brother Lieutenant Keith Smith, two years older, and the mechanics Sergeants Jim Bennett and Wally Shiers.

Although Keith had spent most of his war days as a gunnery instructor in England, Ross had seen enough active service for both of them, landing at Gallipoli on 13 May 1915, joining the Australian Flying Corps in 1917, shooting down eleven planes over Palestine and being awarded the Military Cross twice and the Distinguished Flying Cross three times. He also flew T.S. Lawrence of Arabia around and once famously interrupted his breakfast with the desert commander to jump in his Bristol, take off and shoot down a Turkish aircraft before returning smartly to finish his still-warm porridge. He had barely started on his toast and marmalade when three Turkish Pfalz Scouts appeared overhead looking for trouble, which Smith and another pilot gladly gave them, forcing all three to the ground.

At the end of the war Ross Smith, Bennett and Shiers flew a Handley Page 0/400 from Cairo to Calcutta. By the time they arrived at Hounslow on 12 November ready for departure to Australia, they were familiar with a large section of the route.

After leaving London they immediately ran into snow that blasted them in their open cockpits, and they were driven up to almost 2800 metres by a blizzard. Ice covered their goggles, forcing the aviators to remove them, and the four men endured intense pain as they sat frozen in their seats with their bare eyes smashed by winds of 140 kilometres per hour. At one stage Keith completely lost his bearings, and Ross, his muscles numbed by the aching cold, almost lost control of the aircraft. Somehow they survived to land in Lyons.

The next day Captain Roger Douglas and Lieutenant Leslie Ross took off from Hounslow in their Alliance P2 Seabird named *Endeavour*. Their machine had a huge 450-horsepower Napier Lion piston engine and an enclosed cabin. It climbed into low cloud but was aloft for only a few minutes before entering a spin. It crashed into an orchard at Surbiton just ten kilometres away. Both aviators were killed and the Alliance company ruined.

Bert was dejected about missing out on a start in the big event but consoled himself that he was much better off than the Alliance crew and no worse off than Kingsford Smith and Maddocks, who were jettisoned before the Blackburn Kangaroo took off on 21 November piloted by Lieutenants Valdemar Rendle and David Williams. The mechanic was Lieutenant Garnsey Potts and the navigator Captain Hubert Wilkins, already world famous for taking the first war film in the Balkans in 1912 and for exploring the North Pole. At Suda Bay in Crete, Bulgarian POWs were pressed into service to get their machine out of a boggy landing field, but they might as well have left it there. On 8 December, the Kangaroo took off from Suda Bay bound for Egypt, but a broken crankcase forced her to turn back and she skidded to a stop, wrecked beyond repair, against a mound of earth next to a lunatic asylum.

On 4 December, Captain Cedric 'Spike' Howell, a former Camel pilot with nineteen aerial victories to his credit, and his navigator Sergeant George Fraser, took off in their Martinsyde A Mark 1, the fastest machine in the race, capable of 240 kilometres per hour. They encountered mechanical problems and damage to the machine throughout their trip and, six days after leaving England, both men were killed in a crash near St Georges Bay, Corfu.[12]

Ross Smith's Vimy crew, meanwhile, overcame one obstacle after another. From Lyons they flew to Pisa, where heavy rain made their landing field a bog, and thirty locals were needed to dig their machine out of the slush. Flying down the coast of Greece, they narrowly escaped death when the peak of an island suddenly appeared out of a cloudbank. At Ramadi in Persia the weight of fifty soldiers from the 10th Indian Lancers was needed to stop the Vimy flying away unmanned during a desert storm. Then, while flying through a huge cloudbank surrounding treacherous mountains between Rangoon (now Yangon) and Bangkok, Ross put the Vimy into a dangerous sideslip when he accidentally bumped the rudder bar. Between Bangkok and the Siamese city of Singora the four exhausted aviators were battered by rain with the force of hailstones. Ross had to hand the controls to his brother, and when they finally made it to Singora, after three hours of tag-team flying, they found that half the aerodrome was covered with water and the other half with tree stumps. Somehow Ross landed the Vimy with the only damage sustained being a broken tail skid.

At Singapore the local racetrack was too small for them to make a landing so Jim Bennett climbed out of his cockpit and shimmied down the tail section of the machine, hanging on with all the strength he could summon. His weight forced the tail down sharply and, as Ross brought the Vimy in hard it came to a dead stop within a hundred metres, Bennett riding it like a runaway bronco. At Surabaya the machine was bogged on a field reclaimed from the sea, and it took twenty-four hours of constant work to make a matting tarmac 275 metres long and 12 metres wide to provide traction for take-off.

Despite all the privations and perils, the four men and their big lumbering machine pressed on. By 9 December, they reached Timor and next day crossed the Arafura Sea. Then at 3.50 p.m. on 10 December the Vimy touched down at Fannie Bay near Darwin, having covered 18,250 kilometres in twenty-seven days and twenty hours.[13] The Smith brothers were knighted and Bennett and Shiers were awarded the Air Force Medal and later granted commissions. The four split the £10,000 equally.

Among the first to congratulate them were two other Australian wartime pilots Hudson Fysh and Paul McGinness, who had wanted to enter the event but were unable to buy a suitable machine. Instead they spent fifty-one days in a Model T Ford surveying a route from Longreach to Darwin in case competitors wanted to fly further south after arriving in Australia. A year later Fysh, McGinness and Fergus McMaster, a Queensland grazier and World War I gunner and dispatch rider, registered a company called Queensland and Northern Territory Aerial Services Limited — better known as Qantas.

On 15 December, just a few days after the Vimy arrived in Darwin, Sir John Alcock received a standing ovation as his almost identical Vimy was presented to the Science Museum in London as one of the wonders of the scientific age, an aircraft that had crossed the Atlantic and brought two continents closer through human ingenuity and courage. Three days after that, as Alcock was taking a new Vickers single-engine seaplane, the Type 54 Viking, to the first post-war air show in Paris, he crashed and died trying to land in fog at Cote d'Everard, near Rouen. He had just turned twenty-seven.

Of the six planes that left Hounslow for Darwin, only one other machine made it all the way. Ross Smith's team had already won the £10,000 when Lieutenants Ray Parer and John McIntosh left London on 8 January 1920 in a war-surplus Airco DH.9 sponsored by Glasgow whisky magnate Peter Dawson. They carried with them a bottle of Dawson's finest for Prime Minister Billy Hughes.

The tiny Parer had a heart problem and was not supposed to fly above 3000 metres while McIntosh had only been on a plane once before. They left a trail of broken propellers, bent wings, choked carburettors and burned-out engines as Ray Parer became known as 'Re-Pairer'. They were almost swallowed by the volcanic crater of Mount Vesuvius and had to fight off locals in a Syrian desert, scare off natives they assumed to be cannibals on an island in the Irrawaddy River and fend off marriage proposals in Rangoon. They finally made it to Darwin on 2 August 1920, 206 days after leaving London. They then headed south towards Melbourne, dropped some souvenir charts over Bundaberg and other towns along the way and finally crashed at Culcairn in the Riverina district of New South Wales. The DH.9 arrived in Melbourne by rail, and when Billy Hughes eventually tasted his PD Scotch it had been aged by the best part of a year.

Bert knew that flying from England to Australia was a difficult and deadly exercise. It was much more dangerous attempting the flight alone without a mechanic, navigator or wireless. However, by the time the Smith brothers arrived in Australia Bert had found an even better plane than the Sopwith Dove to annihilate that distance between the Thames and the Burnett.

Chapter 13

*It was apparent even during our first talk that
Hinkler was an outstanding personality; he had
done a lot of flying during the war, but in addition
he had a very fertile and inventive brain. When
he was flying, Bert Hinkler concentrated on the
job in a way I have not seen in any other pilot.*

Roy Chadwick, Avro designer, on meeting Bert in 1919

*Oh my but she's a real flying machine. At
present there is no other aeroplane in the world
of similar performance against power.*

**Bert Hinkler writing about the Avro Baby after
setting his first world distance record in 1920**

The lure of Nova Scotia and the photographic business
after what Bert called the 'washout' over the Dove was
almost irresistible. He was angry at Tommy Sopwith for
selling his machine but, since Tommy had given him his
start in British aviation, there was no way Bert could hold
a grudge. And there was no way that he could really ever
turn his back on aviation, not when he felt so close to

creating history with a solo flight to Australia. Even before he'd been persuaded to switch machines from the Camel to the Dove, Bert became aware of another machine being produced 120 kilometres away where Alliott Verdon-Roe's company, A.V. Roe had set up an experimental works on 120 hectares at Hamble, near Southampton. As Sopwith stared at financial ruin after the war, Verdon-Roe had to let half his staff go but was still making Avro 504 trainers and looking for ways to entice the world's hobby flyers into buying small, low-powered aeroplanes. Verdon-Roe and his chief designer Roy Chadwick came up with an aircraft smaller than the Dove and with a tiny second-hand nine-year-old engine producing just 35 horsepower. Designed with slide rule and pencil, made from wood, wire, canvas and horse-hoof glue, and having less power than most modern-day motorcycles, it was called the Avro Popular but was soon known as the Avro Baby.

The first Baby was born early in 1919 but crashed at Hamble on 30 April, two minutes after take-off. It was rebuilt around the retrieved 1910 four-cylinder Green engine, and the new plane was given the registration K131. The new Baby first flew on 10 May. *Flight* magazine reported that in spite of its relatively small power, the Baby was likely to become popular with pilots who wished to keep a small runabout for their own personal use.

The Baby needed just 45 metres to land or take off. The machine was expected to sell for around £500 — less than many cars of the time — and *Flight* recorded its vital statistics as: Span, 25ft; length overall, 18ft 6in; height, 7ft 6in; weight loaded, 857lb.[1]

Before long the Baby showed its potential under the guidance of Avro's test pilot, Captain Alan Hamersley, a

West Australian fighter ace and Military Cross recipient who had survived a gunshot wound at Gallipoli and the last aerial dogfight of German ace Werner Voss, who was shot down and killed by two of Hamersley's comrades. On 21 June, at Hendon, Hamersley, flying the Baby KI31, won the handicap section of the 1919 Victory Aerial Derby. The following month Hamersley's Baby won the Victory Trophy race at Hendon and in August flew non-stop from Hounslow Heath to Brussels in two hours and fifty minutes before then flying on to the Netherlands.[2]

Bert had watched the Baby perform at Hendon and, as he stood among the joyful summer's day crowd willing away the threatening storm clouds, he was intrigued by the performance of Hamersley's machine. It was the ideal, small, economical machine that could fly all day without too much trouble and one that a good mechanic like him could service on the go. Bert asked magazine editor C.G. Grey to put in a good word for him with the Avro people, and he caught the train down to Hamble to see Roy Chadwick. He put the miniature camera he'd designed into the coat of his suit pocket to show he could do more than fly planes, although flying was the job he wanted.

Despite building some of the most feared war planes ever, the dapper mild-mannered Chadwick told his friends and family that he wanted aviation to bring the world together in peace. And in Bert, the small, keen-eyed Australian with a firm handshake and a modest way, Chadwick immediately felt he'd met a kindred spirit with a shared love of flying. Chadwick recalled years later that he was so impressed by their talk in the Avro offices, and by Bert's 'obviously detailed knowledge of aircraft construction and engine installations' that he persuaded the Avro board to engage him.

Initially the job was as a mechanic with a clause in Bert's work agreement that he could fly the Avro planes whenever time allowed, and Bert made sure that there was plenty of time. Bert and Nance packed up their belongings and moved to Netley on Southampton's outskirts, then in October 1919 took up residence near the area known as the Polygon at No. 4 Havelock Road, West Marlands. Their house was in a row of eight three-storey terraces built sixty years earlier and which shook when strong winds came off the English Channel.

A.V. Roe's experimental works consisted of a large square building with an exquisite parquetry factory floor. There was an office, machine shop, fitting shop, electrical shop, benches for the maintenance of engines, an area for wood craftsman Jack Bradbury to make propellers and a workshop for erecting the aircraft. Behind the building, between it and the tidal estuary called Southampton Water, was a grass airfield from which the finished machines would take to the air and on which cows would graze at other times.

One of Bert's workmates, Ron Cooper, remembered him arriving for his first day on Nance's cycle, a good size for a jockey, with a bag slung over his shoulder containing his dinner.[3] There was a touch of Charlie Chaplin about the humble Aussie in the crumpled clothes and the ever-present oil stains. He was calm and unflappable, always trustworthy, never raised his voice, used 'bally' as his strongest language, was always unassuming and would eat anything that the canteen lady, Mabel Whitcombe, put before him, without complaint. He talked little but smiled a lot. And he worked and worked and worked. From early morning to late at night, taking his lunch of a sandwich while still peering into motors of varying shapes and sizes.

'Very modest man, very modest,' was how Claude Bevis, a fitter at the Avro works from 1915 to 1926, remembered Bert. 'He was a very warm sincere character. Great sense of humour too, and he had pretty good physical endurance.'[4] Bert loved his new job and quickly settled into a regular routine. He left Nance's bike at home, and each morning he and his workmate Jim Laver, a fitter, would walk down Kingsbridge Lane to the West Railway Station for the journey through Northam, St Denys, Bitterne, Woolston, Sholing and Netley, where they would alight and walk a kilometre to Hamble.[5] He and Nance, known to everyone as Mr and Mrs Hinkler, were regulars at Southampton's ancient Holyrood Anglican Church singing up a storm in the front row after a short walk from Havelock Road every Sunday morning. They were also regulars flying the Baby, too, as Bert infused Nance with his passion for flying.

Bert knew he had to wait his turn at Avro. Alan Hamersley was the chief test pilot, and he was assisted by Captain Terence Tully, so Bert busied himself learning everything he could about the Baby and all the other machines Avro was building. He was hardly ever out of his oil-stained overalls, spending his days either at the experimental works or in the design office, tinkering with engines, studying blueprints and helping in the assembly of aircraft. He was convinced of the merits of the Baby and made up his mind to make it his Baby, testing it and exploring its true potential.

'Soon after he joined us he told me of his ambition to fly to his home in Bundaberg, Australia,' Chadwick recalled.

'At that period long-distance flights were heavily financed [but] Hinkler's ambition was to do the job on his own without finance or obligation to anyone.'

Bert set out a course on Southampton Water, making sure he had a long stretch of beach to land on whenever he pushed the Baby's engine so hard that it gave out. Many times he and a team of mechanics would have to carry the plane back to its hangar and begin the investigation into what went wrong, but Bert believed the machine could give him an even greater victory than the one celebrated by Ross Smith's team, even if they had taken the £10,000 England-to-Australia prize. The Baby would give Bert the chance to make the great flight all by himself.

> With the England to Australia flight in my mind now almost an obsession, I flew the Baby and studied how to improve the design for long flights at a cheap rate [Bert recalled]. The necessity of trying out some of my ideas in other craft led to further delay in the actual contemplated flight, but the Avro people grew intensely interested in the possibility of my being the first private owner of an Avro Baby, which was to startle the world with its precocity. With the success of the first experimental machine they went into production. My machine was to be one of the first of the new litter. Delays occurred and I grew impatient.[6]

Inadvertently Chadwick helped Bert procure the machine. Chadwick had learned to fly from Fred Raynham and delighted in taking the Baby cross-country. He took it, now dressed in camouflage livery, for a test run on 13

January 1920. Chadwick had been suffering the flu, it was a freezing winter's day and he'd forgotten his flying jacket. He had hardly lifted off when he blacked out, and the Baby crashed into the garden of Verdon-Roe's brother Everard, the Vicar of Hamble. Chadwick was badly injured, and only new bone-grafting techniques saved his limbs.[7] The Baby was nearly as badly hurt as the pilot, but the engine was salvaged and the machine rebuilt from the wreckage and painted silvery-white.

Bert and Nance had saved enough to buy 4 Havelock Road for £875 on 5 February 1920, and a few weeks later, in April, Bert offered a bargain-basement price for the Baby, which now bore the registration G-EACQ. Bert realised that the machine had already seen a good bit of service, describing it later as 'a pretty battered baby ... dissipated beyond its years'. But it was now his Baby, and he loved it like it was his own child.

Bert shared the same love of mechanical things as young Charles Lindbergh, who although he had never been on an aeroplane couldn't stop thinking about his day watching the Aeronautical Trials at Fort Myer in 1912. As a boy of fourteen, long before he was eligible for a driver's licence, he had driven his mother halfway across the USA in his family's Saxon Six automobile as a pointer of things to come. While Bert was taking possession of his Baby, Lindbergh enrolled in the University of Wisconsin ready to learn everything he could about machines and their magic.

At Hamble, Bert and the other mechanics fitted the Baby with a larger petrol tank to increase the fuel capacity from 45 litres to 113 litres and installed various gadgets Bert had designed to aid in a long flight, including a movable needle jet for carburettor adjustment, the Hinkler

Altitude Recorder and the Hinkler Compass.[8] Bert kept his plans away from prying eyes, but all his friends at Avro knew he was getting ready for a long flight. A very long flight. He spent countless hours along Southampton Water and then beyond, testing the engine and the machine's fuel capacity and rectifying the last of the Baby's teething problems. Bert deliberately stopped writing home to his parents because he wanted to arrive on their doorstep unannounced, somehow believing in his naiveté that he could make a world-record flight solo and not have anyone mention it to the press. There was also an Air Ministry decree forbidding flights between Palestine and India until further notice because of an uprising against the French in Syria. Still, Bert figured he'd fly to Egypt first and sort out the difficulties regarding air traffic once he got there.

He painted a flying kangaroo on the rudder and flew the Baby to the new Croydon Aerodrome in South London, which had replaced Hounslow as the city's main airport. Then another mishap. A mechanic starting the engine by swinging the propeller split a large piece off the trailing edge. It was hastily repaired using tape and Seccotine glue, yet Bert found one positive from the damage 'for straight away I saw the necessity of having a machine that wanted no mechanic but which depended entirely on myself'. As soon as the propeller was fixed, the magneto, a 1913 Bosch that felt its age, began to play up, in Bert's words, 'like the very devil, necessitating a complete overhaul'. Would he ever get away? 'I began to think I would get a start in the year 1960,' Bert revealed later, 'with my beard trailing in the wind as I took off.'[9]

Finally on what he described as one raw Monday morning at 4.50 a.m. on 31 May 1920, he decided he'd take the Baby to Australia. No fanfare, no hoopla, no lavish farewells, just as though he were taking a car on a Sunday drive. He'd been suffering a raging toothache for a week, but the conditions were ideal for flying so he thought he might as well get a move on and have the tooth looked at by a dentist in Bundaberg. Under the cover of darkness with a last goodbye to Nance, without a word to the press — for he was still shy revealing his ambitions in public — and with just a few mechanics rugged up against the cold watching and wondering where he was headed, Bert 'hopped off from Croydon', as he described it. He could almost taste the big fat juicy Bundaberg watermelons as the Baby lifted off.

Bert was flying a second-hand wood and canvas aeroplane that had been almost broken in two in a previous crash, and his survival hinged on a ten-year-old engine that had been in at least two serious crashes and had a dodgy magneto. But Bert couldn't stop smiling to himself as he set sail for Bundaberg 20,000 kilometres away. Within thirty-five minutes, with the Green engine purring, he crossed the English coast and was over the Channel at 5.25 a.m. Forty minutes further on he was above the French countryside for the first time since the war.

Well, I was not over France five minutes before the clouds beat me right down practically to the ground [Bert recalled], and, of course, it was a case of compass or *fini*, as I had lost any known landmarks. Anyhow, I practically hedge-hopped right slap-bang into Paris, picking up the Seine at Argenteuil about 8 a.m. Some luck, of course. Even the Eiffel Tower I did not pick out until I was well over the city ... the

> atmosphere was so thick that I lost my bearings
> before I had left Paris 30 miles. To be on the safe
> side I turned back, and making better bearings,
> passed Fontainebleau just before 9 a.m. (Look at
> the map and see how I lost time.)[10]

His little bus could putter along at just 750 revs when cruising, making it extremely economical, and he chugged along at a bit more than 112 kilometres per hour. His toothache was driving him crazy, and he stuck his head over the side of the Baby, sucking in freezing gulps of air in the hope that it would numb the pain. He was concentrating so much on dulling the stabs of agony that time literally flew, and before he knew it he was approaching the Alps. With a practised eye on the weather he considered for a while that it might be safer to land at Lyon Aerodrome. Instead, Bert pressed on. 'Now I started for a serious climb, the clouds hung very thick around the Alps. As I gained altitude I could see those nasty black peaks poking through, and my poor engine! How I hated to keep her up to it, on an almost full throttle! Anyhow, even though my altimeter showed around 10,000 feet, still I had to hoik the bus over one or two bits, and they do look horrible.'

Bert glanced down at the oil gauge, and his heart jumped. Flying over the savage mountains, his bus had sprung an oil leak, and he was losing pressure fast. He figured he had enough petrol to get within 240 kilometres of Rome, but he was sweating bricks about losing height over the mountains. 'My oil had almost all leaked away,' he recalled, 'and I was somewhat afraid my motor would seize up and it was very cloudy and only the tops here and there poking through, so I had to keep full height;

anyhow I managed to jump her over.' Bert passed over the 2000-metre peak of Mont Cenis in France and spied the Italian city of Turin on the other side of the Alps 89 kilometres away. 'You can bet I was delighted.'[11]

He cruised in to land, but his joy at finding a soft spot to touch down away from the jagged peaks was spoiled by the fact that it was just 2.20 in the afternoon and he could have gone another 240 kilometres. As it was, without realising it on 31 May 1920 Bert Hinkler had just flown the longest solo flight in history, 1046 kilometres in nine hours and thirty-one minutes, probably 1150 kilometres with the detours he made. The Italian mechanics and customs officials couldn't believe that Bert had flown all the way from London non-stop in an aircraft so small that it looked like a toy. And what's more, as they examined the engine with him to find the source of the oil leak, they were astounded that he'd come so far with such an old motor, and one that was now displaying a serious valve problem. Frustrated at not being able to fly further while there was still daylight, Bert decided to stay overnight at the airfield and work on his engine the next day. At the same time the Italians told him that things were worsening in Syria; the locals had formed a new government and had begun a conscription drive to build an army; an action that the French colonists regarded as a military coup. It was the same story for the British trying to govern in Iraq, where Muslim leaders demanded a jihad against the infidels.

Bert's love affair with aviation was frustrating and maddening. He still had not achieved his goal of returning to Australia under his own power and that made him feel an abject failure. He sent a telegram to Nance saying that he'd arrived in Turin and 'all was going well', but even that was stretching it because there was a postal strike in Italy and she wouldn't get the message for two days. Then Bert wrote to his parents apologising to them for being such a dolt.

My Beloved Parents [he began], as a son, I suppose
by now you [have] disowned me entirely. And
what can I say for myself after all this silence? ...
Apparently I've turned out a rank failure. For my part
I am almost at the end of my tether. My ambition —
I'm full of regrets in making such an admission —
being so great and far beyond my financial capacity —
getting me best at last. My hopes — Aviation of
course, is by no means a poor man's hobby and while
as you know I'll never give in to your objections to
flying, still before long, if something really serious
doesn't happen, I'm afraid I shall have to try and
forget about such a glorious pursuit.[12]

Bert explained that if he got stuck halfway across the world his funds wouldn't last long.

The bally Arabs are getting wild again round
Damascus so the War Office warns against flying
over that way. A big flight to India and return was
postponed for this very reason... I have been having
a top overhaul today to make sure all is well even
though the motor was running perfectly right after
the last yesterday. Of course I don't know how far
I'll reach because, oh horrors, I am nearly spun
out already. I may return to England and see if the
makers are sufficiently pleased. It would be better to
go broke there then somewhere further on.[13]

He asked his parents to forgive him for his lack of recent correspondence: 'My main reason for silence was to work hard and quietly and fly home and surprise you. Sounds incredible. But you would not have heard until I was nearing Australia because I fixed the papers to agree with me for secrecy of my intentions. With my fondest love and my wholehearted regret if I may have caused you any anxiety while I was trying to get going. As B4 Your son Bert.'[14]

Although he may have been disappointed over the delays surrounding his return to Australia, many others saw Bert's flight to Turin as a glorious triumph. *Flight* said that Bert, quietly without making any fuss, and having spent less than £10 on petrol in a machine that cost the same as a small car, had demonstrated beyond doubt the economy and viability of aircraft for private use.[15] C.G. Grey called it 'the most meritorious performance in the history of aviation'. He declared that Australia should be proud of 'this wonderful pilot'.[16] Grey even wrote to Frances in Bundaberg after hearing of Bert's arrival in Turin to say that she had nothing to worry about with Bert tackling such a great distance to Australia because her boy was 'quite a wonderful mechanic, and a wonderful pilot, and a wonderful navigator, so that if anybody ever had a first-class chance of doing the journey by air, it is your Bert'.[17]

While the Baby was being repaired bad weather struck Turin, making Bert's plan to fly to Rome over the Apennines extremely risky. So he spent three nights in Turin before taking off for to Rome at 9.40 a.m. on 3 June. He arrived there six hours and forty minutes later after spending most of the flight battling a head wind.[18] Rome still loved aircraft as much as it had when the Wrights were there a decade earlier. Only a month after Bert arrived in the Italian capital, Mussolini, now the country's most assertive political figure, would begin the first stage of making aviation a virtual cult in the nation he dreamed of remoulding under his firm hand. Having recovered from his Isonzo battle wounds, Mussolini embraced a movement he called 'Fascism' and declared war on his former socialist colleagues. He saw no more apt symbol of Italy shaking off its postwar poverty and scars than his own virile self in goggles and a flying suit. Mussolini wanted to promote his own fearlessness, dynamism and intelligence, and the nation's aspiring leader saw himself as a brave aviator just like the Australian who had flown from London to Turin non-stop, defeating the Alps along the way. Mussolini first took flying lessons from the pilot Cesare Redaelli in the middle of 1920, and Redaelli described Mussolini as an exceptional, astonishing student with a remarkable attention span (although he was unlikely to offer much criticism).[19]

In Rome, Bert finally decided that it was not much use pressing on to the Middle East where he could be laid up for months. So, after spending four nights in Rome, he left on 7 June at 5.45 a.m., flew a circuitous route to avoid fog over the Gulf of Genoa and, getting the best possible view of the French Riviera, arrived in Nice seven hours and twenty-five minutes later. The next day he took off from Nice at 8.20 a.m., spent a night in Lyon and then flew to Paris. The sightseeing all the way was marvellous. Bert jaunted about in his open-top Baby as if it was a convertible motorcar traversing country lanes. He stayed in Paris for just five hours, made sure the machine was full of petrol, had a pleasant evening snack, then headed back across the English Channel to arrive at Croydon just in time for supper at 8.50 p.m. He spent the night in London and returned to Hamble the next day having covered 3620 kilometres, using 341 litres of petrol and spending 34 hours and 30 minutes in the air. Workers at Hamble remember him returning from his great adventure as though he was just back from an outing along Southampton Water.[20]

The following month Bert's world-record-breaking aircraft was the star attraction at the air show in London's Olympia exhibition. Bert then entered her in the Aerial Derby set down for Hendon on 24 July, going head to head with Alan Hamersley flying a brand-new Baby registered G-EAUG. Bert was installed as second favourite behind Harry Hawker, who was flying a Sopwith with a Dragonfly engine nearly ten times as powerful as Bert's. In the end Frank Courtney set the fastest time, flying at 246.95 kilometres per hour in a 300-horsepower Martinsyde Semi Quaver. Hamersley repeated his 1919 Handicap win but, as he was being congratulated, he turned to lead the applause for Bert, who came in a close second with his ten-year-old engine performing splendidly. Although neither machine topped 80 miles per hour (129 kilometres per hour), the tiny Babies had won the hearts of the big crowd at Hendon, and Bert and Hamersley were paraded in an open-top car as if they were royalty.[21]

When Hamersley's Baby was smashed beyond repair at Ipswich just eleven days later, the reputation of Bert and his hardy little aircraft only increased. He had joined Avro a few months earlier as a mechanic with permission to fly occasionally yet Bert soon earned the highest honour in British aviation. He succeeded 1919's recipient John

Alcock, conqueror of the Atlantic Ocean, as the winner of the 1920 Britannia Trophy from the Royal Aero Club for his Turin flight.

Setting records over great distances was the yardstick by which aviation progress was being measured as pilots risked their lives to shrink the world. KLM Royal Dutch Airlines, in partnership with the British company Aircraft Transport and Travel,[22] had just begun flying passengers and freight between Croydon and Amsterdam in a war-surplus Airco DH.16.

It was near Amsterdam that Anthony Fokker, owing more than 14 million marks in income tax to the devastated German Government, had returned to set up the Dutch Aircraft Factory after the war. Despite the strict disarmament conditions set down by the Treaty of Versailles, Fokker managed to take six trainloads of his old planes and quickly found markets across Europe. Soon Fokker was the most important aircraft manufacturer in the world. By 1921 six airlines were operating services between London and Paris, and at Winton in Queensland the new company Qantas was about to conquer the vastness of the Queensland Outback.

The development of civil aviation could not help the Sopwith Company survive, and it was wound up in 1920 as the government made moves to claim £500,000 in Excess War Profits Duty. Handley Page was also devastated with losses of more than £600,000, and Airco and Martinsyde went out of business.[23] Harry Hawker, Tommy Sopwith, Fred Sigrist and Bill Eyre formed a new company called H.G. Hawker Engineering, making two-stroke motorcycle engines and designing fast cars.

With Alan Hamersley recalled to the RAF as No. 60 squadron flew off to fight rebel tribesmen in the

Northwest Frontier Province of India and Terence Tully off to Canada,[24] Bert was installed as Avro's chief test pilot. While the Avro company had effectively been taken over by the Manchester automobile manufacturer Crossley Motors, the aircraft were being built independently. Bert tested all the new Avro machines. Often on flights across the lush Hampshire countryside his passenger was Roy Chadwick, who marvelled at Bert's talents and his powers of concentration. Chadwick remembered that Bert focused on his task like no pilot he had ever met, glancing incessantly at his compass, maps, controls and the space around his machine. 'One always felt the greatest confidence due to his masterly handling of the aeroplane,' Chadwick recalled.[25]

Bert had arrived as a first-class, fair-dinkum, world-beating, headline-grabbing heart-stopping pilot in what had been a watershed year. But he still hadn't arrived in his own aircraft at Woodbine Cottage as he'd planned, and he still felt unfulfilled because of it. No matter if the Air Ministry ordered him not to fly across the Middle East, he was going to Bundaberg. On 23 September he took out a mortgage on 4 Havelock Road for £500 and the following day sold the property to Nance for £400. That same day Nance took out a second mortgage for £196. Bert now had the funds to carry out his plan. He fixed his steely gaze on flying right up to the front door that he'd left seven years before and planned to break another world record while doing it.

Chapter 14

My brother George was there and with him
running by the wing I taxied along the street right
up to the very front door of our old home.

Bert Hinkler describing to his wife Nance
how he ended a world-record flight in his
Avro Baby at his parents' house in 1921

Bert Hinkler was really the first of the Australian
record-breakers using light machines ... not
only was Hinkler one of our best test pilots,
but he was also a very practical inventor.[1]

Avro founder Sir Alliott Verdon-Roe

As Bert readied for a return to Australia, the situation in Syria was still tense. The death of the Syrian defence minister in a battle with the French only sparked more rebellion and uprising.[2] Further across the desert, the RAF was flying in to quell the Great Iraqi Revolution. Eventually the British tried to bomb the Iraqis into submission, and Lionel Charlton, the reconnaissance hero of the Great War who was now Chief Staff Officer of the RAF's Iraq

Command, was so sickened by the sight of mutilated women and children in local hospitals that he resigned. For Bert there was no way around the bloody hurdles to his flight home other than to dismantle his Baby, pack her into two large wooden cases and put her into the cargo hold of Blue Funnel Line's SS *Ascanius* in Glasgow for the sea voyage to Australia.

There were battles on Bert's home front, too. His relationship with Nance was at breaking point. Bert had been living with her for the best part of three years and seemed to be still smitten but, perhaps because they weren't legally married and Herbert Crossland, the father of Nance's daughter Maida, was causing problems for them with a legal impediment to a formal marriage, Bert kept their union under wraps as much as possible. He asked Nance to do the same.

Nance did not want him to go to Australia — or 'bally Orstralyer', as Bert said she pronounced it — but Bert told her he was going anyway. He had booked his passage on the ship and paid for the Baby to go as cargo. Nance knew the reputation of aviators. They risked their lives all the time, and their relief at not being killed made them party like playboys. Bert was more sober and serious than any flyer she knew, but still the temptations for aviators were everywhere. Nance was on her sick bed at Havelock Road when the morning of Friday, 28 January 1921, rolled around, and Bert said there was a ship waiting for him up in Glasgow. Nance coughed and wheezed as Bert said his goodbyes and asked her not to fret. 'Have a nice time in Australia,' Nance said between coughs. 'Will you ever come back?'

The question rocked Bert to his bootlaces as he headed off to Hamble, flew the Baby to Brooklands and then packed it on a train to Glasgow. He felt like a heel leaving Nance, and he would spend the next four months trying to make amends in daily declarations of love penned from all points between Glasgow and Bundaberg. Such was Bert's discomfort over his marital arrangement and the threat of public embarrassment posed by Maida's father that he tried to avoid the public eye as much as possible and did not seek any pre-publicity over the return to Australia of a record-breaking pilot.

Bert boarded the *Ascanius* in Glasgow on the morning of Saturday 29 January to find that he would share a small, cramped cabin with two other passengers. The ship was still in dock when Bert monopolised his cabin's tiny writing table, adorning it with a large portrait of him and Nance together and another of her looking coy that made his heart race. For the next seven weeks, as the ship travelled to Sydney, Bert spent much of the time writing love letters. In gushing prose typical of the era, he showed that as well as being a practical man and a fearless pilot, he was also a hopeless romantic.

He decorated his letters with cartoons of them together, of Nance, smartly dressed as always, waving to him in his little Avro. He sent her 'all my true love and a heap of kisses' and called her 'the most darlingest wife a man could ever be blessed with'. By the time Bert reached Las Palmas in the Canary Islands a week into the voyage he promised that it would be the 'very, very last time' they would be apart. He asked Nance to rest and regain her vitality so she would be able to give him 'loving looks' when he returned. He told her he wanted to make a great living from aviation so that she could fill her wardrobe with whatever she desired, and he longed for the day when Nance and her 'Ole Man' could live a good life in Australia in a comfortable homestead near Sydney with a two-seat aeroplane in the garage. He promised to teach her to swim because England was too cold for such pleasures. He said he'd persuade some possums to give up their skins so that he could make her a nice coat.

He told her about tramping the ancient streets of Messina when the ship called in there and how he couldn't stop thinking about his wife, how he tossed and turned every night on the ship and not because of the waves. He told her of all the church services he was attending on board and how singing the hymns reminded him of their Sundays at Holyrood Church. All the time, he said, he was thinking of her, missing her so terribly on the 'long, lonely, weary stretches day after day on the water'. He begged her to write to him care of the Sydney GPO to write 'often, good and strong'. 'Write and tell me that you still love me, that you are still mine and mine alone.' He promised that the next year the two of them could return to Australia by air together and, because of them both making history as the first man and woman to cover the distance, 'we should score in all directions, physically, mentally and financially'.

After five weeks at sea he wrote on 2 March: 'And still we progress over this monstrous stretch. We expect to reach Adelaide on 11th March so we've still another nine days of this rotten existence to wade thru.' What sustained him, he said, were Nance's 'great big brown eyes full of lust for me and those lovely lips, oh hasten the time when I shall cover them with kisses again'. But he told her he felt terrible about the 'bally rotten' circumstances of their parting. Nance questioning his love for her and asking him if he planned to come back from 'bally Orstralyer', he said, cut him 'like a knife to bleed the heart'.

> Nance, I've lain awake at night thinking over that and the mountains of sorrow it implied [he wrote]. If you ever for a moment had that suspicion seriously my beloved Nance, my wife, why in the world didn't you charge me with it before? Say a week or so. At least it would have given me a chance to try and do justice to myself having to leave you lying in your bed in illness, with such a fear paramount in your breast. Nance, you have deeply grieved me. It has absolutely cast a gloom over me on this tiring journey. Here I am loving my Sweetheart with all my life, every fibre in my body vibrating to hers and thinking that she loved me just so warmly in return to have such a query thrown in my face, so to speak. Sweetheart, at the eleventh hour you have lost confidence in your lover and under the circumstances a lack of confidence shows that the trust you placed in me is in danger of falling from the pinnacle of true and deep love.[3]

He said the anxiety he felt over their relationship was killing him. He asked Nance how she was keeping busy and suggested different friends she could visit while he was away to keep up to speed with all the local gossip but also warned her to avoid the parties in Hamble of a Tuesday night. 'It seems — so I suppose with all one horse villages — to be a bed of scandal.'

Then he gave a glimpse into the secretive side of their union and the problems bound up with Maida's father, who was said to be planning on remarrying in South Africa, which would allow Bert and Nance to legally wed.

> It would be fine to know how things stood in SA for you [Bert wrote]. So my love give me all parties you can so that I can make enquiries. You see for all we know, changes may have happened that nothing can affect this. You see if we go flipping around together our dials are sure to wander into the papers. And while in our present ignorance that would be fatal to take such chances. Yet were we able to find out as I have said lots may have happened and if all's clear of course I want you to come out in the limelight, as I am so proud of my wonderful wifie.[4]

Bert feared he was becoming too well known to keep his personal life under wraps much longer.

'[Roy] Chadwick showed me some South African papers and they gave me rather flattering notices with the Baby,' he said, adding that even a friend in Chile had read about him. 'So you see my darling,' he wrote, 'if we managed to pull off a little flip to Australia, both of us together, why they'd have you in all the ladies journals and myself pictured from all angles.' But apart from all the 'paper chat' about them and the personal problems publicity might bring to their unconventional union, he told her flying to Australia would be a magnificent experience for both of them and a 'delightful honeymoon'.[5] 'And sweetheart my own,' he wrote at another time, 'I am going to make your happiness complete by making as soon as I return very special arrangements for a certain day. The reason it has been postponed so far my love, you and I my darling understand each other there, but now I want to have your happiness complete and to seal our love I promise you it's on the top of our wonderful future program.'[6]

The *Ascanius* sailed on, and Bert arrived in Melbourne on 14 March. He immediately sought out relatives in Caulfield, who told him that his grandmother in Gympie, Mary Bonney, was paralysed and very near the end but that if he was quick he might still see her alive. In Melbourne he also found that his old commanding officer at Dunkirk, Jimmy Goble, was now director of the Australian Flying Corps, which was about to be re-formed as the RAAF. Bert hoped to sell Avro Babies to Goble for a 5 per cent commission.

On the rare occasions Bert was not pouring his heart out to Nance, he also revealed his plans for long-distance flights around Australia. While flights of an hour or so around Bundaberg might be a good commercial proposition, he told her, it was the big record-breaking feats that would create the headlines. He had been studying detailed maps of Australia. Sydney to Bundaberg was 1500 kilometres and a whopping bum-aching forty-two hours by rail. Brisbane to Adelaide was almost 3000 kilometres by rail, and the trip took the best part of three days. Sydney to Adelaide took thirty-eight and a half hours. Adelaide to Hobart, he figured, was about 1100 kilometres by air but three days by rail and boat. Connecting the capitals would gain him and the Baby more credit, he assured Nance, but he stressed that she must keep quiet about all his plans until he had actually accomplished them. He never wanted to be seen as presumptuous.

Bert arrived unannounced in Sydney on Friday, 18 March 1921, seven and a bit years after he and Charlie

Laffan had sailed out of Sydney Heads for Hamburg. Although the great yawning gap across the harbour was still crying out for a bridge, Sydney was as magnificent as ever as the *Ascanius* made its way towards Circular Quay and Customs House. After all the disappointments he'd experienced trying to fly home Bert still felt like he was walking on clouds when his feet finally touched Australian soil and he heard the old, familiar 'G'day, mate'. The welcoming committee of just one, Bert's brother George, had been a boy of fourteen when Bert had gone to Britain and was now a man of twenty-one eager to help Bert with his precious cargo. The brothers helped load the cases containing the Baby onto the back of two horse-drawn lorries and then climbed on top as the horses ferried them to the Australian Aircraft and Engineering Co., the local agents for Avro, eight kilometres away at Mascot.

A year before AA&E had received twenty 504Ks from Avro and had sold one of them to Qantas, the addition of which stretched the new airline's fleet to one solitary aircraft. Another Avro had gone to John McIntosh, who, seven months after finally making it to Australia with Ray Parer, was giving joy flights in the West Australian wheat belt. AA&E wanted to show Bert's world-record Avro at Sydney's Royal Easter Show, the biggest exhibition of technology, produce, pigs and sideshow freaks in Australia, due to start on Monday, 21 March. Bert and George, his 'hand me up a spanner boy', as George referred to himself, got cracking all weekend in their overalls, dressing up the Baby for another public outing. Bert rented a boarding-house room with two beds for himself and George a mile from the aerodrome for fifteen shillings a week. He was happy for the Baby to take all the attention as he watched quietly in the background. He might have gone totally unnoticed by the press and by the half a million people who attended the show over its ten-day cycle had not Bert's old boss William Hart, the flying dentist, pointed him out to a reporter from the Sydney *Daily Telegraph*.

On Good Friday, 25 March, 100,000 people braved the hottest day of the year — 99.2 degrees Fahrenheit — to pass through the Showgrounds, and Bert estimated that at least 99 per cent of them had given the Baby a good once-over. That night he attended a standing-room-only service at St Andrew's Cathedral in Sydney.

On Easter Sunday, Bert and George walked a mile from their digs to inspect Mascot airfield, which Bert declared to be 'quite a good aerodrome with just a few ruts that can be easily avoided'. One of the local pilots took Bert up for a bird's-eye view of Sydney, which Bert said looked to cover as many square miles as London. That afternoon Bert and George caught a crowded ferry to Manly, Bert telling Nance later that Manly was the 'first rate seaside resort in all of Orstralyer'. The sight of all the boats on a glorious day on the harbour was 'nothing short of magnificent'.

Always mindful of his pennies, Bert was staggered by how cheap Australian fruit was compared with the prices he paid in Southampton, writing home to Nance about the majestic persimmons, pineapples, perfect tomatoes, juicy pears 'as big as your fist' at eighteen for thruppence and peaches 'as big as cricket balls' at fourteen for a shilling. Even at such an expensive place as the Show, Bert related, he bought a shilling's worth of fruit from a stall and ended up with five fat bananas and seven juicy pears, and for sixpence he procured a quarter pound of sugar almonds.

While Bert was enjoying the Royal Show, early in the evening on Easter Monday, 28 March, with the sun still out, John McIntosh and his Avro were at Pithara, 240 kilometres northeast of Perth, trying to cope with a couple of local wheat contractors who'd been quenching a powerful thirst all day. McIntosh was intrepid. Born near Aberdeen, Scotland, he'd stowed away to Western Australia at the age of fifteen and became a well-known axeman before serving as a stretcher-bearer at Gallipoli. He married a young widow named Amelia Taylor in 1916 at Holy Trinity Church in Tottenham and, after he and Parer delivered their aged Scotch to Billy Hughes in Melbourne, McIntosh bought a motorcycle and rode it across the country to Perth where he started his own aviation business.

At Pithara, Alfred Joy and Albert Loughlin each paid three pounds fifteen shillings — half a week's pay — to go for a ride in the 504K with the man who'd flown from England to Australia. It was a quarter to six, and the two locals were yahooing and wrestling over a bottle of beer when they climbed into the rear cockpit behind McIntosh. The pilot's offsiders took the bottle from them, but only after the pair had finished drinking its contents. They soon pulled out another bottle and drank half of that before it, too, was snatched away. McIntosh's mechanic delayed starting the Avro because of the state of the two passengers, and McIntosh told Loughlin to throw away the cigarette smouldering between his lips as there was petrol all around. Finally with Joy and Loughlin having been told for the last time, the bloody last time, to behave, the mechanic yelled: 'Contact', and McIntosh started moving his machine down the runway. As McIntosh lifted the

Avro into the air Loughlin jumped up in the rear cockpit and started waving a red handkerchief to the onlookers on the ground.[7]

At 150 metres the Avro went into a spin and crashed into some scrub. McIntosh and Joy died instantly, Loughlin survived. The tragedy cast a pall over Bert's plans to fly home to Bundaberg, but not for long. He wrote to Nance the day after McIntosh was killed to tell her he was thinking of an initial stunt to promote the Baby, flying down to Mount Kosciuszko, Australia's highest peak, landing on the golf links in front of the big hotel there, then flying back to Sydney all in the one day. There was also talk of him flying the Baby out to Longreach to show potential buyers. AA&E offered to buy the Baby for £600 and pay Bert the 5 per cent commission on any more machines that he sold.

The Royal Show concluded on 30 March, and heavy rain for the next week turned Bert's hangar at Mascot into an island, forcing him to wade through water half way up to his knees. In the brief patches of sunshine Bert tested the Baby with some short flights over Botany Bay to satisfy himself as to its performance and fuel consumption in the Australian atmosphere. He'd increased the capacity to 123 litres because he planned to fly further than any solo pilot had ever done. The going rate for petrol was four shillings a gallon but Bert, always after a bargain, chased a cheaper commercial rate.[8] He and George went shopping for perfumes to take home to Nance, and they marched around Sydney, as Bert recalled, like a pair of country bumpkins in the big city for the first time. Bert sent George back to Bundaberg and told him that when he saw the Baby rolling and diving over Gavin Street, he was to run from Woodbine Cottage and use green flags to mark out an area suitable for landing on Foundry Green, a park next to the great factory. George told everyone back home about Bert's plan and excitement about the return of Bundaberg's world-beating aviator brewed.

Bert was planning to fly from Sydney to Bundaberg in one go to break his London–Turin record, but he was so reticent about revealing his plans publicly that even when interviewed by reporters at Mascot as he waited for a break in the weather he didn't mention anything about it, only about the value of the Avro Babies for Australian conditions because they could take off and land anywhere and the wings folded so they could be stored in a household garage. While the roads were pretty crook in Australia, Bert explained, the climate for flying was usually wonderful despite the rain then lashing Sydney, and it dismayed him that Australia had yet to embrace the new technology the way Europe had. 'I came out to Australia to see what opportunities there are for an aviator making a reasonable living here,' he said. 'From what I have seen I do not think the country is as yet fully alive to the enormous advantages of the airplane and neither the Federal nor State Government is doing much to remedy that. I do not see much encouragement to remain in Australia.'[9] Bert said that after a short holiday visiting his parents and siblings he'd probably go back to England where the aviation industry was still undergoing growing pains but where he was assured of a permanent job in an aeroplane.

Finally the weather forecast for Monday, 11 April, promised good flying conditions, and the fact that it would be a working day in Bundaberg meant many of his mates from the foundry would be going hammer and tongs when he arrived to surprise them all. He sent a telegram home saying he'd be leaving on Monday morning first thing.

Late on the Sunday night Bert dressed in a suit and tie because he wanted to look presentable when he arrived to see his family after so long, and he finished reading a letter from Nance that found him care of the Sydney GPO. His landlady, who he called 'a dear old soul', made him a late-night cup of tea and a snack. He left the boarding house just before midnight with his trusty 100-shot camera and two apples and a piece of apple pie to keep him going.

He walked the mile to the Baby's hangar in about twenty minutes. Then he got busy. Bert dragged the Baby out of her cosy bed and gave her a thorough check, which kept him occupied until 3 a.m. He thought about a nap but, since there was no one around to wake him except a nightwatchman who was fast asleep, he stayed busy, walking around the few buildings at the aerodrome and reading a newspaper he found. A heavy dew had covered the Baby in the time Bert had her out in the open but, despite the dampness, he managed to start her. The noise of the tiny Green engine barely stirred the nightwatchman, and just before 6 a.m. Bert straightened his tie and bounced the Baby along the Mascot grass, avoiding the ruts, and was up and away.

He aimed for the Hawkesbury River, then headed slightly inland towards the Great Dividing Range and stuck to it as though massaging the spine of Australia. He passed over Armidale at about 9 a.m., then the town of Ben Lomond perched on the range 1400 metres above sea level, photographing the heavily wooded, uninhabited areas around it. He crossed Glen Innes at about 10 a.m., still snapping away merrily with his camera to give everyone at Bundaberg a rare bird's-eye view of their country. Some cumulus clouds spoiled his sightseeing, but at 10.47 he crossed the state border into Queensland at Wallangarra and the sky finally cleared. He had a lovely view of Toowoomba and the Darling Downs and then, as he recalled, 'nothing but wild forest as far as the eye can reach'. Flying at 1200 metres, he kept slightly inland and passed over Blackbutt and Kilkivan.[10] 'Somewhere on this final 200-odd miles,' he recalled, 'I crossed a solitary railway, which is practically the only man-made landmark to pick up.'

Then at about two o'clock, as the autumn sun illuminated the vista through the spinning blade of his propeller, Bert caught sight of the cane fields and red-and-green quilt of the landscape around Childers he knew all too well. Almost 50 kilometres further ahead the ribbon of water that was the Burnett stretched from the azure sea through the townscape and underneath the railway bridge he had tried to cross as a boy in knickerbockers. If only those same gulls he had regarded enviously that day were still there to see him now flying among them, faster and higher. Over to the right he eyed Mon Repos and felt the Pacific breeze that had lifted his dreams to reality. Then Bert pushed the stick on the Baby forward and headed for home.

The telegram Bert sent to tell of his departure had only just arrived at Woodbine Cottage, and no one expected him to make it in one day. That was ridiculous. But then Bert appeared in the sky like a sign from heaven. Although he was shy on the ground, in the air Bert could be a showman to rival P.T. Barnum. The Baby's faint cry grabbed the attention of everyone within earshot as aircraft around Bundaberg were still a rarity in 1921. People in the city streets and in their weatherboard homes stopped what they were doing to watch in amazement as the frail machine with the kangaroo painted on its tail suddenly fell from 1200 metres and hurtled to within 60 metres of disaster, then started to climb again.

At the foundry the shout of 'It's Bert' went up as hammers were thrown into the air in celebration, and everyone rushed outside to gape in astonishment. People began to swarm into Gavin Street. Papa Hinkler, in town going about his errands, couldn't believe what he was seeing and hobbled home as fast as his tired old legs could propel him, his long grey beard trying to keep up. Frances, who was tending her vegetable garden and lucerne patch, burst into tears at the sight of her long-lost son returning from the heavens, waving to her and calling out 'Cheerio, Mum' as he buzzed low over her humble home in that shimmering machine. 'Cheerio, Mum,' he called out again. He hadn't seen his most ardent supporter for seven years, and his joy at seeing her was as great as his sense of achievement.

Frances waved back at him with a mixture of astonishment and affection. 'Cheerio, Bert,' she called out, dropping the bunch of carrots in her hand. 'Cheerio.' Then Frances did what any self-respecting mother would do when her son came home after working hard all day. She went inside to put the kettle on.

Bert continued the spiral diving as gasps erupted from the growing crowd. Children were playing cricket on the Foundry Green and quickly ran off to let him land. George had bolted out of the house and had marked out the course but landing still looked a daunting task as telephone wires were everywhere and on one side of the green loomed the great bulk of the foundry itself. Everyone held their breath as Bert circled to come in for his approach. After a slight adjustment in the air as he made sure of his bearings, Bert then swooped the Baby low. He made a perfect landing at 2.40 p.m.[11] Hundreds of people rushed up to congratulate their hero as his machine slowed to a crawl but Bert waved them all to stand clear. He didn't want any Blériot-style decapitations. Then he wheeled the machine around and brought it off the grass onto the dirt track that was Gavin Street, and amid the dust and the noise, taxied the 200 metres along to his old home as hundreds of men, women and children ran or cycled furiously beside him, hollering and whooping as they dodged the gravel being kicked up by the tail skid.

Bert switched off the engine and jumped out of the cockpit as Frances, Jack, George, May and Queenie all embraced him. Queenie was now sixteen, and Bert told her that she was all grown up and that he did not know her at first. As Bert was being swamped and looking around for his father, Papa hobbled into view having limped his way across the longest steel traffic bridge in Australia to hug his son once again. Bert had just made the longest ever solo flight: 1448 kilometres in eight hours and forty-five minutes. He told his father that he had kept his promise made on the doorstep all those years before. 'Papa, look, I'm a fair dinkum aviator.'

Joe Marks, the *Bundaberg Mail*'s reporter who'd been with Bert on the beach with the gliders and who had corresponded with him ever since, stepped forward to congratulate his old mate on a dream realised.

Hundreds of people, many of them housewives who had dropped everything and rushed down to Gavin Street to witness the commotion, now gathered around Woodbine Cottage. Lewis Maynard, the former mayor, told Bert how proud he was of the young man he'd recommended for a flying job a decade earlier. William Gavegan, the new mayor, shook Bert's hand and asked for a bit of quiet to make a short speech. For the first time that day Bert looked uncomfortable.

'Lieutenant Hinkler, welcome back to Bundaberg,' he said with all the formality he could summon. 'I want to congratulate you on what is a world record non-stop flight, to thank you for the heroic part you played in the Great War and for the great service you have rendered to the Empire in other ways. Bundaberg is proud to have such a distinguished airman and your worthy parents are also to be honoured in rearing such a fine son.'[12] He told his ever-expanding audience that had Bert received the necessary financial backing he would have been the first aviator to fly from England to Australia. At this the crowd burst into wholehearted applause and Bert, recoiling from the adulation, seemed to shrink. Gavegan told the crowd that had Bert been 'the son of a duke or some other well-to-do and not merely a working man's son' any amount of money would have been forthcoming for his aviation efforts. 'Hear, hear,' shouted the crowd and then more applause erupted when Gavegan asked his audience to never forget the way Bert had advertised Bundaberg to the whole world.

Bert replied simply, 'Thank you, I'm glad to be home.' He parked the Baby on a vacant patch next to the house, knowing that no one was likely to steal it. He made a brief visit to his old employers in the *Mail*'s newsroom and was offered a special newspaper run. That night he and his family were invited to a performance at the Queen's Theatre across the Burnett, where they were presented to the audience and given three cheers. Bert was now one of the world's finest pilots yet they travelled to the theatre on Papa's horse and cart.

Later, Bert put pen to paper in another letter to Nance.

My old people were really overjoyed by my arrival, and I found them, while visibly affected by the roll of anno domini, still feeling pretty well considering. I found Jack looking very happy with his wife and baby boy Ron. From the way he talks I feel he is well contented and the wifie — Kitty — is quite a decent sort of girl and they should carry on well together. My sister Mayme likewise seems very happy with her lot — a beaming baby boy, Vernon. I must also tell you I've had a long talk with my parents and now you are well known to them. I showed your picture and I could see my dear Mater appreciated my choice.[13]

Chapter 15

*From the time the machine left the shelter of the Mascot
hangar until its return about three weeks later, it was
exposed to all the elements, the best protection it had
during that period [was] offered by a friendly gum tree.*

**Bert Hinkler on the hardships endured by his
faithful Avro Baby in Australia in 1921**

*He never lost heart but pegged away ... his
achievements in the face of adversities are such
as to stamp him the greatest aviator of the day.*[1]

**Bundaberg Mail reporter Joe Marks
on Bert's return to Australia**

The next morning Bert rose early at Woodbine Cottage to
work on the Baby, intending to give the engine a complete
overhaul. He was delighted with her performance; she
had used just 100 litres of petrol all the way from Sydney,
giving him 66 kilometres (41 miles) to the gallon. He
could have gone another 260 kilometres or so — all the
way to Rockhampton. His plan to devote himself to a
full day's mechanical toil was thwarted, by the number of

distinguished visitors who dropped in to the Hinkler home to marvel at the young man and his machine, among them the Queensland Chief Justice and University of Queensland chancellor Sir Pope Cooper, who was presiding over the Bundaberg Circuit Court that week. Bert was more than happy to show them the finer points of the finest machine of its type in the world and he pointed out the glider that first carried him aloft and was now stored under the house. More visitors came the next day and more and more after that. Bert lamented that he couldn't even have his breakfast in peace but rather took it in pieces. Telegrams poured in from his old teachers at the International Correspondence Schools, from his mates at the Water and Sewerage Board in Brisbane and from proud Australians everywhere. Edward J. Hart, secretary of the New South Wales branch of the Aero Club of Australia, sent a message from Sydney: 'Heartiest congratulations, brilliant flight' and asked Bert to attend a dinner in his honour at the plush Hotel Australia in that great metropolis. Bert readily accepted but asked Hart to postpone it because he wanted more time with his folks.

The following afternoon Bundaberg businesses closed early so that 2000 people could attend Mayor Gavegan's civic reception at the new open-air Olympia Airdome,[2] where Bert was also presented with a cheque for £100 from a grateful community. Bert's finances looked likely to receive an even bigger boost in England. While Bert was in Australia, C.G. Grey had a meeting with Avro's general manager R.J. Parrott, who told him that the company regarded the 28-year-old Australian as the 'bright particular star among British pilots'. Grey even wrote to Nance to say that Avro was planning another world record flight for Bert when he returned. 'Parrott and I talked it over and we came to the conclusion that there is nobody else except Bert who would have the patience and the endurance to do it,' Grey wrote. 'If he pulls it off, which I am sure he will be able to do quite easily, for him, he will be the most famous aviator in the world.'[3]

Bert began a series of flights to advertise the *Bundaberg Mail*. Each morning George held the right wingtip of G-EACQ and Jack spun the propeller. When the engine kicked over Jack grabbed the left wing-tip as they guided the plane to the Foundry Green. Dust flew everywhere as the engine roared then, as Bert wheeled the machine onto the grass, he accelerated across it and zoomed off, to the amazement of all watching.

Once in the air Bert tossed copies of the newspaper to subscribers and dropped flyers advertising the technological wizardry of the *Bundaberg Mail* over nearby towns, many of which had never seen an aircraft before, let alone one that could perform Bert's loops, dives and rolls. Bundaberg, Bert said, now had the most modern paper run in the world. He visited Childers, Dallarnil, Cordalba, Wallaville, Gin Gin, Mount Perry, New Moonta and Booyal and buzzed the remote selection in the area known as the Goodnight Scrub that had been taken up by Charlie Laffan. He also dropped advertising leaflets and mail that was addressed 'By courtesy of Lieutenant Hinkler'.

On the way back from Cordalba on 20 April, Bert put on a special show as 6000 eager spectators fought for vantage points on the banks of the Burnett. At 5.30 p.m. Bert appeared high in the sky and did his 'falling leaf' trick, tumbling over and over before righting the machine. He flew so low that he could almost touch the roof tops and, after disappearing behind the foundry, he re-emerged, rocketing along the river just a few feet above the water. Shrieks went up and cries of 'He's going under the bloody bridge', and there was a stampede towards the riverbank as 6000 necks craned to see triumph or tragedy. In a blur Bert went under the spans of the traffic bridge and then the spans of the railway bridge. Soon after he spun the Baby around and, in case anyone missed it the first time, he came barrelling back just over the water and did it all again, sharing the magic of aviation. He endeared himself to everyone, not the least, the children of Bundaberg who climbed all over the parked Baby and hung from the propeller whenever it was in Gavin Street.

Already Bert was talking to Bundaberg's civic leaders about starting an aviation business to service the local area, and he even approached Bundaberg Racing Club for a lease of the racecourse so that he could use it when the horses weren't running. The club's committee approved his idea in principle, but then Bert started to think about the way he'd left Nance on her sick bed and her question of whether he would ever come home. Bert had only been in Bundaberg a week and a half when he told his family that he had a wife he was anxious to see back in Havelock Road. Although they wanted him to stay in Bundaberg longer, he booked his passage home to England via Vancouver on SS *Makura* and spent his final night in Bundaberg, 22 April, at a euchre tournament and dance organised by the North Bundaberg School Committee. After eleven days of handshakes, pats on the back, three cheers *ad infinitum* and a few 'for he's a jolly good fellows,' not to mention £400 in cheques from appreciative committees and a silver teapot for his parents, it was time to say goodbye.

Frances had gone to Gympie on the mail train to farewell Bert there, but he told the rest of his family he'd be back the next year, gave them all hugs and thanked the people of Bundaberg for their hospitality and generous gifts. He really didn't know what else to say since the whole experience had been so overwhelming. Just as he was about to leave one of his admirers rushed up to him with a good luck charm, a magpie in a cage. Bert laughed and tied the cage to the side of his machine. It seemed that all of Bundaberg had come out to see him. With the cheers of what seemed like thousands of people flocking around 69 Gavin Street, Bert climbed into the cockpit at 2.45 p.m. on Saturday, 23 April,[4] asked his audience to stand well back and keep their arms away from the propeller, then he taxied down the dusty road and steered onto the grass.

With his family waving frantically and the big crowd applauding, he took off from the northern end of the Foundry Green and circled the Baby over Rubyanna, then had a last look at Mon Repos. He flew over Nielson Park, where rugby league was being played in the coastal village of Bargara, and gave the crowd a hearty cheerio. He then set course for Gympie to visit his grandparents, passing over Goodwood and Bauple and covering the 200 kilometres in just under two hours. He dived the Baby down to about 150 metres over Gympie's Memorial Park, where returned soldiers were holding a fete, then flew over Calton Hill where James and Mary Bonney lived. He came down to 30 metres to give the town a good look at the Gympie photographer's assistant made good and landed at the racecourse at half past four. He was met by Frances and by James Bonney, proud as punch that while his grandfather had been a convict in chains, his own grandson was the world-famous flying man. 'Good Lord, who'd have thought it?'

The Baby was towed behind a lorry to the fete in Memorial Park, where Bert was welcomed by Gympie's mayor and presented with another cheque for £25. He released his magpie from the cage, but the bird was having such a good time that it wouldn't leave Bert's side so he decided to keep it with him until he arrived in Sydney. He and Frances spent the Sunday making a final visit to his fading grandmother, who had given him so much encouragement as a child, then as a youth armed with his old camera and big dreams. Mary Anne Bonney died two weeks later aged eighty-one, and James then moved to Bundaberg to live out his life in Bert's old room in Gavin Street.

Bert and his magpie left Gympie from the area now known as Archery Park on the Monday morning at 9.25, which was Anzac Day, 25 April. The Gympie paper said his unassuming manner had won Bert a host of new friends and, as he started the engine, a large crowd gathered to give him three cheers. He kissed Frances goodbye and told her he'd be back before she knew it. As the crowd cheered he shouted back: 'Thanks, good luck to you all'. The Aero Club dinner in Sydney was scheduled for Wednesday evening, 27 April, and Bert planned to stay in Brisbane on the way. He took off towards the Mary Valley and travelled south, passing Imbil at about 10 a.m. He soon spied the magnificent formations of the Glasshouse Mountains. Then, eighty-five minutes after take-off, he arrived almost 180 kilometres away in Brisbane on the area called Albion Flats, now known as Windsor Park, just north of the Brisbane River.[5]

He was met by Lieutenant Frank Roberts, who had an Avro 504 based at Albion Flats and had been Avro's test pilot at the company's Manchester base. Bert spent Monday and Tuesday in Brisbane with his old mentor Tom Macleod, who was now a major in the Australian Flying Corps. He wanted to get going before daybreak on Wednesday to make the non-stop flight from Brisbane to Sydney so he stayed with the Baby in its hangar overnight. Heavy rain delayed his start. He'd already postponed the Aero Club dinner a couple of times and later remarked that 'he could not play with them any longer'. Finally he took off at 6.15 a.m., dressed for the dinner in a suit donated by a Bundaberg menswear store for what he knew would be a rough ride.

He'd hardly made it 160 kilometres when he flew into a heavy squall in northern New South Wales, which battered him in the open cockpit. He wished he was back in the wonderful weather of England. The heavy rain damaged the Baby's fabric and propeller. Bert decided to land to fix the damage and came down on a long stretch of sand south of the Clarence River at a place called Brooms Head, a hamlet with a few deserted holiday shacks. He made some running repairs and showed off one of the world's most famous aircraft to a couple of curious locals fascinated by the quirky, drenched little man with the squawking magpie.[6] Before long Bert was on his way again, wondering what he'd say to all the aviation powerbrokers at the Hotel Australia. He felt much more comfortable fighting his way through torrential downpours than making speeches. But even downpours of this sort had him flummoxed.

'Gee, I thought I was out for six several times,' he later told Nance, but he kept pushing through even though he was worried his propeller was going to fall apart amid the bucketing. 'Just nearing Newcastle, only about 90 miles from Sydney, the rain came down in all its fury — absolutely walloping down cats and dogs. I had been beaten down right to the level of the beach, my wheels just almost skimming the waves.' Bert even used a boxing term, telling Nance that 'I had to ring the bell' and stop fighting the elements. 'Luckily there was a good stretch of beach and even though the storm was going at its hardest I found the beach alright and made quite a decent landing.'[7] Bert climbed out of the battered Baby onto the immense length of sand called Stockton Beach that stretched south for 24 kilometres from his position at Anna Bay. He grabbed the magpie in the cage and swung his machine around to avoid the gusting wind as best he could, hanging on to protect his delicate biplane for about an hour. 'This was now about three o'clock and I was miles from anywhere. So during a lull I ran to the top of one of the sandhills to see what form of civilisation existed. Oh my luck, dense scrub as far as the eye could reach. I remembered passing over a house or two some distance further back but I could not leave the bus there.'

As Bert looked over the surrounding countryside from atop the sandhill the only thing that caught his eye was the Baby, gracefully, elegantly but tragically lifting off the ground and swinging on to her nose with a sound of tearing fabric and cracking wood. She then completed the somersault onto her back just out of reach of the tide. Bert sat down in the cruel rain and cried. 'I felt the most wretched being on earth [but] when I regained commonsense as I could do no more for the bus, I began to walk — and a weary walk it was.' Putting on his straw boater and carrying his caged magpie, a rather defective lucky charm as it turned out, Bert went back along the beach for about seven kilometres, then started inland through the bush. 'I shall never forget that slogging trudge through the dense undergrowth, everything soaking wet and I forget how many miles I must have done.'

Bert was so wet and sore that he wanted to lie down somewhere and have a rest, but he was scared that his joints would freeze solid in the cold rain. 'After some hours, just as it was getting dark, I spotted a house. It really gave me new life and I was almost normal again.' But to his horror the 'bally place' was empty. He followed a track nearby and at last found help in a village called Bobs Farm. He rapped at the door and cried out for help. The door opened to reveal Tom Eagleton, a youngster named Charles Cromarty and his mother all staring at an odd apparition. It was a small, rain-drenched man looking not dissimilar to Charlie Chaplin in a soaked suit and a sodden straw boater and with a squawking caged magpie in his hand. They ushered the oddball stranger inside, gave him a cup of tea and, once he'd dried out a bit, took him to the nearby farm of Mrs Lucy Upton, who looked after the rudimentary telephone service for the area. Bert rang through a telegram for his mother to tell her not to be alarmed by his non-appearance in Sydney, then sent a telegram at 5.50 p.m. addressed to HART AERO CLUB HOTEL AUSTRALIA SYDNEY and reading: FORCED LANDING ON BEACH FIFTEEN MILES NORTH NEWCASTLE HINKLER. He handed over the magpie to some of the kids in the area, who fed it worms by hand, and said he hoped it brought them more good luck than it had him. He then hitched a ride on Tom Eagleton's horse cart back to Anna

Bay to secure the Baby against the weather and stayed the night with the Uptons.

About 150 kilometres south in Castlereagh Street, Sydney, amid the grand opulence of the Hotel Australia,[8] Aero Club president Colonel Oswald Watt made a stirring speech before the fifty or so wartime pilots gathered to honour Bert. Watt was a wealthy Sydney businessman, former Blériot apprentice and highly decorated pilot for both the French Foreign Legion and Australian Flying Corps. He praised Bert's brilliant exploits and said his delay was the first time the Baby had let him down. He said the incident demonstrated the urgent necessity for a thorough organisation of civil aviation in Australia, adding that it was outrageous for an important city such as Newcastle not to have a properly equipped aerodrome. Major Norman Brearley, president of the West Australian Aero Club, told the audience that Bert had done a marvellous service to aviation by proving the possibility of a man running an aircraft for just tuppence a mile.[9] Brearley had been awarded the Military Cross and Distinguished Service Order after being shot in both lungs while attacking seven enemy aircraft. He was now tendering to the Australian Government for its first subsidised air mail and passenger contract to operate the 1900-kilometre route between the West Australian towns of Geraldton and Derby and was about to hire five pilots, including Charles Kingsford Smith, to partner him flying a fleet of Bristol Tourers.

Back at Lucy Upton's farm, in the wee hours past midnight, Bert was dejected and in despair at his big night at the Aero Club having been a literal washout. He picked up a pen and addressed a letter from 'Somewhere way in the bush, not far from the beach about 15 miles from Newcastle', on Thursday, 28 April 1921. 'My Darling Sweetheart Nance,' he wrote, 'Oh my Beloved what about it now. My — our — poor baby rests upside down on the beach.' Bert went on to outline his travails over four pages but assured Nance that she had no need to worry because he was as fit as could be expected, given the disappointment. At least the storm was breaking. His major worry, he said, was that because of the damage to the Baby he might get only half of the £600 he'd agreed on with AA&E.

Sunlight saw Bert joined by Tom Eagleton and Neil Cromarty as they journeyed back to where the Baby lay smashed. They hitched five horses to her and dragged her for a slow, humiliating 24 kilometres across the sand to Stockton. It was a surreal spectacle for beachgoers, not used to seeing an aircraft in the sky, let alone one being hauled by horses like a plough along their long stretch of coastline. One elderly lady looked up from her fishing. 'Did ya find that on the beach, did ya, love?' she cried out.

Through gritted teeth Bert replied: 'Yes, Madam, and it's worth £900.'

When the rescue party finally reached Stockton, Bert stayed overnight with Jim Davidson and his wife, relatives of the Uptons. As usual the battered old Baby waited outside in the weather.[10]

The following morning, Friday, 29 April, Bert found an old motor lorry to tow the Baby and, in her wake, a gathering crew of children, gawkers and the bemused as she beat a solemn march from Stockton to the Hunter River wharf where she was again dismantled and her broken pieces packed onto the steamer *Hunter* for transport to

Sydney. Bert gave Tom Eagleton £10 for all his trouble and promised to take him for a flight if he was ever near Anna Bay again.

When he reached Mascot, Bert finally delivered his Baby to AA&E, although both he and his machine looked much the worse for wear, and he left with a lot less than £600. 'I had a fairly exciting time,' he told a reporter, adding later that his dear old machine had copped the worst of it. Bert hadn't sold another plane to anyone, and there were no 5 per cent commissions from Jimmy Goble or anyone else.

On 5 May, Bert, still dressed in his now tattered, oil-stained and crumpled suit and giving his occupation on the passenger manifesto as 'mechanic at aircraft works', set sail for home via Auckland, Suva, Honolulu, Seattle and Vancouver ready for a reunion with Nance and to face whatever dangers A.V. Roe and company threw his way.

Chapter 16

It was quite an experience and I feel bally fortunate
that it should fall to my lot to get this big job.
My luck, how I should like you to have been over
this way and see the big chap for yourself.

Bert Hinkler, writing to his parents on 6 December 1922
after having test flown the most powerful single-engine
plane in the world, the 1000 hp Avro Aldershot bomber

It is the irony of the air that it will let the
flyer do things seemingly impossible and
then kill them when attempting a trifle.

The *New York Herald* after a spate of
aircraft disasters in the 1920s

Bert arrived at Havelock Road in time to repair his relationship with Nance and prepare for the Sixth Aerial Derby on 16 July 1921 at Hendon. He would race a new Baby against Britain's finest with hopes of winning the handicap section. Harry Hawker would be at the controls of the fastest plane in Britain, a Nieuport Goshawk capable of 267 kilometres per hour. Hawker was rumoured to be making £20,000 a year[1] when the average annual wage in Britain was £200. Bert wanted to get a piece of the action as the No. 1 flyer at Avro, even though times were tough and 68 per cent of Avro had been sold to Crossley Motors.

Testing the latest aircraft was a risky business, but Bert had seen enough of life at twenty-eight to know there were risks everywhere. Just two weeks after Bert had left Sydney on the *Makura* his ardent supporter Oswald Watt, who had survived so many scrapes in the Great War, was collecting firewood near his weekender at Bilgola Beach in Sydney's north when he slipped on rocks, hit his head and drowned, aged forty-three.[2]

As the Derby approached, Hawker wanted to display the Goshawk's full speed despite doctors telling him not to fly.[3] His physician grimly broke the news that Hawker had developed a condition called spinal tuberculosis and recommended an operation to save his life, with the rider that it would probably leave him bedridden. Hawker would have none of it. He had passed the physical examination required for the renewal of his aviator's licence in December 1920 and his restless spirit would not allow him to sit still. When Hawker wasn't playing with Pamela and his new baby daughter Mary, named after the ship that had saved his life, he was busy building the H.G. Hawker two-stroke motorcycle. He even set a world speed record of 169 kilometres per hour at Brooklands in a car made by the AC company.[4]

On 12 July, Hawker went out to Hendon to test the Goshawk in the early summer's evening. At 6.20 p.m. he was powering it from the aerodrome towards Edgware at about 1500 metres when spectators noticed flame coming from the exhaust as he passed over Burnt Oak in obvious difficulties. He aimed the Goshawk for a field about 2.5 kilometres from the aerodrome, but as he came nearer to the ground he saw people sitting on the grass. Desperately trying to avoid them, Hawker felt his machine start to spin. As the Goshawk came even closer to the ground it started to sway from side to side, then it ploughed into the earth with a terrifying crunch. Hawker was thrown clear and was nine metres from the Goshawk as it burst into flame, setting the grass all around ablaze. A doctor and some police officers rushed to Hawker's aid and beat out the fire around him. Both Hawker's legs were broken but he was still alive. Barely. Ten minutes later the plucky Australian died as the doctor treated him. He was thirty-two.[5]

Hawker's death cast a long, maudlin shadow over the Derby four days later, but the show still went on. Bert had a dog of a time and had to bring the new Baby down and out of the race at Sidcup as Jimmy James dominated in a derivative of the Goshawk, a Gloster Mars 1.

A postmortem showed a mass of blood on the front of Hawker's spinal cord indicating a haemorrhage, paralysis, then a loss of control of the Goshawk. Hawker's doctor told the inquest that the aviator 'was on his last legs' as it was and that the slightest movement or strain could have caused a rupture leading to the haemorrhage. Had he not died in the crash, he would have died from his condition within weeks. It was a wretched sight just two days after the inquest when Hawker's casket, adorned with wreaths from Muriel and his two daughters, was buried in St Paul's across the road from his house. 'In our sorrow,' *Flight* opined, 'let us be comforted by the thought that Harry Hawker died as he had lived, doing the work he loved.'[6]

Bert also loved his work more and more as he became entrenched as a real character at Avro. He started riding a motorcycle, a single-cylinder vintage Triumph, and later a two-cylinder Matchless, and his appearance always brought a smile to the faces of his co-workers. Even under the mild English sun Bert always looked like he had a tan, seemingly reflecting his sunny disposition. He was small and strong and, although he remained shy and humble, he smiled often. The youngsters at Hamble idolised him, not only because of his heroics in world-record solo flights in dangerous conditions but also because he was invariably the can-do man, fixing his aeroplanes himself and serving as his own mechanic and navigator as he would for most of his career. He was never, ever known to lose his cool, and he got on with the whole team, from Verdon-Roe, still an Avro director, to the cleaners.[7] Although he'd performed some daredevil stunts in Bundaberg, safety for Avro customers and their passengers was Bert's priority, especially after the first-ever collision between two airliners on 7 April 1922 over France killed all seven people on board the machines.

That disaster could not stop the adventurous wanting to fly, however, and in February 1922, Charles Lindbergh quit the University of Wisconsin having just turned twenty and headed to Lincoln, Nebraska, to enrol at Nebraska Aircraft Corporation's flying school. On 10 April 1922, the tall, skinny, diffident youngster flew for the first time, as a passenger in a two-seat Lincoln-Standard Tourabout biplane, and felt as though he'd touched heaven.

In Hamble, Bert was busy ferrying Avro planes between the company's bases to and from Manchester, testing the different aircraft coming off the drawing board and making suggestions for improvements to Roy Chadwick's designs. There were more versions of the Baby, one even for Ernest Shackleton's Antarctic expedition, and there was the Avro 536 and 546, which were the mainstays for joyride pilots in Blackpool and Jersey. The 539 was a racing biplane and the 548 a pilot trainer. Bert tested them all, although not all of the models were successful. The 547 triplane, one of which went to Qantas, proved so inept in the Outback that it ended up as an expensive chicken coop in a Sydney backyard.

Ross and Keith Smith and their mechanic, the newly commissioned Lieutenant Jim Bennett, were doing plenty of testing, too. While Bert put the Avro machines through their paces the knighted brothers were at Brooklands planning to top the England-to-Australia run with the first-ever flight around the world in another Vickers machine. The Smiths planned to take off on their round-the-world trek on Anzac Day 1922 in a single-engine Vickers Viking amphibian, a similar aircraft to the one on which John Alcock had lost his life. They had supervised every stage of their Viking's construction and, on 13 April, Ross Smith and Bennett decided to give it a thorough examination at Brooklands. They were waiting for Keith Smith to join them on their test flight, but he was running late as the Easter holidays played hell with the train timetables. The other two decided to take off without him at 12.15 p.m.

The Viking performed splendidly for the first 15 minutes, climbing gracefully to 900 metres. Keith Smith arrived at the airport, breathless after rushing from the station, just in time to see the Viking's 15-metre wingspan begin to shake and the machine tilt vertically. The huge plane started to spin. It plummeted and, with hearts in their mouths, Keith and the other spectators hoped Ross was stunting, testing the Viking to its absolute maximum. Then the spin became faster and the Viking nose-dived. It broke apart as it flattened an iron fence that ringed Brooklands.

Keith and the others bolted to the scene. Amid the wreckage Ross Smith, the man who had flown with Lawrence of Arabia and crossed the world, was trapped in his seat, a long gash all the way down his face. Jim Bennett was moaning, but by the time the ambulance men extracted him from the twisted metal his moaning, and his breathing, had ceased forever. When the doctor arrived at the grisly scene in a speeding car, Keith stared at him tearfully and pleaded, 'Please look at my brother and see if there is any chance of saving him.' With just one look, the doctor immediately saw that Ross was beyond help and, with his head lowered, returned to Keith, who gravely remarked, 'I see by your face all is over.' Keith fell to his knees and wept beside his brother, who was dead at twenty-nine. Both bodies were loaded into an ambulance and taken to the local mortuary.[8] Keith, whose life had been spared by a late train, had them embalmed and placed on the steamer *Largs Bay* for transport home to Australia. 'No one knew, or ever will know the cause of the catastrophe,' Keith told reporters. 'Everybody who takes up a new bus knows the risk and simply conjures with Fate.'[9]

At about the same time as Keith Smith was burying his brother, Bert was again waiting for a break in the hostilities in the Middle East so that he could at last try his England-to-Australia solo flight. There were plenty of flying adventures while he waited, and there was the whole staff at Avro to take on joy flights.

In May 1922, Avro sold one of its Babies, G-EBDA, to the Russian military. The Russians sent a pilot named Evgeniy Ivanovich Gvaita, a 26-year-old veteran of the Russian Civil War, who had flown with the 1st Soviet Fighter Aviation Group, to collect the Baby from Hamble. The initial plan was for Bert to fly in a second Baby with Gvaita all the way back to Moscow and then return. This would be another distance record for Bert and Avro but there was a last-minute change of plan, and instead Bert went with Gvaita only as far as the customs aerodrome at Lympne, a delightful village on the sea cliffs near Folkestone in Kent. Gvaita left Lympne at 5 a.m. the following day bound for Berlin. No sooner had Bert returned to Hamble than word came through that Gvaita needed help after a forced landing at Tilburg in Holland. The Russian had been over Belgium when he became lost because of the shocking weather. He made an emergency landing in the fields beside Tilburg's Stevenzandsestraat but, because of the boggy ground, lost control of the Baby, damaging the rudder and steering. As soon as Gvaita was found Bert was sent to the rescue. 'I immediately collected spares etc, hopped back into my bus and rushed off to find him,' Bert explained.

Owing to insurance restrictions I was not permitted to fly the Baby out of England so at Croydon I transferred my baggage to a Fokker F.VII [a single-engine plane that carried six passengers in an enclosed cabin] of the KLM Royal Dutch Air Service as a passenger. I reached Rotterdam after about two and a half hours flight from London thence by rail. At Tilburg I found Gvaita and the machine quite all right — the only damage to the machine was a broken rudder caused when she turned over in very soft ground. As I had brought the necessary replacements she was soon ready again for the air, though he had some difficulty in finding even a small ground suitable for taking off and also in getting the Baby to it. We managed the next day and I flew her to a military aerodrome about 10 miles [16 kilometres] away to fill up with fuel and oil.[10]

Bert returned home without incident, although his trip to Europe with a mysterious Russian fuelled whispers for years that as well as working for Avro he had a side job as a British spy.

In Nebraska, Charles Lindbergh needed more money for flying lessons and the required bond should he damage one of the Nebraska Aircraft Corporation's planes. So in June 1922 he started performing for aerial troupes known as barnstormers, flying for a wing-walking stuntman across Wyoming, Montana, Nebraska, Kansas and Colorado.

As Avro's 'bright particular star' Bert became a regular on Britain's air-race circuit and had his heart set on winning the first King's Cup, a handicap race over 1300 kilometres starting on 8 September 1922. It would cover a course from Croydon Aerodrome to Glasgow and back after an overnight stay. But in preparing for the event Bert met with disaster. On 5 September, Fred Bevis, Avro's transport manager, had driven from Hamble to Twickenham, to pick up a Green engine for Bert's Baby, registered as G-EAXL, only to be plagued by a series of mishaps, including a broken axle. The engine wasn't fitted until 6 a.m. the next day. Bert took off in his Baby only for the engine to cut out a couple of minutes after take-off because of another dodgy magneto. Bert pushed the nose down to maintain speed and made a sharp turn trying to reach the beach, but his altitude was too low. The Baby ploughed into Southampton Water. Bert was thrown forward and his head smashed into the compass resulting in cuts about the face, but otherwise he was none the worse for his experience, although he did have to use the swimming skills he'd developed in the Burnett to get back to safety.[11] The Baby was a write-off.

In the end Captain Frank Barnard accepted the King's Cup having averaged 199 kilometres per hour in a DH.4, capping a stupendous week for the de Havilland machines. Just five days earlier Lieutenant Jimmy Doolittle, of the United States Army Air Service, had flown his DH.4 right across the USA from Pablo Beach in Florida to Rockwell Field in San Diego, California, in less than a day — twenty-one hours and nineteen minutes, to be precise — making just one stop to refuel at Kelly Field, Texas.

In Europe the war in the skies was about to start brewing again as the German Junkers company, violating the Treaty of Versailles, secretly established an aircraft factory. In October, Mussolini's National Fascist Party came to power after the march on Rome, making Il Duce, at thirty-nine, the youngest Premier in the history of Italy. He immediately began reorganising the Italian air force, seeing air power as the key to his reign, and soon one of his Fascist gang leaders, Italo Balbo, would be charged with the task of making Italy rule the skies.[12]

By November 1922, Qantas had made its first scheduled flight between the Queensland towns of Charleville and Cloncurry with Hudson Fysh at the controls and one paying passenger for part of the journey, 84-year-old Alexander Kennedy. Bert and Nance were on the move, too. With Nance still the registered owner of No. 4 Havelock Road, they rented a comfortable two-storey house called The Nest at No. 90 St Johns Road, Hedge End, about six kilometres from Hamble. There was room for a tennis court, which Nance used often, and there was an abundance of fruit trees in the garden. Bert kept chickens and ducks as well. Whenever he wasn't tinkering with engines or ailerons, which seemed to Nance almost all the time, they played tennis on the lawn and chatted over refreshments in a cosy corner of their yard appropriately known as the Tea Garden. Bert loved living there, and his enthusiasm spilled over as he wrote to his parents, gushing that even the normally biting winter in Hampshire was much milder than usual. 'At the "Nest" pruning of the apple and pear trees is in full swing,' Bert wrote.

> Nance is very anxious for the same attention to be extended to the roses. Inside we are just about getting comfy. Nance's mater has been with us during the move, rendering no little help while we are all upside down. She speaks of returning home on Saturday as she particularly wants to be in Yorkshire for Xmas. When she goes the house will be full of empty bedrooms, four of 'em. Altho I say empty I really mean unoccupied as we have no end of rubbish in some of the others.

Bert optimistically asked his mother and father — whom he addressed as 'My Dears' — to come and live with him and Nance in England for a year or two, telling them there was more than enough space for everybody. 'And also with the place getting straight it is so inviting that I cannot see how you could refuse to come. It only requires one glimpse and I bet you'd soon be on your way.'

A neighbouring boy named Fred Sharpe remembered Bert as a quiet man who liked to laugh and who amused the district with his antics. One of them was to drop bags of wood chips for Nance as he flew slowly over their house. She would leave a marker out in the yard to aim at, and he rarely missed.[13]

Bert also began experimenting with radio, stretching wires around the house and all over the yard, eventually making the acquaintance of an amateur radio operator from Kent named C.G. Allen, who encouraged Bert's experiments even more. Each day Bert fairly whistled at his good fortune as he made his way to Hamble on his motorcycle or sometimes even in the experimental car that Verdon-Roe had designed complete with bucket seats. Soon he was driving a Willys-Overland.

On 30 November 1922, Bert made history piloting the massive Avro 549 Aldershot bomber, the first ever aircraft with a 1000-horsepower motor and enthusiastically wrote home to tell his parents that its power was equivalent to the locomotive engine in the Brisbane mail train. Roy Chadwick remembered that, although Bert was small in stature, he was very strong, energetic and keen minded 'and the way he flew large aeroplanes such as the Avro Aldershot was remarkable'.[14] In more ways than one.

He had long ditched his straw boater and began to eschew the leather flying helmet in favour of a bowler hat more suited to a City of London businessman. Bert started wearing high heels on his boots, but he was still so small and the Aldershot so big that he needed a stack of cushions to sit on so that he could reach the controls. Wooden blocks were attached to the rudder bar so that he could work it with his feet. Once when flying the Aldershot with a flight engineer in the front cockpit, Bert took the cushions out from under his seat in the rear cockpit and ducked low in his own confined space while, at the same time, giving the stick a flutter to make the giant aircraft wobble about. The startled engineer spun around in his seat to see the source of the problem only to find an empty cockpit where the little Australian pilot had been sitting. Just as the engineer panicked at being alone in the sky, Bert's bowler hat started to rise into view like a turtle's head coming out of its shell, a huge spread of gold teeth splitting his face.

Bert was always busy, testing and delivering such machines as the 555 Bison fleet-spotter, the 557 Ava torpedo bomber, the 561 Andover, an air ambulance version of the Aldershot and the almost weightless 562 Avis light plane. He became a favourite at all the big air races, usually in the handicap events, with his Baby going up against the monster powerplants now propelling aircraft well beyond 320 kilometres per hour. His desire to make the long voyage in his bus from London to Bundaberg only increased with the news that over two days in May 1923 American pilots Oakley Kelly and John Macready flew a Fokker T-2 across the USA non-stop from Long Island, New York, to San Diego in a just under twenty-seven hours.

One of the most important races for British flyers became the Grosvenor Cup held for the first time at Lympne on 25 June 1923. It was a handicap event for British-built aeroplanes of not more than 150 horsepower contested over a course of 650 kilometres.[15]

Bert lodged with his friends Henry and Maggie Staines, who had a bungalow named Ingleside next to the Lympne airfield, and whenever he wanted to take off he just climbed over the back fence and strolled out to his machine. He was a big hit with all the kids of the village and those who flocked to the air meets, and he let them take turns listening to his new whiz-bang radio through special devices he called 'earphones'.

Nine pilots took off for the inaugural Grosvenor Cup race with the favourite being the newly married Major Ernest Leslie Foot, in a Bristol Monoplane with a 100-horsepower Lucifer engine. Bert fancied his chances in the Avro Baby registered G-EAUM and was the first to take off at 10 a.m. By the time the planes arrived before a crowd of 25,000 enjoying a carnival atmosphere at Bristol's Filton aerodrome, RAF ace Flight Lieutenant Walter 'Scruffy' Longton was in the lead on a Sopwith Gnu, but Bert was just six minutes behind. When Major Foot landed after them at Bristol he said he felt dizzy from petrol fumes, and mechanics got busy repairing the leak. In the end Longton held on to win the race with Fred Raynham second and Bert third.

In a stark understatement, the local paper later reported that a good day's sport was rather ruined when Major Foot was burned to death. He had covered 480 kilometres when his machine crashed onto Stonehill Road near Chertsey between Bristol and Croydon. Both his legs had been torn off at the thigh, and he was burnt beyond recognition.

At the *Daily Mail* Motor Glider Competition at Lympne in October 1923, twenty-eight low-powered planes were entered, and Bert took out the prize for the most reliable machine, flying 1600 kilometres around a 20-kilometre circuit in an Avro 560 ultralight. The engine had been derived from a motorcycle.

On 6 February 1924, Bert's paper, 'Flying in Australia', was presented to the Engineers Club in Coventry Street, London. In it Bert appraised the various start-up airlines in Australia, observing that Norman Brearley's Western Australian Airlines led the way but that the new company operating in central Queensland called 'Quantas' provided a 'particularly useful' service linking a number of Outback railheads, a service that had previously been the tiresome domain of the stagecoach: 'The route, Charleville–Cloncurry, inclines one to use superlatives for its description. Ideal flying country with vast stretches of open downs, level as a bowling green, an equable climate, a district blessed with prosperity.' He told the story of the first 'Quantas' passenger, Alexander Kennedy, the owner of Buckingham Downs Station and a resident of Queensland for sixty-three years, who made the Longreach–Cloncurry trip in four hours flying time. His first trip to Cloncurry in the 1870s, Bert related, had taken eight months by packhorse.[16]

Bert's old commanding officer, Jimmy Goble, had a first-hand look at the vast distances Australian aviation could service when he and another RAAF pilot, Flight Lieutenant Ivor McIntyre, left Point Cook on 6 April in a Fairey IIID seaplane, one of six the new air force had bought from Britain. In their open cockpits Goble and McIntyre were pioneering a route between Melbourne and Thursday Island, surveying the Great Barrier Reef and testing the new machine in all sorts of weather. They survived mosquitoes, sand flies, sunburn and infections to land at St Kilda Beach forty-four days later to rapturous applause as the first aviators to circumnavigate Australia.

Three months later British-born Horace Brinsmead, Australia's first Controller of Civil Aviation, led a three-man party on an around-Australia flight in a DH.50 land plane, taking off from Point Cook on 7 August for Darwin along the inland route. The trio rounded Australia in just twenty-three days.

Bert was also celebrating. On 4 October 1924 at Lympne, he piloted a tiny Avro 562 Avis to the Grosvenor Challenge Cup — a 160-kilometre test for light planes with engines no bigger than 1100 cc. The race took eight laps of a 20-kilometre course that was set up so that the aeroplanes were in view of the crowd the whole time. With Nance among the throng cheering for her hero and telling the spectators around her that it was the most exciting race she'd ever seen, Bert pipped Flying Officer S.H. Gaskell in a Westland Woodpigeon on the last lap.

Already Bert and Nance, as happy a pair as their friends had ever seen, were planning to move out of their rented house and build their very own dream home together, a cottage among the majestic oaks and silver birches on an acre or so in a nearby subdivision called Thornhill Park Farm Estate. It was just off the Southampton–Portsmouth Road, and Nance had bought the land for £105 on 19 August 1924, signing the deed as Mrs Nance Hinkler, wife of Herbert John Louis Hinkler, Pilot of Aircraft.

While Bert concentrated on his work for Avro and the big air races, Australia was becoming a beacon for long-distance flyers from Europe. Mussolini had restructured the Italian air force, making the Regia Aeronautica, a powerful tool for Fascist propaganda, encouraging Italian pilots to cross the world. So it was that Marquis Francesco de Pinedo, a 35-year-old nobleman pilot, embarked on the greatest aerial journey ever attempted. He and his mechanic Ernesto Campanelli took off in a Savoia S.16 flying boat with a monstrous 450 horsepower engine and a pusher propellor from Sesto Calende in northern Italy on 20 April 1925 bound for the Great Southern Land and Tokyo in a round trip that would cover almost 55,000 kilometres.

They touched down in Broome on 31 May 1925, having covered the first 16,900 kilometres of their adventure. They were the first aviators to reach Australia from Europe since Parer and McIntosh five years before, and Stanley Bruce immediately sent the pair a congratulatory radio message, then a telegram to 'Signor Mussolini, Prime Minister of Italy', which read: 'We feel that in emulating the success of our own countrymen Commandant de Pinedo has added one more link to the common bond of interest and friendship which unites Australia and Italy.'[17]

From Broome the Italians flew to Perth and then across the Great Australian Bight to Melbourne where a civic reception greeted them. They spent five weeks enjoying the charms of the city, then flew on to Sydney for another three weeks beside the harbour before flying north to Queensland, landing on the Brisbane River and mooring at Kangaroo Point. They called in at the northern centres of Townsville, Innisfail, Cooktown and Port Kennedy, then flew to New Guinea and the Philippines, finally reaching Tokyo on 17 October. Then on 7 November, to a fanfare worthy of Caesar's homecoming, they landed on the Tiber in Rome. Their journey had taken the best part of seven months. Mussolini heralded de Pinedo as Italy's Lord of the Distances and called upon him to become his nation's '*messaggero di Italianità*', declaring that his voyage of discovery was just the start of a career conquering skies on every continent.

In England it seemed that after de Pinedo's achievements the 1925 King's Cup on 3–4 July would be a non-event yet heavy fog, high speed and near misses kept the pilots sweating throughout Britain's premier distance race over a course of almost 1300 kilometres. Bert flew an Avro 504N that was no match for the weather. Of the fourteen machines lined up for the 6 a.m. start at Croydon on Friday, 3 July, six failed to complete the first stage of 300 kilometres to Harrogate and four more dropped out within the next stage to Newcastle. Even Bert, one of the four survivors, found the going almost impossible and decided that in trying to penetrate the early morning fog it was 'absolutely suicidal to attempt to continue'[18] so he landed at Worksop and waited for the weather to clear. As great clouds of fog wafted over, Bert borrowed a bicycle and pedalled as fast as his legs could go to the nearest telephone office and waited for what seemed an eternity on the line to find out weather conditions further along. With news that the fog was clearing, he pedalled furiously back to his Avro and took off for Harrogate. At Renfrew, 620 kilometres into the journey, Bert and Major Harold Hemming, in his DH.37, raced to the finish line of that stage together but from opposite directions. In the thick fog, they averted a certain fatal collision by a mere 4.5 metres.

Back at Croydon after the first day's racing Bert landed in a heavy rain shower just before 10 p.m. with the help of flares, smashing his undercarriage. He had lost so much time due to the weather that he withdrew, and Frank

Barnard took the cup the next day. Bert and his tiny Avis placed third in the following month's Holiday Handicap at Lympne after Bert ran out of petrol on the way to the start from Hamble. He landed in a field eight kilometres from Lympne's aerodrome, walked to a garage, bought a nine-litre tin of fuel, filled his machine and continued to the start line.

It was just that kind of versatility that won Bert a start as the reserve pilot for Great Britain's assault on the Schneider Trophy in 1925, although he had minimal experience with the experimental racing machines that were usually the domain of military pilots. Bert spent a couple of weeks practising at the Marine Aircraft Experimental Establishment at Felixstowe in Suffolk. Great Britain and Italy were set down to challenge the trophy holders, the USA, whose ranks boasted the irrepressible Jimmy Doolittle, at Bay Shore Park near Baltimore. The pilots would cover a triangular course of fifty kilometres seven times.

Britain entered two pilots. One was Henry Biard, who had obtained his pilot's certificate way back in 1912, at the Grahame-White School at Hendon. In Baltimore Biard would fly the Reginald Mitchell-designed Supermarine-Napier S.4, a streamlined sensation that looked like it had come off the pages of a science fiction magazine. It was as futuristic as a moon rocket, a sleek monoplane mounted on twin floats, with a 12-cylinder Napier Lion VII engine blasting out a gargantuan 700 horsepower and capable of 385 kilometres per hour. The second pilot was Captain Hubert Broad who, like Bert, had been with the RNAS in Dunkirk, and had become chief test pilot for de Havilland. He would pilot the Gloster III, a pugnacious-looking wooden biplane with white wings and a light blue fuselage that was shaped like a fat round .45 calibre bullet. It also had the thundering Lion VII powerplant.

There was a festive atmosphere as the British pilots boarded SS *Minnewaska* at Southampton on 26 September for the ten-day voyage across the Atlantic, travelling with an extended crew of mechanics, riggers, engineers and aircraft manufacturers such as Verdon-Roe, Gloster's Henry Folland and Mitchell, the boy genius at Supermarine.

On his immigration form Bert advised the US authorities that he had been in the USA briefly in 1921, at Seattle, on the way home from Australia and, no he was not a polygamist, no he was not an anarchist, he was not a cripple nor a criminal, his next of kin was Mrs N. Hinkler of Hedge End, Hampshire, he had grown to five feet four and a quarter inches, he had dark complexion, dark brown hair and blue eyes and his fare had been paid by the Gloucestershire Aircraft Co. of Cheltenham. He intended to stay in the USA for two months.

Early in the voyage the team hit a rough patch when Biard slipped on the deck and injured his wrist. Then in Baltimore, after Bert and his two team-mates had spent a couple of weeks testing the machines, a hurricane hit Chesapeake Bay and nearly wrecked their planes in their makeshift tent hangars. A falling tent pole badly damage the Supermarine's tail, and seventeen US Navy seaplanes were either strewn across the beach or sunk.

On Friday, 23 October, Biard, who had been suffering from a chill, still went up in the Supermarine to complete the trophy's navigability and mooring tests, but he encountered trouble almost immediately and crashed into the water, his futuristic craft somersaulting onto her back and quickly going under. Hubert Broad taxied over to the wreck in his Gloster and threw Biard a lifebuoy. With the Supermarine out of the race, Bert was hailed by the American press as 'the airman with the wonder hands' and was given his chance to fly a back-up Gloster, despite the Italian team protesting that his replacement machine hadn't been readied in time for qualifying. The machines were finally sent on their way on Monday, 26 October.

Bert shot up into the sky and brought the Gloster down for his first taxiing test, but in the raging water he managed to go only about 90 metres when what he later described as 'the terrific pounding of the waves' caused the undercarriage struts to give way and the wings to fold in. The Gloster had to be towed back to the sheds, and Bert's race was over.

In the end Doolittle's 600-horsepower, black-and-gold Curtiss R3C-2 twin-float biplane, hitting 374.27 kilometres per hour, proved harder to catch than speeding bumble bee.

The Schneider Trophy was a disappointment for Bert yet in New York he managed to check out all the landmarks, buying postcards of the Brooklyn Bridge, Broadway, St Patrick's Cathedral and the Manhattan Municipal Building. Bert wrote to Joe Marks saying that the race was a great pity and that, although the British team couldn't win, he figured on lapping at about 346 kilometres per hour in the Gloster.

What Bert didn't tell Joe or Nance or his family in Bundaberg, or anyone else for that matter, is that while in the USA he'd met a pretty stenographer named Catherine Rose at the British Consulate. She lived with her parents and a younger brother in a small, modest apartment at 900

8th Avenue in Astoria on Long Island in a neighbourhood that was home to cab drivers, carpenters, tile fitters and printers like her father, Robert. She was twenty-three, ten years younger than Bert, and younger than Nance's daughter Maida. She was also a couple of centimetres taller than Bert, but it was less noticeable when Bert wore those big heels on his boots. Catherine, who always spelt her name Katherine, had bright blue eyes, shiny brown hair and a smile that Bert couldn't get out of his head. She told him all about her life, how she'd been born in Edinburgh and gone to New York when she was five with her mother Isabella, an older sister named Jean and a brother named Robert Jr. Her father had travelled to New York a few months earlier in 1906 to stay with his brother George on East 69th Street and find work as a printer's compositor. Bert said that was a job that once interested him in Bundaberg. When Isabella had brought the children over in 1907 to join Robert, the Rose family lived in a rented apartment on West 144th Street. There Isabella had given birth to another boy named James. They had then moved to another rented apartment in the Bronx on 173rd Street.

Katherine was fascinated by this small, bright airman, his shyness, his bashful smile, his funny accent, sort of British but more earthy, his cheeky sense of humour. She was astounded that such a humble, quiet fellow could control the most powerful flying machines in the world.

Katherine told Bert that her sister Jean Rome, who was two years older, had worked as a stenographer, too, at a shipping company but had married young to a ship's captain named William Brown Rome, who was in charge of great vessels for the Cunard Line such as the *Tuscania*. Jean travelled often between a home in Glasgow and

New York with her boy Billy. Sometimes Katherine went, too. They were very close and sometimes, because their surnames were so similar, people called her Katherine Rome. She loved travelling and hoped to visit Britain again, soon. They had just met, but Katherine would linger like a love song in Bert's head, and no matter where he went the tune stayed with him.

Chapter 17

Bert Hinkler had a natural gift for flying. He did not seem to fly the machine but rather to be actually part of it. Just as the legs of a trained athlete obey his brain, so the wings of an aeroplane answered Hinkler's instinctive control. He was a master one could not hope to copy, but to fly with him, as I did, gave an insight into the ways of a pilot who was undoubtedly a genius.

John Leeming, Lancashire Aero Club
chairman and record-breaking pilot

Bert returned to The Nest from New York on 8 November 1925 aboard the Red Star liner SS *Lapland*. Although Katherine had made an indelible mark on his heart, he did not outwardly show it as life with Nance returned to normal. They went ahead with their new home on the Thornhill estate and, on 9 December 1925, the day after his thirty-third birthday, Bert submitted plans for the construction of the two-storey detached cottage of brick, Baltic pine, European red wood and a Welsh slate roof on Nance's one-acre allotment. It was given the street address of 29 Lydgate Road. H.W. Small, a builder in Bitterne, turned the first sod on 15 January 1926. In Italy Prime Minister Mussolini was also getting his house in order, and on 23 January he became the head of Italian aviation, taking over the ministry of the air as well as the portfolios of foreign affairs, army and navy.

Throughout 1926, while a team of workers carted in the bricks, cement render and glass for the new Hinkler house, Bert was almost always up in the air testing and delivering the new Avro machines and working on the new helicopter-like autogyros Avro was developing in conjunction with the Spanish engineer Juan de la Cierva. He also had the hope that Katherine would visit her relatives in Scotland before long.

He still had time to be the dutiful husband for Nance, in practice if not name. Early in March 1926 they attended the Ideal Home Exhibition at London's Olympia together like a couple of newlyweds looking at the latest furniture and gadgets to equip their Thornhill home. They bought a long, white enamel tub for the upstairs bathroom where Bert could stretch out and relax after a long day covered in oil splashes and windburn. Bert wrote home to his parents that he and Nance were so excited by all the wonderful displays of the latest wood stove kettles and gas cookers that their legs worked overtime and grew weary long before their 'peepers'. On some weekends he and Nance, together with their Scotch terrier Rufus, would drive in the Willys through the night to visit Nance's mother at Royston in Yorkshire and finish the weekend by driving back with her through the night down the Great North Road to The Nest. It helped prepare Bert for the long journeys into night that lay ahead.

On 16 April 1926, five days before George V celebrated the birth of a granddaughter named Elizabeth, Bert was at Avro's aerodrome at Woodford on the outskirts of Manchester for the presentation of a 504 Gosport to the Lancashire Aero Club. He gave demonstrations of the aircraft's speed and manoeuvrability, taking up the club's young chairman John Leeming as his rather terrified passenger. Leeming almost threw up as Bert rolled and dived his aircraft as if it was a rollercoaster off its rails. The festivities finished with a mock bombing of a model Arab fort by a posse of the new de Havilland Moths with sacks of flour being aimed at Boy Scouts dressed as Arabs pretending to pray to Allah. Apparently it was quite a hoot.[1]

The last window was put into place on the Hinklers' new home on 7 June and, never one to waste a penny, Avro's chief test pilot filed a claim for a £100 new home subsidy grant four days later. He and Nance talked over a name for the idyllic country home, and in the end there was just one that was fitting, 'Mon Repos', the place of rest where Bert's love of flying had taken root half a world away. They had a plaque painted with the name and hung it beside the front door. A neighbouring farm provided them with fresh milk and eggs. Avro's coppersmith John Dunkerton gave them a copper kettle for Nance to keep in her state-of-the-art kitchen where she would prepare morning tea for the many visitors, especially Roy Chadwick, who would occupy the sitting room for hours discussing aviation with her man. Bert also acquired a smart Riley car, and he built a driveway of brick rubble through the copse to the house with his great friend Jim Laver.

But there was a nagging sense of unease around Bert, and only part of it was the desire to see Katherine again.

The great long-distance solo flight to Bundaberg was never out of Bert's mind, and he even tried in vain to persuade the Borough Council Works Committee to name a new Thornhill street after a village near Bundaberg called Woongarra, an Aboriginal word for sleeping place. Bert was still wrestling with the feasibility of a flight to Australia when Alan Cobham, de Havilland's chief pilot and Bert's constant rival in all the British air races, cut Bert's nerves red raw.

On 26 June, Bert had test flown the Avenger, a Roy Chadwick-designed, all-metal biplane that Avro believed would be the fastest fighter plane in the world at 290 kilometres per hour. Just four days later, as Bert was still getting used to his new home, Cobham and his mechanic Arthur Elliott left the River Medway at Rochester near London under the power of their DH.50's 385 horsepower Armstrong Siddeley Jaguar engine with the intention of flying to Australia and back to survey air routes.

Cobham, seventeen months younger than Bert, became a veterinary sergeant in charge of horses during the war in France, then thumbed his nose at a lack of formal education to finish the conflict as an RAF flying instructor. After winning the 1924 King's Cup he and Elliott had flown from Croydon to Rangoon, Burma, with Britain's Director of Civil Aviation, Sir Sefton Brancker, and had then surveyed another route between Croydon and Cape Town. For the flight to Australia, their aircraft was fitted with steel floats because Cobham believed that the facilities for land planes were totally inadequate between Calcutta and Darwin.

A lack of suitable landing fields was really the least of their concerns, however. Cobham and Elliott ran into a mess that no one anticipated on 6 July while flying in temperatures higher than 40 degrees Celsius across the 800 kilometres from Baghdad to Bushire (now called Bushehr) on the Persian Gulf. They took off from the Tigris River, with Cobham at the controls and Elliott inside the four-berth passenger cabin. A raging sandstorm forced Cobham to bring the machine down to just 15 metres and, at one stage, to land on the Euphrates River. He and Elliott made another take-off and were about 190 kilometres from Basra, still flying low because of all the dust, when over the roar of the engine Cobham heard an explosion. He looked back through the cabin porthole and saw Elliott's face ashen and blood spurting from his arm and chest. A bullet from a Bedouin rifle had torn through the fabric of the fuselage, gone through a parcel of photographs of the drawn Second Ashes cricket Test from Lord's bound for Australian newspapers, burst a petrol pipe, ripped through Elliott's arm, broken one of his ribs, blew apart his left lung and lodged in his back. Cobham was aghast. With the dust storm having kicked up again, the DH.50 leaking petrol and Elliott gushing blood, he flogged every one of the 177 kilometres per hour he could get out of the aircraft until they reached the British air base at Basra. Cobham beached his machine on the Shatt al-Arab waterway, screamed for help and some locals waded into the water to put his wounded mate onto an improvised stretcher. Elliott underwent surgery but died the following night.[2]

Although Cobham was so distraught that he wanted to fly home, Sergeant Alan Ward, an RAF engineer stationed at Basra, said he could handle the DH.50's big engine. So, a week after Elliott's death, Cobham and his new mechanic were on their way to Darwin. They arrived three weeks later, on 5 August, beet red from the sun. They spent the next two days telling terrifying stories about enormous dragons with claws that could eat horses. They had seen the huge beasts breathing smoke-like fumes on an island in the East Indies called Komodo.[3] The floats on the DH.50 were replaced with wheels and by the time Cobham and Ward neared Melbourne on 15 August public interest in their flight had reached a frenzy. The city experienced one of its first traffic jams as cars clogged all roads to the Essendon Aerodrome. By the early afternoon an estimated 150,000 jostling, cheering Melburnians, said to be the biggest crowd the city had ever seen, wrestled each other for the best vantage point as just forty police officers tried to hold them back. When Cobham and Ward touched down the huge crowd pushed past and, in many cases, knocked over the constabulary and charged onto the landing ground like excited football fans after a nail-biting Grand Final. Many barely avoided the whizzing propeller. Women and children were crushed by the charging hordes. Many of the police used their fists to subdue the unruly masses as a group of RAAF men ran to protect Cobham and carried him shoulder high to the safety of the aerodrome's reception room. In the end the only fatality was a quail, killed by Cobham's propeller. Its headless body was taken home as a souvenir by a policeman.[4]

After a month of celebrations in Australia, Cobham and Ward left Darwin on 4 September for a comparatively uneventful return journey to complete a round trip that had extended to more than 44,000 kilometres. By the time Cobham, dressed in a suit and tie, brought the DH.50 down on the Thames near the Houses of Parliament on 1 October 1926, his knighthood was just days away.

While Cobham and Ward had been flying into history Bert had flown a Gosport from Manchester down to Croydon to demonstrate its capabilities for foreign air attachés and gone to Bournemouth for yet another aerial show, giving the crowd what *Flight* said was 'a really thrilling exhibition of stunt flying. [Bert Hinkler] executed some of the slowest rolls we have ever seen, without, apparently, the slightest effort. He also did some remarkable "autogyring", at times hovering almost motionless over one spot'.[5]

But no amount of flying around England though could ease Bert's longing to reach Australia. His spirits lifted in September with the arrival of Roy Chadwick's latest masterpiece, a small two-seat, wood and fabric biplane called the Avro 581 Avian with a five-cylinder, 75-horsepower Armstrong Siddeley Genet engine. Bert flew it in the *Daily Mail*'s two-seater light aeroplane competition at Lympne. It was just the light, economical machine to rival the de Havilland Moths. Bert's Avian, registered as G-EBOV, was a joy to handle, but at Lympne it sprang a leak in the petrol tank. Although the mechanics patched it up by plastering the tank with cakes of soap, they couldn't stop Bert from being eliminated when he broke a magneto spindle.[6] On 18 September, at Lympne, Bert won 200 guineas flying the patched-up Avian in a handicap race organised by the Society of Motor Manufacturers and Traders. At Bert's suggestion some adjustments were made, the engine was worked on, the rudder altered and the wingspan reduced from 9.75 metres to 7.92 metres to make it quicker. Bert also fitted the Avian with a metal Fairey-Reed propeller from a Westland Woodpigeon and demonstrated the all-new Avian package to a crowd of 20,000 at the Lancashire Air Pageant.

Across the Atlantic the long-distance achievements of Bert in the Avro Baby and more latterly by Cobham had reignited interest in Raymond Orteig's $25,000 prize for a flight from New York to Paris. Although the Atlantic had now been crossed several times, no one had yet flown from the USA to the European mainland non-stop. For seven years Orteig's challenge had proved too daunting. The massive amount of fuel needed for the journey meant that just getting off the ground was a dice with death, and the costs of mounting an attempt were usually far greater than the prize. From late 1926, however, there was renewed interest, and a number of flyers said they were willing to risk their lives to make the crossing.

Even young Charles Lindbergh, the most unlikely of candidates, wanted to give it a go. After a year of military flight training in San Antonio, Texas, which saw him nearly killed when he collided with another Army SE.5, he had been working since October 1925 for Robertson Aircraft Corporation out of St Louis, Missouri, delivering the US Mail between there and Chicago. Lindbergh was flying the same sort of de Havilland DH.4s Bert had learned to fly on with Charles Sproatt. He liked to fly at night because he believed it sharpened his skills, and he was tested frequently by bad weather and unpredictable machines. The early air mail planes were given the nickname 'Flaming Coffins' and on 16 September 1926, Lindbergh was forced to escape his machine in a parachute near the town of Wedron, 96 kilometres southwest of Chicago.

Other flyers seemed much more likely to claim the $25,000 prize. Five days after Lindbergh and his parachute landed next to his wrecked machine and some sacks of undelivered mail in a farmer's field, the diminutive French fighter ace René Fonck took the controls of his 30-metre-wide, three-engine S.35 biplane in New York. The machine was designed by Igor Sikorsky, who had left Russia for a new life in the USA. As Fonck revved the engines at 6 a.m. he was confident that he and his three crew members would be in Paris the next day, and they gleefully loaded the $100,000 machine with luggage and gifts. Along with more than 10,000 litres of petrol, the S.35 was about 4500 kilograms over its suggested take-off weight. A thousand people were at Roosevelt Field as the plane gathered speed down the runway. The S.35 hadn't gone far when a wheel came loose, and the plane crashed into a gully and burst into flames. Fonck and his co-pilot managed to jump to safety, but radio operator Charles Clavier and mechanic Jacob Islamoff were incinerated.[7]

The incident was still making headlines around the world when Bert received the news that his grandfather James Edmund Bonney had died in Bundaberg Hospital on 2 October. Bert consoled himself and his mother with the notion that at eighty-nine, old grandpapa had enjoyed a good innings. Bert hoped that he could live as long, and he planned to, even though he was presented with a new and unique challenge by Avro. This scheme of unprecedented risk was hatched by two of the most important aviation identities in Britain at Chez Victor, a fashionable club off London's Bond Street. The imperious Sefton Brancker and his young guest John Leeming, from the Lancashire Aero Club, had been discussing plans to build Britain's first purpose-built municipal aerodrome in Manchester when Brancker dropped the idea for a 'propaganda' flight.

Leeming had been enjoying the brandy so much that he wasn't thinking straight when Brancker, stroking his moustache and flashing his monocle, said the best publicity for aviation's safety was to land a plane on a seemingly impossible location. Like a mountain, for instance. Yes, Brancker declared, raising a glass to his lips, 'What a shot in the arm for British aviation if you could land an aircraft on a mountain, then take off again and land at Manchester. Even the worst of those bally sceptics would be won over.' Leeming's head was still spinning a few days later when he realised that Brancker had spoken to the press and there were newspaper reports announcing that Leeming would attempt to land an aircraft on Helvellyn, at 950 metres the highest point in the English Lake District, and a favourite place of inspiration for the poet William Wordsworth.

Leeming, who'd made a small fortune from recycling oily rags, wondered how the hell he'd let himself be roped into this lunacy. Realising that he was boxed in, Leeming decided that if he was going to risk his life Bert was the best man to train him for the stunt and to partner him on the journey, especially after he'd given the rich young businessman his rollercoaster ride a few months earlier. Bert was eager to attempt the flight because landing on a British mountain was something that not even Sir Alan Cobham had achieved. So Bert flew up to Woodford to test a new Gosport fitted with an experimental 100-horsepower Alpha radial engine, which Leeming was to fly. The days blurred into weeks as Bert made short take-offs, short flights, short landings, testing, testing, and readjusting. He tried to reassure the always-anxious Leeming that he'd had a good look at Helvellyn and there was nothing to worry about.

Leeming's friends also tried to dispel his fears and assured him that the top of Helvellyn was a plateau as flat as a billiard table. Leeming wanted to find out for himself. At just thirty he was already enjoying sedentary bliss, and Wordsworth's love of the outdoors was something he didn't share, often remarking that mankind had not been given legs to misuse with exercise. Nevertheless he and a friend decided to climb to Helvellyn's summit and see the tiny landing patch for themselves only to quickly end up red-faced and wheezing, crying out for a good lie down and likening the whole, agonising experience to that endured by Scott of the Antarctic. Leeming said he suffered more actual pain and physical misery on that climb than at any time in his life.

When he finally made it to the top the summit was indeed as flat as a billiard table but, as his eyes widened, he realised that it was also about the same size. He wanted to cancel the whole blasted nonsense then and there but felt he would die from the public ridicule if he did, regardless of the fact that he could also die in a smashed aircraft on a snowy mountain.

'Hinkler sensed the deterioration that was taking place in myself, and rallied around like the good friend he was,' Leeming recalled,[8] remembering how Bert encouraged him to 'just keep flying' to steady his nerves, practise his landings and take-offs and even try some stunts over Woodford to assure himself that he and the machine could do the job. Bert pegged down a newspaper on the runway and, in their dual-controlled machine, took turns with Leeming at seeing who could land closest to it. It was a trick Bert often practised at Hamble, touching a handkerchief on the airstrip with one wheel and then coming back to touch it with the other. To Leeming the practice, reassurance and eye for detail were invaluable.

'I remember how [Bert] once said: "Every landing is a forced landing. Every time I land I pretend I haven't got an engine."'[9]

Across in Chicago Lindbergh was finding out what it was like to land without a plane. On 3 November, just six weeks after his previous crash, he bailed out of another 'flaming coffin' in the dead of night near Bloomington, Illinois.

Bert and Leeming were ready to attack Helvellyn in two planes on 8 December, but they had to wait a week for the weather to improve. The *Manchester Guardian* made the flight front-page news and asked Bert to take up their best photographer with him. Leeming feared that it would be to photograph the wreckage of his machine and his mutilated corpse on the side of the mountain. Nevertheless on 15 December the two planes took off, Leeming flying solo and Bert with the photographer. The winter sun shone brilliantly over snow-white fields, but the patches of mist soon turned to fog. Before long the sky was the colour of lentil soup and the planes were being bombarded by hailstones. The planes climbed higher into the storm but hit perilous vacuums of air pockets that forced their rapid descent. One of Leeming's wings dropped as though some great weight had been suddenly hurled onto it, and his machine yo-yoed all over as though being assaulted by monstrous, invisible fists. Leeming wasn't waiting around for more. He pushed the Avro up and over the green scummy stormclouds and headed for Manchester. Bert took the hint and went with him.

It wasn't until 21 December that a fine weather report allowed them to try again, but Bert's Gosport wouldn't start. Bert and Leeming decided to go it alone in the one plane and leave their disgruntled photographer behind. Official watchers had already set out from the village of Wythburn to verify the landing on the summit. By the time the flyers reached Lancaster, ice was forming on their wings and a gale was starting to blow. They were within a mile of Helvellyn but, although they flew towards it at nearly 160 kilometres per hour, the wind rushing back to meet them was so strong it felt as if the Gosport was stationary. Both men knew trying to land in that wind meant certain death. So they headed back to Lancaster. Leeming wanted Bert to stay the night in a hotel and leave the Gosport overnight to make an attempt first thing in the morning, but Bert insisted that the open field was no place for an Avro in the middle of winter so the two climbed on board to go back to Manchester.

Bert was at the controls. Leeming later said that if he'd been flying they would have both been dead. The Gosport had risen just six metres when the engine died. A bank of telephone wires was right in front of them. Bert acted instantly, pushing the nose down and swinging around in a vertical turn back towards the wind. A fraction of misjudgement or the slightest hesitation and they would have crashed. Instead Bert made a perfect landing.

Bert inspected the engine and found sediment in the carburettor. It was too late to fix the problem properly so they borrowed some sacks from a nearby farm and covered the Gosport as best they could, then set off on an excruciating five kilometre foot-slog to the nearest hotel, in the freezing dark with a wind of 60 kilometres per hour blowing them backwards at times. They tried to stop some passing cars to hitch a ride but were nearly run over. Leeming moaned the whole way, and when they finally arrived at the nearest inn they were cold, hungry, dishevelled, devoid of luggage and dressed in clothes splattered with snowy muck and oil. 'To complete our discomfort,' Leeming recalled, 'both of us had lost our handkerchiefs and we had no cigarettes.'

The hotel manager eyed them suspiciously as the two flyers sat down for a steak dinner. Halfway through their hearty meal both felt sick. They both realised they'd left their wallets behind. Bert seemed more worried about this predicament than anything that had happened in the Gosport and quickly calculated the cost of the two steak dinners, two bedrooms, baths and breakfasts. And oil and repairs. 'And don't forget a taxi back to the Gosport, too,' Leeming said. 'I'm not walking back there again.'

Bert had a sleepless night fretting over the financial dilemma and, as Leeming was getting dressed the next morning, Bert kept knocking on his door to whisper advice on the best way to approach the hotel manager. Bert was so concerned that he was totally disinterested in the various scathing newspaper reports about their failure to conquer Helvellyn that Leeming was reading over breakfast. As Leeming chewed on his toast he told Bert to keep his trap shut and that he'd handle the manager.

Leeming sipped the rest of his tea, tut-tutted about the bally press reports then, with Bert close behind, went to explain their rather odd spot of bother to the hotel manager, which he tried with a 'Now, see here my good man'. Instead of being impressed by Leeming's pomp, the manager mentioned something about fraud being an indictable offence.

Bert then jumped in with a rambling, stammering account of their flight the previous day, and about

Helvellyn and Gosports and Avros and air pockets and wind drift and horsepower. He finally blurted out that not only did they not have the money for their rooms and board but also they'd like a loan of two pounds please, so that they could get back to Manchester. The manager said he was calling the police. Leeming had a few pennies in his pocket and as a last resort made a call to the local Atkinson's garage, told the owner that there was a £1500 Avro Gosport parked in a nearby field that needed urgent repairs, told them who he was and how much he was worth, asked the garage man to settle their hotel bill, then asked for a loan of not two but three pounds with the promise that it would all be repaid with interest. To Bert's amazement, the garage man couldn't get there quick enough.

Leeming turned on his heel and told the hotel manager that he wouldn't be staying in this rather rummy establishment again. And by the way, no tip. Bert, who had avoided a near fatal crash without the slightest sign of emotion the day before, mopped his sweaty brow as they were leaving and said that the whole bally hotel business was the closest call he'd had in years. 'I'm all shaking,' he told Leeming.

After the mechanics fitted new spark plugs and filters Bert and Leeming decided to have another crack at the mountain since the visibility was good and the wind was a manageable 48 kilometres per hour. There would be no official watchers to record the event, but Bert had his pocket camera to prove they'd done it.

Once airborne, visibility went from good to excellent as Bert in the front cockpit and Leeming working the controls surveyed all before them, the brown and purple hilltops, the green fields and darker green of the pine forests, the flashes of snow and the silvery lakes and rivers. All was going smoothly until they arrived over Newby Bridge later. The engine began to cough as though it had TB. The machine came good but, five minutes later, when they started to follow the sliver of Lake Windermere at Bowness, the engine started to wheeze and splutter again. Bert pointed to a small patch of green and Leeming froze. There was no way he could land on that. Then the engine died. Bert had cut the throttle.

'Leave it to me,' Bert shouted, and in a long series of S-bends he brought the Gosport down gently onto a tiny playing field at a children's sanatorium. 'Nothing to worry about,' Bert said as he climbed out, 'just some more dirt in the petrol filters.' Bert cleaned them quickly and, with a tiny field to negotiate, got the Gosport back in the air before handing the controls to Leeming once they were on their way to Helvellyn and well clear of sharp obstacles. When they were 1200 metres over Grasmere more air pockets pushed Leeming's seat belt deep into his flesh and sent Bert bouncing so high that his seat cushion flew out of the cockpit. Even in the rough, treacherous weather with both their lives on the line Bert still let Leeming control the plane because he knew how much landing on Helvellyn meant to him.

Then, as they neared the summit, not only did the bumps stop but also they saw a mountain climber, an eyewitness, near a cairn of stones on the plateau. It was a double bonus. A strong wind brought the landing speed down to just 24 kilometres per hour and, concentrating so hard he thought his brain would pop, Leeming made the Gosport touch down. It came to an almost immediate halt 27 metres from the edge of a precipice above a 150-metre drop. Bert turned around to give Leeming the thumbs up, but they had landed facing upwards on a slight slope. Before they knew it the Gosport started rolling backwards, pushed by the wind. Leeming leapt out and put stones behind the wheels and was soon joined by the mountain climber, who turned out to be the esteemed Irish scholar E.R. Dodds, professor of Greek at Birmingham University. Leeming produced a bill from a pocket and Dodds, pressing it against the Gosport's wing for support, wrote: 'I hereby certify that an aeroplane, GEBPH, pilots Bert Hinkler and John Leeming, has landed on the summit of Helvellyn on Dec. 22, 1926.' They took some photos as further proof.

Then came the tricky part: getting off the mountain. Leeming only had about 25 metres before they hit the precipice, and they couldn't let the Gosport roll back down the slope any further to give them more room or there'd be no chance of stopping it. So Bert paced out the runway and told Leeming to throttle the hell out of the engine and pray that the machine was airborne by the time it reached the edge. Instead of taking the controls himself and making sure of the job Bert let Leeming loose on a take-off that could kill them both. They shook hands with the professor who wished them luck, because they'd need all they could get, then the two pilots climbed into their machine. Bert turned around from the front cockpit to give Leeming the nod, Leeming opened the throttle as far as it would go and the machine rattled along the rocky surface, bumping and thumping as it gained speed. Four metres from the edge the wheels were still on the rocky ground, and Leeming's heart was going like the Dickens. The great chasm yawned in front of them like an open grave. The Gosport's wheels touched the precipice and the nose dipped towards the jagged rocks below. Then, as though some mighty hand had caught them, the Gosport lifted with a great surge as Leeming and Bert rose towards the clouds and headed home. In the front cockpit Bert turned around and gave Leeming a thumbs up. He didn't need to say a word.

In later years Leeming would look back on the best day of his life and always remember how Bert whistled a tune called 'Brown Eyes' as he prepared the Gosport's engine for that final ascent. 'I hear that tune sometimes,' Leeming wrote years later, 'and it never fails to bring back a picture of those days before Helvellyn — and Bert Hinkler: Bert, the best pilot I ever knew, the cheeriest of sportsmen, who went his way quietly getting on with his job, unassuming and unafraid.'[10]

Chapter 18

*What kind of man would live where there is no danger?
I don't believe in taking foolish chances. But nothing
can be accomplished by not taking a chance at all.*
Charles Lindbergh, transatlantic aviator

*Bert Hinkler and Charles Lindbergh were soul mates.
They were the pioneers of aircraft development by
opening up new routes. As a pilot Hinkler would
have been the equal or better than Lindbergh
because Hinkler's technical skills were wonderful.*
Lang Kidby, Australian adventurer and solo flyer, 2011

The Gosport had been just the plane for the Helvellyn
landing, and the Avian was just the machine Bert was
looking for to make the flight to Australia, especially after
the Genet engine was replaced with a more reliable four-
cylinder Cirrus II from Airdisco, the Aircraft Disposal
Company.

Bert wanted to get back to Australia as soon as possible
to see his father, who'd been crippled with arthritis for
years and whose health was in sharp decline. He began

experimenting with the design of the Avian — the size and shape of the wings, the rudder, the set-up of the undercarriage, the size of the fuel tanks and the propeller — making modifications that he believed would allow him to fly for 1600 kilometres a day for two weeks on end. Soon word spread about the changes Bert was making, and before long the news reached Australia with newspapers reporting on Monday, 21 February 1927, that Bert was making plans to fly a two-seater plane to Australia. Long-distance flights had become a craze. Cobham was gearing up to circumnavigate Africa, de Pinedo had left Rome for Buenos Aires and US Navy officer Richard E. Byrd, who'd claimed a flight over the North Pole a year before — although many did not believe him — was chasing the Orteig prize with the backing of department store magnate Rodman Wanamaker.

Avro decided that as Bert had so much work at Hamble they would hire Captain Sam Brown, who'd spent the previous six years teaching Spanish naval pilots in Barcelona, to look after all the machines coming out of the Manchester factory. When Bert's contract with Avro ended in 1926 he did not leave on happy terms. He went freelance, testing Avro's Hamble machines but also picking up work from other manufacturers.

Much had changed over the years, and Avro was more than ever just one piece of a larger company that Crossley was about to sell to Armstrong Siddeley. Alliott Verdon-Roe would soon resign from the company he had founded to form Saunders-Roe with a base on the Isle of Wight. Bert did not have enough of a head for business to follow all the mergers, share sales and company politics. He saw his future emulating the likes of the great distance flyers, and the papers reported that he was planning to move back to

Australia with his wife. Bert had still not married Nance, but he was no longer so secretive about their life together and proudly called her his wife at every opportunity. The papers quoted Bert saying: 'There is no better way of going home than by flying', and that he planned to make twelve-hour hops each day in the Avian over a shorter, more direct route to Australia than Cobham's.[1]

The news reports picked up momentum, saying that it was 'fairly definite that he would start the journey in the first week of April',[2] Messers C.C. Wakefield & Co. Ltd, manufacturers of Castrol motor oil, were laying down supplies at his landing points at Darwin, Newcastle Waters, Cloncurry, Longreach, Bundaberg, Brisbane and Sydney,[3] and he was about to make the most daring flight yet undertaken to Australia in a silver machine that looked for all the world like a big streamlined flying fish.[4] Bert planned to give the Avian a thorough long-distance test on 29 March 1927 leaving Croydon for a day's flying that would take him almost 1700 kilometres around Britain in eleven hours.[5] He had enclosed the front cockpit and converted its passenger seat, a hollowed-out metal drum, to use as a 210-litre additional fuel tank. With the 90-litre tank already fitted into the centre section of the top wing, the Avian could fly 2900 kilometres without refuelling. Rain and wind sunk his plans to test the Avian on 29 March, but Bundaberg was fully expecting him to start for Australia soon. Mayor William Gavegan cabled the city's best wishes to Bert, who sent a reply back saying, 'Greatly appreciate your good wishes. Press announcements rather premature. Departure date yet unfixed.'

In New York, Richard E. Byrd was having plenty of his own problems with the $100,000 Fokker C-2 monoplane named *America* that he intended for Paris and the $25,000 Orteig prize. In a test fight at New Jersey's Teterboro airport on 16 April, with the designer Anthony Fokker at the controls, the C-2 crashed on landing. Fokker escaped without a scratch, but Byrd suffered a broken wrist and his co-pilot suffered a broken collarbone, broken leg, dislocated shoulder and serious head injuries. Ten days later two other Orteig prize hopefuls, American naval pilots Lieutenant Commander Noel Davis and Lieutenant Stanton Wooster, died when their big yellow Keystone Pathfinder tri-motor crashed on a test flight at Langley Field, Virginia.

For Bert, the British aerial racing circuit was just as dangerous, and the meeting over the 1927 Easter Weekend at Bournemouth's Ensbury Park presented a whole new peril in the shape of Trelawney Dayrell Reed Esq, a big red-bearded ruddy-faced local. Incensed by the noise of aircraft upsetting him and his livestock, Reed fired both barrels of his favourite grouse gun at a Blackburn Bluebird being flown by Scruffy Longton, now a squadron leader. Remembering how Arthur Elliott had died from gunfire near Basra, Longton brought the Bluebird down in a hurry to find forty-eight small holes in his lower wing.[6] Bert immediately flew off in the Avian to find the culprit, ignoring the fact that he might be shot as well. Reed later beat a charge 'feloniously, and of malice aforethought shooting with intent to kill and murder', saying he hadn't meant to hurt anyone, just to stop the blasted noise.[7]

Bert and the Avian won three of the races that weekend — the Killjoy Cup, the Hotels Handicap and Holiday Handicap — but, more importantly to him, he also demonstrated that his aeroplane was as versatile as a car, flying home the 65 kilometres to Mon Repos every night after the racing rather than stay in accommodation at the airfield.

Work still stalled his plans to fly to Australia, and for much of the first half of 1927 he was testing autogyros, surviving one crash when the hovering mechanism failed and he and his passenger came down from 75 metres. Bert made sure the passenger was unhurt, but his own head was swathed in bandages when he emerged an hour later from the hangar to demonstrate the autogyro again.

In April 1927 he acquired the Avian from Avro having really only flown it on loan until then. He knew that, if he was to fly to Australia solo, he would have to service the 85 horsepower engine himself in remote areas and began modifying it with what Roy Chadwick remembered was 'his usual ingenuity'. 'Hinkler suggested an alteration to the undercarriage arrangement which would enable the machine to be easily lowered so that he could work on the engine without the use of ladders or trestles,' Chadwick recalled. 'I worked out this idea for him and it was incorporated and worked very well. Numerous little gadgets were produced by Hinkler to facilitate servicing of his machine. Many of these devices he made himself and neatly stowed in the cockpit and the locker of the Avian.'[8]

When parked the wings of the Avian could be folded back by removing quick-release bolts. As the wings came back the wheels spread out, lowering the engine so that Bert could make repairs as though he were merely lifting the bonnet of his car. With the wings folded it was also easier to wheel the machine around by hand. The idea was such a hit that Bert eventually patented it. The wider track of the new undercarriage softened the landings on rough surfaces. Bert replaced the original circular rudder with a triangular fin and finally settled on a wingspan of nine metres with curved tips. He installed a compartment behind the pilot's seat to house an inflatable boat and paddles just in case.

Halfway around the world in San Diego, in a converted cannery that still smelled of fish, Lindbergh was also making modifications to a new plane. Somehow, despite his crashes and a quiet, unassuming manner not unlike Bert's, he'd managed to persuade a consortium of St Louis businessmen to sponsor his attempt at the Orteig prize. Lindbergh had left his job on the mail run in February 1927 and travelled to San Diego to oversee the design and construction of a plane he named *Spirit of St Louis*.

The Ryan Aeronautical Company was just about the only manufacturer that didn't laugh at Lindbergh's request to build him a machine capable of flying across the Atlantic. Their designer, Donald A. Hall, believed that it could be done by reshaping a Ryan M-2, a mail delivery aircraft with an enclosed cabin, into what would basically be a flying petrol tank. Lindbergh believed that a small, single-seat monoplane with the ever-reliable nine-cylinder Wright J-5C Whirlwind radial engine cranking out 223 horsepower had a much better chance than any of the monstrous multi-engine biplanes lining up for Orteig's money. With Lindbergh supervising, the Ryan team spent sixty days building the Ryan NYP (New York–Paris), increasing the wingspan from 11 to 14 metres and strengthening the undercarriage so that it could take the weight of 1700 litres of petrol weighing more than a tonne.

The main fuel tank was placed in the forward section of the fuselage between the engine and the pilot, meaning that Lindbergh would only be able to see out of side windows and, when he was on the ground, through a small periscope. His flying seat would be a wicker chair and the cockpit just 90 centimetres wide, 80 centimetres high and 1.3 metres long. He would not be able to stretch out his long legs. Lindbergh was adamant, though, that the vast open spaces of the Atlantic held no more terrors than the night mail run in bad weather around Chicago. This time he needed to save weight and would leave his parachute, radio and sextant at home. Five sandwiches and a few candy bars would be his only companions.

Lindbergh's aircraft cost $10,580 and flew for the first time at Dutch Flats in San Diego on 28 April, two days after Noel Davis and Stanton Wooster died. Before he left San Diego for New York to begin his transatlantic quest, Lindbergh asked the Ryan factory's owner, Benjamin Franklin Mahoney, how much the fare would cost him from Le Bourget airport into the city of Paris if he made it across the ocean.

While Lindbergh prepared to make his start, two Frenchmen thought they'd beat the Americans and make their crossing from Paris to New York. On 8 May World War I ace Charles Nungesser and co-pilot François Coli took off in a Levasseur PL-8 biplane, heading for the Big Apple. They were never seen again.

By mid-May 1927, Bert had another reason to delay his flight home. Britain's Schneider Trophy team had bypassed their own specialist pilots at RAF High Speed Flight in Felixstowe and asked him to test the Short Crusader, the backup aircraft for their attempt to regain the trophy in Venice. Italy's Mario de Bernardi, heavily backed by Mussolini, had won it the previous year in Norfolk, Virginia, and the Italians were favoured to retain their title. In the end a Supermarine S.5 piloted by Sidney Webster took out first place, reaching a top speed of 453.281 kilometres per hour before 200,000 awestruck Italians lining the Lido, but Bert's involvement with the high-speed machines demonstrated his versatility in handling every type of aircraft Britain produced.

In Australia, the Hinkler and Bonney clans were thrilled to bits over his career. His aunt Beatrice Bonney reckoned Bert wanted to settle in Australia and, without him knowing about it, cut out a newspaper article about his work for the Schneider Trophy team and wrote to Major General William Glasgow, a graduate of One Mile State School, Gympie, who had become Minister for Defence after being an ardent proponent of the firing squad for deserters during the Great War. Aunt Beatrice told Glasgow she knew just the chap to be appointed Australia's next military aircraft expert, a lovely fellow and a wonderful aviator who had flown during the war in England, France and Italy and could send a machine whizzing around at 400 kilometres per hour for Britain's racing team. Five days later Glasgow wrote back to say that he wasn't sure what position Aunt Beatrice was talking about but that, if 'Mr Hinkler' was interested in a position with the Australian military, he should submit an application and it would be given due consideration.

In May 1927, however, Bert had other things on his mind. He unveiled the Avian's new undercarriage at the Hampshire Air Pageant in Hamble and kept an eye fixed on all the British newspapers for news of the Orteig prize. He didn't have to wait long. With six men having already been killed trying to win it, and after a nervous, sleepless night, Lindbergh rose at Roosevelt Field on the gloomy morning of 20 May. Success or death awaited. Many of the 500 spectators that morning expected to see a man commit suicide, and newspapers were calling the gangly youngster 'the flying fool'. In the wind and the rain his *Spirit of St Louis* was towed by hand from its hangar onto the grass runway made soggy by overnight rain. The total weight of man and machine was 2327 kilograms, and just getting it in the air would be a remarkable feat, let alone flying almost 6000 kilometres before he saw the Eiffel Tower — if, in fact, he could see it through that narrow porthole on the side of the aircraft. 'When I enter the cockpit,' he said, 'it's like going into the death chamber. When I step out at Paris it will be like getting a pardon from the governor.'[9]

Lindbergh said goodbye to his mother and at 7.51 a.m., with the Wright Whirlwind engine buzzing, the chocks were pulled away. The field was so soggy that the machine hardly budged so spectators were called in to give Lindbergh a push. He moved off at 7.52 and struggled along the sodden runway as if he was driving through rubber, the weight of all the petrol straining the reinforced landing gear. He bounced up and came back down and finally bounced into the air and stayed there, passing over the telephone wires at the end of the runway by a mere six metres. He lumbered along towards Long Island Sound on his way to Cape Cod and Nova Scotia, skirting the coast of Newfoundland, the last piece of earth he expected to see before Ireland.

Before long the turbulence became so violent that Lindbergh was afraid the wings would snap with all the twisting and bending, but he battled on through a thunderstorm. Shortly after leaving Newfoundland, he began to see icebergs and within an hour was at 3000 metres flying over storm clouds. Sometimes the fog would force him down to three metres above the Atlantic waves. He was cramped and tired and all alone. Soon he was so weary that his eyes felt as hard and dry as stones. He was afraid that if he closed them for a moment he would go the same way as Nungesser and Coli. He stamped on the floorboards and flexed the muscles in his arms and legs. He screamed at himself to stay awake and punched himself hard. As he journeyed into the night his eyelids felt like tonne weights, and he had to keep them open forcibly with his thumb. Death was waiting if he didn't press on.

After twenty hours flying, a dreamy calm floated over him, and he felt at peace. He punched himself again, harder. After twenty-eight hours cramped, cold and alone he saw land through the porthole. Or thought he did. Was it a mirage? He blinked hard and stared at it. It *was* land. The west coast of Ireland at Dingle Bay. Lindbergh was only five kilometres off course and two and a half hours ahead of schedule.

The crowds began to gather at Le Bourget early on 21 May with the news that Lindbergh was coming, although he was still hours away. He crossed southwestern England and the Channel and followed the Seine to Paris, where he circled the city before recognising the airfield. By the time his machine reached the lit runway at 10.22 p.m., Lindberg had been flying for 33 hours, 30 minutes and 29.9 seconds. He was not sure how much longer he could have lasted. Seeing Le Bourget, he said, made him know how the dead would feel to live again. A crowd of Parisians estimated at between 100,000 and 150,000 shouting: '*Vive Lindbergh*' and '*Vive l'Américain*' were at the aerodrome to see history. Not since the Armistice had there been scenes of such unbridled joy. Lindbergh, like Cobham in Melbourne, had to taxi through the huge crowd of people in ecstasy. He breathed a heavy sigh as he pulled up.

'Well, here we are. I am very happy,' he said, but before he knew what was happening Lindbergh was dragged out of the cockpit and carried shoulder high around the crowd for half an hour. Instantly, he had become the most famous man in the world. The $25,000 Orteig prize was small change. The *New York Herald Tribune* estimated that he'd earn a million dollars within a year from appearances, books and film deals. He wouldn't need to worry about the cab fare to the city of Paris after all.

Huge, adoring crowds followed Lindbergh everywhere as he paid his condolences to Nungesser's mother and dined with Blériot. From Paris, Lindbergh flew to Brussels for more adulation, then to Croydon on 30 May where another crowd estimated at 150,000 threatened to swallow him up. The next day Lindbergh packed up the Spirit for shipment back to New York, met the British Prime Minister Stanley Baldwin, was grilled by the King and Queen about every aspect of his journey and played with their granddaughter, the adorable Princess Elizabeth.

That night at a Savoy Hotel dinner organised by the captains of British aviation Lindbergh told his audience that the basic principle of navigation for the journey was simply to have enough fuel in case he was blown off course. For Bert, who had never been so focused in his life, the advice was just what he wanted to hear.[10]

As Lindbergh headed home on USS *Memphis*, for a reception that surpassed anything in American history,

Bert and his regular rivals on the air-racing circuit headed back to Bournemouth that week for the Whitsun meeting organised by the Royal Aero Club. Trelawney Reed and his shotgun had been subdued, but the Ensbury Park aerial circuit with its tight corners and bends presented more dangers than ever. On Saturday, 4 June, even before the races commenced, a DH.37 slammed into the scoreboard and killed a passenger, Claude St John Plevins. Two days later in the first race of Monday, 6 June, twelve machines took part and, after several almost collided on take-off, they screamed around the aerodrome in a bunch like duelling stock cars. A Westland Widgeon, flown by the honeymooning Major Lawrence P. Openshaw, flew past Bert's Avian. All the way around the course the machines narrowly avoided bumps and scrapes. Openshaw went past Hubert Broad's Moth and was rapidly gaining on the leaders when he and Scruffy Longton collided.

Fire devoured everything within minutes, and the two pilots' young wives witnessed them being consumed by the massive blaze. Remarkably, when the charred bodies were removed and the debris cleared away, the racing continued that afternoon and, two weeks later, Bert dominated the events at Filton Aerodrome in the Bristol and Wessex Aeroplane Club's first air pageant, winning the Utility and De Prez cups. Just as he had shielded his parents from the horrors of war a decade earlier Bert avoided the disasters of Bournemouth when he wrote home to 'My Darling Parents' from Manchester on 14 July.

> My luck, see how sorry I am that I have missed writing again for such a long time [he said]. Partly

because my plans are so unsettled and I have not been able to look even a month ahead. My latest experience is the testing of the Autogyro. No doubt you have read of this particular contraption. I am sending you some pictures so you will be able to see what it looks like. It certainly looks a bit of a curio. The inventor of the autogyro is Spanish and his name is la Cierva. I hope I am not saying too much when I tell you he seems awfully pleased with my flying of his machine.

Well I have not prepared my start for home and beauty yet. The blessed papers have made too big a story all too soon and sort of queered my pitch, so when it is quiet I'll just come toddling along.[11]

Bert's King's Cup assault in July 1927 was a fizzer. The new Alpha engine he'd used on Helvellyn wouldn't start in another Avian because of a crack in a carburettor. Captain Wally Hope was declared the winner, but not only did ten of the sixteen starters withdraw because of the handicaps they were given but two days before the event Frank Barnard, the winner in 1922 and 1925, was killed testing his Bristol Badminton.

It was just as dangerous in the big races in America where Hawaii's 'Pineapple King' James Dole offered $25,000 for the first civilian plane to fly from California to Honolulu. Three entrants were killed just getting ready for the race and, after about 100,000 people saw the start of the event at Oakland on 16 August, seven more, including the elfin school teacher Mildred Doran, would be lost over the Pacific during the next few days.

Still, aviation records were tumbling everywhere. Charles Kingsford Smith and Charles Ulm had flown a Bristol tourer around Australia in just tens days and five hours, halving the time of Brinsmead and his crew three years earlier. Bert had a mind to fly much further but needed to test the Avian on a significant journey. He was finally given the chance to take it a great distance on 27 August, although not south to Bundaberg, where he knew everyone, but east to the city of Riga in Latvia, where he knew no one and couldn't speak the language.

Nance had flown with Bert many times around England and she even called the Avian by a nickname, 'Liz', after the young Princess Elizabeth. This time, however, Bert would be flying solo, and Nance would have to get used to him being away from Mon Repos for long stretches that would strain their relationship. Bert had taken on a job for the Glasgow aircraft builders William Beardmore & Co., who were trying to sell their Beardmore WBs to the Latvian air force. Part of the deal was that Beardmore would provide a test pilot, and Bert figured that the quickest way to get to Riga was to fly the Avian there non-stop. All year he had hoped to entice a backer to sponsor his trip to Australia but, given the mortality rate among the world's elite flyers, it was hard going. Every door he knocked on gave him a knockback. He figured that another world-record solo flight might attract a benefactor and, with that in mind, he stayed at the hotel at Croydon Aerodrome overnight on 26 August, rising at 4.30 a.m. after a policeman woke him with a cup of tea.

Bert wanted to attract publicity as a dashing aviator, but he saw being in the public eye as a necessary evil, merely as a means to fund his enterprises. And he didn't like to make a noise until the job was done. He arrived at the aerodrome with no word to the press that he would be attempting a world-record flight, to surpass the records he set flying to Turin and Bundaberg.

With just a *Times Atlas* as his guide to the airways of Europe, aviation's international man of mystery headed out to Airdisco's Croydon hangars where the Avian was housed. Just as dawn was breaking he managed to persuade a sceptical nightwatchman to help him open the iron doors guarding his machine. Bert put 273 litres of petrol into the Avian's tanks — he wouldn't need any more — and casually wheeled her out of the cocoon. Bert had fitted a double-action pump of his own design to gravity-feed the engine and an extra oil sump to keep the workings lubricated with 23 litres of oil for long flights.

He had a light breakfast, bought a copy of the *Daily Express*, donned his leather helmet and goggles and warmed up the Cirrus engine, letting the four cylinders breathe. He took some long deep breaths himself as he prepared to fly into the great unknown. 'There were no spectators,' Bert wrote later. 'I had no record-breaking intentions as I was simply going about my business.'[12] At 5.42, he was racing down the Croydon runway, up, up and away.

Thirty-nine minutes later he was 1200 metres over Ramsgate on the coast of the English Channel. Almost before he knew it he had crossed the Channel and was over the sea wall called the Mole of Zeebrugge on the Belgian coast. He was forced down by heavy fog to just 30 metres over parts of Belgium, but the weather and his altitude had improved by 11.25 a.m. as he passed New Brandenburg in Germany. By the early afternoon he was looking down at sunbathers enjoying a beach at Swinemunde. As he approached the Free City of Danzig he took a wide berth, realising that it was no-fly zone, and headed into black storm clouds over the Baltic Sea. He aimed for Memel in East Prussia. He was over land in Lithuania again at 2.49 and sailing briskly at more than 160 kilometres per hour towards Riga. His *Times Atlas* had a scale of 50 miles to an inch (80.5 kilometres to 2.5 centimetres) and there was no aerodrome marked for Riga, but he figured it wouldn't be hard to find. With his legs painfully stiff from the confined space and his goggles feeling like a tonne weight on the bridge of his nose, it was a welcome relief when he saw a long stretch of grass that was Riga's Spilve Aerodrome five kilometres north of the city.[13]

He brought the machine down at 4.12 p.m. and wrote in his log that the flight's duration was ten and a half hours. He still had 91 litres of petrol left. The solo non-stop flight of more than 1900 kilometres was a milestone for the future of the light plane. The *Guardian*'s Major F.A. de V Robertson wrote, 'Nothing to compare with this non-stop flight of 1200 miles in a tiny aeroplane has ever been accomplished before. Hinkler's pluck is famous, and his exploits in comparative "dud" planes have proved him to be perhaps the world's most skilful pilot of the ordinary, common [aeroplane] such as the average citizen can afford to fly.' Bert had used just 182 litres of fuel at 48 kilometres (30 miles) to the gallon, and he still had 18 litres of oil remaining.

As he taxied the Avian towards a small collection of hangars, military officials dressed in both French and German helmets rushed out to meet him, none too happy about the unannounced and uninvited intruder. As the

▲ 1906: Bert, aged 13, with his father John, mother Frances, sisters Queenie (the toddler) and May, and his brothers Jack (at front) and George (on the tricycle). Bert, interested in mechanics from an early age, took this photo with a timer mechanism. *Courtesy Hinkler Hall of Aviation Memorabilia Trust*

▶ 1911: Bert at 69 Gavin Street, Bundaberg, reading about the latest aircraft designs in *The Aero*. Even though Bert had not yet seen an aircraft, he became obsessed with aviation and would always spell the word with a capital 'A'. *Courtesy Hinkler Hall of Aviation Memorabilia Trust*

1912: Bert (left) in his backyard at Gavin Street, building a glider to fly at Mon Repos beach. *Courtesy Hinkler Hall of Aviation Memorabilia Trust*

1911: Bert, aged 18, with his mother and siblings, transporting his glider by horse and cart for testing at Mon Repos beach. *Courtesy Hinkler Hall of Aviation Memorabilia Trust*

1912: Bert, aged 19, at the controls of his glider on Mon Repos beach near Bundaberg with (from left) Charlie Laffan, Charlie Griffin, May Hinkler, Charlie Macklin, Scamp the dog and newspaper reporter Joe Marks. *Courtesy Hinkler Hall of Aviation Memorabilia Trust*

1912: Bert (right) with one of his early mentors, 'Wizard' Stone (centre), when the Wizard was in Brisbane. Bert volunteered to be the daredevil's assistant in order to learn everything he could about flying. *Courtesy Hinkler Hall of Aviation Memorabilia Trust*

▲ 1915: Bert (second row, right) at RNAS training in Whitley Bay, Yorkshire. *Courtesy Hinkler Hall of Aviation Memorabilia Trust*

◀ 1917: Nance Hinkler, Bert's English first wife. Although they were not officially married, he often referred to her in letters as 'my little wife'. *Courtesy Hinkler Hall of Aviation Memorabilia Trust*

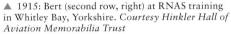

1921: Bert's triumphant return to Gavin Street in the Avro Baby. He had flown from Sydney to Bundaberg on what was then the world's longest solo flight. His brothers Jack and George guided the Baby down Gavin Street. *Courtesy Hinkler Hall of Aviation Memorabilia Trust*

◄ 1922: Bert, as a dashing young test pilot at the Avro works at Hamble, has the world at his feet. *Courtesy Hinkler Hall of Aviation Memorabilia Trust*

▼ 1923: Bert in 1923 with two of his favourite aircraft, the Avro Baby and the mighty Avro Aldershot bomber. *John Oxley Library, State Library of Queensland Neg: 19522*

1926: Nance in front of the home she shared with Bert in Thornhill, Southampton. It was called Mon Repos, after Bert's beloved beach in Bundaberg. More than half a century later the home was dismantled and rebuilt in the Bundaberg Botanic Gardens by Bert's admirers. *Courtesy Hinkler Hall of Aviation Memorabilia Trust*

1927: Bert with Robert 'All-weather' McIntosh, ahead of their world record attempt to fly 7000 kilometres non-stop in the *Princess Xenia*. *Courtesy the* Courier-Mail, *Brisbane*

1928: Bert put comfort above style when he landed at Winton on his way from London to Bundaberg. He was wearing a coat and tie, ladies' shorts and tennis shoes. *Courtesy Hinkler Hall of Aviation Memorabilia Trust*

1928: Bert and his mother Frances after seven years apart. *Courtesy Hinkler Hall of Aviation Memorabilia Trust*

1928: Bert being presented with £2000 on behalf of a grateful nation by Prime Minister Stanley Bruce at Parliament House in Canberra. *Courtesy Hinkler Hall of Aviation Memorabilia Trust*

1928: Huge crowds came out to see Bert and his Avro Avian paraded through the streets of Brisbane after his record flight from England. *Courtesy the* Courier-Mail, *Brisbane*

1928: Bert and Nance flew in the Avro Avian around England and Australia. Nance called the little plane 'Liz' after Princess Elizabeth, the future Queen. *Courtesy Hinkler Hall of Aviation Memorabilia Trust*

▲ Left: 1930: Bert and Rowland Bound, his partner in Ibis Aircraft, and the machine of their dreams. *Courtesy Hinkler Hall of Aviation Memorabilia Trust*

▲ Right: 1932: Katherine Rose, a Scottish-born New Yorker, was working in the British Consulate when she met Bert in 1925. She and Bert married in secret on 21 May 1932. Bert didn't tell anyone: not Nance (who was still known as Mrs Hinkler), not even his mother. *Courtesy Hinkler Hall of Aviation Memorabilia Trust*

1931: Bert arrives at Hanworth Air Park on 7 December 1931 after a 17,700km flight from Toronto via New York, Jamaica, Brazil and the first solo crossing of the South Atlantic from South America to Africa. *Courtesy Hinkler Hall of Aviation Memorabilia Trust*

◀ 1932: One of the last photos taken of Bert, with his friend the radio operator CG Allen beside the ill-fated *Karohi*, adorned with Cupid's arrow. *Courtesy the* Courier-Mail, *Brisbane*

▼ 1933: He had been at the forefront of aviation technology but after his final flight, Bert and his smashed aircraft made a humble descent from the mountains. *John Oxley Library, State Library of Queensland Neg: 148842*

1933: The streets of Florence were crowded with admirers as Benito Mussolini awarded Bert a state funeral as one of history's greatest aviators. *National Library of Australia*

Avian came to a standstill in front of their steely faces, Bert cut the motor and gave them a nervous wave. He could not speak the Latvian language, Lettish, and they had no idea who he was. He looked around for someone from Beardmores, the aviation company, to help him but all he saw were angry faces.

'Bert Hinkler,' he said, pointing a thumb at his chest and waving a hand vaguely towards the clouds from which he'd just descended. There was no response. Only a silence heavy with foreboding. Finally some representatives of Beardmores arrived and acted as interpreters. They told the various officers crowded around the wary Australian that this was the famous aviator who had come to test and demonstrate the Latvian air force's new British machine. No one could believe Bert had left London only that morning, and they were stunned when he showed them how the Avian's wings folded back so that the little aircraft could be moved around like a car. A Riga newspaper's report of Bert's stay said: 'Light and easy like a bird in the air Lieutenant Hinkler flew over the Riga aerodrome. In the presence of the Chief of the War Office, General Roushkevitch and Colonels [Janis] Indans and [Arvids] Skurbe. Our flying officers were astonished by the fact that the plane with a comparatively weak motor, rises quickly into the air.'[14]

The Latvians put on a lavish dinner and introduced Bert to a wicked tipple called vodka, which gave him an insight into why there were so many revolutions in Russia. Colonel Indans told Bert all about how he'd been drafted into the Red Army back in 1916 and how he deserted and formed a band of partisans to fight the Bolsheviks and how he helped form a Latvian air force with planes abandoned by the Germans. He was great company. Bert stayed in Riga two weeks and had the time of his life. So did the Latvians, who were treated to Bert's aerial acrobatics in his remarkable biplane.

The local pilots all wanted to test the Avian, too, but Bert fobbed them off diplomatically, saying that his deal with Avro allowed only him to be in the cockpit. The Latvians didn't seem to mind and awarded Bert the golden eagle breast decoration of the air force of Latvia, a medal that featured a gilt eagle suspended by silver chains from a red enamel swastika. They told him he was the only foreign pilot ever to receive the honour. Bert finally left Riga on 9 September. Taking off at 10.25 a.m., he headed into a strong westerly wind for Berlin more than a thousand kilometres away. The flight took eight hours and twenty-nine minutes. The same strong wind was blowing the next day when Bert left Berlin's Tempelhof aerodrome at 8.02 a.m. and flew for eight hours and twenty-eight minutes to cover a similar distance back to Croydon. The wind and rain trapped Bert over the Channel for an hour, but to him it was all practice for the terrors that might lie ahead between the Thames and the Burnett.

Chapter 19

*Hinkler is small of stature but stout of heart.
There are few, if any, better test pilots in the
country and no wiser head on any airman.*

The *Daily Telegraph*, London[1]

*Whether outwardly or inwardly, whether in space
or time, the farther we penetrate the unknown,
the vaster and more marvellous it becomes.*

Charles Lindbergh, transatlantic aviator

Bert had only been back in England a few weeks when
his mother sent him the news he'd been dreading. There
was no need for him to rush home to see Papa because, on
13 October 1927, at the age of seventy-two, the life that
had begun in an impoverished village in Prussia ended at
Woodbine Cottage. The official cause of death was old age.
Although Bert had not seen him since 1921, his father had
kept a keen eye on his achievements and, according to the
Bundaberg Mail, he died a proud man, his son's success
being what it called 'a big factor in assisting him to weather
his indisposition in the hope of seeing his son once again'.[2]

While Bert's trip to Australia was still being delayed by work commitments and an absence of sponsors, others were beating him to the start line. As Papa was being buried in Bundaberg's General Cemetery on 14 October, Bert was at Croydon wishing the very best of bally luck to Bill Lancaster, RAF captain, and his companion, Mrs Jessie Miller, who were about to start their own England-to-Australia attempt. The 29-year-old Lancaster was born in Birmingham, spent time working as a jackaroo in western NSW and was in Sydney when he enlisted for the Great War. He had stayed in England after the Armistice and, like Bert, wanted to make a grand flight to Australia only to be thwarted by a lack of funds. That was until he was partying one night in London and met Mrs Miller, a pocket-sized whirlwind whose friends called her 'Chubbie' because of her tiny, petite figure. She was born in the most Australian of towns, Southern Cross, Western Australia, in 1901 and had gone to London for an adventurous life after leaving her husband, the Melbourne journalist Keith Miller. She found a kindred spirit in the dashing, hard-up and very married Lancaster, who had two children and whose wife of eight years, Kiki, was a close friend of Nance Hinkler. Chubbie said she'd be willing to help finance Lancaster's great adventure, but only if he let her come too as the first woman to fly from England to Australia. Chubbie and Bill took off in a silver Avian that Bert had test-flown and which Lancaster named *Red Rose* after a charity for ex-soldiers that was his mother's passion. It was the start of a wild ride for Lancaster and Miller that would soon become a scandalous love affair and culminate in one of the most sensational murder trials of the age.[3]

Just five days after they left London, with Chubbie clutching a bunch of white heather for good luck,[4] Bert was at London's Olympia along with a group of well-wishers that included Phyllis Von Alwyn, Miss Australia 1927, for the send-off of adventurer Francis Birtles. Displaying a sign that read 'To Melbourne, 16,000 miles', Birtles putt-putted off on the longest road trip ever attempted to show the reliability of a motor car called the Bean 14, then one of the more popular brands in Britain. As Bert shook Birtles' hand he told him to keep his eye in the sky because at some stage Bert would fly past him.[5]

While he was in London Bert also shared a beer with Captain Robert McIntosh, a fearless pilot known in the aviation world as 'All-weather Mac' because he could fly through any conditions. He always had a huge opinion of Bert and remembered him as small, slim and wiry with a round, almost cherubic face that contained a twinkling eye and a famous grin. As Bert sipped his beer and wondered out loud why the Poms couldn't make it cold like they did in Australia, Mac told Bert he had a very interesting proposition.

He'd bought a bright-blue plywood Fokker F.VIIa high-wing monoplane with an enclosed cabin from KLM. He had fitted his big monoplane with a nine-cylinder Bristol Jupiter radial engine that produced 450 horsepower and called the plane *Princess Xenia* after the Greek wife of the New York tycoon who helped him buy it.[6] Despite the Xenia's grand title, however, McIntosh had been forced to turn back from a transatlantic attempt in mid-September, just 480 kilometres after leaving Dublin. Winter over the Atlantic made another attempt impossible for months so All-weather Mac latched onto the idea that he and Bert could set a world distance record by flying the *Princess Xenia* almost 7000 kilometres non-stop. At the time the record was 6294 kilometres established by Clarence Chamberlin on his flight from Roosevelt Field to Eisleben, the hometown of Martin Luther in Germany, just two weeks after Lindbergh's great feat. Was Bert interested? The cheeky Aussie looked at his fellow aviator over the froth on his warm beer. 'Hell, Mac, it's what I've been waiting for,' Bert replied, 'course I'll come.'

Within a couple of weeks Bert and Mac caught the train to Bristol and were testing the Fokker. As soon as the press got wind of the plan, they speculated that the pair would then fly on to Singapore, then on to Darwin. Bert said that was all a lot of bally rot and that he wanted to be back in England within a fortnight to organise his own solo trip to his mother's front door in the Avian.

Just like the *Spirit of St Louis*, McIntosh's machine was transformed into a flying fuel tank, carrying 3640 litres, although there was provision for a mattress so that one of the pilots could take a nap while the other was at the controls in two-hour shifts. A hole was cut in the roof for using a sextant at night.[7] As Mac and Bert flew the Fokker from Bristol to the military airfield at Upavon on 10 November to begin their flight, the *Red Rose* was flying Lancaster and Chubbie out of Baghdad on the next leg of the journey to Australia, and Bert wished that he was in his Avian chasing them. On the crisp afternoon of Tuesday, 15 November 1927, with a fresh westerly wind blowing, with three tonnes of petrol on board and with fire crews stationed all around the runway, the *Princess Xenia* rose into the air at 1.12 p.m. after an 800-metre run along the grass. The weather forecast was for mostly good conditions with a wind following and some sleet and snow over northern Germany. By their calculations Mac and Bert would be almost 7000 kilometres away in Delhi within two days, following a route over Ramsgate, Berlin, Warsaw, Odessa, the Caspian Sea, the Khyber Pass, then across the Himalayas.

When reporters asked Nance how she felt about Bert flying over great tracts of country uninhabited except by possibly hostile tribes and through bad weather over mountains, she said she would spend the whole time watching his route on the map with her radio loudspeaker turned on.[8] Two days later the headlines read: 'HINKLER AND MCINTOSH MISSING' and 'FORCED LANDING FEARED'.

Nance wrestled with the notion that after so many perilous adventures the odds had finally caught up with Bert. The bad weather had started at Flushing (now called Vlissingen) on the Dutch coast and soon went from bad to worse. Storms near Amsterdam rendered Mac and Bert as blind as bats. Soon the snow began falling hard, making the airspeed indicator useless. Then the wing succumbed to the elements and the Xenia sideslipped violently. With Mac fighting the controls the Fokker started sinking fast. Ice in the carburettors.

Princess Xenia started to spin. The altimeter needle sunk further ... 1300 metres, 1200 metres.[9] It was freezing inside the cockpit but Bert and Mac were bathed in sweat. The plane was in a death roll. The needle spun out of control. She sunk to 1000 metres, 900 metres, 700 metres, 300 metres. They were about to crash. They plummeted to 150 metres. Then Xenia's nose lifted. She sensed life. They managed to bring the plane out of the spin thirty metres from the trees below.

Mac and Bert were exhausted. Their eyes were red and sore from squinting into the dark void. Their fingers froze into claws. They thought about warming themselves with hot coffee but in the excitement of take off they'd forgotten to fill the Thermos flasks. Bert remembered he had some caffeine tablets to keep awake so they swallowed them like lollies, and soon they were having heart palpitations. After fifteen hours of flying they thought they saw stars above through the clouds. Instead the glow was really lights from a village. They were flying along the side of a steep mountain, lower than the houses. Mac put the machine into a turn. They almost ran into the side of a mountain that leapt at them from the mist. Mac pulled back on the stick with everything he had, and *Princess Xenia* clipped some trees as she came up the side of the peak.

'Keep turning,' Bert bellowed above the engine's roar. 'We're in a valley and there's mountains all around us.' Bert figured they were in the Carpathian Mountains. For two hours Mac and Bert took turns keeping the Fokker circling in the dark. Finally dawn arrived and they were able to see a safe path out of the danger. Mac climbed through a solid layer of grey cloud above them. *Princess Xenia* shook violently from side to side, but at last they burst through to the safety of a pale-blue sky above. Below them dark cloud stretched out as far as they could see, broken only by jagged peaks stabbing through. Mac turned the Fokker north to return to their original course. They kept flying at full throttle and, after being in the air for twenty-four hours, they were on a course towards Astrakhan near the Caspian Sea. But fighting the rotten weather had used up more petrol than they could afford. Bert did some sums in his head and figured that they had only enough fuel left to make it to Afghanistan. They would never see Delhi, not on this flight, anyway. Bert shouted out to Mac: 'No good, there isn't enough petrol, we've had it Mac. Better make for the Polish border.'

After a day and night of enormous physical and mental stress the two spent pilots surrendered to common sense and decided to head towards Warsaw, where they knew the Poles would be much friendlier to a pair of British flyers than the Bolsheviks in Russia.

They flew on for nearly three more hours without incident, resigned to their defeat, and hardly spoke a word out of a combination of disappointment and fear of what might happen if they landed in Communist Russia. As dusk was falling, however, the *Princess Xenia* became trapped in cloud again. Visibility was zero. Danger extreme. Mac and Bert knew they had to descend and land as soon as possible or they'd crash into a mountain. At 150 metres they were assaulted by another heavy snowstorm. Below them in the fading light were what seemed like flat, snow-covered fields. Mac decided that it was now or never and, using the drifting snow to gauge the wind, he brought the Fokker down with a jolt on the uneven ground. White powder erupted all around them. As the Fokker abruptly came to a stop, Mac switched off the big engine and said, 'I hope to hell we're not in Russia.'

'Sit tight, Mac,' Bert replied. 'There's damn all we can do about it now.'

The machine was soon approached by a group of angry-looking bedraggled men with fierce moustaches. The men came no closer than a few metres and, as Bert called out to them in English, they disappeared behind a new curtain of falling snow. The two weary flyers, just happy to be alive, thought about going for help, but it was snowing too hard. Nightfall was approaching, and they soon fell asleep in their seats from exhaustion. They enjoyed the bliss of silence only briefly. Mac was woken in the dark by a fearful scream from Bert and, as he sat bolt upright, he saw his co-pilot having his arms pinioned by a bearded giant who was dragging the little Australian out of the cockpit and through the plane's cabin.

Peasants with sticks and pitchforks ordered Mac outside, and in the darkness, as the snow continued to fall, a large group of men in military uniforms carrying flaming torches had the two aviators surrounded. The one who seemed to be in charge waved a revolver and barked in a language Bert couldn't understand.

'*Angielski?*' demanded the leader, asking them if they were English. Bert gave Mac a plaintive look.

'Hollandish,' the pair replied in unison, having already decided that no one anywhere was at war with the Dutch.

By the light of their captors' flaming torches, Bert and Mac, already lost in a blur of exhaustion and bewilderment, were marched to a cold, stinking barn and thrown heavily onto the musty straw. The effect of the caffeine tablets was only making Bert and Mac more twitchy. The two frightened aviators huddled together on the straw to stay warm and to reassure each other they'd be OK. There was no sleep. At the dawn of 17 November 1927 light filtered through a rough window and a posse of men with rifles returned and started shouting at them. Mac feared the worst, but his voice was steady as he said, 'Bert, old boy, I think this may be the end.'

Bert pulled himself upright and gripped Mac's arm in a show of solidarity and defiance.

Soldiers herded Mac and Bert into an open, horse-drawn sleigh, and they were taken through the snow to a small town and marched into a dank, grim building where army officers in grey uniforms sat stone-faced around a table waiting for them. The officers spat words at them that neither could comprehend. Mac tried to tell the men that he and Bert were Dutch. After several minutes with the foreign barks growing louder and the two pilots growing more afraid, one of the soldiers stepped forward and in perfect English said, 'Gentlemen, please identify yourselves.'

Mac told his story and confessed that they were really English — well, he was. Bert was from Australia, but that was like England. Almost. To their amazement the officer smiled broadly at them. 'I believe you,' he said. 'Sorry for the rough treatment but we thought *you* were Russians.' He held his hand out to both of them. 'Welcome to Poland, gentlemen. Would you like coffee? Or perhaps vodka, yes?'

Mac and Bert had come down between Pidhaitsi and Bialokrynica in eastern Galicia not far from the Russian border. The soldiers who had dragged them out of the Fokker also thought Bert and Mac were Russians, the memory of the Russo–Polish War still fresh in their minds. The two pilots were treated to a feast in front of a roaring fire in the police station. After dinner Bert and Mac bedded down in a Pidhaitsi hotel to sleep for thirteen hours. They didn't have time to bathe, thinking they'd best be on their way as quickly as possible, and the next morning they went back to their stranded machine to find it covered by 30 centimetres of snow. Using sign language and his trademark smile, Bert persuaded the locals to clear a path almost 400 metres long for them to take off and surveyed it all to make sure it was clear of ditches and ruts.

They took off in the Fokker bound for Warsaw, but an hour and a half later more shocking weather caused another forced landing, at Mshana, near Lemberg, now the Ukrainian city of L'viv. This time the Fokker's propeller and undercarriage were damaged and so, too, were a pair of farmers who got in its way as the big noisy beast scared the hell out of everybody in the village as she plunged out of the sky and rumbled along the ground.[10] One of the injured men told a reporter from the British United Press: 'The aeroplane headed towards me at great speed. I could not escape and one of the wings knocked me to the ground. The doctors tell me that one of my legs is fractured'. Bert and Mac had to empty their wallets to placate the furious wives of the injured men and as their victims headed for hospital the two aviators hitched a ride on the same sleigh into Lemberg. Bert and Mac alighted at the best hotel in the city, the Krakowski, but in the opulent foyer they presented a sorry sight. They were dirty, unshaven, unkempt and wearing filthy, wet flying clothes and boots covered in slush. The manager appeared and staying well upwind of the two men, who hadn't had a bath in four days, told them that regrettably the grand establishment had no vacancies. Bert momentarily lost his famous cool. He'd had a bally gutful, he said. 'Listen cobber, get on the blower now and bally ring the bally British Consul.'

'Cobber, what is cobber?' the manager said, with a frown of incomprehension.

'Just phone the consul, mate, and they'll give you the drum.'

'Why they give me drum?' The hotel manager was still mystified by all these foreign terms and the little man's funny English accent, but the consul eventually put him right.

Despite the consternation they had caused, Mac and Bert were treated like visiting royalty by the Poles once the authorities recognised their names. Even the country's Prime Minister Marshal Jozef Pilsudski organised a luncheon reception for them in Lemberg. They stayed as honoured guests at the Krakowski,[11] and their suite had the biggest, deepest, hottest bath Bert had ever seen. The Poles even offered to lend them a plane, but Mac and Bert left their machine where it was, took photographs of the damage to satisfy their insurers and left for England by train on 28 November.

Four days later on the evening of 2 December 1927 Nance was among a group of friends and supporters at London's Liverpool Street Station to throw her arms around her husband and say, 'Bad luck Bert, better luck next time.' It would be four months before Mac would return to Poland without Bert to fly the Fokker home.

Bert had missed out on the long-distance record. But he later revealed that he wasn't all that disappointed. He saw distance flights, he said, as just a means to an end to promote the aviation business, which was his bread and butter. He never saw flying as heroic, just the most convenient means of transport, and it was always his dream to see aircraft become as common as automobiles. Looking back on the years leading up to his flight to Poland he recalled that since 1920 or thereabouts he had got into the habit of 'flipping all over England' in the Avian 'bus' or one of the other light planes always at his disposal.

My wife was always my passenger [he recalled]. She was an English nurse, and terribly keen on flying. We would think nothing of flying 100 miles

[160 kilometres] to drop in on a friend for afternoon tea, and our weekends were generally spent knocking about different parts of the English atmosphere. It was in this way that flying became second nature to us. It is only by such continual use of a plane for everyday purposes that the silly 'hero' stuff can be knocked on the head. It is not heroic to fly. It is just useful and cheap, pleasant and easy. As long as the general public believe that it is plucky to go up in the air it will be left only to the few to use the cheapest and best mode of travel there is.[12]

Bert's real disappointment over the Poland trip was his dashed hopes that an arrival in India would net him a benefactor for the Avian flight to Bundaberg.

I could not expect anyone to help me without some prospect of return [he wrote]. Philanthropists are few and far between. We airmen build castles, plenty of them, but mine have mostly nosedived before I could enter into residence. You remember how many disasters followed the successful flights of Lindbergh and Chamberlin. It looked as if a suicide club had been formed in air circles. Women as well as men went to their deaths. I cannot say for certain but it is likely that backers were wary of helping more adventurers to their deaths.[13]

Bert had every confidence, however, in the Avian and the Cirrus II engine to cope with whatever nature threw at them. After he arrived home from Poland he had a couple of months of down time to check and recheck all the additions he had made to the aircraft since 1926. Chief among them was a refuelling system that would allow him to avoid the labour-intensive method of climbing out of the machine and lifting petrol drums over the wings to fill up. He developed a double pump system with gauze fitted over a tube to catch any impurities. He also devised a strangler system on the carburettor that made it perfectly safe for the lone pilot to start the machine by swinging the propeller despite the fact that the Avian did not have brakes or wheel chocks. His folding undercarriage made it simple for the born mechanic to work on the machine no matter where he found himself, and the folding wings would avoid any repeat of his Baby somersaulting on Stockton Beach.

In the long, thin white enamel tub of the upstairs bathroom at Mon Repos he would take turns lying in icy water then in almost scalding heat to toughen his body for the rigours of the changing climatic conditions between London and Bundaberg. To stay fit he hit golf balls into the neighbouring paddock, and he rigged up a bar on a tree on which he would do chin-ups and gymnastic exercises. He was always building up his shoulders and forearms by swinging an axe for firewood or out in the fields wailing away with a sickle and scythe, cutting the long grass the way he had once cut sugar cane.

By the end of 1927, Bert realised that he would have to finance his great venture alone. He'd made some money in prizes from the air races and from testing the Crusader for the Schneider Trophy team, but his nest egg was well short of the £2000 he needed just in case he was stuck along the route to Australia, through another war in Syria, foul weather, forced landings, Bedouin snipers, boggy landing fields, no landing fields, malaria or any of the other problems facing a long-distance aviator. Remembering that it had taken the Smith brothers and their Vimy nearly twenty-eight days to make the journey to Australia in 1919, a milestone that still endured, Bert came up with a plan by which a newspaper would reward him for each day he took off the record.

'No payment would be made if I took the full 28 days,' he explained, 'but a day saved would net me £1, each further day doubling the amount. I thought a newspaper would meet me on those terms, but all listened coldly to the proposal.'[14] A friend suggested that the insurance agents Lloyd's of London would bet on anything and advised Bert to put the proposal to them. If he could make it to Darwin in sixteen days he stood to win £2048.

> They bit at once, but the premium they asked, £150, was beyond me. They thought it was a ridiculous proposal, and said so, loudly and frequently. Lloyd's would not pay beyond 16 days. Unfortunately all I had was £150, and I could not use that for a premium and fly on nothing. I could fly on air, but not live on it, so I gave up the idea.[15]

Nance had developed a real taste for flying with all her trips in the Avian, and she wanted to accompany Bert all the way to Bundaberg just as Chubbie Miller was a passenger on the *Red Rose*. Lancaster and Miller were spending Christmas in Rangoon, and Nance thought flying to Australia with Bert would be the grandest thing she could dream of.

'My commonsense revolted against the idea of a woman with me,' Bert wrote later, without regard for political correctness, 'because she can be of no assistance, and therefore can only hamper. Publicity is served by it, but I was not looking for publicity. My idea was simply to fly home, and my failure to raise the insurance premium had removed my last hope of making the flight turn me in any profit. I would see my mother and the family, and would save steamer fare. That was my main thought.'[16]

Bert didn't have £2000 but he figured that, if all went smoothly and he wasn't delayed during his journey, he could get by with the money he had. With that in mind he checked into the hotel at Croydon Aerodrome on Monday, 6 February 1928, and prepared the Avian to fly all the way to Australia the next morning. He had already informed the Air Ministry of his intention to fly abroad, with a detailed plan of where he would land, and asked Shell and Castrol, whose products were so named because they contained castor oil, to provide petrol and oil along the route. The ministry had cabled the officials of each country and asked formal permission for Bert to fly there. It had cost him about twenty quid in cables, bally expensive but that was red tape for you. His passport was ready, his log book was up to date.

As Bert waited at the Croydon hotel, Nance was meant to drive up to London to meet him. 'She had to use this out-of-date method of travel, as a plane was not available,' Bert recalled with a laugh. 'I waited nervously for her in London, knowing that anything can happen with a motor. Hour after hour went by, and I began to worry.' While he waited Bert went across to the aerodrome and fussed about with the Avian to pass the time. From 6.30 p.m. to 11.10 p.m. he waited, wondering whether Nance would turn up and whether he would be able to make a start.

331

'Then, on enquiring at the Aero Club, I found that the blessed car had broken down, and she had been forced to take a slow train.' Nance finally made it, and at 1.30 a.m. the pair went back to the aerodrome to double-check the Avian. Nance was putting on a brave face, quite cheerful and confident, her only sadness, Bert remembered, 'arising from the impossibility of coming with me'.[17] Although a couple of the London papers had floated that Bert was planning his great flight, there were no cheering crowds, no Lindbergh-like scenes of mass adulation for his departure. He and Nance went back to the hotel to pass the next few hours.

At 4.30 a.m. Bert rose again, looked out the hotel window at the raw, wet darkness outside and, realising that his judgement needed bolstering, finally decided it was now or never. The weather was freezing even in a lounge suit underneath a woollen pullover and a heavy overcoat.

For an hour he walked around the Avian as Nance waited nervously. Bert had barely survived a nightmare flight over Poland a few weeks earlier. He'd seen flyers as experienced as himself killed left, right and centre but, then again, he hadn't seen his mother and family for seven years, and he'd spent a decade promising himself and his nearest and dearest that one day he'd fly from England to Bundaberg. The Avian was a tiny machine that cost just £730, less than some cars, yet he was contemplating the greatest solo distance flight of all time across lands and seas he had never seen, with no radio, no mechanic and just the same map a schoolboy might use for his homework.

Bert had flown more than 12,000 kilometres in the Avian since 1926, and now he was planning to fly more than that distance within a couple of weeks. He thought for a while that maybe the task was just too great. Then Bert thought about all the promises he'd made to himself and to his family and finally he came to a decision. 'Hang it,' he said to Nance. 'I'll go. I've waited ten years for this. Not another hour.'[18]

Chapter 20

Twice I said 'bother' and once 'dash'

**Bert Hinkler outlining his frustrations at trying
to stop his map flying out of an open cockpit
over the coast of Egypt as he fought to keep
his aircraft steady with the other hand**[1]

*I would a thousand times rather be in the air with him,
however risky the thing that he might be attempting,
than wait at home for news of his progress daily.*

**Nance Hinkler on the stress of following
Bert's epic flight from home**[2]

Bert prayed for peace in Syria as the grey fog swirled around him under a waning half moon, adding a chilling touch of suspense as he and Nance prepared to say their farewells at Croydon Aerodrome.

The monumental task before Bert presented many dangers, but dying of hunger was not one he was willing to face. He loaded the narrow cockpit with some Ovaltine chocolate, a few biscuits, sandwiches and a Thermos of hot coffee. He also had a greasegun to work on the engine rockers and undercarriage, a miniature case of whisky that Dewar's paid him to deliver to Australia, a bottle of Burgoyne's port for a tipple now and then, 400 Greys cigarettes, a copy of a new contract between British and Australian cinema interests he was delivering by the quickest airmail in the world, and photographs of Malcolm Campbell's racing car from Dunlop Rubber bound for the Australian press.[3] He also had various official letters, including one from Granville Ryrie, the Australian High Commissioner in London, to the Australian Prime Minster Stanley Bruce. His personal toiletries were limited to a razor and toothbrush because every item left behind was an item not weighing him down. To point the way he had the detachable pages of his *Times Atlas*. He hoped to be back in England by July for the King's Cup.

Bert took one long last look at Nance and the world he was leaving and kissed her goodbye. 'All the best of luck, Bert,' Nance said. 'Good weather and safety. It won't be long.'

'Thanks Nance,' he replied. 'Don't worry.'[4] He pulled down his Luxor goggles and with a last wave Bert was in the air at 6.50 a.m. as the lights of London seemed to wink encouragement at him through the mist. The air was cold and biting as Nance and Croydon grew smaller and smaller. Bert swung the Avian around and headed east towards Australia.

Visibility turned bad. Bert reached the Channel between Hastings and Dungeness at 7.21 and climbed to 900 metres in an effort to beat the fog, then maintained that altitude for three hours or so until he was halfway across France, although he couldn't see any of it. He crossed Lyon at 11.46. Gradually the fog began to thin over the splendour of the

Rhone Valley vineyards. The Cirrus engine ticked over sweetly, and soon the Avian was at 2400 metres as Bert rose above the Alps, only to hit a headwind that made him feel as if he was running on the spot. He came down to just 30 metres to escape the headwind and buzzed over grazing cattle in glorious sunshine. He was as happy and confident as five-year-old Bertie Hinkler skipping along past the ibises to North Bundaberg school. He climbed high again as the Avian reached the Mediterranean at Saint-Raphael on the Riviera at 2 p.m., and he saw another plane for the first time on the journey, shimmering below him.[5]

Bert sipped his coffee through a glass tube he'd fitted through the cork, but it was difficult even to reach for the sandwiches and chocolate in the confined space. He began to think of nightfall and wondered where he could have his dinner. He remembered that the tucker was pretty good in Rome and thought he might as well be the first man to fly solo non-stop from London to the Italian capital. He planned to cut across the Mediterranean beyond Genoa, crossing over Corsica, but a stiff breeze from the southeast slowed him again, and he figured he'd make better time if he skirted the coast. There were at least four aerodromes he knew of before reaching Rome — Nice, Genoa, Livorno and Pisa — so that if the darkness beat him he'd still have a safe place to land.

He flew with one eye on the sinking sun and the other looking for aerodromes. He could still see for about 24 kilometres ahead, but there was only a thick haze beyond that and everything was growing dimmer. Below him he saw a steamer and an old lugger with brown sails that hardly seemed to move. Their images were growing fainter as the sun came down. Bert started to have a conversation with himself in his mind. 'Better get along and make Pisa,' said one voice.

'Don't be a fool,' answered the other. 'Get on for Rome. You can do it on your head.'

'Exactly,' said the first.

Bert felt certain that if he stuck it out he'd make Rome in spite of nightfall. He'd been in Rome in the Baby eight years earlier and remembered it pretty well. He guessed the aerodrome would now be one of those ultra-modern ones with flares or even electric lights.

Darkness descended as the fog rose and, while it had been easy to be optimistic in the sunshine, he was now on his 'Pat Malone' with night fast approaching and only a guess at where he would land. It was pitch black in the open cockpit, and he couldn't see the dials on the dashboard. As he bobbed around in the dark he took out his pocket torch and was heartened by the skinny beam of light. He passed over a couple of seaside towns and looked down to see the distant headlights of a few cars. He was glad of the company.

A brisk wind whipped up, and the Avian bucked and jumped in disapproval. Bert couldn't soothe her protests, and there was nothing he could do but press ahead. The moon rose behind him like an old friend. Bert saw a blinking red light and, certain that it was Rome's Centocelle military aerodrome, turned inland towards it. The moon seemed to be shining a light on the course as he passed over forest, river and hills. But as he came nearer he saw that the flashing light was a great neon advertising sign. Bert did a double take as his pulse quickened. For half an hour he flew around and around over Rome like a bird that had lost its nest. He combed the city from the southeast, zig-zagging right and left. He began to fear the aerodrome had been sold off and that he'd have to wait until dawn to ask a milkman for directions. Finally, aided by the moonlight, he made out the very hangar where he'd parked the Baby back in 1920. Bert circled at 300 metres trying to get his bearings so that he didn't crash into the wireless towers with their piddling warning lights. There was neither a light nor a soul below where the landing field should have been, so Bert kept circling in the darkness, fluttering, as he said, like an angry moth, trying to attract attention. The minutes seemed like hours.

He took out his pocket torch and flashed a feeble SOS, hoping someone would send up the flares for a night landing. Nothing. He made a couple of approaches as though he was going to land, hoping the Romans would take the hint. Again nothing. He had now been airborne for twelve hours and forty-five minutes and decided there was nothing for it but a shot in the dark. With the moon at his back he came in a third time, relying on the Avian's wide undercarriage to help eliminate the slight drift caused by a crosswind.

He touched the ground with a thud and finally, after he was rolling along to a standstill, flares were lit. Bert taxied towards a hangar as soldiers rushed out of the darkness to surround the machine. Newspapers in Australia would later report that Bert was arrested and thrown into jail for landing at a military airfield. But Bert later put the story right.

A babble of voices demanded to know who he was and where he'd come from, and it was an hour and a half before he housed the Avian, then another long wait for the customs man to inspect his papers and the machine.

At 11 p.m., after a flight of 1750 kilometres, Bert, guided by an aerodrome worker, caught a tram into Rome's centre to change some money and send some cables to the press agencies paying him a small fee for daily progress updates. He had his first real meal since leaving London and crawled into bed at a small hotel at 1 a.m. His last thoughts before a blissful sleep were that the lights of a big city looked wonderful from the air.

Day 2, 8 February

Bert had just four hours rest but felt energised by the Roman sunrise and caught another tram back to the aerodrome to check his engine and fill the tanks. He shuddered when he saw radio masts with their wires all around the path he'd taken on approach, realising that he had just missed slamming into them. The spreading rumours that he was flying all the way to Australia had drawn an eager audience and it was 9.07 a.m. before he could take off, bound for Valetta on the island of Malta, more than 900 kilometres away. He'd decided not to risk going further than Malta on his second leg because it was more than 700 kilometres from there across the sea to the North African coast and there were no guarantees of the weather. In Rome it was a sunny morning, and air traffic in Italy had progressed so much that the locals were using what Bert called a 'glorified traffic cop' in the middle of the aerodrome to guide planes queued behind him for the Rome–Venice and Rome–Brindisi runs.

Flying down the Italian coast, Bert gazed with awe at the crags and valleys of the Apennines on his left. He'd hate to come down there. An hour and a half from Rome he was over the Bay of Naples. A stiff breeze straight from the cold heart of the mountains made the going bumpy. Then he flew right through the stinking sulphur fumes coming from Mount Vesuvius, slayer of Pompeii, and was flying blind again. Bert tried not to heave up his breakfast at the smell of rotten eggs.

Eventually visibility returned and the stench passed, and Bert enjoyed the splendour of the Tyrrhenian Sea and its cliffs, rocks and sandy inlets. Just before noon he picked up one of his navigation marks, the island of Stromboli with its three active volcanoes, and at 1.10 p.m. he was over Messina on the Sicilian coast. Bert flew low, following the same streets he had walked in 1921 when the Baby was in the cargo hold.

The Sicilian coast was glorious but Bert suddenly gasped with fear. Sixty-four kilometres beyond Messina, towering into the sky higher than he was flying was the biggest heap of dirt he'd ever seen, the ominous volcano Mount Etna, bold and proud at 3000 metres and covered with snow. Bert let out a whoop at nature's majesty. It became awfully lonely flying solo, and often he would have conversations with himself, sing at the top of his voice or scream to no one just to hear a human voice over the non-stop churning of the engine. A stiff northeast wind sprang up propelling the Avian at 200 kilometres per hour past Catania and Syracuse and over the hundred kilometres of water to the rocky Maltese coast and the stony ground of the farms below.

At three o'clock Bert received a warm welcome from British airmen as he landed at the RAF base eight kilometres from Valetta. He pushed the Avian into a canvas hangar where the servicemen helped him with his checks and refuelling. He was then driven to the officers' mess for a sumptuous dinner over war stories that lasted until nearly midnight. The wind and rain were howling but, as Bert undressed for bed, a forecast for fine weather the next day was slipped under his door and the wind and rain became like a lullaby.

Day 3, 9 February

The next morning at 7.50 a crowd of servicemen watched Bert take off from a runway of red soggy earth made sticky by the rain. He was packing new sandwiches and a Thermos of fresh coffee from the officers' mess but had more than 700 kilometres of water to cross and knew that it would be many more after that before he'd be able to again enjoy the fellowship of British airmen. The officers said that if Bert was lost at sea they'd come looking for him but, rather than comfort him, the idea made Bert lonely and dispirited. The really arduous part of his journey was about to begin, and he knew that for hour after hour, day after day, he would only have himself to talk to and to lift his spirits. Lindbergh had done it for a day and a half, Bert would have to do it for two weeks. He felt a terrible sense of longing, almost of heartbreak, as he left Valetta and aimed for the African coast.

For six hours the Avian droned on and on and on over the blue Mediterranean, flying in an arc as Bert made allowances for wind blowing him off course. Finally, Bert sighted the African coast at Benghazi, a city that had endured fierce persecution from Mussolini's forces. He arrived just eight kilometres off his planned course and told himself, 'Well done.' He touched down briefly to ask British officials there to notify his new pals in Malta that he'd made it, then set off again for Tobruk, 400 kilometres further east. Flying conditions were changing; the skies became more intensely blue and the air much hotter. The African coast was rugged, with great gorges that looked as though a giant's fingers had gouged out the earth and rocks. As hills seemed to rise, trying to grasp Bert's undercarriage, he saw that the orange sun was sinking much faster than he anticipated. Bert knew nothing about Tobruk and dared not arrive at night. He was only about 60 kilometres away but darkness was not so much creeping as leaping upon him. A safe landing in the fading light was better than an unsafe one in the dark. The ground looked flat but, as he went low for a better view, he found it pockmarked with camel thorn. A couple of times he wanted to land but, at the last moment, the Avian kicked up her wheels as though they'd been pricked by the thorns. Finally he came down on a long stretch of sand.

'Thank you, Lord,' he said as he jumped out to survey the Avian's condition and found it undamaged. A couple of sandwiches and some coffee fed his resolve, and he was glad to stretch his legs. He had more room than he'd counted on, with miles of nothing everywhere he looked, and it was now pitch dark. Remembering how Arthur Elliott had been killed on Cobham's flight, Bert wasn't game to light a cigarette in case another sniper was about. He spoke to his little bus as if it was a faithful watchdog. 'Keep an eye out for danger, old girl,' he said, 'that's a good bus.'

He gave the Avian an affectionate pat, then took out the cockpit seat to use as a pillow, removed the inflatable boat and pumped in the air. He couldn't see why he should be the only one out there with the wind up him. He set his alarm clock for an hour before dawn. The rubber boat was two metres long and upturned it made a marvellous bed. Bert fell asleep hoping that he wouldn't have his throat cut during the night.

Day 4, 10 February

Bert crawled from his inflatable bed as the North African sun lit his surrounds. Sand and camel thorn weren't his only neighbours. There were rocks everywhere blocking the path of the Avian's escape. In the distance he saw two Arabs heading towards him on horseback. Soon they came up to Bert, giving signs neither of friendship nor hostility, as though they were reserving their decision. They were more interested in the Avian, and Bert guessed that they had never seen a plane. Bert tried to communicate that he needed help to clear a runway, but they did not understand English and he was no mime artist. To their amusement, Bert trotted around the area pretending to clear rocks and bushes, flapping his arms like a bird. The Arabs laughed at him but finally got the message. For almost a hundred metres they pulled up the thorn bushes and, although the ground was uneven, it was possible to take off. To save weight on the rough runway, Bert dumped most of his petrol, keeping just enough for the half-hour run to Tobruk.

He started up the Avian and the Arabs jumped back. Their bemused glee over this funny little man turned to apprehension. It was a great test for the aircraft to take off from such a short run, and Bert wasn't the only one who was amazed that he did it. He said later the Arabs must have been tickled to death because as he lifted off they were both scratching their heads, and as Bert rose over the Sahara he realised just how lucky he'd been to land where he did. Not another piece of desert for the next 60-odd kilometres seemed hospitable. Then he saw that the wireless towers at Tobruk's aerodrome, as insidious as those in Rome, would have been catastrophic in the dark.

Bert landed on the hard, hot gravelly airstrip and found that Mussolini's Regia Aeronautica had three machines wheeled out ready to start a search for him as he had been a day overdue from Benghazi. The Italian aviators were delighted to see him and, although the language barrier proved tough, their friendliness over coffee made up for the communication difficulties. Bert explained as best he could that he had no time to linger because he wanted to reach Ramla, in Palestine, 1600 kilometres away, by sunset. The Italians helped him refuel quickly, and he was touched that they sent two escorting planes to fly the first 80 kilometres beside him. After that he was on his own and, since Bert had not given Egyptian authorities the mandatory fifteen days' notice of his intention to fly over their territory, he bypassed the land of the pharaohs for fear that he'd be arrested like a motorist without a licence. The daylight hours had been reduced by his late start from Tobruk, and he knew he could not possibly reach Ramla that night. He was tired and uncomfortable from the cramped cockpit, the endless whirr of the engine and the hot wind hitting his face. He studied his *Times Atlas* map as best he could, but the wind rushing past at nearly 160 kilometres per hour made it almost impossible to hold it with one hand, and he feared it would be wrenched from his grasp at any moment.

At dusk, Bert looked around for somewhere to place his head for the night. With Ramla still more than a hundred kilometres away, he picked out what he thought was an ideal spot and came down. With a petrifying shake the Avian almost toppled over in the loose sand. Again Bert's luck was in, and he clambered out in one piece. He knew he would need a much firmer surface for a take-off the next day and, as he wondered how he might drag his tiny bus to a suitable site, a sea of Arabs suddenly materialised as though they'd been hiding under the sand. Bert approached one who looked like the silent movie star Rudolph Valentino and, using his sign language, managed to assemble a whole gang of workers in exchange for his Greys cigarettes. The Arabs carried and pulled the Avian across the soft, hot sand to harder ground.

Fascinated by this little man and his machine, the Arabs then refused to go home and instead lit bonfires, sat down and talked to Bert for hours, although he had no idea what the conversations were about. He was out in the middle of the desert with a group of armed strangers and hoped their friendliness lasted. With the dew as heavy as rain, Bert inflated his boat and went to sleep under the shelter of a wing. The Arabs bedded down in the sand. Bert tried to rest with one eye watching them, but eventually fatigue made him doze off. During the night he was woken by a rustling noise and, with his heart thumping like the Avian's pistons, he raised one eyelid cautiously to watch two of the Arabs circling his plane and running their hands all over the smooth, lacquered fabric. He thought about making a run for it if trouble started. But the Arabs could not have been more helpful. Bert remarked later that the Avian was nothing more than a wonderful curiosity to them. He drifted off to sleep again and at daybreak watched his new friends shaking the sand from their clothes, ready to help him on his way. As Bert took off across the hard ground they waved excitedly to him yelling out what he imagined was 'Good luck'.

Day 5, 11 February

Bert hugged the Mediterranean that morning and followed a straggly railway line for the hundred-odd kilometres to Ramla. Occasionally he flew low to look at Bedouin camps and the curious faces turned upward, but mostly he kept the Avian at between 2400 and 3000 metres. To his left the sea shone like a sapphire, and ahead Ramla looked green and cool against the desert surrounding it. A squadron of the RAF armoured car section was based there, and Bert planned to do a quick check of his engine before bypassing Baghdad for Basra about 1400 kilometres away. It was Saturday morning and the troops were on parade, delaying his arrival onto what he called 'a splendid landing ground'. His hopes for a quick engine check and exit were spoiled by the excited welcome, and the RAF men wouldn't hear of him doing any work on the Avian until they had given him a bountiful breakfast.

Palestine was plagued by diphtheria and, since Bert didn't have the necessary medical clearance, he was rushed into Ramla's township for an examination then rushed back to the aerodrome, only to find the longest and most detailed customs forms he'd ever seen. The formalities gouged a hole in Bert's flying time, and the chances of him leaving for Basra that day evaporated. The RAF men persuaded him to stay in Ramla, have an early night and wake refreshed for a full day's flying in the morning. Instead of an early night, however, Bert found himself with some rather boisterous RAF chaps in the nearby city of Jaffa, home of Jonah and his whale and a famous line of oranges, carousing the night away with officers and their wives until 1.30 a.m. Bert was amazed that a few hours later when he left Ramla many of the very same officers and their wives were at the aerodrome fresh as paint to wave goodbye. He hoped that there might be a few people just as interested in his journey when he finally arrived in Bundaberg.

Day 6, 12 February

Bert felt an odd sense of surrealism that morning as he journeyed over the places he'd heard about in church — Bethlehem, Jerusalem and Jericho — and discovered that they were not places of legend but rather real cities and towns, although not particularly attractive ones, and that the countryside over which so many of the great figures of the Bible walked was barren and cruel. He pressed on over the valley of the Dead Sea, its foothills gradually smoothing out to become more of the flat, unforgiving desert. The fierce heat of the wilds of Assyria was intensified by the ringing in his ears from the noise, the numbing cramp of his legs and the soreness of his bones, stuck in one position for hour after hour. Finally the endless sea of sand was broken by what he called a 'muddy little stream which is one of the most famous rivers of history and fairy tale — the Euphrates'.

Further on came the Tigris and, as the two rivers merged at Basra, Bert thought that even when they came together they still didn't make one river half as grand as the Burnett. He had thought about detouring to Baghdad to see where the Hanging Gardens of Babylon had once blossomed but reminded himself that he was not a tourist. He wanted to reach Bundaberg as quickly as possible. He flew near the place where Elliott had been shot, but the few Bedouins aimed nothing more than curious looks at him. At 4.40 p.m he landed at the Shaibah Air Base run by Imperial Airways near Basra and taxied to the tin hangar in a cloud of dust and, with help from the maintenance crews, worked on the Avian's engine until after midnight.

Day 7, 13 February

At dawn Bert took off towards Jask, 1400 kilometres away. Underneath, through a developing fog, stretched the ugly mud flats of the Euphrates before they gave way to the placid blue of the Persian Gulf, dotted with hundreds of small fishing boats. A couple of hours into his flight Bert passed the ancient city of Bushehr and was tempted to land for a closer look. 'Don't be a fathead,' he barked to himself. 'Carry on. You're not on a sightseeing excursion.'

The view from the air was magnificent enough, and Bert had never seen a coastline like it, comparing the deep fissures in the sandstone cliffs falling straight to the sea with melted cracks in a giant sugar cube. Then a sandstorm hit, but up a few thousand feet the particles were too small to sting and the only hazard was a fog-like vapour. Bert flew on across the gulf over the triangular peninsula of Oman, and thought that he should recommend air travel wherever he went as a way to teach geography to school students.

In mid-afternoon, just beyond the Strait of Oman, he reached Jask, a desolate outpost that survived as an Indo–European telegraph station and transit point for flights from Europe to India. Hundreds of locals made a beeline for the plane, and the British Commissioner came out to greet him. Bert was offered a ride into town yet

Jask seemed to have no motorcars and no roads. He was given the choice of riding a donkey or bicycle. He took the bike, he said, because the animal's rudder control seemed defective.

Day 8, 14 February

Bert later described Jask as a godforsaken hole. He was not sorry when he rode his bike back to the Avian before dawn. He started to refuel with petrol and oil but was shocked to see a drip coming from the main fuel tank. Like a skilled surgeon, he investigated the innards of the tank and tried to stem the flow of its lifeblood. Then he carefully counted the drips like a doctor taking a pulse. He reckoned that, even with the rate of fuel loss, he could still make it down the Arabian Sea and cover the thousand kilometres to Karachi.

Bert asked the Shell representative in Jask to organise a supply of fuel in Ormara about three-quarters of the way to Karachi, just in case the petrol drip became a geyser. He set off once more in his leaky 'boat' for a day's flying east, passing over beachgoers enjoying the delights of the warm water and warm sun, thinking to himself that people all over the world were really the same inside, with the same hopes, desires and dreams.

Bert's attention swung back from the sunbathers to the Avian's fuel gauge. The needle was dipping faster than his calculations allowed. He normally kept his eye on his watch and every two and a half hours switched from one 45-litre tank in the top wing to the other before pumping up another 45 litres from the main tank in the fuselage. Now he was emptying the tank much faster than the mileage accounted for. It was a race against time. He was leaking sweat as fast as the Avian was leaking fuel. There was a sublime stretch of blue water below him but Bert felt no relief until about 240 kilometres before Karachi when he felt a giddy exhilaration. He knew he would make it with petrol to spare.

Bert arrived at 1.43 p.m., after a seat-of-his-pants flight of seven hours and three minutes, to find that the Karachi RAF base was one of the biggest airports in the world, about 10 kilometres from the city and gearing up for the India-to-Australia air service proposed by Imperial Airways. The RAF boys greeted him enthusiastically and were only too happy to start the overhaul on the Avian. The fuel tanks were lifted out and examined, the leak put down to the engine 'panting' or expanding in the heat. Bert joked later that the tanks were fitted with braces to prevent further problems with the 'pants'.

Bert sent some telegrams, including one to his mother saying he'd see her soon, and finally hit the sack at 1 a.m. He was up again at 3.30 to start all over. He had set another world record for the longest flight ever in a light plane. The papers in London, New York, Sydney and Bundaberg were now calling him 'Hustling Hinkler'.

Day 9, 15 February

The sand around the aerodrome was doused in used oil to prevent dust flare-ups from the aircraft propellers and Bert took off just before dawn for the 1500-kilometre trip across India to Cawnpore (now Kanpur). He looked an odd sight as he left. He had replaced his leather flying helmet with a white pith helmet, or topee 'tiger shooter', because the RAF men had persuaded him that he needed better protection against the Indian sun. Although the pith helmet might have stopped sunstroke, it didn't allow

Bert to plug his ears the way his flying helmet did, and before long he felt he was going deaf from the constant rattle of the Avian, the noise of the wind and the incessant, maddening hum of the Cirrus II engine.

More than a hundred kilometres after leaving Karachi Bert sighted the muddy Indus, snaking its way through the dry rocks that soon became grim, ugly mountains devoid of life and full of dread. The ringing in his ears made Bert's head spin and gave him a screaming headache. He had travelled close enough to 1200 kilometres before he finally found a city of any size at Gwalior, and he felt as sick as he had at any time of his life, so nauseous that he feared he would pass out. Finally the waters of a Ganges tributary, the Yamuna, cooled his mood because it meant that Cawnpore and its airfield was nearby. Bert landed there soon after. He was stone deaf. Although it was only five o'clock, he collapsed into bed.

Day 10, 16 February

At daybreak, the bus was airborne again. Bert's hearing was coming back and he felt that no matter where he travelled, the world always looked shiny and new with the first rays of morning. He was heading for Calcutta, about a thousand kilometres away. He passed over Allahabad before being bumped about in mountainous country. Eighty kilometres or so from Calcutta, Bert passed over the Hooghly River and the most thickly populated area he had seen since leaving Italy. People seemed to be everywhere on the river's green shores, working behind weary buffalo.

The surrounding jungle and fields made a wonderful landscape and a refreshing change from the drab earth that had occupied so much of the trip. He landed on Calcutta's dry, dusty Dum Dum Aerodrome, 16 kilometres from the huge impoverished city, the Avian scratching up thick dust as she arrived.

News of Bert's progress had spread around the world, and hundreds of coolies, most of them near naked, surrounded the plane to welcome him. Two locals running an air taxi and aerial photography business were proud to show Bert their very own Avro Baby just like the one that had once served him so well. They helped Bert work on the Cirrus II until after midnight then took him to lodgings in the city, although, given the traffic Bert encountered the next morning, he wished he'd slept beside his machine. The roads were gridlocked with water buffalo, cars of all makes, dog carts and buggies.

'You can accelerate nothing on that road, except language,' Bert recalled. 'No man with hardened arteries should attempt to travel on it.'

Day 11, 17 February

At 6.42 a.m., Bert was bound for Rangoon in Burma, 1200 kilometres away. He flew over the muddy estuary of the Hooghly and headed for the open sea of the Bay of Bengal, making for Akyab, intending to turn southeast from there and cruise down the Burmese coast. Turbulence from the heat forced Bert to 2000 metres, and a grey haze was made worse by jungle fires. With visibility poor Bert flew by compass until just south of Akyab when he saw an entrancing vision that only airmen could ever behold. Before him was a formation of cirrus and cumulous clouds, so thick as to appear solid as earth. He swooped down on the clouds in wonder. He looked down immense cloud gorges, their sides made of solid gold, burnished by the sun. Bert flew into the clouds and felt as though their great golden walls were falling in on him like majestic waterfalls going over an escarpment. Another canyon seemed to lead him to new beauty.

It was as if he was in a dream he hoped would last forever. All around him the colours were changing with the angle of the sun. Great billowing cliffs gaped before him, and he rocketed down them to come racing up again through the shadows into the light, the sun gleaming on his wings. All the dangers and pitfalls of aviation were worth it for those few minutes of mind-bending bliss.

Bert arrived at Rangoon at half-past two, thought briefly about continuing to Tavoy or even Bangkok but then decided he might be risking another night-time landing in unfamiliar territory. So he put down on Rangoon's new racecourse, which from the air looked like a green pond in a vast garden. He had been wearing the same suit for a week through all sorts of heat and dust, and his early arrival at Rangoon meant that he could have a lie-down while the natives washed his kit. The local Shell representatives put on a dinner for him. Bert left early to get some rest.

The Australian papers now predicted that Bert would obliterate the Smiths' England-to-Australia time and, while Bert was thrilled, his joy was not shared by the Australian Government, which was sick of foolish flyers killing themselves and damaging aviation's reputation. Australian Prime Minister Stanley Bruce put out a warning, declaring that Mr Hinkler might get away with it but facilities would not be provided at government aerodromes, nor would special weather forecasts be provided for any more unauthorised journeys. In fact all powers would be invoked to penalise such flights. So there.[6]

Day 12, 18 February

Bert couldn't have cared less about bureaucracy as he left Rangoon at 6.30 a.m. Fifty or so horses had to be shooed away from the take-off area until he was in the air and heading towards the village of Victoria Point (now called Kawthaung) more than 900 kilometres away on the Malay Peninsula. A rain storm chased him all day.

Bert wanted to fly low to spot a tiger, but the heat forced him up to the cooler climes of 1500 metres. At 2 p.m. he circled the village at Victoria Point, home to two white rubber planters and a hundred local workers. He then headed for the aerodrome, a clearing hacked out of the jungle. A car came out to meet him, and one of the rubber planters told him that his hangar would have to be the shade of a big tree. Bert secured the Avian and covered her with a tarpaulin against the rain that arrived in haste just after him. As thunder and lightning roared, Bert and a helper huddled under the tarp and used flash-lamps to work on the engine. The bright light attracted hordes of flying ants that stuck to the oily parts of the aeroplane so that it looked like a big piece of flypaper. When the work was complete Bert was taken to one of the rubber planters' bungalows while pet monkeys and small, pretty wood pigeons serenaded him. He was glad to finally go to sleep in a comfortable bed at a decent hour.

Day 13, 19 February

Singapore beckoned more than 1300 kilometres away as Bert left the rubber plantation aerodrome at 6.15 a.m. Although he expected a thick haze common in the tropical summer, he passed over Georgetown on Penang in brilliant Sunday noon sunshine and saw four RAF flying boats moored below, surrounded by other, more ancient craft. The perfect weather couldn't last, and the sky began to darken ominously as though nature was waiting to ambush Bert and the bus. The rain opened fire, and Bert peeled off as though Richthofen was in pursuit, turning sharply off course, to dodge the first attack. But he was surrounded. The rain hit him hard in the face, the windscreen all but useless. Bert hurtled towards the storm clouds at 145 kilometres per hour and the rain fired back behind an eighty-kilometre-per-hour wind. The downpour hurt like blazes. Bert put his head down and charged ahead, billy goat style. Flashes of lightning split the huge black clouds, and the roar of thunder shook him to his bones. Bert turned north and went 80 kilometres off course to dodge the worst of it, flying just above the jungle to see the way. He could find nowhere to land safely. Ahead of him fleecy clouds just over the tree tops looked like bits of cotton tangled on a hedge. The scene was so lovely that Bert momentarily forgot his troubles. Although his first look at Singapore was through a violent rainstorm, he could make out the city well enough and circled it before descending to the official landing ground as he'd been advised in England. Bert was drenched. He was promptly told that he should have landed on Singapore's racecourse. He took off again and landed as a hundred coolies welcomed him. In their midst was a pair of familiar faces, Bill Lancaster and Chubbie Miller who, faced with danger and excitement on their own remarkable journey, had fallen madly, hopelessly in love.

Theirs had been an emotional journey. After leaving Lympne on 14 October, Bill and Chubbie reached Egypt in two weeks, then Baghdad in early November. Over the Arabian Sea they had almost crashed into the shark-infested waters, an episode so traumatic that in the endorphin-rush of relief they made love for the first time that night under the Persian stars.[7] Later in their journey Arabs shot at them and, flying out of Rangoon, Chubbie discovered a poisonous snake at her feet. She broke off the control stick in her cockpit to kill it, and they barely managed to reinsert the stick and regain control of the *Red Rose*. Then a blocked fuel line sent them crashing into Muntok off Sumatra and, although they survived with only minor injuries, they had been stranded in Singapore for six weeks awaiting repairs. They were only too keen to help Bert minister to his weary bird by lamplight under umbrellas. The trio then went into Singapore for dinner and to swap yarns about their many Avian adventures. Lancaster happily conceded that Bert was about to beat them to Australia and become the pilot of the first light aircraft to make the journey. But he had no hard feelings and said Bert could have the 'strip maps' for the Darwin–Katherine–Camooweal route that had been prepared for the *Red Rose* by Australia's Department of Defence. The maps were on rolls of linen like crepe bandage that could be rolled out as the distances were covered and were much easier to use in a cockpit than the *Times Atlas*. When the three aviators returned from their dinner Lancaster sat in Bert's plane all night to guard it while his friend slept soundly.

Day 14, 20 February

When Bert filled the Avian's tanks the next morning her wheels sank eight centimetres into the soggy ground. It was still raining and it would be a difficult take-off, yet if Bert didn't make a start he could be bogged for days. He opened the throttle full out but the Avian wouldn't budge from the mud. Lancaster and Miller led a crowd of coolies giving Bert a push but he was flat out doing 32 kilometres per hour across the sodden airfield and was almost about to abort the take-off when he hit a firm patch and the Avian kicked underneath him like she'd found an extra gear. Bert let out a yell as he cleared the first fence, then the trees surrounding the racecourse. He dug in the spurs and headed for Java.

The rain pelted down into his open cockpit all the way, and Bert took the Avian to just over 2000 metres, watching the heavy clouds dropping rain beneath him. After about 480 kilometres he saw a hole in the clouds and went through to see what lay beneath. He was over the island of Bangka off the coast of Sumatra and beneath him were steamers heading for Singapore. The weather improved, and he soon came upon the chain known as the Thousand Islands off the coast near Batavia (now Jakarta), in the Dutch East Indies.[8] They looked like precious jewels in a sapphire sea. Bert arrived over Batavia at 12.45 and found it surrounded by heavy clouds. Earlier in the day, Sir Josiah Crosby, the British Consul General, received a Reuters telegram from Singapore saying that Bert had started for Batavia that morning, but all he really knew about Bert's plans was what he'd read in the newspapers.

The Vice Consul, General W.H. Newbould, was dispatched to the landing ground at Batavia to join an army officer and a gathering of local reporters. But as they waited anxiously for Bert to arrive, constantly scanning the grey skies for the Avian, Bert decided the clouds were too heavy and instead headed for the aerodrome at Kalidjati about a hundred kilometres away.

On the way Bert saw a thinner patch of cloud and headed through it. The deluge still hit the Avian so hard that it felt like an assault with small twigs. Bert cruised back and forth for more than an hour looking for ways to outsmart nature. He came around the back of the storm at about 450 metres and landed drenched to the bone at Kalidjati at 2.22 p.m. He was met by the commandant of the Dutch Flying School and his charming wife, who both spoke some English. Later that afternoon as the official welcoming party was still waiting in the belting rain at Batavia, they were joined by an air force officer who flew in from Bandoeng (now called Bandung) 145 kilometres away, hoping to shake the hand of the famous airman. Among the sodden officials, there were feelings of dread over what Bert's non-appearance meant. Finally, towards evening they received the news that while they'd all been standing in the rain for the day, Bert was having a nap after his detour to Kalidjati.

Consul General Josiah Crosby was ropeable. He wrote that Bert arrived totally unexpected at Kalidjati and had 'literally descended from the clouds'. 'The greatest admiration is felt in this country for [Hinkler's] feat and the local press has paid him glowing tributes, stressing in particular the absence of any attempt on his part to advertise his flight or capture public attention,' Crosby wrote. 'Having said this I draw your attention to the confusion created by the omission to notify the authorities in the Netherlands East Indies beforehand of his impending arrival.' Crosby pointed out that all airfields in the area were owned by the military and not available freely to private aviators — even record-breaking ones. If authorities weren't notified, he warned, the local airfields were likely to be populated by grazing cattle and buffalo when visiting aviators made their surprise appearances and that a serious accident could ensue.

Bert didn't realise the trouble he was causing in Batavia, and, soaked to the skin after his ordeal, it's likely he didn't care much. He was on a mission, and no distractions were going to faze him.

Day 15, 21 February

Although Bert didn't have a great deal of time to look around, he described Java as the most fertile land he had ever seen before he was off again at 6 a.m. heading for Bima almost 1400 kilometres away on the island of Sumbawa.

He flew a straight line to Semarang and at 3000 metres gazed awestruck at nearby volcanoes, which were puffing out smoke like giant chimneys over the sea. He flew underneath a great ceiling of cloud and felt the Avian being pushed up by the warm air over the Java Sea. Even when Bert shut the engine off he did not lose height for some time and maintained the same forward speed. He arrived at Bima's aerodrome amid another throng of coolies at 2.47 p.m. The local Dutch commissioner drove Bert into the town 18 kilometres away, and Bert was able to luxuriate in his new friend's concrete Roman bath. They then returned to the Avian, and by the time Bert had finished checking her they were working by lamplight, attracting every mosquito on the islands, or so it seemed. Bert recalled that the insects were so big that four hefty ones could have swung the propeller. He finished his maintenance at 11 o'clock and turned in for the night on the veranda of a native hut on a bed furnished with mosquito curtains. 'Some of the mosquitos, afraid of the bigger ones, crept in with me and had their tea,' Bert recalled later. 'I did not sleep a wink all night.'

Day 16, 22 February

After a breakfast of two bananas, the only food Bert trusted, he started off in the half light before daybreak on the 1450-kilometre run to Darwin, the last leg of his monumental journey. He had a long day ahead, more than ten hours of flying, half of it across open water, but he felt euphoric. With his exhaust pipe red-hot and gleaming, he headed out over the rice paddies and made a tricky climb with a full load of fuel over nearby mountains. He headed for the Savu Sea and crossed Kupang on Timor at about 10.30 a.m. Then came five hours across the Timor Sea, the body of water that threatened to be the most treacherous of the whole flight, the last long lap. There was no turning back and not a ship anywhere. It was the most desolate stretch of water Bert had seen, but he no longer felt lonely or alone. He was almost home.

Bert had hoped there might be a few people to shake his hand when he reached Australian soil. He had no idea of the emotion that had been building in his home country day after record-breaking day.

There had been some confusion over the time difference at Bima, and authorities in Darwin expected Bert to arrive at about 2 p.m. Hundreds of new admirers — men wearing topees and white suits, women in knee-length dresses and cloche hats despite the summer heat and humidity, started heading to the aerodrome at Fannie Bay, not far from the town centre just after midday,[9] gathering around the prominent memorial to Ross Smith. There were dignitaries, photographers and a cinematographer. The sun beat down, and the crowd grew restless. As the Wednesday afternoon wore on and the humidity became stifling, more people arrived until it seemed that all of Darwin's populace was on the coast, sweating together. There was a beer strike on but the mayor, Douglas Watts, better known as Jim, had a bottle of Melbourne Bitter on ice because he suspected Bert could do with a drink when he arrived. The weather was unusually dry for February, and Darwin baked like a slow-cooking roast. There was no sign of Bert, and the only thing buzzing were the flies. The beer strike made waiting that much worse. Something bad must have happened. Murmurs grew loud. There was nowhere to land in the Timor Sea. At five o'clock a grim message was sent to the aerodrome from the cruiser HMAS *Melbourne* steaming north on the same track as Bert was expected to fly. There was no sign of him. Not a peep. The crowd groaned. Some, teary with emotion, turned for home.

Then just before six o'clock a man with a telescope saw a speck in the sky glinting in the late afternoon sunlight over the jungle to the north. 'There's somethin' up there,' he yelled.

'Is it him? Is it Hinkler?'

'Dunno. Too far away,' he replied. 'Looks like a beetle, a big silver-back beetle.'

The silver beetle was moving like a silver bullet. Then, almost in unison the crowd shouted, 'Here he comes. Here comes Hinkler.'

Bert's first sight of Australia was Bathurst Island, and he punched his fist in triumph. He saw Darwin in the distance at 5.40 p.m. and, as he neared the city, he came down to 600 metres before dropping sharply to glide in.

He twice circled the Ross Smith memorial at the end of the landing strip. Bert had sunburn across his face where the leather helmet couldn't protect him but, despite the pain, he couldn't stop smiling. No one had ever flown from England to Australia alone before, and no aircraft had ever done it so quickly. He had almost halved the previous best time as aviation entered a new age. Bert knew how Blériot, Lindbergh and the Smith brothers all felt.

He wondered what all the people were doing underneath him as he came in to land and figured that Darwin must have been having some sort of holiday picnic. As he came down out of the hot sky, Bert's heart felt as light as a feather. He and the Avian had flown 17,710 kilometres (11,005 miles) in just fifteen days, two and a quarter hours after leaving Croydon, and the newspapers were calling him the Monarch of the Air. Bert landed at two minutes to six and climbed out of the machine, looking dishevelled in his crumpled double-breasted suit coat but with the relief of a man who'd seen both heaven and hell and lived to tell the tale.

The first person to approach him was a local doctor in his official capacity as quarantine officer. He gave Bert a bone-crunching handshake and a quick once-over and declared him OK as the Government Resident, Lieutenant Colonel Robert Weddell, and Mayor Watts pumped Bert's hand. A customs officer inspected Bert's meagre luggage to declare officially that he wasn't a smuggler and then, dazed by all the attention from the big crowd, Bert took off the leather helmet and put on his wide-brimmed tiger shooter topee. With his creased jacket and sunburnt face he looked for all the world like some eccentric hunter who'd just woken up in the desert. He was tired and his head kept wobbling from the vibrations in the plane as he signed the necessary customs and medical documents with a shaky hand. Once again he was partially deaf from the noise of the engine and the buzzing in his ears felt like they'd been invaded by swarms of angry bees. His face was already bright red, but he blushed even more as he was surrounded by cheering men and women. Mayor Watts pushed the bottle of Melbourne Bitter into Bert's hand and, although his favourite beverage was ginger beer, Bert guzzled down the amber fluid.

It was just on sunset, but it was slowly starting to dawn on Bert that he was now the most celebrated aviator in the world.

Chapter 21

*Hinkler's flight was a greater individual
performance than even that of Lindbergh.*

**Sir Robert Horne, Britain's former
Chancellor of the Exchequer**

*In many respects Hinkler's is the most
remarkable flight that has ever been made.*

The *Daily Telegraph*, London

No special arrangements had been made for the care of the
Avian in Darwin so it was consigned to the safekeeping of
the police under a tent-fly stretched between two mangrove
saplings. Bert's head was still wobbling and shaking as
though he was punchdrunk. Mayor Watts took him into
town in his car, gushing all the way about the historic
feat and how all Australia had been on tenterhooks. He
escorted Bert into the handsome Victoria Hotel, where the
Smith brothers and Cobham had stayed after their much
slower journeys to Australia.

Bert was given the same room in which Cobham had
slept[1] and presented with a bag containing 476 telegrams

of congratulations from world leaders, captains of industry, old friends and the Avro workmen at Hamble. He'd been squinting at the horizon since first light and put the telegrams aside to read later, telling Mayor Watts, 'Thanks, but I'm pretty well worn out.' His mission was accomplished, but there wasn't much time for rest. Bert sent off a cable to Nance that read: 'Australia at last. Great congratulations. Love, Bert', then had a bath. After flying 1450 kilometres through the day he still had a big night ahead.

King George sent a message through Lord Stonehaven, the Governor General, that declared: 'Please convey to Mr Hinkler the expression of my warmest congratulations on his splendid achievement. I have been following his flight with the keenest interest and I am delighted that he has been successful.' Another telegram came from Stanley Bruce, the Australian Prime Minister: 'I am proud indeed that the honour of being first to fly this long journey alone in a Light Aeroplane and with such speed has fallen to an Australian-born pilot.' Offers of lecture tours and a season on J.C. Williamson's Tivoli circuit arrived, but Bert was too beat to study them.

In London huge lunchtime crowds gathered before a window in the Strand that displayed Bert's route. Newspapers put out early edition posters. The *Daily Express* said Bert's achievement left all other aerial records standing still and the *Christian Science Monitor* proclaimed that just as the locomotive had revolutionised land transport, Bert's 'daring, resourcefulness and mechanical ability' had marked an important stage in aviation, revolutionising global travel. Northcliffe's *Daily Mail* said there had never been a more impressive feat of individual skill, courage and endurance.

Castrol boss Sir Charles Wakefield, the former Lord Mayor of London, sent a message that began with the words 'Advance Australia' and called the flight 'a landmark in Empire unity', adding that Bert had achieved a personal triumph unaided and 'unostentatiously'. A.V. Roe described the journey as 'the most historic feat in the annals of flying',[2] and *The Times* said Bert had now opened the way for bigger, faster planes with passengers, cargo and mail.

Nance was staying at Cricklewood in London when a press reporter knocked on her door to break the news. 'I am the proudest woman in the world,' Nance said. 'I simply could not sleep. It was not fear or anxiety. My faith in Bert is too strong for that. All the time I knew he could do it, but womanlike, I could not help lying awake accompanying him in spirit, taking off with him, and enjoying the thrill of it all. I really have been flying all the time. Tonight, I shall have my first sound sleep in a fortnight.'[3] Like Bert, Nance was uncomfortable in the spotlight and to fob off the press she said she planned to celebrate with friends on a quiet weekend in the country where she could not be contacted. She sent Bert a cable: 'Congratulations. Bubbling over with joy and pride. Much love Nance.'[4] Instead of heading for the country, though, she went shopping in London, had lunch with friends and afternoon tea with Kiki Lancaster, whose husband was still in Singapore with Mrs Miller. Then friends treated Nance to a big night of celebration at a West End hotel.

In Bundaberg, in the modest house where she'd lived for thirty-six years, Frances told reporters she was immensely proud of her son and was looking forward to seeing him for the first time since 1921. With her dark, alert eyes dancing with delight behind her wire-rimmed spectacles she read the constant stream of telegrams from around the globe being delivered by boys on muddy bicycles. From a cupboard she pulled out all her treasured letters from Bert and, to show a reporter, plucked out one from 1918 when Bert first told her he wouldn't be satisfied until he flew home from London to her door. She never doubted that he'd eventually do it.

Bundaberg needed a boost to its morale as the month of February 1928 was one of the bleakest anyone could remember. Only a week before Bert left Croydon the last of a dozen children, including all three in one family, were buried after a botched immunisation program for diphtheria. And a few days after that former mayor Lewis Maynard, who had once written a glowing reference for Bert, drew a .36 revolver from his coat, shot dead his wife Alice while she was eating an apple, then put the hot barrel in his mouth and pulled the trigger.[5]

Bert still hadn't had time to sift through his telegrams when Mayor Watts' car pulled up to take him to a civic reception at Darwin's Town Hall. All Bert had to wear was the dusty suit that had been soaking up sweat for the best part of sixteen days but it would have to do. Because of the beer strike the unions had declared any beer served that night as black, but it still tasted pretty good as Watts invited Darwin's leading citizens to congratulate an aviator he described as a superman who had condensed the world into a very small place. The Mayor said he was proud to shake hands with 'the bravest man in the world'.[6]

Bert was barely able to keep his eyes open as he was shunted from Darwin Town Hall to a banquet at the Soldiers Hall where his health and that of the King and

Commonwealth were toasted with more union-banned black beer.

Front pages were being prepared in newspaper offices around Australia, and Shell and Castrol were quick to cash in with full-page advertisements highlighting what could be achieved by a lone pilot in a tiny machine with the right fuel and lubricants. Mayor Watts sent off a telegram to Carlton & United Breweries declaring that Bert's first drink on arrival in Australia was Melbourne Bitter Ale. The brewery used the telegram in its advertising campaign and later donated the princely sum of £25 to a fund for Bert for his unwitting endorsement.[7]

Back at the Victoria Hotel Bert flopped into bed at about midnight. Not being one to sleep in, he was up again just three and a half hours later for a ride down to Fannie Bay to check the Avian. Sandflies were everywhere and the mosquitoes just as pugnacious as the ones in Bima, but the engine was in top shape and Bert was ready for the run home. He decided, though, that it wouldn't hurt to give the Avian a complete overhaul and to have more of a rest at the Victoria.

The next day Frank Forde,[8] Federal Member for Capricornia, the electorate that included Bundaberg, dashed off a letter to the Minister of Defence, William Glasgow, urging the Federal Government take steps to recognise Bert's 'wonderful achievement and the great impetus he has given to aviation between England and Australia' and went on to highlight Bert's milestones in a machine with less power than many motor cars:

1   the fastest time from England to Australia
2   the first non-stop flight from England to Rome

3   the fastest time from England to India
4   the longest solo flight ever made
5   the longest flight in a light plane.

After lunch at the Victoria, Bert seated himself on the hotel's balcony for another press interview. He heeded the advice of the locals to ditch his thick woollen suit for something more comfortable, but all that could be found to fit him were a pair of khaki drill shorts that belonged to Miss Stella Nelson, the daughter of a local parliamentarian. Bert conducted the interview barefoot, dressed in a singlet and Stella's shorts[9] and sporting a bandage where his goggles had chafed a hole under his left eye. He had a cigarette in his hand. He said his only regret on the trip was that he couldn't raise the money to back himself with Lloyd's because he would have won more than £2000 by completing the journey within sixteen days.

The next day, Friday, 24 February at 7 a.m., the man who had usurped Lindbergh's place at the pinnacle of aviation left Darwin for Cloncurry 1600 kilometres away carrying his sack of telegrams and wearing a double-breasted suit coat, ladies' shorts, a pair of white tennis shoes and black ankle socks.

Bert's arrival in Australia came as the whole country was gripped by the excitement of aviation. As Bert made his way across the arid Northern Territory the navy was celebrating the launch of Australia's first seaplane carrier, HMAS *Albatross*, at Sydney's Cockatoo Island and at the same time, in the Coo-ee City dancing hall at the Sydney Sports Ground, a handsome Norwegian, Lieutenant Haakon Quiller, was making the final cut from

600 applications he'd received from women desperate to become the first Australian female parachutist under his direction. Quiller had advertised for volunteers, and an almost endless stream of beautiful, daring young women were said to have banged on his door at the Hotel Sydney at all hours, declaring they'd do anything, anything, to jump out of a plane with him. Quiller never did take a woman parachuting with him in Australia, but his advertisement proved to be a great way to meet and impress them.[10]

Bert flew for a couple of hours without incident and passed over Katherine at 9.18, dropping a note of good wishes. But the heat was so intense that Bert felt he was flying into the open door of a blast furnace. He feared that the sun would soon set fire to his face. Bert was expected at Brunette Downs, 320 kilometres northwest of Camooweal, at 4 p.m. but didn't arrive. At 5.40 p.m. when there was still no news the alarm was raised. At Cloncurry, another 580 kilometres further on, several planes had been arranged to escort Bert into the landing field in triumph that evening, but now they sat forlornly as more than twenty cars were arranged with their headlights on in case Bert came in for a night landing. The drivers all waited in vain for the sound of an aircraft engine to break the pitch-dark, eerie silence of the Outback.

There was still no word from Bert the next morning as newspapers around Australia tried to calm readers by telling them that a safe landing was possible in the Never-Never as 'Q.A.N.T.A.S. planes often come down in isolated places'.[11] Colonel Brinsmead, who was on his way to Bundaberg for the huge reception being planned, said Bert had probably just missed the track to Cloncurry and that it was easy to do with the dense forest around the

Katherine River. If he'd encountered engine trouble there were plenty of places to land safely.[12]

It was estimated that Bert had enough food for four days but wouldn't be able to survive long without water. Following Frank Forde's plea for Bert's achievement to be recognised, Stanley Bruce had announced that the Commonwealth would present him with a £2000 reward, but many Australians wondered whether the brave airman would survive the Outback to spend it.

At 10.30 a.m. on Saturday, 25 February, Qantas pilot Arthur Affleck, who would soon fly the first mission in a DH.50 for the Revd John Flynn's Royal Flying Doctor Service,[13] took off from Cloncurry bound for Camooweal with his eyes peeled. He flew a more direct route than the normal Qantas path and disregarded his own safety to see whether Bert had come down in inhospitable terrain between Cloncurry and Mount Isa. He looked everywhere but by the time he pulled into Camooweal there was still no sign of Bert. Another Qantas pilot, Charles Scott, known as C.W.A. Scott, the imposing former RAF heavyweight boxing champion, took off from Cloncurry with a man from British Imperial Oil just after midday and started his own search. Still nothing.

In Gavin Street, Frances was now being comforted by a never-ending stream of relatives who had arrived in Bundaberg for what they hoped would be Bert's crowning glory only to hear the dismal news. To have come so far only to crash so close to home. What a tragedy. But Frances told each and every one of them that she had complete faith in her boy and that he would pull through.

When Affleck arrived at Camooweal he received word that a day earlier Bert had landed at Brunette Downs, halfway between Katherine and Cloncurry, eaten some lunch and taken off in plenty of time to reach Camooweal by nightfall. No one knew where he'd disappeared, but at least the search area had been slashed in half. Affleck refuelled and went into the town of Camooweal about 2.5 kilometres from the landing ground to gather supplies. He had just returned to the airfield when he heard a faint buzzing noise off to the west. He squinted into the sky and made out a speck that was getting bigger and louder as it approached. He soon realised that it was the missing world-beater.

Bert touched down at Camooweal at 12.12 p.m. and, while he was delighted to meet Affleck, wondered what all the drama was about. He'd simply slept the night in the desert just as he had done twice on his way to Australia. Bert was hot, tired and thirsty, and he did what any red-blooded Australian would do in such a situation — he looked for a pub. He and Affleck headed across the sunburnt, treeless plain for Reilly's Hotel. Young Dooley Reilly had seen the Smith brothers when they'd passed through Camooweal nine years earlier in the Vimy, but the sight of this strange apparition approaching was more than a shock. She and her elder sister were working at the hotel when this odd-looking little man in an open-neck shirt, ladies shorts, ankle socks and tennis shoes walked towards the hotel.

We kept our eyes fixed on the stranger as he neared our hotel where we were watching from the bar [she recalled]. We saw a leather flying helmet in his hand ... All I could say in an incredulous voice was 'you're Hinkler'. To say we were overjoyed would be an understatement. We served him cool beer on the house.[14]

Dooley's parents threw Bert a back-from-the-dead party that night, and all had a grand time, especially the Reillys, who charged six shillings for a bottle of beer on the banquet table.

Amid steady rain in Bundaberg the fire bell rang long and loud to announce that Bert had been found safe. Bundaberg's council decided to name a street near the landing ground in Bert's honour.

That night, sharing a room with Affleck at Reilly's Hotel, Bert revealed that despite Bill Lancaster's intricate strip maps and his reputation as a brilliant navigator, he had become hopelessly lost after Brunette Downs. Even the best pilots could make mistakes, after all. He took a wrong track and flew around for a couple of maddening hours in the blazing heat, dying for an ice-cold drink and looking for some sort of landmark that he could cross-reference on the map. All he found was blazing dust, dirt, rock and scrub. The sun burnt his face all day then, in near darkness and facing a powerful headwind, he decided to land near a windmill where an astonished stockman was pumping artesian bore water from deep inside the earth for his parched cattle. Bert dashed off a note for the stockman to give to the manager at Brunette Downs saying, 'As there may be some anxiety owing to my non arrival at Camoweal [sic] if you have a wire would you be kind enough to inform Bundaberg that I am quite OK and landed at No. 6 Windmill after a very trying time. Hope proceed Camoweal [sic] for petrol first thing in the morning. Many thanks. Sincerely B Hinkler.'

Bert had decided to camp with the stockman and his herd for the night, taking out his old standby, the inflatable raft, for a bed, well pleased that the mosquitoes hadn't followed him south. Like his bovine companions, Bert was so thirsty that he guzzled down mouthfuls of the bore water with its sharp metallic tang. It didn't taste too flash, but he was not in a position to complain. Halfway through the night, though, Bert was woken by the rumbling in his stomach and to the great amusement of the stockman spent the next few hours making frequent and rapid trips to a hole he'd dug in the ground. By first light on 25 February, as Australia held its collective breath over his fate, Bert had felt well enough to fly on and, with directions from the stockman, headed out to find the main road to Camooweal. Soon after take-off he had spotted the settlement of Alexandria Station, a large cattle ranch, and landed for breakfast with an astonished station manager, who not only shared toast and tea with one of the most famous men in the British Empire but was also handed the latest London newspaper for his trouble. 'Crikey,' the manager said, 'I've got the paper quicker from London that I get one from Camooweal just up the road.'

Bert took off again for Camooweal but was still about 60 kilometres away over a small village now known as Ranken when his stomach started playing up again. He made his fastest landing since the war and, roaring the Avian up the one wide street in town, ran into the backyard of the nearest home, unfastening Stella Nelson's shorts as he called out a hurried apology on his way to the outside toilet. With the lady of the house and about twenty of her neighbours — virtually the whole population of the village — banging on the outhouse door, Bert barricaded himself in and told them he was very, very sorry but nature was calling and making plenty of noise in her demands. Lindbergh had never made an entrance quite so dramatic.

After the party at Reilly's Hotel, Bert was up again before sunrise on Sunday, 26 February, and at 6.28 a.m. left Camooweal for Cloncurry accompanied by two Qantas aircraft piloted by Affleck and Scott. They arrived three hours and twelve minutes later to see the whole of Cloncurry and more than a hundred cars beside the landing field. After another official welcome, a quick morning tea and more hand-shaking, Bert was off again at 11.20 a.m. bound for Longreach 500 kilometres away, with stops en route at McKinlay and Winton. By the time he arrived at Longreach at 4.50 p.m. a band was playing 'See the Conquering Hero Comes' and people had arrived from all over western Queensland to see a national hero, even if he looked ridiculous in ladies shorts and tennis shoes.[15] Some were too enthusiastic in their acclaim. One woman was nearly trampled in the stampede to greet him, and another had a close shave with the propeller. When the Avian had stopped others plonked their babies on the delicate fabric of the silver wings.

A local lout grabbed Bert's goggles as a souvenir and dashed off, but after Bert protested to the crowd that they were a treasured item, the goggles were returned. Bert made a speech thanking the people of Longreach from the bottom of his heart for the reception and asked them to be kind to his machine. Someone suggested Bert fit the Avian with a button that when depressed would shoot out protective spikes all over the machine like the quills of an echidna. Bert didn't think that was practical as it would add unnecessary weight. He was taken to his lodgings at the Imperial Hotel. Bundaberg's former mayor William Gavegan telephoned Bert to say that his old hometown was planning the biggest reception it had ever seen. The Foundry Green was no longer safe for landing with all the electrical wires and telephone cables around it, but all Bert had to do was follow the railway line at Bundaberg to the freshly mowed North Bundaberg Recreation Reserve, which Bert had known as a millet paddock near his old school. 'You know where it is Bert,' Gavegan said. 'We used to call it Aiken's paddock.'

'Yeah, I know where it is now,' Bert replied, 'I used to catch bullfinches there in the old days.'

Bert had dinner with the local bosses of Qantas and British Imperial Oil, and just after nine o'clock at the Shire Hall he took another long-distance phone call, this time from the home of the new Bundaberg mayor Barney McLean, where a large gathering of the Hinkler clan and assorted friends, including Joe Marks and a local dentist named Otto 'Joe' Grüter, who had once stayed with Bert on a trip to England, gathered eagerly. McLean handed Frances the receiver, and she was almost overcome with emotion when she heard her eldest son's voice for the first time since 1921. 'Is that you, Bert?' the tiny woman shouted down the phone as though she was trying to yell at him right across Queensland's Outback. 'I'm so proud that I can hardly speak to you.'

Frances handed Queenie the receiver. 'Oh Bert, I'm so glad,' she said. 'I don't know what to say dear. It's splendid. What's that you say? The flight was nothing much?'

McLean asked Bert whether he'd like to ride in an official car from the landing strip to his mother's house or ride on the back of a lorry, and Bert said he'd go with the truck. 'Now, Bert we'd like you to get here before five o'clock. Give the old bus some juice and see if you can get here by four o'clock on Monday. What? You will. Good boy!'

McLean gave the receiver to Bert's brother Jack, who shouted down the line, 'Hello, Bert. Congrats, boy. We are all delighted.' The mayor then gathered Bert's cheer squad together to sing a rousing rendition of a song composed by a local pianist Arthur Harper that included the line 'Bert, you bobby dazzler'.[16]

Thousands of admirers flocked to Bundaberg to see Bert arrive, including Civil Aviation boss Horace Brinsmead and the Queensland Premier, William McCormack. Visitors started arriving in the rain from the mining fields of Mount Perry and the sugar towns of Gin Gin and Wallaville in mud-splattered jalopies, old sulkies and pushbikes. Special trains were organised from Childers and Maryborough. More people would have come from remote areas if not for swollen rivers and creeks. Photographs of Bert were in every shop window along Bourbong Street, and Australian flags flew proudly. Warnings were posted saying that, along with Bert, a number of undesirables were also expected in town for the big event, including pickpockets, so Bundaberg was told to be on guard and not to leave valuables in cars.

Bert planned to escape the oppressive heat with another early start from Longreach. He had worked on the Avian's engine for an hour on the Sunday night and, according to eyewitnesses, not a single nut on the aircraft or speck of dirt escaped his close scrutiny. He finally turned in after midnight at the Imperial Hotel and was up again after just three hours sleep. He put the shorts, tennis shoes and tiger shooter hat in his compact suitcase and dressed in his suit for the grand welcome.

With a large crowd waving him off, Bert was away from Longreach at 6.32 a.m. on Monday, 27 February, accompanied by two Qantas planes piloted by Arthur Baird and Charles Scott, who had a beaming passenger, Bert's old supporter Major Thomas Macleod, now a Qantas director. Bert circled the landing ground, waved goodbye and headed off into a strong headwind towards Barcaldine almost a hundred kilometres away. After twenty-five minutes of flying as the three planes passed over Ilfracombe, Bert joined his hands over his head to signal to the others that he would now go it alone. He followed the railway line east towards Rockhampton. He passed over Barcaldine at 7.45, crossed over Alpha and, just before 11.30, flew over the town of Dingo. The word spread through Rockhampton 150 kilometres away that Bert planned to land at the cricket ground there at one o'clock. Nearly every building in Rocky displayed the Australian flag in tribute to him. People climbed onto rooftops to obtain the best vantage point for his landing while thousands of others gathered around the boundary line of the cricket field. Business was at a standstill. One o'clock came but there was no sign of Bert, only a huge collective groan with the news that he had changed course, turned off before Rockhampton and gone over Baralaba Hospital a quarter of an hour earlier as a favour to his aunt, Matron Jessie Hetherington, Frances' younger sister.

In Bundaberg the fire bell and the bells of Christ Church and Holy Rosary Church rang to announce that Bert was well on his way and that Monday, 27 February

1928, would be the proudest day in the history of the town. Businesses shut down and thousands of people began to line the landing area next to the cane fields about a mile from Woodbine Cottage. Police and 400 volunteer marshals, many of them brawny cane-cutters in black singlets with official white armbands, were kept busy stopping ground invaders sneaking through holes in the cordon. Cumulous clouds filled the sky, but the heavy rain had gone and a strong southwest wind was blowing. A small shed served as an impromptu grandstand, and some children climbed telegraph poles to act as lookouts. Cars and lorries, festooned with flags and banners proclaiming Bert 'the world's bravest man' and 'Australia's hero', formed a long procession and the roads to North Bundaberg were choked. The Hinklers travelled to Aiken's Field in an automobile bearing the number plate Official Car No. 1 decorated with sticks of sugar cane and carrying a huge floral banner on the roof that said 'Bravo Bert'. Outside No. 69 Gavin Street the Australian flag flew proudly beside the Union Jack and the Cross of St George. On Aiken's Field three bands, including a Scottish pipe band, warmed up. At 2.43 word arrived that Bert had passed Miriam Vale about 110 kilometres away, and the excitement intensified. Oil fires were lit to show Bert the exact location of the runway, still soggy from the recent rain, and, just in case, the spot was also marked with a white calico cross.

Jack Hinkler's son Ron was then a boy of seven, but eighty-three years later he vividly remembered the excitement of that day: how he had never seen so many people in one place, how the anticipation built and built like the heavy atmosphere before a cyclone.[17] The photographers were everywhere, and there was a lorry for the men filming with motion picture cameras. Everyone gasped when someone yelled out that they could see Bert coming in the distance, but groaned when it turned out to be a far-off crow.

One of the lorries contained radio-transmitting equipment for the ABC's Brisbane station 4QG, and listeners around Australia in those more innocent times were treated to lots of swearing in the background as Bundaberg's populace jostled for position and voiced their frustration at more false alarms. Just after four o'clock, and after much persuasion, Frances gave a nervous radio interview and told the announcer, 'My son's wife and myself are the two happiest women in the world. I thank you all for the wonderful reception you are giving my son and for the thousands of messages received.'

It was then 4.11 p.m. Through a V-shaped break in the clouds almost due north Bert and the Avian appeared as a small dot high above. Frances almost fainted. 'I see my son coming,' she told the radio host, breathlessly. 'Goodbye.'

The Avian looked magnificent backlit by the sun and framed by the white clouds. 'Here he comes, here he comes,' the crowd shouted. Bert swooped down to see a huge audience below him. Bundaberg had a population of only 8000, but police estimated the crowd at Aiken's Field to be nearly double that. The whistles of the sugar mills and every locomotive in the railway yard shrieked in unison, and hundreds of people rang cowbells or blew car horns. Those people watching from the surrounding rooftops stamped their feet in unified joy on the hot tin. The Scottish band assaulted their bagpipes, and the band leader put his busby on his baton and waved it triumphantly in the air.

Men shadowboxed in delight to release all their bubbling excitement. Bert looped the loop and the noise from the crowd seemed to rustle the cane stalks like a heavy wind. Frances, Queenie and May jumped up and down on the spot, clapping their hands. Mayor Barney McLean waved his hat around his head in joy.

Bert half circled the ground then dipped the wings and coasted down over some electricity poles on which children were perched. He made a perfect landing at 4.15, pulling up the Avian within 180 metres after a bump or two over the uneven ground. Despite the heavy security measures and barbed wire protecting the long strip of grass, the crowd was soon out of hand, charging across the field to touch the man and his machine. Bundaberg had never seen anything to resemble the wild scenes. As Bert pulled off his leather flying helmet and his thick black hair blew about in the breeze, he gazed about for his mother while imploring the crowd not to jump on his plane. Girls leapt out to kiss him, and it felt as if his shoulders were being dislocated by men tugging at him to shake his hand. Bert's dark complexion was darker still from all the engine grease that had sprayed everywhere not protected by his goggles and helmet. He was badly sunburned and still had the sticking plaster across the cut under his eye.

With considerable difficulty a wedge was created for Frances and the family to greet Bert at the side of the Avian. 'Hullo, Mum,' he called out to the tiny woman he hadn't seen for seven years and who seemed to have grown even smaller in that time. 'My Bert,' she gasped as she planted a big kiss on him and fell into his arms. Tears flooded Bert's eyes and Frances kept taking her glasses on and off as though blinking to make sure it wasn't all a mirage. Bert reached out to greet Jack and May and Queenie and young Ron and all the other nephews, nieces, cousins, aunts and uncles lining up. But there was no escape from the fawning throng. As a circle of young ladies tossed flowers at him, a posse of male admirers lifted Bert onto their shoulders and carried him to the flag-draped lorry as one of the bands, managing to extricate their brass instruments from the heaving weight of humanity, struck up the familiar refrain of 'See the Conquering Hero Comes', which Bert now knew by heart. Felt hats and umbrellas were thrown into the air like confetti, and an enormous golden smile split Bert's face.

From the back of the lorry advertising Shell Oil, Bert waved to the crowd as Premier McCormack spoke into the microphone declaring that Bert had given Queensland the greatest advertisement it had ever received. There was more wild cheering when McCormack said the whole country now had the chance to do for Bert what America had done for Lindbergh and handed him a cheque for £500, calling on the audience to donate to a fund in Bert's honour in recognition of his 'great and noble deed'.

Barney McLean pointed to the applauding thousands and told Bert that among them were men and women who had been his boyhood chums and who had seen him rise from obscurity to worldwide fame. A somewhat bemused Colonel Brinsmead welcomed Bert home on behalf of the Federal Government and, to more cheering, told the crowd that Lindbergh had been well and truly usurped as the world's champion aviator.

Bert, choked up by all the euphoria, told his new army of fans, in the well modulated tones that he'd been rehearsing for public occasions: 'I am afraid that this overwhelming reception which you have accorded me leaves me absolutely at a loss for words.' The cheering was so loud that Bert could hardly be heard above the din. 'I would like to tell you how truly glad I am to be home again in Bundaberg amongst you all.' And then in a nod to his early religious training he said: 'I feel I owe it all to God, who guided me safely through these unknown and difficult places.'

With the police guarding the Avian, the lorry began rolling towards Gavin Street in a triumphant procession, passing through an archway of flags to the Hinkler family's cottage. Running beside the lorry was Bundaberg's brilliant young cricketer Don Tallon, a twelve-year-old wicketkeeper who would become one of the finest players of the twentieth century and whose dad Les was an iron moulder at the foundry. In a statement issued to the press Bert said that the sight of Bundaberg had stirred him even more than seeing Darwin after the long flight across the empty Timor Sea. His message to Australia was reprinted in the newspapers the next day and continued:

I only wish I could shake each one of you by the hand for it is the proudest moment of my life to have successfully reached Bundaberg and home. As an Australian I am proud that my flight has brought England nearer to Australia than ever before. As a Briton I am particularly proud that only British workmanship and British organisation have been utilised the whole way. Almost every night I came down in a different country, and I was astonished to find the British flag so strongly represented at every stop. It made me realise that British genius and enterprise are still on top for there is no other single nation which could so completely link up the ends of the earth.

At 6.15 p.m. Bert and nine other family members gathered for a small private dinner at Wooster's Café, and later that night Bert, wearing boots that made him an inch or so taller, attended a civic reception in Bundaberg's council chambers, where McCormack said it was men like Bert who moved the great mass of people along the road to progress and made the world a better place. Brinsmead said it was a day that he would remember for the rest of his life and, since Cobham had recently been knighted, it would not be long before Australia's great aviator was known as Sir Herbert Hinkler. He apologised to Bert if he'd been gibbering following the landing and said it was all due to the incredible excitement of the moment and the many, many times Brinsmead had drunk to Bert's health that afternoon.

Interviewed by the national press, Bert said his plane cost less than many cars, had used 2000 litres of petrol at a cost of just £45 and another £10 for oil. He figured that the whole trip had cost a bit more than tuppence a mile. He said the flight illustrated how cost effective and safe air travel could be over long distances. According to the *Daily Express* being read in England as Bert winged his way towards Bundaberg, the flight illustrated much more than that, a triumph for the whole Empire. 'These Antipodean giants help us to look even a Lindbergh in the eye,' the paper said. '[Hinkler] provides history a hundred years hence with an excuse for saying that there were giants in those days.'[18]

Chapter 22

*Change wheels for wings, let us make the air
a broad highway for every one of us — not
merely a speedway for a privileged few. If we
all keep this in mind and act on it, flights to
Australia should be commonplace events.*

**Bert Hinkler in a radio address to
Australia after his 1928 solo flight**

*There must be pioneering in everything and
record flights help to establish the worth of
human stamina, the worth of machinery and I
am satisfied if record flights were abandoned
the English nation would become decadent
and the pioneering spirit would disappear.*

Charles Kingsford Smith

It had been seven years since Frances had seen Bert, and
that sight became increasingly fleeting. He was so busy
with official functions in Bundaberg that she rarely had
a chance to sit with him, and she complained to Mayor
Barney McLean. Bert gave his old glider the once-over

again under the house, but he had official lunches to frequent, tribute dinners to eat, soldiers to greet, concerts to hear, hospitals to visit, bowling greens to grace, photographs to sign, cancer charities to support, factories to tour. There were radio broadcasts, press interviews, photo shoots, speeches. Bert even dropped into the local swimming carnival and a euchre night now and then, and he toured schools and inspired children. At Bargara school he was shown a tree planted in his honour in 1921, and at North Bundaberg the children gave him three cheers after he told them to study hard to build up their minds, play sport after school to build up their bodies and make Bundaberg proud. He wrote handwritten notes of thanks to all those who welcomed him, including children who gave special talks or read poems in his honour.

A day after his arrival Bert had received more than a thousand letters and telegrams from the broad spectrum of humanity, ranging from the King to Dame Nellie Melba, Fokker to Fairey and A.V. Roe; from prime ministers, governors, mayors, old workmates and the Batchelor Admirers of Port Augusta whose telegram asked rhetorically: 'You ball of muscle; are you any good?'[1]

Nance wrote succinctly but passionately: 'Bravo Beloved. Please do rest awhile. How proud I am. Wonderful reception. My love mate all longing [to] know when you are returning. I need you so much.'

There were invitations to visit local councils all over Australia and all sorts of job offers and business proposals: £10,000 for a lecture tour of Australia, a five-year offer at £5000 a year to manage an airline and a twelve-week deal for £100 a week to appear in a film. He mulled them all over but, with Horace Brinsmead advising caution, was reluctant to rush into anything. Advertisers used his name in their sales pitches whether Bert liked it or not, and many prominent citizens voiced the feeling that he was being exploited by all sorts of interests from which the 'King of the Air' would not receive a penny,[2] although Wrigley sent him boxes of chewing gum and Greys cigarettes wished him good health with 2000 of their strongest. He endorsed Shell, Castrol, Mastertouch music rolls, Uka ant repellents, Ovaltine and Arnott's. He posed beside the cars of Studebaker and Austin, Vauxhall and Dodge, usually just as a favour to the photographers.

Barney McLean gave Bert a temporary office in the Bundaberg council chambers and, with the assistance of a stenographer, the three set about sorting through all the correspondence. Having a stenographer made Bert think of Katherine Rose, the secretary he'd met at the British Consulate in New York back in 1925. He corresponded with Katherine and said he'd like to see her again. But what was he thinking? He had a wife back in England, and she was coming out to Australia soon after the Orient Steamship Company offered free passage in recognition of Bert's achievement.

The Avian went on show at Marles & Son, the Bundaberg agent for the Ford Motor Company, and Bert went on show all over the country. He had only been in Bundaberg a few hours when he started working out an itinerary for his flight to Canberra and the planned meeting with Stanley Bruce and that fat, juicy cheque for £2000 that would be the icing on the cake for his Tour of Triumph.

Newspapers around Australia reported on Bert's every move in tidbits called Hinklerisms. Scenes of crowd euphoria were called bouts of Hinkleritis. Sightings of him were Hinklings. Music stores began selling the Tin Pan Alley song 'Hustling Hinkler' penned by Hollywood composers L. Wolfe Gilbert and Abel Baer. In dance halls around the country flappers in tight-fitting bonnets sold as 'Hinkler Hats' did the Hinkler Quickstep with their partners proudly displaying Hinkler badges that bore the image of Bert as an officer in the Great War and the words 'Australia's super airman'.

Housewives everywhere baked the Hinkler cake, and their husbands started wearing homburgs because one had started to appear on Bert's head. The British magazine *Punch* published a cartoon by Bernard Partridge celebrating Bert's achievement with the caption 'Hinkle, Hinkle little star, 16 days and here you are'. New breeds of dahlias and carnations were named in his honour.

Bert managed occasionally to escape the clamour for his attention by hiding out at the seaside home of Joe Grüter at Bargara, just down the coast from Mon Repos. He frolicked in the bright-blue surf, a luxury he missed in England, and three days after his arrival Dr Grüter's wife Ada put on a huge spread for about twenty of Bert's family and friends. His appetite had well and truly returned as he devoured a whole spring chicken like a ravenous wolf before flopping onto a couch to read the week's papers.

Flight compared his courage with Lindbergh's, saying that his achievement must rank among the 'very finest in the history of flying' pointing out that, while Lindbergh had covered a much greater distance in one flight, Bert stuck at his task for day after day, working on his machine every night before having any rest for himself.[3] In trumpeting the achievement of British technology the magazine pointed out that the Avro machine was built in England with a British ADC Cirrus engine and all its components were British: BTH magnetos, KLG plugs, Hobson carburettor, Fairey-Reed metal airscrew, Shell aviation spirit and Wakefield Castrol oil. The machine was doped with Titanine, had a Tecalemit grease gun and carried British air in its Palmer tyres.

Even as far away as Alberta, Canada, newspapers lauded Bert with one declaring that 'without in any way robbing Lindbergh of the glory of [his] flight what Hinkler has achieved is far more of practical value in the uses to which aviation can be turned. The practical nature of the flight of Hinkler ... is the most important contribution to aviation that has yet been given'.[4]

Bert remained meticulous about the condition of the Avian, taking her to pieces and reconfiguring it to accommodate a passenger. He had pieces of the machine all over the back of Frances' veranda. Neighbourhood kids would help him service it, and any time Barney McLean or any of the other Bundaberg bigwigs came by Bert would give them the job of cleaning the carbon off the pistons.

For a special service of thanksgiving on Bert's first Sunday home Anglican Archbishop Gerald Sharp travelled up from Brisbane to Christ Church to praise the Lord for the way in which Bert, seated proudly in the front pew with his family, had transformed the planet, showing the courage of the Australian fighting men from the Great War and giving the world a special gift, the ability to turn a journey that had once taken months into one of a few days.[5]

Bert spent whatever free time he was allowed with his family often in friendly banter with Jack Hinkler's wife Kitty, who was forever teasing him. 'Wait till I get you in my plane,' Bert would shoot back. 'We'll see how cheeky you are then — you'll soon change your tune.' Kitty wouldn't give in, and her son Ron was at North Bundaberg school one day when the headmaster, Bill O'Shea, took him outside, saying, 'Come and have a look at this.'

'We sat out on the edge of the school and we watched Bert up in the air twisting and turning and doing all these loops,' Ron remembered. 'I was fascinated. When I got home I found out it was Bert trying to make my mother scream for help — but she still wouldn't give in.'[6]

Bert gave all the adult relatives a ride — even Frances — but he left out any of the trick flying with her in case he got a clip over the ear.

A newspaper syndication group, Herald Feature Services, signed a deal with Bert and ghost writer Frank Russell to serialise the exclusive story of his flight for Australian newspapers. They offered £300 for the Australian rights, £200 for foreign rights and a further £200 for a subsequent book with tuppence per copy sold in royalties. But Bert's genius did not extend to business. He was too slow snapping up many of the offers that came his way and, halfway through the newspaper series, unwittingly spoke to another newspaper organisation, thereby wrecking the deal. He ended up with just £150 and no book.

Realising that the paperwork was too much for him, he appointed the local office of British Imperial Oil to manage his affairs. He made preparations for his Tour of Triumph but sent off a telegram to the boss of British Imperial saying that he would not accept gate money from the crowds. His only purpose was to greet the people of Australia for the kind wishes they had sent him.[7]

As Bert woke on the morning of Tuesday, 6 March, to begin his national tour, war was raging again in Libya and Iraq, but he was in high spirits as 9000 people gathered to see him off from North Bundaberg Recreation Grounds. He gave them a final 'cheerio' and dropped a bottle of champagne from the air to christen the ground with its new name Hinkler Park, the same name the Warringah Council was giving the area around Sydney's Manly Lagoon. Frances and Queenie had already left on the train to meet him in Brisbane. The Avian was a source of wonder as it passed over schools, farms and small towns on the 320-kilometre journey south to the Queensland capital where all roads led to the racecourse, the lorry jostling with the limousine and the motorcycle on the congested thoroughfares. Just after 2 p.m., and wanting to avoid the bog at Brisbane's Eagle Farm aerodrome, Bert glided into Eagle Farm racecourse to the cheers of 12,000 people, many of them schoolchildren given a half-day holiday. The tall and commanding Governor, Sir John Goodwin, towered over Bert as he led him to the judge's box where the crowd's hero gave a short speech imploring Queenslanders everywhere to embrace aviation because it was the tool to annihilate distances. With the wings of the Avian folded back she was towed behind a lorry with a mounted police escort as Bert led a motorcade through the streets seated next to Frances in an open-top Armstrong Siddeley limousine. Buildings were decorated with placards and bunting, and children waved Australian flags and Union Jacks all the way from the racecourse to the city of Brisbane 10 kilometres away.

The procession was travelling slowly along Wickham Street at about 3.30 when a section of the crowd rushed at the car and spooked one of the police horses. It lashed out and kicked the front of Bert's vehicle, breaking the battery and caving in one of the panels. But Bert arrived at the City Hall unscathed, and Lord Mayor William Jolly introduced him and Frances to one of the biggest and noisiest crowds the city had seen. The Avian went on display at the showroom of British Dominion Motors in Adelaide Street, and Bert went to a lavish reception at the City Hall, then spent the night as a guest at Government House.

The next day at the salubrious Tattersalls Club, as 500 members sat down to dine with Bert and many more watched from the gallery upstairs, he was presented with a cheque for £261/1/9 from members in recognition of his effort, as well as a £150 Salonola, a revolutionary gramophone with a record changer housed in an ornate timber drinks cabinet. Bert unveiled the cardboard box of miniature bottles of Dewar's whisky he'd carried from Croydon, handing them to the Brisbane Dewar's representative and declaring that the first case of whisky air-mailed to Australia, undamaged and aged by just two weeks, was further indication of the myriad applications of air transport.

From there it was lunch with the Royal Automobile Club members at Rowe's Banqueting Hall in Edward Street and more adoring crowds on the footpath shouting 'Bravo'. Bert told the auto club's guests that in the future the car would be used only for driving around town and that distances of more than 300 kilometres would be undertaken by air because the pilot would not have to worry about flooded creeks, bogs or logs on the road. The days of mankind 'crawling about on the face of the earth' were over.

The following day Bert visited the offices of the *Brisbane Courier* to collect a cheque for £1000 from reader donations. The Premier hosted yet another dinner for him, and at a reception put on by his old employer, the politically incorrect Water Board, he was lauded for the magnificent service he had rendered to the white race. Frances's cousin Harry Bonney, who had done very well out of making leather goods, invited the Hinklers to lunch with him and his vivacious wife of a decade, Lores, at their home on a hill overlooking the Brisbane River. Lores was keen to make an impression and, dressed in a French frock of net and fine lace with an embroidered basket of flowers at the waist and a wide black hat, she hung on every word as Bert told her of his travels. Having already lived in South Africa, England and Germany, Lores was keen to see more of the world whether Harry — or 'Hubs'[8] as she called him — liked it or not. Soon Bert would take her into the air for the first time in the Avian, and sixty-three years later she would remember it as 'the answer to my dreams. I adored birds and there I was literally feeling like one'.[9]

As the Hinklers lunched at Lores' palatial home, Nance was being farewelled at Australia House in London as she departed to Toulon in France to board the *Orama* bound for Fremantle. Her arms full of bouquets, she told the press she would have loved to have flown out with Bert but hoped they could fly together on the return journey to England.[10]

Dominion Motors handed Bert a cheque for £373/13/3 from the donation boxes placed around the free exhibition of the Avian. He planned a Sunday flight to Melbourne, thus sparking outrage from church groups, which then harangued Victorian Premier Ned Hogan over such disrespect for the Sabbath. The locomotive union complained that drivers would have to work an extra Sunday and said the whole business set a dangerous precedent that, perish the thought, might see Melbourne planning more public events on Sundays.

Ned Hogan, however, was not one to take criticism well. The former farm labourer, timber-cutter, rabbit-catcher and caber-tossing champion almost put his fist through his desk and said it had to be Sunday because there were other important religious services to observe on the Saturday — namely the Flemington races and the St Patrick's Day parade. If Bert arrived on the Monday most of Melbourne's workers would have to miss the big show, and Bert's achievement was too important to Australia not to allow everyone the chance to see him. The Federal Government announced that any money Bert made from his national tour would be tax free.

On Saturday, 10 March the *Brisbane Courier* published a thank you message from Bert and his mother to all of Queensland for their support, and that morning, before another big crowd of admirers at Eagle Farm aerodrome, Bert took off at 6.33 a.m. into the kind of national adoration and acclaim rarely seen in Australia before or since. True to form, however, his appearance took a battering. In a hurry to get going he cut himself shaving and his collar was stained by droplets of blood. Six hours after he left Brisbane on that Saturday morning, and a full hour ahead of schedule, he circled the Newcastle racecourse before making a graceful landing, taxiing to within a metre of a large white cross marked on the ground opposite the members' stand. It was a much more successful landing that the one he'd made in the Baby at nearby Stockton Beach seven years before.

Despite his early arrival several thousand people gave him a thunderous reception. At the request of Alexander

Peate, president of the Newcastle Jockey Club, Bert went up again at 1.45 and made a second landing so as not to disappoint the thousands more who had arrived to see him at the advertised time of 1.30. He stayed at the track to watch three races that afternoon. He was tipped two 'certainties' that proved to be anything but and had £5 on another hot tip only to see it follow the leaders home.[11]

At 2.30 it was time to go. The crowd cheered vigorously. 'Thanks awfully,' he said, blushing. 'I've been asked to stay for the next race, but for two reasons I can't. I've done my last fiver and they expect me in Sydney in an hour.' Bert walked out on to the course, tucked the tail of the Avian nonchalantly under one arm, swung it into the wind, and soon became a speck in the southern sky. He was still peeved about his collar.

About 160 kilometres to the south people had begun arriving at Mascot aerodrome early in the morning, and by early afternoon thousands of cars surrounded the field in tightly packed groups. The traffic was murder, even for 1928. Several thousand more people waited at Sydney's Domain for a glimpse of the Avian in flight. From 2.30 p.m. fourteen escort planes began ascending and performing stunts for the crowds. Loudspeakers dotted around Mascot announced the names of the various loops and rolls the aviators performed. Jazz music blared and stalls sold balloons, Hinkler buttons, booklets, ice-cream, sweets, cigarettes and soft drinks. Photographers raced around with their cameras clicking, and the police ordered cinematographers perched on the roof of the New South Wales Aero Club to get off.

Bert swooped low over Gosford for a close look at the picturesque town and its waterways, and at 3.17 the jazz music at Mascot was interrupted by the announcement that Bert was over Dee Why. Within minutes there was a fleet of aircraft in the sky and in the middle of them was a small silver machine. Below it was a crowd of 80,000 people, among them the New South Wales Premier Thomas Bavin, as well as Frances, Queenie and Jack, Bert's newly appointed national tour manager.

Thousands of car horns screamed as Bert glided down in front of the Mascot club house. Eighty thousand voices chanted, 'We want Bert, we want Bert.' The little man with the mop of dark hair and blood-spattered collar standing beside his aged mother and siblings was visibly overwhelmed by the sea of faces. He was lost in the middle of them and was asked to climb a photographer's ladder so the people could see their hero. He then climbed down and approached a microphone with far more trepidation than he had approached the air journey and said: 'From the bottom of my heart I must thank you. More I cannot say.' The crowd shouted their approval.

Five hundred metres above, the Norwegian parachutist and ladies man Haakon Quiller jumped out of a plane hoping to honour Bert with a perfect parachute landing on the airfield. Unfortunately Quiller took so long to find a pilot who'd take him up that most of the big crowd was leaving as he started his descent. Very few people saw him drift off course and plop into the soggy bank of a canal at Botany. Even fewer saw him emerge covered in head to toe by a brown ooze.

From Mascot, Bert visited returned soldiers at Randwick Hospital, met the Governor and waved to the huge crowd outside the Botanic Gardens as wellwishers surrounded his car. He then attended a reception at Sydney

Town Hall where, lighting a cigarette before making his speech, he told the packed crowd of 2500 he hoped his flight showed the value of aircraft in bringing the countries of the world together.

More adulation, more cheques, more crowds and more dignitaries followed, and King George V announced that Bert would receive the Air Force Cross as rumours of an impending knighthood made headlines throughout the Empire. Bert took contest winner Miss Gwen Fowler for a flight over Sydney in an Avian belonging to war pilot turned aircraft designer Edgar Percival, was cheered by 25,000 on a visit to Parramatta and recorded the story of his flight at the Columbia Graphaphone Works at Homebush for a £100 fee plus a thruppence royalty on every copy sold.[12] He was the special guest at a performance of the new Rodgers and Hart musical *The Girl Friend* at Her Majesty's Theatre, and the cast worked a rendition of 'Hustling Hinkler' into the first act. Several times during the performance Bert had to rise in his box to acknowledge the cheers of the crowd.

By now it was estimated that Bert had been offered £30,000 in business opportunities but had yet to accept any of them.[13] He was preoccupied with visiting as many Australians as he could to show them that flying was the way of the future and that with the light aeroplane everyone could travel vast distances with no more effort than driving a motorcar.

Over the next few weeks he ate more fancy food than he'd ever imagined — from turtle soup and *croute au sardines* at Australia's Parliament House to *oysters à la Hinkler* with the South Australian Premier. He also saw the inside of the country's most exclusive hotels, dining rooms and government houses and collectively hundreds of thousands of Australian battlers just like his own family came out to thank Bert personally for what he had done.

On Wednesday, 14 March, Bert left Sydney to fly to Canberra where his family had again journeyed by train. Despite persistent rain over the embryonic capital, at 2 p.m. Canberra presented a majestic vista for Bert as two RAAF machines escorted him over the handiwork of the city's architect Walter Burley Griffin. A year before, the Duke of York, with the assistance of speech therapist Lionel Logue, had harnessed his stutter to deliver a stirring speech at the opening of Canberra's new Parliament House.

As Bert landed on the Review Ground, now known as York Park, thousands rushed the Avian only to be held back by a cordon of police and 150 returned soldiers on security patrol. The RSL men joined hands to form a human wall but one intrepid fan managed to break though, a four-year-old girl holding a bouquet of flowers.

Bert carefully laid a tarpaulin over his Cirrus engine before a group of Diggers escorted him through a guard of honour formed by cadets from Duntroon Royal Military College to a rotunda where Stanley Bruce, his wife, a group of federal ministers, their wives and Frances, Jack and Queenie were sheltering from the rain. Bert went all bashful when one young woman leapt from the crowd to embrace him.[14]

At three o'clock Bruce called for an adjournment in the House of Representatives so that the whole parliament could attend an official welcome on the House steps fifteen minutes later. The rain stopped long enough for Bert to be driven to the ceremony in an open-top car.

The aristocratic Bruce, himself a Great War hero, spoke of Bert's courage, enterprise and ingenuity, saying he had 'contributed greatly to the science of aviation'. 'But, above all,' the Prime Minister continued, 'you have strengthened our faith in the future by the amazing demonstration that men of Australian birth possess all the qualities that make the greatness of a nation.' Bruce presented Bert with the cheque for £2000 — about eight years wages for a foundry worker — and Bert was shaking with emotion. 'I am doing my best to maintain a calm exterior,' he told the PM, 'but I assure you there is a lot going on inside.' He then handed Bruce the letter he'd carried from the London office of Granville Ryrie, saying he'd transported it from one of the oldest capitals in the world to the newest.

That night Bert and Jack attended a dinner for 200 along with most members of parliament, and Bert was also presented with a gold cigarette case engraved with the Australian coat of arms. Then the Prime Minister stood to toast Bert's health on behalf of a grateful nation. Jack told guests that when flying long distances solo Bert fashioned an old alarm clock, which he fastened to his neck in such a way that when his head lowered in sleep it would ring and wake him up. Bert explained to Bruce that soon there would be regular long-distance flights at night to allow passengers to see the sights by day before climbing back on the aircraft to take off at sunset.

On the Review Ground, Bert's 'little bus' spent that night under guard but still exposed to the wind and rain. Still, she was none the worse for wear the next day when Bert showed her to the Governor General, Lord Stonehaven, before going on a tour of Duntroon. Later in the day Bert was accorded the rare honour of a seat on the left of the President of the Senate and that evening he and his family had a private dinner at the Prime Minister's residence, the Lodge.

More receptions, lunches and tours followed. Bert spoke to about a thousand children at Telopea Park school and told them to obey their teachers because it was the best way to get ahead in life. At an RSL function, where Bert told of his experiences chasing Zeppelins armed with just a rifle, Bruce presented him with an Australian war gratuity of £153/3/9 despite the fact that Bert had technically forfeited his claim on the money by staying in England after the Armistice. At the Capitol Theatre Bert and the PM sat through a newsreel screening of his arrival in Sydney to deafening cheers and then a screening of *Wings*, the Clara Bow and Gary Cooper silent movie about fighter pilots, which Bruce declared the finest film he'd ever seen.

On Saturday, 17 March, Bert left Canberra at 2.30 p.m. farewelled by a group of dignitaries led by the Prime Minister nattily attired in plus fours. Bert arrived at Cootamundra at 3.30 for a cup of tea, a scone, a mayoral speech, some rousing cheers from a crowd of 4000 and a cheque for £100 collected from donations. He took off again for more of the same in Wagga Wagga 90 kilometres away, landing at the showground at 4.35 to find that special trains had brought thousands from surrounding towns. He spent the next morning at the showgrounds working on the Avian's engine and at midday took off for Melbourne 400 kilometres to the south.

Newspapers around the world were reporting that all hope had been abandoned for British fighter ace Captain Walter Hinchliffe and heiress Elsie Mackay, who were trying to cross the Atlantic in a Stinson Detroiter, but the mood of Melbourne was one of joyous exuberance when the crowd caught sight of Bert approaching over the city's north just after three o'clock escorted by two squadrons of RAAF bombers. Although Bert could not hear them over the roar of the engine, 70,000 people were giving him a standing ovation as he came down low and slow to give the vast Flemington crowd a good look at man and machine. He and the Avian glided along the straight where the country's greatest racehorses competed for the Melbourne Cup. Bert was then driven around the Flemington course standing in the back of an open-top car, dapper with homburg in hand, as the multitude waved hats, handkerchiefs and parasols in approval. So many people wanted to shake his hand that already, at Jack's suggestion, he was wearing a bandage around his right hand to politely fob them off, although many admirers crushed his left hand instead.

Frances received almost as big a cheer when she was introduced to the crowd and seemed to be revelling in her new role as a national celebrity. Half of the £1700 from the gate takings for the day went to Bert, the other half to charity. The Hinklers moved into the Menzies Hotel and spent the next week doing the rounds of official tours and functions. Bert went to the Princess Theatre to see the Hollywood star Betty Ross Clarke in the play *Tarnish* and happily posed with the cast. Miss Clarke told him she was a huge fan and even went up with the 1919 England to Australia pilot, Skipper Matthews to photograph Bert in flight.

On 20 March, while Bert was still in Melbourne, Bill and Chubbie arrived in Darwin to begin their own tour of victory. Bert spent time working on the Avian, which was moved to Essendon Aerodrome, and he visited the ultimate in scientific wizardry, the new television and radio laboratories in Queen Street where he saw scientists engaged in the astonishing work of transmitting photographs by wireless. He dined with his old CO Jimmy Goble and with Sir Keith Smith made a radio broadcast from his hotel room via station 3LO to Nance on the *Orama*. He went to the Moonee Valley horseraces and had three bets only to confirm that he was a better pilot than punter.

To at least one journalist Bert seemed utterly devoid of ego and a 'candid, friendly, amiable, quiet-voiced little man' who had 'none of the pompous secrecy of the inventor'.

He chooses his words well, and speaks slowly and deliberately. In conversation, however, he talks often with great rapidity, especially on technical matters, when that aviation enthusiasm of a lifetime blazes up in those dark eyes.[15]

Bert took Queenie and two aviation enthusiasts who'd each paid £25 at a charity auction to ride with him for flights in another Avian at an air pageant at Essendon. On the following Tuesday, 27 March, 10,000 people greeted Bert in Geelong despite the fact that he arrived only as a passenger on another plane.

Bert hadn't seen Nance for nearly two months and, although he thought often of Katherine, it was his partner of eleven years who still had his heart. He very much wanted to see Nance as soon as possible, and on Friday, 30 March, he took off from Essendon at 6.05 a.m. to meet her right across the country in Fremantle. Late that evening the Shell company received a message from its agent at the South Australian railway outpost of Cook on the Nullarbor Plain 130 kilometres from the West Australian border saying: 'Hinkler arrived at a quarter to five o'clock this afternoon central time. Had a good trip, and made a perfect landing. The actual flying time was 12 hours 5 minutes. The distance was 975 miles [1569km] as the crow flies which is an Australian record. The actual flying distance was between 1000 and 1100 miles [1609–1770km].' In making the flight Bert had reclaimed the national long-distance record he'd set in the Baby between Sydney and Bundaberg but which had been overtaken by Kingsford Smith and Ulm in their 1927 flight around Australia and by Frank Neale in a flight from Melbourne to Warwick a year later. Bert's new record coincided with the Federal Government's announcement that he was to be awarded the honorary rank of RAAF squadron leader.

The following morning Bert left Cook at 6.40, waved to passengers on the transcontinental train at the Deakin railway siding an hour later and finally landed at Merriden in Western Australia's wheat belt after a flight of eight hours that covered almost 1200 kilometres. The following day, Sunday, 1 April, Bert prepared for the short 270-kilometre flight to Perth despite the Revd Neil McDonald, Moderator Elect of the Presbyterian Church in Western Australia, declaring from the pulpit that if Bert were as strong morally as he was physically he would not desecrate the Sabbath.[16] Roman Catholic Archbishop Patrick Clune saw it differently, remarking that Bert was something of a miracle worker, making the whole of Perth look to the heavens for the first time in the city's history.

Bert left Merriden at 1.18 p.m. and breezed into Perth two hours later, coming out of the clouds behind a three-plane escort led by Norman Brearley to land on Loton Park, now called Perth Oval, which was crowded with 20,000 spectators. He quickly made his headquarters at the Savoy Hotel and two days later was in Fremantle to greet Nance on the *Orama*. With him at Victoria Quay at 9 a.m. were the Mayor and Mayoress of Fremantle, press reporters, photographers and a cinematographer, and held back by barricades, thousands more spectators hoping to catch a glimpse of the aviator and his wife. So eager was Bert to see Nance that even before the vessel had properly berthed he leapt from the wharf, across the chasm to the water and onto the ship's deck. He trotted inside the ship's foyer to greet her in private. When the happy couple finally came down the gangplank, the crowds cheered and wharfies wolf-whistled, one calling out, 'She looks all right, Bert', which made them both blush.[17]

Reporters described Nance as being a sweet, shy retiring sort of woman of medium height, slightly taller than Bert and with a slight build, black curly hair with dark eyes and wearing a Paris model frock of cream georgette. She told reporters she was born in Sheffield, and they wrote that she had 'fresh English colouring' and 'the most charming smile'. She said she felt like Alice in Wonderland because it was like some wonderful dream with all the attention being lavished on them, and she was quite unprepared for such a welcome.[18] Bert had made her the proudest woman in the world, she said, and she was proud of the fact that she was about to become the first woman to fly from Perth to Adelaide and would see the vast nation as no woman and very few men had ever seen it. The Avian had been reconfigured for passenger travel and, although it meant less petrol capacity and shorter flights, there would be more stops and more people to meet.

After a week of festivities, tributes and shilling donations to the 'Bob in for Bert' fund, and Bert's purchase of a small block of land at Johnson Street in the new Perth housing estate of Wembley for £70, the Hinklers left Perth from Maylands Aerodrome.

They flew to the Northam racecourse about a hundred kilometres away, then to the Boulder racecourse 4.8 kilometres from Kalgoorlie. They followed the trans-Australian railway line for more than 600 kilometres until, running short of petrol because of a strong headwind, Bert brought the bus down at the Forrest railway siding to refuel. The railway fettling gang he was relying on was missing. With the sun scorching Nance's 'fresh English colouring', she waited beside the Avian in her red leather flying helmet thinking hell couldn't be much hotter. Bert took off on foot for about three kilometres to find a startled ganger, who told him there was no petrol at the depot even for the King's favourite aviator.

Bert and Nance flew just another 135 kilometres before the sun had almost sunk, and Bert decided to stay overnight at the Hughes railway siding instead. The small community there turned on the hospitality and, suitably refreshed the next morning, Bert and Nance headed for Cook. They refuelled there and, after refreshments and declarations by Nance that she wouldn't have missed the trip for the world, they left at 12.25 p.m. Nance kept her eyes peeled for kangaroos but didn't see a jolly one, only dozens of rabbits scurrying about. They visited Ceduna on the Eyre Peninsula, and when one of the residents asked if she would like to settle there Bert piped up to say there was plenty of dust to settle there instead. The next afternoon more than 500 kilometres away in Adelaide another crowd of 20,000, including Frances and Jack, were at Morphettville Racecourse to welcome Bert and Nance to the South Australian capital. They landed at 3.30 p.m. on Saturday, 14 April, after a journey of four hours forty-five minutes, which normally took two days by car. It was the first time Nance had met Frances, and they embraced affectionately. Nance impressed with her elegance, but Bert looked as dishevelled as he had been in Darwin, although a cardboard box containing eggs he delivered to the Lord Mayor, Lavington Bonython, were in immaculate condition, a testimony, he said, to the safety and comfort of air travel. The Hinklers did the usual round of civic ceremonies and toasted the success of South Australian country boy Hubert Wilkins and his American pilot Carl 'Ben' Eielson, who had just completed a twenty-hour trans-Arctic crossing, an achievement that would see Wilkins knighted. Surely Bert's knighthood was close behind.

Bert and Nance stayed in Adelaide until Wednesday, 18 April when they headed off from Parafield aerodrome towards Melbourne with stopovers at Nhill, Stawell and Ararat. On Saturday, 21 April, they headed to Ballarat and the City Oval, where fifteen years earlier Bert had watched Wizard Stone crash into telephone wires and almost die. Not much had changed there. As the Avian circled the oval preparing to land, Bert realised he was travelling too fast to avoid the big crowd, pulled the nose up and just missed the phone wires. He headed down the road to the Miners racecourse instead.

They left Ballarat the next morning and spent two weeks enjoying the hospitality of Melbourne, where Bert and Jack fitted the Avian with another, smaller oil tank. In latter years Jack would tell the story of how he found a piece of cotton waste that looked like it had been deliberately pushed into the oil pipe as an act of vandalism or even sabotage. Although Bert privately told his relatives that he figured he would have been way out over Bass Strait when the motor started to play up, he never mentioned the incident publicly,[19] and no culprit was ever found.

Instead Bert was in fine spirits at 11 a.m. on Saturday, 5 May, when he and Nance took off from Coode Island at the meeting of the Yarra and Maribyrnong rivers in Melbourne. Nance was embarking on the most daring flight she had yet undertaken, a four-hour journey across Bass Strait to the Elphin Showground in Launceston. Another crowd of 10,000 was waiting, and many followed the Hinklers to their lodgings at the Brisbane Hotel. In Launceston the Hinklers met up with Bill and Chubbie, and Bert was reunited with his uncle Ted Bonney, an underground foreman at northern Tasmania's Aberfoyle tin mine. Ted had last seen Bert sixteen years earlier on a visit to Bundaberg and, given the young man's enthusiasm for flying and the dangerous nature of his hobby, he assumed the naive aeronaut was not long for this world. He was glad Bert had proved him wrong. At a reception hosted by returned soldiers at the Masonic Hall, Bert stood on a chair so that the audience could see him and said that aviation was Australia's best defence against war but also a tool for peace because if we remained 'in our own little coop',

we don't understand the other fellow's viewpoint, but
if we could have more personal contact with other
nations it would help wipe ill-feeling away. Australia
has the biggest coastline in the world to protect, and
aviation would be our best defence if the time ever
came.[20]

Bert visited some of the Bonneys 50 kilometres away in
Deloraine, and the next day he and Nance thrilled another
crowd of 10,000 with a spectacular flight down the straight
of Elwick racecourse in Hobart. The Hinklers made short
flights all over the northern part of the state, landing at
Bothwell, Scottsdale, Devonport, Burnie, Wynyard and on
the beach at Ulverstone. Then on 14 May, Bert and Nance
left Wynyard for Melbourne little realising that for the
next three hours their lives would hang in the balance. The
trouble started with buffeting winds that sent marmalade
oranges rolling violently around the cockpit. Then things
got really bad. The blinding rainstorm was terrifying for
them both.

'Hang on, Nance,' Bert cried out from the front cockpit,
as they started bouncing through the sky over Bass Strait.
Nance shrieked in terror at the wildest ride she'd ever had.
The rain lashed them, and Bert feared the Avian would
crash into the water below at any moment. He reached
down and passed Nance the inflatable life raft in case of
disaster. Every few minutes Nance would reach around
to wipe the water from his goggles. After a nightmare
journey they finally made it back to Melbourne shaken but
alive and Bert was ready to go up again.

After five more days in the Victorian capital they
began the journey back to Bundaberg.[21] They landed at

a sports ground in Albury during the big football match against Beechworth and then flew to Canberra for dinner with Billy Hughes, the former Prime Minister Bert once criticised for his 'big, wide Welsh noisy mouth'.

From there it was a trip to Goulburn, then Bong Bong and finally Sydney on 22 May. Over the next week Bert gave more lectures on aviation, and the pair visited schools and took in the sights of the Blue Mountains. On 23 May they attended a function in their honour at David Jones emporium in Sydney while, across the Pacific Ocean, Charles Kingsford Smith and Charles Ulm were enjoying the largesse of a rival retailer, Sidney Myer. For months the two pilots had been planning the first flight between America and Australia. Myer, the Russian peddler turned retail tsar, had given Kingsford Smith and Ulm £1500 to help fund their mission, and they had fitted three new Wright Whirlwind engines each of 220 horsepower to a massive Fokker tri-motor they'd bought, minus instruments or engines, from Hubert Wilkins. They called the machine the *Southern Cross*. Six minutes before nine o'clock on the misty morning of 31 May, the pair along with Americans Jim Warner, the radio operator, and Harry Lyon, navigator and engineer, cruised out of Oakland, California, past the Golden Gate — the great expanse of San Francisco Bay that was awaiting its new bridge — and began the first transpacific flight to Australia. The fate of the Dole flyers who had died on their way to Hawaii was very much in their minds as they stared at an ocean even wider than the Atlantic.

Bert told the Sydney press he'd be delighted to fly up to Brisbane to meet the *Southern Cross* crew on their arrival, although he realised that he now faced serious threats to his throne as the Empire's greatest aviator. Maybe Brisbane wasn't big enough for both of them. In the King's Birthday honours that week Captain George Hubert Wilkins became Sir Hubert Wilkins, sparking demands among Bert's supporters — and they were everywhere in Australia — as to when his knighthood might be arriving. Wilkins had flown across the North Pole as part of a team, but stone the bloody crows, mate, Bert had flown around the world. And solo!

There was anger and outrage in the very same Federal Parliament Bert had graced only a few weeks before as, first, western Sydney's Percy Coleman then 'Red' Ted Theodore, former Premier of Queensland, grilled Stanley Bruce on why he had recommended Wilkins for a knighthood and not Bundaberg's Monarch of the Air. Bruce could only reply that he declined to give any information or discuss the matter.[22] But rumours abounded. Some said it was because Bert was very much a working-class man. Others said it was because of the German name with the war still fresh in the minds of Australians, especially those whose sons had died on the Western Front. There was also the gossip that Bert's swarthy features and thick black hair were due to a 'touch of tar' — black blood — somewhere in his past. In Bundaberg there was even talk of a love child, a daughter, though there was never any public proof. And of course there was the question mark over Bert's marital status. Was he in fact married or 'living in sin'?

Soon, however, the furore over the King's blessings gave way to a new wave of euphoria in Australia. Twenty-seven hours and twenty-five minutes after leaving Oakland the *Southern Cross* arrived at Wheeler Field near Honolulu, after a flight of more than 3800 kilometres. The four crewmen stayed at the Royal Hawaiian Hotel on Waikiki Beach, and Kingsford Smith and Ulm posed in bathing suits for photographers, having a great time in the sun. They then flew to Barking Sands Beach on Kauai Island to fill their tanks with 6365 litres of petrol for the flight of almost 5000 kilometres to Suva in Fiji through a savage lightning storm in which they became hopelessly lost. From there they flew towards Brisbane nearly 3000 kilometres west.

Just after ten o'clock on Saturday, June 9, a crowd reported to be anywhere between 10,000 and 25,000 — including Bert's mother — was at Eagle Farm to see the big blue *Southern Cross* circle the aerodrome three times before completing a flight of almost 12,000 kilometres. The huge Fokker taxied to the enclosed barricade on the left of the Qantas hangar as Kingsford Smith appeared above the cockpit waving heartily to the crowd. He climbed out, lean, handsome, suntanned and as confident as Douglas Fairbanks. He acknowledged the cheers of the crowd with a broad smile and a shout of 'Hello, Aussies.' The nation had a new monarch of the air. As Brisbane went mad with aviation hysteria for the second time in three and a half months, Kingsford Smith worked the media for all it was worth and before long was generating an estimated £50,000 from the flight and planning to sell his machine to the Australian Government for £3000. The next day, Sunday, 10 June, at five past three the *Southern Cross* landed at Mascot in Sydney. Police estimated the welcome party to be 200,000.

Bert and Nance had no desire to be bit players in the Kingsford Smith story so, while the *Southern Cross* stole the headlines, they were in Cessnock after having visited

Maitland on their scenic tour north. Bert was still pulling crowds, but the big business offers had dried up.

As Kingsford Smith took over Sydney, Bert stayed in Cessnock, saying he had to fit a new tailskid to the Avian. He and Nance left on Monday, 11 June, and headed to Armidale and Glen Innes just as Francis Birtles made it by ship to Darwin in the Bean car after his eight-month drive from London. In Stanthorpe Nance said Bert's ultimate aim was to live in Australia but first he had plans to design a new light plane in England. In Toowoomba 5000 people met them at Clifford Park racecourse. Finally, back in Brisbane and staying at Lennons Hotel, Bert, Nance and Frances visited the Exhibition Grounds on Saturday 16 June to see the Queensland rugby league side led by Tom Gorman defeat the touring British Lions 21–7.

While they were in Brisbane a 29-year-old tomboy from Kansas named Amelia Earhart became the first woman to fly the Atlantic, although she was really just a passenger for pilot Wilmer Stultz and co-pilot and mechanic Louis Gordon, admitting after landing at Burry Port, near Llanelli, Wales, that 'Stultz did all the flying. I was just baggage, like a sack of potatoes.'[23]

On 21 June, Bert and Nance flew into Gympie Showgrounds where thousands of children, granted a half holiday for the event, were there to cheer them. Bert sustained a sprained ankle in a jarring landing and hurt it again when they visited Maryborough. He needed a walking stick to get around when he finally flew back to Hinkler Park on Saturday 23 June to introduce Nance, resplendent in a long, black velvet ensemble complete with skunk fur collar and cuffs, to his hometown.[24] Bert announced that his tour was over and he would soon be returning to England, but he wasn't done with public appearances. On Wednesday, 4 July, with his ankle healed, he led the Bundaberg rugby league team onto the field for a match against the touring Englishmen and performed the ceremonial kickoff. Although he gave the local boys a pep talk, England stormed all over them 61–13.

The Avian was kept in a makeshift hangar at Hinkler Park, and Nance did the rounds of family and friends. When young Ron Hinkler wasn't giggling at Nance's 'funny, posh accent' he spent many hours after school climbing into the cockpit of one of the world's most famous aircraft imagining he was flying over the seven seas.

In England Sir Alan Cobham told a luncheon at the Air League of the British Empire that Bert's single-handed flight was 'a physical feat which I, personally, would be unable to undertake'. Still the job offers for Bert were scarce.

In London Katherine Rose had arrived to visit her relatives in Glasgow and spent the next few weeks there enjoying the British summer. She loved England and Scotland and decided she wanted to see a lot more of them — especially the charming, funny little pilot she'd met in New York and whose letters touched her heart.

There were no more public functions in Australia for Bert but there was still a lot of travelling. On 7 August, he drove a Dodge Six from Bundaberg to Brisbane, singing the car's praises along the journey as he visited Childers, Biggenden, Goomeri, Nanango, Toogoolawah and Ipswich. He went to the Ekka sixteen years after his glider had gone on display there and watched the woodchopping events with the Governor. Bert was sounded out by an American company that wanted him and Ray Parer to pilot

Dornier-Wal flying boats on a route between Sydney and New Zealand, but nothing came of it. Bert was frustrated at having not taken up some of the big offers while they were hot.

A.V. Roe began advertising Avians for £600 and an order for twenty of them was received from the USA. Soon there was another order for fifty more, but Bert and Frances were disillusioned that the Australian Government had not given him a position promoting Australian aviation. To make matters worse, Kingsford Smith and Ulm were stealing all the press and had just made the first non-stop flight across Australia, flying the *Southern Cross* from Point Cook to Perth. 'You would have thought the Government would have offered him something here in Australia,' Frances wrote in a private letter to a friend that made its way into the press. 'I feel very disappointed. My son will have to go back from his native soil as no job is offering to keep him here and take his machine with him.'[25]

Bert and Nance flew down to Brisbane for a ball on the *Orama*, and two days later Bert flew to Southport School's annual sports day as a guest, landing on the Southport golf course. Bert was still talking about flying back to England in early September, something that terrified Frances, who believed he couldn't keep chancing his luck in those tiny, flimsy planes. Kingsford Smith had the right idea, she said, a big plane with plenty of engines and other men to help him. On 11 September, Smithy, Ulm, navigator Harry Litchfield and radio operator Tom McWilliams landed at Wigram Airport near Christchurch, New Zealand, after the first trans-Tasman flight 2500 kilometres from their starting point at William E. Hart's old airfield at Richmond.

If Bert wasn't feeling bad enough already, at 3 p.m. on Wednesday, 12 September, when he and Nance flew back to Bundaberg from Brisbane, Bert struck a rut landing at Hinkler Park, damaging one of the Avian's wings and the undercarriage. Bert said he would have his bus fixed within a few days, yet he had a good think about things and decided there was nothing keeping him in Australia. The *Orama* had already left Brisbane, and Bert and Nance decided to catch the train to meet it in Adelaide on its way back to London. Bert said he'd be back in Australia within twelve months and that he wanted to help establish a regular air service between England and Australia.

The Avian, he said, was still as good after more than 50,000 kilometres — 20,000 of them in Australia — as the day he'd left England. He said he had all sorts of schemes for aviation in Australia, although the schemes would be useless, he lamented, without government backing. All he could do was look to the younger generation of Australians to embrace aviation as the mode of transport for the future.[26]

The Avro Avian G-EBOV, which had set world records and opened the way for regular flights between England and Australia, was placed in a shed that Jack Hinkler built in his backyard on Kolan Street a couple of blocks away from Woodbine Cottage. On the afternoon of Thursday, 20 September, Bert and Nance set sail for England, looking the picture of domestic bliss, although that was about to change. The trip had made Bert about £10,000 tax free and he already had a plan to spend it.

Chapter 23

We are a race of fighters, descended from the War Gods.

**Bert Hinkler leading the Australian rugby league
war cry before the match against Wales at
London's Wembley Stadium, 18 January 1930**

*Of all the characters that aviation produced — and
there were hundreds of them in those adventurous
and formative twenties — Bert Hinkler stood
out head and shoulders above the rest.*

**Robert McIntosh, aka All-weather Mac, one of
Britain's most celebrated aviation pioneers[1]**

While Bert's seat at the dinner table of public acclaim in
Australia might have been yanked from underneath him by
the boisterous arrival of Kingsford Smith, the committee
of the Fédération Aéronautique Internationale was meeting
in Paris to decide the successor to de Pinedo, Cobham
and Lindbergh as the outstanding aviator of 1928. The
committee members nominated three Australians. Britain
put forward Bert. Holland, with its Fokker connection, went
for Kingsford Smith, and the USA chose Hubert Wilkins.

Spain tossed up Juan de la Cierva for his work on the autogyro, while Mussolini was confident about the chances of Captain Arturo Ferrarin. Together with the ill-fated navigator Major Carlo del Prete, who was killed in a crash just a few weeks later, Ferrarin had set a long-distance non-stop record by flying the absurd-looking Savoia Marchetti SM-64 pusher-propeller monoplane 7000 kilometres from Rome to the South American coast. The favourite in Paris, however, was Frenchman Captain Dieudonné Costes, who, with Lieutenant Commander Joseph le Brix, spent six months flying around the world, covering almost 55,000 kilometres in a Breguet 19GR biplane bomber.[2]

Bert and Nance arrived back in England on 24 October 1928. They'd had enough press attention to last them a while and, after first setting foot in Plymouth, managed to dodge the few photographers and reporters waiting for the ship. A photographer from the *Daily Sketch* got a shot of Bert and Nance when the *Orama* finally berthed at Tilbury, but there were no crowds. Eight months after Bert's record-breaking flight time had marched on. Newspapers said it was obvious that Bert was in dire need of a publicity agent if he wanted to experience the fame and fortune of Cobham.[3]

On 29 October, Bert was interviewed by the Australian Press Association and ventured the opinion that the best way to transport passengers between Britain and Australia was by using twin-engine machines capable of carrying ten people on a journey of two weeks. The trip would involve ten landings, and most of the flying would be done by night, allowing the passengers to see the sights during the day. The fare would be somewhere around £800, the price of a luxury car.[4]

After his monumental flight Bert should have expected a comfortable life endorsing the products of A.V. Roe, Castrol, Fairey or Shell but, while he had spent so long meeting and greeting in Australia, the aviation scene in England had changed and long-distance daredevils carried much less clout than the corporate heavyweights now calling the shots. In any case Bert told reporters he now wanted to be his own man. 'Numerous propositions have been submitted,' he said, 'but I won't tackle anything unless I can be absolute director running things in my own way.'[5]

Sir Charles Wakefield hosted a dinner at the Savoy for Bert, Nance and more than 300 guests on 28 November, and pointed out that one of the most remarkable features of Bert's great flight was his extreme modesty, departing in silence and returning to England unobtrusively. Sir Sefton Brancker agreed, saying that Bert was one of the world's greatest airmen yet few people knew him.[6] At a later time All-weather Mac said that, despite Bert's short stature, he was a giant compared to over every other aviator of the time and was a tough, courageous man who was popular wherever he went.

Bert began a long letter to his mother on 10 December, saying he and Nance were able to 'hang out' down at Mon Repos at weekends and, while his time was being taken up by one function after another, he was at last making some headway in building 'the machine of my dreams':

But I must hasten to add that in the midst of all this running about I am not collecting fees right and left. One or two schemes for that purpose I have had to turn down or else I should be delayed much long [*sic*]

in the pursuit of my chosen objective. When we were
leaving [Bundaberg] I told you we should be returning
as soon as possible and there are many reasons why
we should still stick to this course. If I thought there
was going to be any delay I would suggest you coming
over the coming summer, the winter I am afraid
would be rather too severe on you. The last few days
the cold has been so great that even I, climatised [*sic*]
as I thought, feel so uncomfortable that I should give
a lot for just a wee bit of warm Australian sunshine.[7]

Back at the Avro works in Hamble Bert gave a lecture
with illustrations on his Australian flight to his fascinated
former workmates in the staff canteen, an appearance that
effectively brought down the curtain on his involvement
with the company. He contributed to a symposium in the
Evening Standard on what aviation would be like twenty-
five years hence in 1953 and visualised that, while design
principles would generally remain the same, the methods of
streamlining monoplanes would make machines faster and
with a much longer range. Reliability would be so improved
that accidents would greatly decrease. Navigation would
be by wireless. Multi-engine aircraft of the private touring
type would be used in larger numbers, having enclosed
cabins, and would be as luxurious as the best cars. A non-
stop flight to Spain or Italy would be taken with the same
ease as a trip to the South Coast of England, a boon to
businessmen who wanted good weather for weekend golf.
And there would be special instruments to ensure easy
flying in fog and bad weather.[8]

A couple of days before Christmas 1928, Bert travelled
to Buckingham Palace to receive his Air Force Cross

from the future king, Edward, Prince of Wales, and he started 1929 with great optimism. In Paris the seventeen committee members of the Fédération Aéronautique Internationale met on 12 January to decide their brightest star. It was a close-run thing and, after five ballots, there were just two airmen left in the race, Costes and Bert. There was much deliberation and much discussion. Costes had flown around the world, but he'd had six months to do it and a navigator to help. Bert had flown more than 17,000 kilometres by himself. The committee voted again and, after a count and recount, the winner nine to eight for the greatest aviation feat of 1928 was Squadron Leader Herbert John Louis Hinkler of Bundaberg, Australia. He was invited to collect his award that June at a ceremony in Copenhagen.

With Alliott Verdon-Roe becoming Sir Alliott Verdon-Roe in the New Year's Honours list Bert felt that his own knighthood must be in the works, although he was much more interested in building his new plane. He envisaged a new aircraft called the Ibis, a safe comfortable touring machine that combined the best features of planes he had flown on long-distance flights and which could be easily adapted for land or amphibian use. Flying across Australia had convinced him of the need for a machine that could land where there were no aerodromes and only rivers or lakes. He selected the aeronautical engineer Rowland Bound, who had worked as a designer for A.V. Roe, to put his ideas onto proper blueprints.

The pair decided that the best sort of wing would be like the one Basil B. Henderson had designed for the Hendy Heck, a four-seat monoplane built by the Parnall company. Bert was willing to spend a good portion of his cash to make his dream machine fly and constructed a large, shed-like hangar behind Mon Repos. Soon it was enveloped by the sound of wood being hammered and shaped and the overpowering smell of varnish dope. A poker-faced Yorkshireman, Jack Hudson, a woodcutter for Avro who seemed to always have a pipe between his lips, was called in to assist. All Bert needed was a mulberry bush and he could have been back in Bundaberg making another flying machine from timber, metal, fabric, glue and dope. Soon his backyard team moved into one of the old Avro buildings at Hamble to continue their construction, and when the Ibis had reached a satisfactory stage, Bert brought it home behind his Riley car, taking off the wings, putting them on his roof rack and towing his machine as he had once towed his glider behind the horse and cart through the cane fields.

Years later Bound recalled that Bert said 'it should be an amphibian and as nearly immune from forced landings as was humanly possible':

> For that reason we decided to have twin engines mounted in tandem above the top of the wing. This reduced head resistance and meant also that in the event of failure of one engine, we did not have to fly with one dead engine, and rudder turned against the one that was still providing power. This little aircraft was of timber construction and the hull was skinned with 1/16-inch ply wood, coated with about six layers of dope to make it as waterproof as possible.

While Bert busied himself with his dream machine he also took freelance work for other aircraft manufacturers.

On 20 February 1929, he and Nance took part in an experiment by the Australian Press Association in which Bert took a Bristol fighter biplane over Croydon to receive a broadcast from 3LO in Melbourne on a six-valve super-heterodyne wireless, belonging to his friend C.G. Allen.[9]

Bert announced that he would be chief test pilot with Bristol, although he seldom worked for them. He toyed with the idea of a sponsored flight to Australia but, when the organisers would not use Wakefield's Castrol products, he abandoned it.[10] Instead, in May, he asked Jack to take the Avian out of his shed and, through his friend Len Pike, the Queensland Agent-General in London, donated his 'little bus' to the Queensland Museum as a gift to all Australians. Frances took the news hard. She loved that plane. Bert wrote to her, asking her not to feel disappointed. 'As a matter of fact I have no further use for it,' Bert said, 'and it would not do much good leaving it to deteriorate in a shed. Owing to the sentimental interest of a generous public I couldn't very well have sold it to anyone, so I think handing it over to the Queensland Government was about the best thing I could do under the circumstances.' Frances bit her lip and said goodbye to the silver machine, but not before writing to the government to ask whether it would it be all right to come to Brisbane to visit the Avian now and then.

On 20 June 1929, Bert made a short but momentous flight to Copenhagen where, in the Danish Parliament building, the president of the International Air Congress, Comte de La Vaux, presented him with the 1928 FAI gold medal for the best flight of the year. Delegates from twenty-one nations applauded long and loud[11] as Bert became just the fourth winner of aviation's most coveted prize. He would be in England only a month or two, he said, and then would be going off on another sensational exploit, the nature of which could not yet be disclosed. It was just the start of a phase of obsessive secrecy that would cloud the rest of Bert's life.

Under the signatures of de Pinedo, Cobham and Lindbergh, Bert signed the International Gold Book of Aviation, and while in Copenhagen he attended a function at the Aviators Club where the King of Denmark, Christian X, presented him with the Golden Air Cross. He also visited Jacob Ellehammer, the 'Danish Edison', and went on a flight with the Danish air force hero Lieutenant Bjarkow. After five days in Denmark, Bert took off for Stockholm, then London where his second Britannia Trophy awaited, following his 1920 win for the London-to-Turin flight.

Bert's time for the distance between England and Australia was eclipsed in the reverse direction by Kingsford Smith and Ulm, together with their wireless operator and navigator on 10 July 1929, when the *Southern Cross* landed at Croydon twelve days, twenty-one hours and eighteen minutes after leaving Derby in Western Australia as part of a round-the-world flight. Commentators agreed, however, that there was no comparison between what Kingsford Smith had done in a huge plane with a four-man crew and what Bert had achieved solo. Ulm emphasised that by saying the success of the *Southern Cross* would have been impossible without the pioneering achievements of the Smith brothers and Bert, 'whose lone voyage as his own navigator, pilot and mechanic could be described as truly wonderful' and had made their task easier.[12]

Bert and Rowland Bound were working around the clock on the Ibis. It was a unique design, a small, compact high-wing monoplane with a fuselage in the shape of a boat and an upturned nose. The machine had two seats side by side in a tight, enclosed cockpit and, to save weight, had a single joystick between the seats, which either person could operate. The engines were two Salmson AD.9 radials laid back to back, which cost £175 each and could develop 40 horsepower at 2000 revs per minute. Piano wire linked the controls rather than heavier push rods and bell crank levers. The undercarriage was made from two legs taken from an Avro 504K with rubber bungee cord as shock absorbers, and it could fold away when the plane was used as an amphibian.

On 28 August Bert wrote home to wish his mother a happy sixty-third birthday and told her of his progress. 'I am really right down hard at it and at last we are beginning to show something for our time and work,' he said. The machine embodied everything he wanted in an aircraft, a plane that was 'at home in all three elements':

whether flying in the air, landing on the ground or else on the water. The many difficulties I had to put up with in the Avian have fully demonstrated to me what to design for, what to avoid, and how to arrange these things all together so as to produce the first really useful small aeroplane. Perhaps you had time to notice in your little flip the uncomfortable force and rush of wind, the noise from the motor and all the rest of it so that you could not hear yourself speak.

All that would be different in the comfort of the Ibis, he assured Frances, explaining that 'you'll hardly know you're flying until you look out and see the country far below'. He promised her that for her next birthday she would be flying in his new plane.[13]

On the last week of October it was announced that Bert would fly up to Leeds to perform the ceremonial kickoff for the second rugby league Test between England and the Australian side led by Tom Gorman on 9 November. However, all week there was a simmering undercurrent in the atmosphere that made a looming football match in Yorkshire seem irrelevant. Bert was spending less and less time with Nance as he took freelance work and scoured London for backers for the Ibis. Because he was spending so much time away from home, he took a London flat at 26 Chichele Road, Cricklewood, near Hendon Aerodrome. But his domestic difficulties only mirrored the foreboding climate of the world.

The global trouble had started on 24 October 1929 when, after a huge share market run to cap off the excesses of the Roaring Twenties, the Dow Jones Industrial Average fell 9 per cent, sparking two days of panic selling on New York's Wall Street. Then, on Black Tuesday, 29 October, the Dow crashed 23 per cent, sending the world's financial markets nosediving into the Great Depression.

Bert had been in worse jams before, and the day after Black Tuesday he wrote to his mother to say the biggest crisis he faced was a shortage of hours to work on the Ibis. Even then the machine was coming together, and the Salmson engines, 'two real dinky spinning tops', had arrived from Paris. 'Have you seen any of the latest machines that the Quantas [sic] are using on the Brisbane to Charleville route?' he asked Frances.

These machines are fitted with the famous Jupiter 9-cylinder radial motor. Well the Salmson motors that I am fitting to the Ibis are very similar but of course very much smaller. The nine tiddley cylinders round the crankcase are like so many teacups with gills on. Just imagine the difference it would have made to the Avian, or perhaps I should say the difference it would have made to me, had I been able to land either on the water or land at will during my tootle around Australia last year.

Bert still presented a happy home life. At Mon Repos, he and Nance entertained friends and played records on the Salonola, Nance with her collection of Gilbert and Sullivan tunes and Bert with his stirring marching bands. Bert told his mother that he and Nance had enjoyed a wonderful summer, 'and here we are just heading into a hard winter. It is already getting darn cold. Nance usually finds plenty of amusement in the garden. Love from us both.' He wasn't about to let even his oldest supporter in on the secret about Katherine and the fact that he was now seeing her whenever she visited her Scottish relatives. He was often away from home, flying here and there, and it was not hard to meet in secret.

With the world facing the greatest economic setback of the twentieth century Bert couldn't have designed a revolutionary new plane at a worse time. Unemployment in Britain would soon reach 2.5 million. Across the Atlantic it was even worse. Hundreds of thousands of Americans became homeless. More than 5000 banks went under. Still Bert and Bound ploughed on. They registered Ibis Aircraft Company on 11 January 1930, and Bert taxied the machine around the farm field next to Mon Repos. The prototype was registered as G-AAIS.

The Australian rugby league side was seething on 4 January 1930 as the third Test at Swinton ended in a 0–all draw after a last-gasp try by Sydney's Eastern Suburbs halfback Joe 'Chimpy' Busch was overruled. On 15 January, England sealed the series 2–1 with a nail-biting win in the dying stages, and Gorman's Aussies were desperate to save face against Wales. So they called in their little big man. Three days later Bert jogged out onto London's Wembley Arena in his suit and tie before a crowd of 16,000 with the Australian rugby league team behind him. Bert promised to convey the *Daily Mail* Cup for the game home to Australia in the Ibis if they won. The players formed a crescent and linked arms as Bert led them in what was a feature of pre-match international rugby league until the late 1960s, the Kangaroos' war cry, a ritual that still has echoes in the Maori haka.

The speed and passing of the Australians ensured a 26–10 victory, and Bert invited Australian team manager Harry Sunderland,[14] who was reporting on the game for the *Brisbane Courier* to visit Mon Repos to show him what he was doing with the Ibis. 'If Bert's hopes are realised he has the ideal machine to suit Outback pastoral conditions for Australia,' Sunderland wrote later, 'and one that will reduce risk to a minimum.'[15]

On 22 January, Bert and Nance were at Southampton to farewell the Kangaroos as they sailed for home. Tom Gorman's team were so chuffed by Bert's support that they gave their champion a rousing dockside war cry. The shouts of 'Coo-ee' from the players could still be heard wafting across the water as the ship was well on its way.

* * *

In May 1930 Bert towed the Ibis to Hamble behind his car and test-flew it around Southampton Water, reaching a top speed of 177 kilometres per hour and taking his mate Jim Laver up for a spin as well.

No man had yet been able to break Bert's solo England-to-Australia record, but that same month the remarkable 26-year-old London secretary Amy Johnson came close in a Gipsy Moth. Flying a more direct route than Bert's, she was ahead of schedule until a series of crashes and bad weather over Siam wrecked her plans. Bert told reporters: 'All records are made to be broken. Even if Amy does not quite manage to break mine, she has shown that she can, and no doubt some day she will.' Even with the delays the intrepid Miss Johnson arrived in Darwin on 24 May, nineteen days after leaving Croydon, and immediately became the darling of the flying world.

The following month, as shares continued to wither, and Don Bradman surpassed Bert and Kingsford Smith as Australia's most celebrated hero with his batting on the 1930 Ashes cricket tour of England, another two, inexperienced young aviators decided to give Bert's record a shot.

On 20 June, Sydney-born Eric Hook, twenty-seven, and Jack 'Buller' Matthews, twenty-eight, who had worked for many years alongside Bert as a mechanic for Avro, left Lympne in a Gipsy Moth. Hook had grown up in Stanmore in Sydney, the son of a proofreader at the *Sydney Morning Herald*, and Bert told reporters: 'Matthews is a good chap and a skilled mechanic. He is quite up to the job he has undertaken. With good weather and if their luck stands they have a good chance of beating my record. Matthews was with me at the Avro works for some years and accompanied me on many test flights. I wish him the best of luck. I have given him the best advice I could relating to the project.'

Shortly before his flight Hook wrote to his parents in Sydney to tell them he believed he and Matthews could better Bert's record, despite the fact that both of them had received their pilots licences just a few days earlier.[16]

Hook had his whole future riding on the plane he called the *Dryasel*, and he and his young wife Dorothy, the mother of his two babies, had spent their every penny on it. For nine days, the two pilots made rapid progress until 29 June 1930 when violent winds on the way to Calcutta forced them to turn back to Allahabad. They were a day behind Bert's mark when they finally made it to Calcutta and, on 3 July, left the Burmese city of Akyab for Rangoon. They were halfway there flying through monsoonal rain over the Yoma Mountains when the Moth's engine became waterlogged. They crashed into a huge clump of bamboo, but the thick foliage saved their lives. The plane hung suspended in the dense crop before sliding to the ground. As Hook and Matthews scrambled out they were relieved that, despite a few cuts and bruises, they were remarkably uninjured. They decided to look for friendly villagers. Through the heavy rain they walked and walked and walked, their skin cut and torn by the thick undergrowth as leeches dropped onto them from trees and insects feasted on their bare skin. Finally after hours of struggle through the jungle they found themselves, exhausted and bleeding, right back beside their wrecked machine. They wailed in frustration. Then, composing themselves, they decided to follow the Buyo Chaung stream, believing that it must pass a village somewhere. For the next eight days they were like the walking dead trying to find help.

While they were struggling through the jungle, Bert acted as navigator for Charles Barnard in the 1200-kilometre King's Cup race around Britain. Bert's aircraft was one of the new de Havilland DH.80As, known as the Puss Moth, a high-wing monoplane with an enclosed cabin that could take two passengers. Made from fabric-covered steel tubing and with wooden wings, it was one of the fastest private planes available with a top speed of 206 kilometres per hour from its 115-horsepower, four-cylinder, in-line, air-cooled Gipsy III motor. It wasn't fast enough, however, and following the adulation around Amy Johnson's flight to Australia it was timely that on 5 July 1930, 22-year-old Miss Winifred Brown, the daughter of a wealthy Salford butcher, beat eighty-seven other competitors to become the first female winner of the event, pushing her Avian so hard it threatened to disintegrate.

In the Burmese jungle, Hook became ill with fever. He and Matthews had to swim across the Buyo Chaung several times, and that only made Hook weaker. They were hopelessly lost but had to go on. Walking the swampy ground was excruciating on their jellied legs. Terrified of eating poisonous fruit, they chewed only leaves for nourishment. Finally Hook collapsed. Matthews carried him for a while, but Hook begged him to go on alone to find help. Matthews pressed on and, covered in mud and muck and blood, finally found a village. A search party was organised.

Nance sent Dorothy Hook a message of support from one aviator's wife to another and, with Bert, visited

Matthews' fiancée. Then, a week after Matthews' escape from the jungle, the Australian press began running reports that Hook had been found alive. Dorothy, who had just turned twenty-two, was overjoyed.

The reports were wrong. A British search party, wading for days through swollen rivers and creeks, finally found Hook's body washed up eleven kilometres from where Matthews had left him. Hook had been so badly mauled by a tiger or leopard that his corpse was virtually a skeleton.

When Matthews finally returned to England after recovering from his wounds and a bout of malaria he told reporters that Bert had been his inspiration. 'He has been a great pal to me,' Matthews said. 'The last letter I received before we left Lympne was from him. It contained heaps of useful advice. I saw him in London previous to that and he gave me plenty of information and help. And during the time we were lost in Burma, he came and saw my people and comforted them.'[17] After the horrific ordeal he'd been through, would Matthews ever attempt such a flight again? You bet, he said. 'I should not think twice about having another crack at it.'[18]

By the end of July there was great speculation in Australia that Bert and All-weather Mac were planning to fly an Avro 10 Tri-motor, a very similar plane to the *Southern Cross*, from England to Australia, circumnavigate the continent and return to London all within a month.[19] But no matter what he said to stay in the news, Bert had other plans. He told the newspapers he wanted to make the Ibis a viable business and that was his sole focus. Secretly, he was breathless with anticipation at seeing Katherine again. She arrived in Plymouth on the *Tuscania* on 18 August 1930 and gave her address in London as the Metropole Hotel on Northumberland Street, a few kilometres from Bert's flat in Cricklewood.

Katherine was only in London five days before she headed back to New York on 23 August. Bert was on the same ship. The skipper was Katherine's brother-in-law, William Brown Rome.

In press interviews, Bert claimed he was going to New York to find financial backing for the Ibis, but that was not the only reason. In fact, while Bert was living in England in a very public relationship with his partner of thirteen years, a wife in all but certificate, he was now involved with a young woman on the other side of the world. He became even more secretive about his dealings at the same time as trying to launch a new aviation business at the worst possible era in American corporate history.

His frustration was apparent when he wrote to Rowland Bound on 18 September 1930 from the Hotel Fort Shelby, a skyscraper boasting 900 rooms and 900 baths on Lafayette Boulevard in Detroit. Bert related how he had gone to the Curtiss-Wright office in New York:

Mr Chas. Lawrence, I think he is Vice President or something like that, showed a great interest in the 'Ibis' and thought that the chief of their Keystone Works should have it brought to his notice. Hoping the best but fearing the worst, in any case to be prepared for any eventuality, I wired you to know the position. A few days later I went to the Keystone plant at Bristol [Pennsylvania]. But although the particular guy I wanted to see was away, I did not feel much elated at the views expressed by his subordinates.

Bert's disappointment was masked by his excitement at all the new aeroplanes he was sampling in America, and he admitted the exhilaration had him in a 'dither'. He had just spent an afternoon at Detroit Aircraft Corporation's airport flying Lockheeds. 'Oh Gee boy and aren't they dandy,' he wrote.

> I think I am well on the way to making a good deal with Lockheed, as a matter of fact, keep it to yourself for the present until the job is fixed, but I am negotiating for sole Lockheed Representation and the preliminaries have been so satisfactory that I am most confident it will come off. Already there are arrangements for me to deliver some Lockheeds to various parts of the States to get me more acquainted with the ship and their methods. The other day I was over at Ford's and my luck one pair of eyes is not enough.

Bert related how he tested a pair of Ford Tri-motors and they were so good they brought any airline pilot 'down to the level of bus driver'. 'The pilot only has to come on duty while taking off and landing,' Bert wrote, 'he doesn't even require an office boy on duty while he goes off and soothes the passengers.'

He then told Bound the story of how a 'private pilot to some wealthy guy' took him in a Bellanca aeroplane to Bristol, from New York's 'exclusive Aviation Country Club aerodrome at Hicksville, Long Island about 20 miles from NY': 'We travelled bang over New York, fine sight, and made a call at Teterboro Airport, where Fokker's Eastern plant is located. Here was another feast for my eyes. I met

Fokker's pilot Bernt Balchen — that is the chap who flew [Commander Richard E.] Byrd over both the North and South Pole and he very kindly showed me around.'

At Teterboro he had a good look at Fokker's amphibian but said it looked better in photos than it did in reality and thought the Ibis a better craft. He was more impressed by the huge, four-engine Fokker F.32 and the Bellanca monoplane powered by a 300-horsepower Whirlwind engine. He said he'd flown the 'Fairchild cabin job' with a Wasp motor. 'She flies alright,' he said, 'but the take-off, well, it's not very brilliant, something like your old Moth with [the] Mark I Cirrus [engine] and with the top speed just getting into three figures. Well it seems to be a waste of [a] good engine.' The Curtiss Robin, he said, 'flies as nice as the rest, but the main thing about it is that you can buy them very cheap. The other day at Buffalo I flew all around over the Niagara Falls in one of the [Consolidated Aircraft Corporation's] Fleetster ships. Like a Lockheed but with a 575HP Hornet motor.' Bert signed off by telling his business partner: 'I'll keep you posted on any happenings so that if any opportunity shows up we are on it.'[20] Rowland Bound would be waiting a long time for news.

Back in England, the race continued for aviators trying to break Bert's record to Australia despite the tragedy of Eric Hook and the crash of the world's biggest airship R101 in France, which killed British airship travel as well as forty-eight people, including Sir Sefton Brancker, Director of Civil Aviation, and Lord Thomson, Secretary of State for Air. By mid-October four aircraft were all somewhere between London and Darwin with their pilots looking to topple Bert's milestone.

F.R. (Froude Ridler) Matthews was chief instructor at the London Aero Club, and after having taught Amy Johnson to fly figured he was more than capable of a crack at Bert's fifteen-day mark. His Puss Moss was much faster than Bert's Avian. He was on track to break the record but, on 27 September, he left Rangoon heading for Bangkok when he crashed in bad weather. He finally made it to Darwin on 18 October, having taken more than twice the time of Bert's flight.

Queensland Flight Lieutenant Cedric Hill left Lympne in a Gipsy Moth named *Jane* on 5 October and was passed by Major Charles Pickthorne and Flying Officer Charles Chabot in a Puss Moth. They eventually abandoned their flight in Karachi after a forced landing and passport problems delayed them in Persia (now Iran).

Hill had flown for thirteen days when he arrived at Atambua on the west of Timor. He only had the trip to Darwin left but, when taking off on the short, soaked runway the next morning, his wheels clipped the fence and the Moth crashed. Hill was still surveying the damage later that day and making plans for the machine to be shipped to Surabaya for repairs when out of the clouds came a new, faster model of the Avian called the *Southern Cross Junior* with Kingsford Smith at the controls. Hill conceded defeat and the next morning gave Smithy his inflatable boat just in case he had problems across the Timor Sea. He even swung the Avian's propeller for him as Kingsford Smith, powered by a 120-horsepower de Havilland Gipsy II motor and revised wings, completed the England-to-Australia journey on 19 October. He arrived just ten and a half days after he had left Heston Aerodrome, in London's west.

The first telegram Kingsford Smith opened upon arriving in Darwin was from Bert in New York, who told the press: 'I am happy to add my congratulations on Kingsford Smith's very fine show.':

> I am very glad he had the benefit of modern equipment, whose reliability has been a wonderful demonstration of the progress we are making with small touring aircraft. The few extra miles per hour available on their speed, because of added power and advancement in design, is a tremendous aid in negotiating longer hops. I never dreamed that my little run home nearly three years ago would remain a standard for so long, but the progress of aviation is sure and definite. We who knew Smithy expected him to put up such a good showing, and our expectations have been fully justified.[21]

Kingsford Smith told listeners of Brisbane's radio station 4QG that Bert still stood 'very high' in his estimation and that he had the advantage over Bert with two or three years of advancement in the science of aviation, a better aircraft and a more powerful engine with greater cruising range.[22]

Bert was having no success in finding backers for the Ibis. However, with the airfields of the USA making him feel like a kid in a toyshop and Katherine making him feel like the luckiest man in the world, he still found ways to enjoy himself, testing American planes and flying as a passenger on commercial airlines. He went over to Toronto to talk to the de Havilland company about the Ibis then, on 6 November, made his way through a snow storm to Montreal where he met one of his old buddies from the Italian Front, Captain Roy Foss, now director of the Montreal Light Aeroplane Club. Bert told Foss that the Ibis was the perfect machine for the private pilot to cover the vast distances of Canada and that he thought he could push the plane's top speed up 16 kilometres per hour to 193 by replacing the two Salmson engines with a single Gipsy. On 30 November, he caught a Canadian Colonial Airways flight from Montreal to Albany, New York, then journeyed on to see Katherine in Astoria.

Back in Australia, on 10 December 1930, Cedric Hill landed his patched-up Gipsy Moth in Darwin and *Jane* was sold to Harry and Lores Bonney. Lores had stunned all her friends and family by announcing that she had learned to fly in secret. She couldn't drive and at weekends, while Harry was playing golf, she would hitch early morning rides with her milkman to Eagle Farm eight kilometres from her home and take to the air. Harry eventually found out about the lessons but surprised Lores by supporting her love for aviation all the way. She renamed Hill's Moth *My Little Ship* and planned some great voyages.

In America Bert was also giving out flying lessons, most famously to the cartoonist John Held Jr, who designed many covers for *Life* magazine and the *New Yorker*. Late in 1930 Bert decided to head south to sunny Florida to see his old friends Bill Lancaster and Chubbie Miller. He had stayed in touch with them after he'd returned to England and knew they had not found the success that their exciting adventures and breathless romance promised. Bill and Chubbie had been invited to Hollywood with the promise of a movie about their flight to Australia, but the project was abandoned partly because of the scandal surrounding their relationship. Kiki Lancaster wouldn't give her husband a divorce, and Lancaster's star had waned while Chubbie's had risen. She had gained her pilot's licence in New Jersey and had gone on to compete in the first Powder Puff Derby for female aviators in 1929, flying from Santa Monica to Cleveland against the likes of Amelia Earhart.

Chubbie's exploits and those of her fellow female aviators only added to the drama surrounding the pending release of the new Jean Harlow movie, *Hell's Angels*, one of the most expensive films made to that time in which maverick producer Howard Hughes told the story of World War I fighter pilots and their battles with the Zeppelins. Chubbie became a test pilot for Curtiss-Wright, set women's records for flights across the USA and survived being blown off course on one journey from Miami to Havana. She was initially reported lost, presumed dead, but turned up safe in the Bahamas.

Chubbie was preparing to fly from Jacksonville, Florida, to Washington DC when Bert flew into town in a Puss Moth, with two passengers. He arrived just in time to see Chubbie crash from a height of 15 metres when her fuel pump failed. The aircraft was completely wrecked, and Chubbie suffered serious internal injuries.

On 16 December 1930, newspapers around the world reported that one of Bert's passengers in sunny Florida was John Held Jr and the other was Bert's wife. That was news to Nance Hinkler, the woman the world knew as Bert's wife, as she was still in England, shivering through a miserable winter. Three days after the reports appeared, Nance sailed from Southampton on the *Ausonia* bound for New York. She wasn't happy.

Chapter 24

During one of the wildest nights I have ever spent I
ran into every kind of weather and wind imaginable.
Then into the worst electrical storm I have ever seen.
I battled it for six full hours. I was completely blinded.
At one point I came down so low [over the ocean]
that a mountainous wave brushed just below me.

Bert Hinkler, quoted in the *New York Times*
on 4 December 1931, describing his solo
flight across the South Atlantic

Kingsford Smith said he was proud to claim
Bert Hinkler as a brother Aussie.

***Flight*, 25 December 1931**

The turbulent economic winds of 1930 had thrown Bert
completely off course, and the situation with Nance
and Katherine yanked the stability of the home life he'd
enjoyed at Mon Repos right from underneath him. He
was convinced that with the right financial support the
Ibis could be a winner, but the twin engines laid back to
back caused some handling problems, and more work was

needed to refine it. Bert talked up the plane's innovative brilliance every chance he had in the USA, but the money-men weren't listening.

For the first time in his life, Bert's friends were noting signs of stress and depression. He and Nance had smoothed things over after her arrival in New York four days after Christmas 1930, but it did not auger for a happy new year. The chief test pilot at Westland Aircraft, Harald Penrose recalled that at this time Bert was becoming so headstrong that his forceful opinions on aircraft and their design made him difficult. And there were other worries.

He and Nance were dining in a restaurant in Detroit on 30 January 1931. Bert told her he was planning to spend a lot of time in the USA, and he had many of his personal possessions with him, or thought he did. Outside the restaurant they saw that a small leather trunk containing Bert's medals and trophies worth an estimated £4000 had been stolen from the rumble seat of his car. There was some consolation twelve days later when four men, three with long police records despite their youth, were arrested after one of them pawned Bert's diamond ring.[1]

Bert told the press he intended to base the Ibis company[2] in the USA (which would keep him close to Katherine). However, if he thought his record-breaking flight of three years earlier would open doors for him Stateside, he was wrong. The glow surrounding his England-to-Australia trek was losing its lustre. On 10 April C.W.A. Scott, the former Qantas pilot who'd gone looking for Bert around Cloncurry in 1928, reached Darwin just nine days and four hours after leaving Lympne in a Gipsy Moth, breaking Kingsford Smith's mark and shattering Bert's time by six days.

The world was sinking further and further into turmoil. Italian police had thwarted an assassination plot against Mussolini. Adolf Hitler, preaching fanaticism as the ladder to success, was gaining a toehold in German politics with the help of the once-dashing Hermann Göring, by now a violent and bloated morphine addict whom a psychiatrist had labelled 'hysteric and unstable'. Japan was considering an invasion of Manchuria.

Bert thought about buying a plane and doing air-taxi work for wealthy businessmen, but wealthy businessmen were few and far between after the Wall Street meltdown. He knew he had to do something spectacular to get his name back in the headlines as more than a has-been trying to flog a plane no one wanted, and on 16 April Canadian authorities issued him with a Commercial Air Pilot's Certificate.

He tried to buy a Westland Widgeon at a discount but found the company uncooperative so, with some financial help from Castrol's Charles Wakefield, he flew to Toronto to talk to de Havilland about a Puss Moth. They had just the one. It had been assembled at de Havilland's Downsview Airport in Toronto on 13 September 1930 and looked magnificent with silver fuselage and red struts. It was test-flown on 27 April 1931 and registered to Bert two days later as CF-APK. Reporters in Toronto speculated that he was planning either a monumental journey to South America then across the South Atlantic, a flight to Australia via Vancouver or a North Atlantic flight from Canada to London.[3]

Bert named his Puss Moth *Karohi*, which he told some reporters was an old American Indian word for 'wanderer' and others an Australian Aboriginal word for 'lone wanderer' or 'lone hand'. Even Nance believed it, although 'Karohi' actually was a combination of abbreviations: Ka for Katherine, Ro for Rose and Hi for Hinkler. Bert even had an artist adorn the name 'Karohi' with Cupid's arrow on the side of the aircraft.

Most days Bert would be in his overalls at Downsview Airport, face greased and oiled, tinkering and modifying the *Karohi*. De Havilland workers remembered him as being very quiet and polite and a man who kept to himself, apart from his long discussions with de Havilland engineers over changes to the plane. So intent was Bert on saving weight that he even removed the plane's navigation lights. The interior was stripped almost bare to fit a long-range fuel tank custom-made by a firm in New York. Built to Bert's specifications, it would give him twenty-four hours in the air. Imported bracing wires replaced the original set to give the machine's fuselage greater strength. The only provision he made for safety was to install a backup compass.

Bert and two veteran engineers worked out a way to replenish the engine oil based on the mechanics of the water cooler in the de Havilland office. But he took on so much of the logistical preparations that he had no time to promote himself and his mission to attract funding. Whereas Lindbergh and Kingsford Smith had been able to find lucrative sponsorships, Bert was again working on the cheap. Once again he shunned a radio because it was unnecessary weight.

As Bert toiled away on the Puss Moth in Toronto, the handsome Norwegian Haakon Quiller was trying to establish his parachute act and meet adventurous women in New Zealand. On 2 May, he was performing at Oamaru on the South Island where 1400 people had gathered on a Saturday afternoon to watch the 35-year-old bail out from 1950 metres. Quiller jumped spectacularly from the machine, but the crowd watched horrified as his parachute failed to open and he fought frantically to get the bloody thing working. 'His body was smashed to pieces,' said one news report.

Three days later Lieutenant Commander Glen Kidston and Captain Thomas Anthony Gladstone were flying a Puss Moth, like Bert's, on a tour of South Africa at a height of 300 metres between Johannesburg and Pietermaritzburg when their machine flew into a gale and thick clouds of dust. Children playing in the area saw a wing break loose. The machine nose-dived into the ground among rocks and thick bush. Both men were killed.

On 5 May 1931, the day of the Puss Moth crash in South Africa, Bert flew out of Toronto in a cloud of mystery. That afternoon at 2.30 he arrived in Buffalo, New York, and although he was polite to local reporters he had a firm 'no comment' when pressed on his future movements.

From New York Bert flew to Pawtucket, a few miles from Providence, Rhode Island, and under more questioning from reporters scoffed at suggestions of Buenos Aires and Africa. 'You see, whenever I take a plane off the ground they get the idea that I must be going somewhere,' he said. 'If I have not decided where I am going they decide it for me.'[4]

In Bundaberg, Frances was just back from a tour of the countryside around her home in her new Ford Model A and told her friends she would not be surprised to see Bert fly back to Gavin Street. However, the rest of the Hinkler family had caught his secrecy bug and weren't revealing much. 'Members of the family are reticent regarding the movements of the famous aviator,' the *Rockhampton Morning Bulletin* reported, 'and dismiss all questions with a smile, adding "Bert does not like publicity."'[5]

At the end of May 1931, Bert farewelled Nance from New York on the Cunard liner *Lancastria*. She headed back to the Mon Repos house, and Bert headed for Katherine. His life was taking unexpected and sudden turns, and his private life was becoming as turbulent as the storms he'd encountered over Sumatra. He was embarrassed in the spotlight as it was, and the thought of being portrayed by the press as a two-timing ladies' man must have terrified him. The clandestine relationship with Katherine added to his furtive behaviour over his flight plans, now all the more urgent as he was quickly running out of ready cash. Bert flew back to Toronto and took the Puss Moth out for test flights after each modification, but when the weekends came he almost always headed for New York 800 kilometres away.

On 24 June 1931, he wrote from Pawtucket to Edward J. Hart, now editor and owner of *Aircraft*, official journal of the Australian Aero Club in Sydney, to tell him of his Puss Moth purchase and his hopes to resurrect the Ibis 'under the Stars and Stripes':

> My finances being what they are I am prevented from the great joy of just flying for pleasure [Bert complained]. Of course I cannot stay in this part of the world for all my life, someday I suppose I must return to the land of smoke and fog. Perhaps you

may know what a bad sailor I am and how I dislike
the discomfort of travel as provided by the various
shipping people. If my own Ibis was ready there would
be no more to say about it. I have considered using
the Moth for the purpose and have already worked
out satisfactory figures as to the practicability of
such a return.[6]

With a pencil and paper Bert had plotted a course
from New York to Trinidad and on to Maricaibo in
Venezuela. He needed to get a move on if he was going
to regain public attention as, on 6 August 1931, a tough,
hard-drinking Scottish playboy named Jim Mollison,
who had been flying in Australia for Kingsford Smith's
ANA Airlines, took just eight days and nineteen hours
in a Gipsy Moth to fly between Wyndham in Western
Australia and Pevensey Bay in East Sussex. One of the first
people to send a congratulatory telegram was Mollison's
future wife Amy Johnson, who had just flown to Japan
from England. Mollison later said he got on much better
with the flamboyant Kingsford Smith than he did with
Bert, whose reserved nature was at odds with Mollison's
carousing.

A week after Mollison landed in England, Bert had
lunch in New York with the Tasmanian flyer Harold Gatty,
the man Lindbergh referred to as the Prince of Navigators.
Gatty had just been honoured with a tickertape parade
through Manhattan after he and the Texan adventurer
Wiley Post had flown for 24,000 kilometres from Roosevelt
Field in New York across Europe, Russia, Siberia and
Canada and back to Roosevelt Field. Gatty's description of
his journey fired Bert up for his next adventure.

Despite the time he was spending in the arms of Katherine, Bert still considered Nance his wife and was determined to see her right if anything happened to him. On Monday, 19 October, he made a visit to his Toronto attorney, Alfred Bicknell, a King's Counsel, and asked him to knock up a will for Herbert John Louis Hinkler, 'at present residing in the city of Toronto (formerly of Bundaberg, Queensland)' and naming his 'said wife' Nance Hinkler as the executrix and sole beneficiary of his estate. The next day Bert took off from the Downsview airfield with no advance notice and landed in New York City. He was not in a good mood after having had a spat with de Havilland over his account. A de Havilland director in Toronto insisted that the money for the Puss Moth be paid immediately in case anything happened to its pilot. Bert later told Nance:

> The blessed [de Havillands] in some ways are blasted cold hard dollar snatchers. If they want me they will have to catch me.

Bert eventually sorted out his financial arrangement with the aircraft company but, with seemingly no idea of the commercial potential for another record flight, he fobbed off all media enquiries and secretly began preparations for his most audacious journey yet. On Wednesday, 21 October, he spent the day confirming the oil and petrol arrangements for his travels to South America with Castrol then, on the Thursday, spent every waking hour checking and rechecking the *Karohi*. 'Gee, she is in good nick,' he wrote to Nance. 'Even the men while at de H's came round and told me they thought my ship was in the best condition of any of the Puss Moths, oil, plugs, valves, magneto, filters and everything that makes it go all perfect.'

On Friday, 23 October, for the very first time, Bert did some gas-load trials to make sure the machine could carry the massive amount of petrol it would need for a flight that would stun the world. Bert put 254 litres into the wing tanks and another 150 litres into the specially designed tank for the cabin and took off from North Beach Airport (later named LaGuardia) at Queens, near Katherine's home in Astoria. The Puss Moth initially struggled with the weight of fuel. 'Although we did not go off like a skyrocket, still the results were very encouraging,' Bert told Nance. He landed and put another 76 litres into his machine. 'The gas load was beginning to be noticed getting off but once in the air Oh boy!'

Bert listed the distances for the start of his flight so Nance could follow his progress: New York to Kingston, Jamaica 2890 kilometres; Kingston to Maracaibo, Venezuela 998; Maracaibo to Trinidad 1135; Trinidad to Georgetown, British Guiana 628; Georgetown to Cayenne, French Guiana 725; Cayenne to Natal, Brazil 2400. He said he'd find a place to land somewhere between Cayenne and Natal when he was closer to his destination. And then he tried to put Nance's mind at rest.

'Oh look, My Darling Always,' he wrote on 25 October, 'as I told you before I left Toronto I got all things put in order. [Attorney] Bicknell was very good, in fact I think he got quite a kick in attending to my affairs. I have also given him a Power of Attorney. I'm sorry the way I might have hurt your feelings on past occasions over this very same matter.' Although he had not told the attorney he and Nance weren't legally married, Bert reassured

Nance that it was a mere technicality as far as his estate was concerned. 'I, naturally, have not thought it necessary to enlighten Mr Bicknell, but you need not worry, he is your man and should the need arise he will carry out my instructions to look after your interests.'[7]

The following afternoon Monday, 26 October, at 2 p.m. Bert said goodbye to Katherine and amid much secrecy, left North Beach, New York, and headed south. With no navigation lights he had to get out of American jurisdiction by nightfall. Bumpy winds gave the Puss Moth a severe test. Bert felt dread until the winds abated, but then he ran into heavy clouds and a storm at 10 p.m. about 240 kilometres over the Atlantic. He flew by the clock to escape the weather, going in one direction for a certain time, then changing course in the opposite direction for an equal amount of time. Twice he brought her down low to escape the weather before recovering altitude. Then he climbed back to around 2400 metres in the clouds, and found moonlight brightening the sky at 3000 metres.

'It was a great aid in reading the instruments,' he recounted later. 'The good ship *Karohi* ran perfectly, and we landed on the polo ground at Kingston in time for breakfast.' After a flight of eighteen and a quarter hours in which he covered 3000 kilometres because of the detours for weather, Bert landed just after 8 a.m. on 27 October. *Time* magazine duly reported that the *Karohi* was the first land plane to touch Jamaican soil.[8]

Bert completed the various immigration formalities in Jamaica, proving that he had recently been vaccinated against smallpox and that his name did not appear on any criminal records. He was given the royal treatment after adding a touch of breathless colour to the planned inauguration of Kingston's new airport with his unannounced arrival. A couple of days later he was honoured at a slap-up dinner at Kingston's Manor House Hotel hosted by the mayor, George Seymour Seymour. There the Jamaican Trade Commissioner stood to announce that while in England he had climbed the ominous mountain Helvellyn to find a stone tablet announcing that Kingston's most honoured guest had landed an aeroplane on that very spot, the only mountain in the world upon which an aircraft had landed. The following day Bert was again the special guest alongside the Jamaican Governor in a crowd of 4000 at Sabina Park where the Jamaican soccer team ran the legs off their Cuban rivals, who were still a quarter of a century away from communism.

While Bert was delayed in Jamaica by bad weather, Arthur Butler, a British-born pilot raised in Lithgow, New South Wales, shaved two hours off C.W.A. Scott's England-to-Australia record, making the journey in a tiny Comper Swift in nine days and two hours. Finally, Bert hopped off again from Jamaica on 9 November and headed to Maracaibo in Venezuela. He passed over one ship an hour out of Kingston, but for most of the journey saw nothing but an endless stretch of water punctuated occasionally by the sinister dark shapes of monster sharks. Only the constant hum of his Gipsy III engine kept him company as he covered the distance of almost a thousand kilometres across the Caribbean Sea in six hours.

The next day, 10 November, Bert landed on Piarco Airdrome in Port of Spain, Trinidad, just after noon, ending a journey of six hours and fifteen minutes. He spent two days in Trinidad as the guest of Sir Charles Belcher, an Australian lawyer and bird-watcher who had just been made Trinidad's Chief Justice.[9]

Bert had mapped out a route to Brazil in easy stages, but the journey was tougher than he imagined. And more intriguing. He marvelled at the bird life, including great flocks of scarlet ibis that only made him more determined to make his own Ibis a success. He estimated that he spent an hour flying across the mouth of the Amazon. On 13 November, he arrived in the Brazilian city of Belem after a flight from Paramaribo in Dutch Guiana. He had a standard line for reporters who asked him about the rumours that he was about to embark on the first flight west to east across the South Atlantic. Other pilots had come the other way — even Mussolini's right-hand man, General Balbo — had led twelve S.55 flying boats from Italy to Rio earlier in the year, but no one had gone in the more dangerous reverse direction. 'I have no plans owing to my resources being insufficient to cover the flight I desire to make,' Bert said. 'My future arrangements are very indefinite.'

He was giving the same minimalist line after he flew nearly a thousand kilometres across impenetrable rainforest to the Caera State aerodrome in the Brazilian city of Fortaleza on 14 November. But then as police surrounded his plane, demanding his visa and authorisation to fly over Brazilian territory, which he did not have, Bert started talking — and fast. He was taken into custody immediately and dumped in a jail for illegal immigrants. Bert smuggled out a note appealing for help from Fortaleza's British community, ultimately resulting in officials of Booth Steamship Line approaching Brazil's British consul. Bert was released and, while he waited for the necessary official permission to fly over Brazil, copious apologies were proffered. He later described his incarceration as nothing more than going for walks and drinking beer and wine with the Governor.

On 23 November, he journeyed to the nearby city of Natal, about the closest point to Africa in South America. On the morning of 25 November, the Puss Moth was loaded to the gills with petrol so that it was about 225 kilograms overweight. Bert told very few people that he was about to attempt one of the greatest aviation feats of all time. He sent Nance a cable that read simply: 'Here's hoping for all.' When she received it at home at Mon Repos, Nance thought he was flying to South America's Patagonia region for some sightseeing.

As he was preparing his plane, one of the few people to see Bert off gave him a small female marmoset monkey as a good luck charm. It was love at first sight between the little pilot and the undersized critter, just 15 centimetres long. Its two brilliant eyes, like black marbles, shone with what Bert took as affection and, although some people found its screeches annoying, Bert was glad to have a companion on his great quest into the unknown. It reminded him of the magpie he'd been given on his final flight with the Baby, but he was sure this odyssey would turn out better.

Bert put the marmoset on the passenger seat next to him and revved up the Gipsy III, an engine with just half the power of Lindbergh's *Spirit of St Louis*. 'Hang on, girl,' he said to the monkey as he aimed the Puss Moth for Gambia 3000 kilometres across the South Atlantic with its cyclonic winds, roaring waves and demons of the deep. Bert took off at 9.52 a.m. Behind him was the immense Amazon rainforest looking like a vast motionless green sea. In front of him a great grey rolling ocean just spoiling for a fight. At best he had enough fuel to take him 3500 kilometres, giving him a very small margin of error to fly around bad weather.

The overloaded plane struggled into the air over Natal and lumbered towards the oncoming clouds to the northeast. Bert had hardly lost sight of the Brazilian coast when the first storm hit. He tried to gain altitude but the Puss Moth, with all its petrol, was too heavy. The wind steadily forced her down towards the stormy sea. With the marmoset having a great old time screeching with laughter, Bert wrestled the joystick with all the strength in his brawny forearms, but not even Hercules could have stopped the plane from falling. Before he knew it, Bert was just above the furious Atlantic waves. One monster wave leapt up at him and rolled just 1.5 metres under the fuselage like a thousand black runaway freight trains racing end to end. Spray lashed the Puss Moth, and Bert was ready to swim at any moment. He hadn't brought a life raft because he couldn't see the point way out here. For the next few stomach-churning hours he rocketed along just above the ocean's surface, trapped between the water and thick black clouds as spray splashed his fuselage. Chain lightning as thick as telegraph poles flashed left and right and zig-zagged across the sky, and the marmoset hid her pretty little face. Bert was now flying blind in the worst weather he'd encountered. The plane had burned up a few hours of petrol so he was able to gain height, but the rain clouds were so thick and heavy that it felt like he was running into blocks of concrete. He could not rise above the weather, and he feared he'd hit the water if he stayed low. So he took the clouds on right through the middle. He had no navigation lights and the moon was obscured, so the sensation was like being in a speeding car going blindly through a black tunnel and not knowing whether he was about to hit a wall at the far end. For the next six hours he died a thousand deaths as the tiny Moth lurched side to side, up and down. All he had to guide him were two compasses, one thankfully luminous, which he'd glance at occasionally as he tried to stop the plane spinning out of control. He wondered how long it would be before a bolt of lightning sliced through his frail plane.

He feared that, with the engine's workload, his petrol would run out before he saw Africa. But finally, after ten hours of heart palpitations, the monstrous weather began to taper off and the moon finally emerged from its hiding place to reveal the tiny outcrop of the Saint Peter and Saint Paul Archipelago almost a thousand kilometres from Natal. Bert cheered at the sight of it because it meant that, despite the shocking weather and flying blind, his navigation was spot on. As dawn broke Bert spotted the Portuguese steamer *Nyassa* and swooped down low to thank it for proving to him that he was still on the right course. Soon Bert spotted the Bissagos Islands on the far horizon and before long the coast of Senegal beyond. He gave the marmoset a banana and patted her cute head.

After everything he'd been through, flying twenty-two hours and covering 3000 kilometres, he was just 16 kilometres off the course he'd charted. He finally brought the Puss Moth to a halt on the airstrip in Bathurst, Gambia, at 8.30 on the morning of 26 November 1931. It was the first west-to-east crossing of the South Atlantic, the first transatlantic flight in a light plane and the first solo flight across the South Atlantic. Bert only had enough fuel for another two hours. He cabled Nance: 'Landed at Bathurst, Gambia, OK Bert.' She was more shocked than anyone as she suddenly realised that Gambia was on the west coast of Africa with only a huge ocean between it and the place from where Bert had sent his previous telegram. 'It is a magnificent achievement,' Nance told the *Evening Standard*. 'I am thrilled at his great success for only one other man, Colonel Lindbergh, has succeeded in flying across the Atlantic alone. I think he has done wonderfully, but then he is a wonderful husband.'[10]

After a day's rest in Bathurst, Bert refuelled, bought his marmoset some more bananas and flew on to St Louis in Senegal. With his great feat achieved he could now take his time and enjoy the ride home. He flew on to Port Etienne in Mauritania then on to Cape Juby and Casablanca in Morocco, where he worked on the Puss Moth and on his golf for a week, soaking up the sunshine. Bert was a huge hit with the French officials in Casablanca, who saw in him the spirit of Roland Garros and René Fonck. The French Commissioner even presented him with the Moroccan Cross for his great journey. When he flew to Rabat on 1 December Bert emerged from the *Karohi* cradling his monkey like a tiny baby.

Back in Bundaberg Frances said Bert's wonderful flight was adequate compensation for the fact he wouldn't be home for Christmas, but she was sure he would be back in Gavin Street sooner rather than later.

From Rabat, Bert flew to Madrid where he went sightseeing across the red Andalusian plains. He told the press there that once across the South Atlantic was enough, and he would never try anything so hazardous again. He headed for Paris but had to land at Tours until the weather cleared. When he was finally welcomed by an enthusiastic crowd at Le Bourget in Paris, across the Channel All-weather Mac McIntosh was declaring Bert's Atlantic crossing to be the single greatest flight of all time. *The Times* said Bert had stamped himself as a pilot of exceptional skill, daring, and judgement.

> He appears to have a genius amounting almost to a sixth sense for discovering navigational facts, which ordinary pilots are able to discover only by means of elaborate tests [it wrote]. His extraordinary faculty for correcting drift by estimating the strength and direction of the wind, which he is able to detect in the shapes and movements of the clouds, brought him safely to the end of a perilous journey.[11]

The *Daily Express* said Bert had rounded off the biggest thing achieved by one man in the history of flying and that he had done it without advertisement and bravado 'which doubles the value of his triumph' while Britain's *Daily Telegraph* said simply that Bert was 'truly a wonderful little man'.[12]

Finally, on 7 December 1931, at three minutes past two in the afternoon, just three minutes late for an official reception, Bert and the Puss Moth flew across the bright blue of a crisp winter's day in London to land at Hanworth Aerodrome after a flight that had taken them 17,700 kilometres from Toronto. Commentators remarked that Britain hadn't really yet grasped the enormity of what this small man had done, flying a more dangerous path than Lindbergh in a machine with half the muscle.

As mechanics grabbed hold of the Puss Moth's wing tips to steady the plane, Bert taxied into an open enclosure. He was wearing his blue serge suit, crumpled as usual, and with the obligatory grease and oil stains that almost always dotted his clothing. Underneath his suit coat was his favourite striped woolly sweater. As Bert emerged from the cockpit he was carried shoulder high to a platform where Nance, dressed immaculately in a black hat and black coat with a white fur around her neck, waited beaming with a bouquet of carnations. She embraced Bert and twice kissed him passionately on the lips. Bert was handed a telegram from his mother, which said: 'Proud of your achievement. Wonderful.' He made a short speech of thanks and praised the Puss Moth then asked for a glass of milk.

A mechanic took charge of his marmoset, which, wrapped in a silk handkerchief, panicked at the scent of strange hand and bit through the mechanic's thumb.

Bert spoke to the press for as long as they wanted, a glass of champagne in one hand and a cigarette in the other. 'Scared? Oh yes, I was scared right enough,' Bert revealed. 'After it got dark I'm afraid I must confess that my hopes of growing into a nice respectable old man with long whiskers seemed as though they weren't going to be realised. But I had to go on, you see. There was nothing else to do. After some hours of weary waiting the land showed up and I was very pleased to see it.'

One of the people to welcome Bert back to London was Sir Arthur Whitten Brown, who had flown the Atlantic with Alcock in 1919. 'Wonderful,' Sir Arthur said when asked what he thought of Bert's flight. 'Put any superlatives you like into my mouth and they will not be too great.'

Later in the week, with the pioneer aviator John Moore-Brabazon, now a Conservative MP, as his guide, Bert visited the House of Commons. He was made a life member of the British Air League and awarded the Aero Club's Gold Medal, and on 12 December he and Nance were afforded a civic reception at Atlantic Park in Swaythling, a few kilometres from Mon Repos. The guests included Jack Matthews, recovered from his ordeal in the Burmese jungle.

Edward, Prince of Wales, who also owned a Puss Moth, invited Bert to York House in St James Palace to relate tales of his flight. Bert spent the time wondering whether he should ask about that knighthood. That evening he was treated to another slap-up dinner at the Royal Aero Club where the guests included Kingsford Smith, who had just arrived in London in his Avro X *Southern Star* — virtually a copy of the *Southern Cross* — with the first Christmas airmail from Australia. Smithy jokingly reprimanded Bert for the enormous risk he'd taken over such a big ocean in such a small plane and asked him if there was any big flight he was not going to do because he himself would like to have due notice and a chance to try it instead.[13]

Bert was hoping that his great achievement would be the salvation of the Ibis, but he was sorely disappointed. The *Daily Express* reported that he would probably return to the USA to work as a commercial pilot, adding that 'it seems there is no room here for a man who, after serving in the Royal Naval Air Service during the war, flew on some of the most spectacular pioneering flights'.[14] Bert said he would only wait a month for a job offer in Britain before returning to the USA, and there was talk of him joining Harold Gatty there in a commercial venture. 'So far I have found nothing to do in England,' he lamented, 'although I have undertaken flights boosting British aviation all over the globe. I hate the idea of boosting foreign aeroplanes, but flying is my bread and butter, and I must live.'[15]

While Lindbergh had become a rich man and one of America's best known celebrities, Bert was waiting for the phone to ring with a job offer. Still, at the end of December he was named the world's greatest aviator by the French newspaper *L'Auto*, and on Boxing Day his star protégé Lores Bonney flew from Brisbane to Wangaratta in northern Victoria, a distance of 1600 kilometres, to visit her father in the longest flight ever made by an Australian woman.

Australian papers pushed for Bert and Smithy to be given special roles with the RAAF because of their inspiring, historic feats, but Defence Minister Sir George Pearce, who had knocked back Wizard Stone for a government aviation job two decades earlier, sparked outrage when he said that Bert, who was thirty-nine, and Smithy, who was thirty-four, were already too old for RAAF positions. Bert retorted:

I hope to fly for another 40 years, even if I have to build a plane specially fitted to carry crutches. A woman is as old as she looks, but a man is old when he ceases to look. If I am too old Sir George ought to alter the Australian old age pension regulations enabling me to qualify now instead of at 65. Flying is a game for people of all ages who are physically fit and possess common sense and judgment.[16]

Bert and Nance retreated to Mon Repos as Bert considered his next move. In the wooded countryside around the two-storey house the marmoset found a new home, although the weather was a lot more rugged than the Amazon jungle. The little monkey made friends with Mickey, a three-legged black cat Bert had rescued from a rabbit trap in the neighbouring woods and nursed back to health after fashioning it an artificial leg. Sometimes, though, the monkey seemed cold and lonely.

Hardly before he knew it Bert was back in London accepting the Segrave Memorial Trophy as the British subject who had accomplished the most important feat of 1931 on land, on sea or in the air. He would also garner the Johnston Memorial Silver Plaque for his astonishing navigational feat and his fourth Oswald Watt Medal for the finest performance by an Australian aviator.

Racing driver Sir Malcolm Campbell described Bert's flight as the sort of feat to fire the ambition of the youth of Britain and the Dominions. Soon Bert would also be awarded his third Britannia trophy. But while he publicly put on the face of the devoted husband, Bert's relationship with Nance had withered just like Bert's monkey, who was struggling to cope with a savage English winter.

Early in February 1932 the marmoset, thousands of kilometres from its humid home, succumbed to the Hampshire cold. Nance placed the forlorn creature in a flower-covered box and buried her in the garden. A week later, on 10 February, Nance farewelled Bert on the White Star liner *Majestic* from Southampton. He and All-weather McIntosh were heading to the USA to explore business opportunities. After landing in New York on 16 February, Bert told the press that he was in the USA 'on behalf of a powerful English syndicate' to establish a new long-distance air service from London. 'Next to safety, speed will be essential,' Bert said. 'I am figuring on an average of 200 miles an hour. Undoubtedly the continents will be as easily and as quickly connected as now the transcontinental cities are served by railways.'

Bert and McIntosh were also looking at launching a high-speed air service of four and a half days between London and Cape Town in all-metal aeroplanes. Anglo-African Airways was sponsoring the service, and Bert and McIntosh were to be the managing pilots. They were given a Lockheed Vega on loan and flew together all over the northern states of the USA, but he and Mac quickly realised that, with banks closing everywhere and people queuing for soup in Times Square, such a venture was years away.

Bert gave a series of talks on CBS radio about his Atlantic flight, and there were also rumours that he was planning another across the North Atlantic, via the Arctic route, or maybe that he would even partner Sir Hubert Wilkins in an England–Canada airline venture.

Nance left Southampton to join Bert in New York on 15 March, and in Toronto Bert was issued with a new Canadian passport three days later. Talk of Bert's future flights was consigned to the small print for some weeks, however, after Charles Lindbergh's baby son, Charles Jr, was kidnapped from the family mansion in East Amwell, New Jersey, and later killed in what the press decried as the most despicable crime of the century. A month later Australia was only interested in the news that another Australian flyer, the great racehorse Phar Lap, had died in suspicious circumstances at a ranch near Menlo Park, California.

In the first week of May, with their business venture going nowhere, Bert farewelled All-weather Mac from

Montreal as his friend sailed home alone to London. Mac's wife Betty was about to give birth to a son. Bert's personal life was chaotic and his career was in the doldrums, but he told himself that at least he was faring better than his old mate Bill Lancaster, who by the middle of 1932 was facing the electric chair for murder.

How had it come to this? Like Bert, Lancaster and Miller had been unable to fully cash in on their aviation exploits and by 1931 were living and fighting in a cheap bungalow in Coral Gables, Florida, dodging their landlord, surviving on grapefruit from a tree in their yard and on the occasional chicken or rabbit Lancaster would steal from their neighbours. When Lancaster was lucky, they'd eat duck. Desperate for cash, the lovers decided to sell Chubbie's life story and hooked up with a 26-year-old ghost writer from New Orleans named Haden Clarke, who neglected to tell them he was a bigamist with a venereal disease.

While Lancaster was out looking for work in America's west, Clarke and Chubbie drank bootleg gin and began sleeping together. They then made plans to marry. On hearing the news Lancaster drowned his sorrows with a bottle of Scotch, sent the pair a telegram insisting on being the best man and bought a long-barrelled Colt .38 revolver.

While Lancaster was flying back to Miami, C.W.A. Scott was on his way once more from Lympne to Darwin in his Gipsy Moth, breaking the record again, this time in eight days, twenty hours and forty-seven minutes.

Clarke and Chubbie picked up Lancaster from Miami Airport on the night of 20 April 1932, and all three went home together for a heart to heart. The men began drinking and arguing, and Chubbie went to bed alone. At 2.30 a.m.

Lancaster pounded on her door shouting, 'A terrible thing has happened. Haden has shot himself.' Clarke was still alive, barely, as Chubbie mopped the blood from his head with a rag. He died a few hours later in hospital without telling police what had happened.

Lancaster and Miller were questioned for two and a half days. Two suicide notes were found beside Clarke's body, but Lancaster finally confessed he had forged them. He said he'd been woken by a shot and when he saw Clarke with a hole in his head he panicked. While his rival for Chubbie's heart was bleeding to death, Lancaster sat down at Clarke's portable typewriter and wrote two notes — 'Bill, I can't make the grade' and 'Chubbie, I can't go through with it'. But hell, I never pulled the trigger, Lancaster said. Few believed him.

So it was with the sordid revelations of these Australian aviators in the news that Katherine's family told Bert to do the right thing by their daughter. Nance was in New York, well aware of Katherine's place in Bert's heart, but Katherine's family said Bert had been dilly-dallying long enough. He and Katherine were obviously in love. Katherine adored her brave, cheeky flying man, and Bert finally obtained a marriage licence on 16 May.

Even in this most important life event Bert was more secretive than ever. Whether it was to avoid humiliating Nance, his partner since the Great War, or because of his general disdain for attention to his personal life, Herbert John Louis Hinkler, AFC, DSM, used the name Herbert Bonney when he married Catherine Rose, also known as Katherine Rose, Kathy Rose and sometimes Katherine Rome, before a Justice of the Peace in Stamford, Connecticut, on 21 May 1932. Their marriage would remain a public secret for a long time. Bert didn't tell Nance that he had a new wife and, a couple of days after the wedding, Nance boarded the White Star liner *Baltic* in New York for the journey to Liverpool.

In Boston the ship picked up Bert and another passenger who was still using the name Catherine Rose. The 29-year-old new Mrs Hinkler, who couldn't admit publicly to being Mrs Hinkler, the 50-year-old former Mrs Hinkler who'd never really been Mrs Hinkler officially, and a world-weary pilot with one monumental headache, all set sail together for Liverpool a week away across the Atlantic. It was not the wonderful honeymoon Katherine had been expecting. When they arrived in England on 31 May, Katherine checked into London's Metropole Hotel. Bert and Nance maintained a façade of domestic normality and his home for the record remained Mon Repos in Southampton, but Bert visited London as often as he could and Glasgow when Katherine travelled north to see her relatives.

Bert had problems with his private life, but it looked as though, soon, Bill Lancaster would have no life at all. On 2 August 1932 in Miami he went on trial for murdering Haden Clarke. A packed courtroom was salivating at the salacious details, and reports were being wired around the world by the hour. Chubbie took the stand as photographers almost blinded her with their flashbulbs. She told the court she hadn't loved Lancaster for two years but still wanted to defend him because he was innocent. The prosecution tore her testimony to shreds, portraying her as a tart, a liar and a drunk until finally she stumbled from the witness box hysterically sobbing: 'They're crucifying me! They're crucifying me!'[17]

Throughout the trial, Lancaster was a model of cool British elegance. Although Old Sparky was being charged up in readiness, Lancaster treated the proceedings as no more hazardous than a rough flight, even when women fainted as ballistics experts examined the dead man's shattered skull in the courtroom. On 8 August, Lancaster marched to the stand and began to charm the courtroom. The defence painted Lancaster as a war hero and aviation pioneer, Clarke as a cowardly, dope-smoking, disease-riddled depressive bigamist. The jury deliberated for nearly five hours. And Lancaster's female admirers burst into tears at the verdict. Not guilty. Chubbie was in an adjoining room when the verdict was delivered to sustained cheering. She gave a whistle through her teeth and told reporters: 'I knew old Bill would come through.'[18]

That same month word leaked out that Bert was making plans for another flight to Australia. Since September, when Charles Kingsford Smith had been knighted and promoted to air commodore for his services to aviation, Bert's Puss Moth had been at a hangar belonging to Savage Skywriting Co. at the Hendon Aerodrome. Bert's friend Major Jack Savage was the man credited with turning the sky into a billboard by adapting the technique of low-level battlefield smoke screens for aerial advertising.

Bert was replacing the Gipsy III engine with a Gipsy Major that could pump out 145 horsepower at 2550 revolutions per minute. He reckoned he could extract around 3000 kilometres a day from his machine and was rumoured to be chasing down C.W.A. Scott's time by making Darwin in just four days with four hops. He gave the Air Ministry a proposed itinerary, although it was nothing quite as ambitious, starting at Croydon on 14

October, taking him over Vienna, Sofia, Constantinople (Istanbul), Koya (now called Koi Sanjaq), Aleppo, Baghdad and Bushehr.

Whether he wanted to add mystery to spice up his mission or whether the situation with the two Mrs Hinklers had made Bert especially cautious, he told the *Barrier Miner*: 'The time to discuss the flight will be after it is accomplished, not before.'[19] Bert had, however, penned the first chapter of his memoirs, which he had called 'Eighteen years of flying: Dips into My Diary. Boyhood Dreams and Manhood Thrills'. He had completed chapter 1, 'The soaring ambitions of youth', and had finished it by promising 'Thrills from his time in the great war ... to be continued'.

With winter looming Bert altered his planned route to take in France and Italy. In late November he farewelled Nance and her daughter Maida on the *Rangitata*, bound for Australia via New Zealand, and there was a great sadness in their parting. Nance knew the place that Katherine had in Bert's heart even if she didn't know about the secret marriage. Bert wanted to be in Bundaberg on 8 December, his fortieth birthday, the first he would have in his hometown for twenty years. Delays, however, made that impossible. Katherine spent time in London with Bert but, although they were legally married, their meetings were clandestine. The last thing Bert wanted was a scandal, and he didn't want to humiliate Nance. He was still thinking of ways to break the news to her and planned to meet up again in New York with Katherine as soon as he did.

Katherine caught the train from London to Glasgow to stay at 17 Falkland Mansions with her sister Jean,

Jean's husband William and their ten-year-old son Billy. On 7 December 1932, Bert sent a telegram home from freezing London to the sun-kissed 69 Gavin Street, North Bundaberg, telling his sister Queenie the day before their shared birthday: 'Many happy returns confidential coming home soon so please save my share cake love and kisses Bert.'

He had told Nance that he would make a start for Australia as soon as the Puss Moth was ready and the rotten weather improved, but there was still a lot to be done on the machine. Australian aviation authorities required the Puss Moth to be strengthened before leaving for Australia because of a design fault that resulted in wings collapsing during rough flights. The machines had actually been grounded in Australia because of the structural weakness of the wings.

On the fortieth birthday that he'd hoped to spend in Bundaberg, Bert was instead in a meeting with the Air Ministry's Director of Civil Aviation, Lieutenant Colonel Francis Shelmerdine, discussing the need for permission from the French to fly across their airspace, and Shelmerdine shook his head, saying that once again Bert had been so wrapped up in his machine that he had left the paperwork until the last minute. Four days later Katherine sat down in Glasgow and wrote Bert a love letter.

Nance and Maida arrived in Auckland on 21 December, but it was obvious they wouldn't be spending Christmas with Bert, and Nance wondered whether she'd ever spend Christmas with him again. When Bert was beset by delays in London, he sent Nance a cable suggesting that she and Maida tour the North Island of New Zealand until he was on his way. They would meet again in Australia, he said, and have a fine time together just like the old days, although he had something serious that he needed to discuss.

Nance didn't know that Bert was now married to someone else but she knew that she was losing him and, deep in her heart, she suspected that soon Bert would be gone forever.

Chapter 25

*Bert Hinkler had indeed been the
loneliest of all the great flyers*
Jim Mollison, record-breaking Scottish aviator, 1937

*Imagine a motorist whose accelerator has jammed
so that he cannot travel at less than 80 miles an
hour, a motorist with a strip of muslin across his
eyes so that he can see no further ahead than 20
or 30 yards and you have some idea of a pilot's
feelings when following the ground in bad weather.*
John Leeming, *Airdays*, 1936

Bert continued to play coy about his next great adventure right up to the first week of January 1933, telling anyone who asked that he wasn't going anywhere special, just 'somewhere where the sun is shining'. His extraordinary double life was taking a toll, and his furtiveness now bordered on paranoia. He was depressed about his inability to make the Ibis a success and his failure to find regular flying work.

But he embarked on a plan to charter aircraft to fly British cricket fans to Australia to watch Don Bradman take on Harold Larwood in the Bodyline series at £400 a passenger. He needed forty passengers to make it work but could only find twelve.[1]

With yet another business black eye, Bert instead finished off the four-month preparation of the Puss Moth, making repeated trial flights and dismantling the engine in search of faults. He checked and rechecked all the gadgets he'd installed himself: the inverted glass bottle that delivered clean oil to the engine, a flow meter to check petrol consumption with a stop watch, and a faint blue light under a hood on the illuminated instrument panel to prevent windscreen glare. But with no attempt to secure corporate backing or media support he prepared for the longest flight of his life: from England to Australia then on to Toronto. He'd wanted to leave England before the arrival of the northern winter, but delays installing the Gipsy Major engine then setbacks with bad weather kept him grounded until the New Year. The Mon Repos house had been locked up, and a neighbour was looking after Mickey, the three-legged cat.

Finally, first thing on the morning of Friday, 6 January, Bert went to see his old friend C.G. Grey at the office of *The Aeroplane* at 175 Piccadilly. They talked about all Bert's great flights of the last thirteen years and how Grey had believed in him before anyone else in the aviation world. Bert said cheerio then called on Len Pike at the Strand office of the Queensland Agent-General. He had time to fly the Puss Moth from its hangar at Jack Savage's business in Hendon the 130 kilometres down to a send-off at the Hampshire Aero Club in Southampton. He did not tell anyone there that he was leaving the next day, only that he planned to hop off soon. After the festivities Bert called on his old workmate from Avro, Jim Laver, and they had a coffee and a bun together beside the cable ferry called the 'Floating Bridge', which crossed the River Itchen to Woolston.

The old friends said their goodbyes, and Bert flew back to London, landing at Croydon at 3 p.m., presenting his Canadian passport and going through the customs formalities ahead of his big trip. He then flew across London to land at 4.15 on the 60-hectare plot of land in West London that aircraft builder Richard Fairey had bought for £15,000 three years earlier. Fairey was developing his Great Western Aerodrome there, but locals knew it better as Heath Row.

Bert supervised the refuelling of the machine, and one of the aerodrome workers washed mud from the wings. Then, carrying some luggage and six bottles of stout, Bert entered the rooms of the aerodrome's caretaker, Mr Harris, to make some phone calls. He called Joe Taylor, the aviation officer for Shell Mex, at 5.17 p.m. to make sure his fuel arrangements were in order along the route and carried out checks on his engine until 7.30 when he ate a light dinner prepared by the caretaker's wife. He gave her one of the bottles of stout as a thank you. Over dinner he told Mrs Harris that he was aiming for Athens by nightfall the next day but would stop for the night at Brindisi on the heel of Italy if time beat him. He had to calculate his departure perfectly, he said, because he didn't want to approach the Alps while it was still dark. 'Five years ago it took me 15 days to reach Australia in the Avian,' he told Mrs Harris, 'but I reckon I can do it this time in six if all goes well.'

Bert had painted over the name *Karohi* on the Puss

Moth. When he finally did arrive in Australia he didn't want to answer any questions about its real meaning.

At 11 p.m. Bert dialled the operator and asked to be connected to Jack Savage at Savage Skywriting Co. to tell him that all was in readiness for a take-off before dawn and ask him to come over to Heath Row with one of the skywriters, Captain 'Dopey' Lingham, to help with the take-off. Then Bert made the last call of the night, asking the operator to connect him with Glasgow Western 5560 for a late-night heart to heart with Katherine at Falkland Mansions. After Bert spoke to his very secret wife and wondered about the painful parting he'd have with Nance in Australia, Mr Harris prepared a bed for him in the aerodrome's sick bay. Then Bert had a drink of stout from one of the bottles, which he put beside his bed.

He asked not to be disturbed until 1.15 a.m. At 1 a.m. on what was now a bitterly cold Saturday, 7 January, Jack Savage arrived from Hendon in his Rolls-Royce with Dopey Lingham following. The fog around the airfield was so thick that the headlights from their two vehicles were visible for only a few metres. With Bert asleep, Lingham and Savage waited in an adjoining room until Bert rose, washed, shaved and dressed in a suit and thick flying coat. He placed the cigarette case Stanley Bruce had given him in his suit pocket and put on a gold watch.

Mr Harris made a pot of tea, and Bert drank a cup and then another. He prepared all his personal effects and started stuffing his pockets with fourteen maps covering the route he'd take, a small pocket atlas, a licence to carry a firearm, a small case containing his petrol authority to use at Shell depots, a piece of writing paper with his distance calculations for the flight to Athens and two

British newspaper cuttings. Close to his heart he put Katherine's love letter from 12 December, which began 'My Darling Beloved', and next to it ten small photos of Katherine standing beside the Puss Moth. In his wallet he had £122, 75 *lire* and a few coins.

Mr Harris helped Bert load the last of his provisions into the Moth's cabin, the remaining four bottles of stout, some sandwiches that Mrs Harris had made — one of egg, two cheese and three tongue as well as three Thermos flasks of unsugared black coffee and a Thermos of water. The Puss Moth was wheeled from the hangar. Even in the gloom the little plane looked gorgeous with its silver fuselage, red struts and lettering. Bert had hoped to get away at 2 a.m., but the thick fog hung around.

Bert decided to warm up the motor. He climbed into the cockpit while one of the aerodrome workers named Clifton went through the drill to start the engine. 'Contact,' they yelled to each other, and the engine fired. It was now 2.20 a.m., and Bert was anxious to get going.

Dodging the whirring propeller, Harris removed the chocks from the wheels, and Bert eased the machine forward towards the grass runway. He taxied the Puss Moth towards the southeast corner of the aerodrome and was soon enveloped in fog. Heath Row had no lighting for night flying so Savage and Lingham took their cars out beside the field to illuminate the black runway with their headlights and parked almost 300 metres from him. When Bert had reached the southeast corner he turned the Puss Moth back towards the wind but, just as he did, another cloud of fog came over, and visibility evaporated. He waited in the eerie darkness with the engine running for forty full minutes as Fairey Aviation Company's ambulance stayed nearby. Far away beside their cars Lingham and Savage could see nothing, and the only sign of life was the far-off sound of Bert's engine. Suddenly the fog began to lift, and the engine noise reached a higher pitch. The silvery machine leapt out of the churning fog, brilliantly lit by the Rolls-Royce headlights, and, like a ghostly flash, tore past them into the air halfway up the runway, a flame exploding from the exhaust as it left. Then, as quickly as the aircraft was upon them, it was swallowed by the great black void above.

It was 3.10 a.m. and Bert had disappeared.

Like the mist outside the plane, Bert's emotions swirled inside him as he headed towards the English Channel, but his messy personal life and career crisis had to take second place to the immediate goal of arriving in Australia in one piece. The delay in take-off meant that he had burnt up an hour's fuel on the ground, and he would likely have to stay the night at Brindisi rather than Athens about 725 kilometres further along. He made his way across the Channel and passed over Le Bourget airport in Paris, looking down at the city of light glittering in the dark, with Gustave Eiffel's tower off to the side where Santos-Dumont had once flown. How sad it was for Bert when he'd heard the news that his boyhood hero, sick with multiple sclerosis and despondent at the use of aircraft in war, had hanged himself in São Paulo. But Bert had his own life to worry about, all alone up there in the dark.

He flew on and was over Sens three and a quarter hours after leaving London. He headed towards Macon, the engine ticking over like a precision watch. A forester heard Bert fly overhead in the darkness but could see nothing and thought it was foolish for a man to be flying in the dark, cold morning. Four hours and thirty-five minutes into the flight Bert passed Macon and headed towards Mont Cenis. After flying for a little more than six hours he was near La Spezia, south of Genoa, on the Italian coast. Bert imagined that the view below would be spectacular if he could see anything. He took a compass bearing and turned for Florence, flying over the sort of mountainous Tuscan countryside he had once traversed in the Sopwith Camel with all guns blazing. He wrote in his log that he planned to cross La Verna and the coast of the Adriatic Sea to Brindisi. He took a quick look at the map he'd marked in red and blue ink.

At 11.05 Italian time, seven hours after leaving Heath Row, Bert could see Florence and the Arno River through the clouds. He came down out of the mist to get his bearings and to see the lie of the land. The Pratomagno mountains, part of the Apennines, were nearby, rising from the Arno Valley and topped at 1592 metres by the peak known as Croce di Pratomagno, the Cross of Pratomagno. It was a mountain adorned with a great iron cross raised for the Feast of the Assumption five years earlier. The religious icon dominated the skyline and looked down over another mountain called Poggio del Lupo, the Hill of the Wolf.

The noise coming from the Puss Moth on that gloomy Saturday morning startled villagers in the ancient terracotta-coloured Tuscan homes nestled in the sharp hills. They came outside hoping to see a plane flying along the Valdarno valley towards the great cross. Aircraft were not often sighted in that treacherous part of Italy, at least not since the war. More than sixty years later, Pia Bettini Camiciottoli, one of those villagers, revealed in the ABC documentary *Hustling for Hinkler* how she was surprised by the engine noise overhead and was afraid for the pilot because the machine seemed to be very low.

Bert passed by the Cross of Pratomagno, swathed in fog, a few minutes later as the wind twisted the Puss Moth. The poet Dante had written about the evil, menacing storms in these mountains, and Bert was experiencing them first-hand. Downdraughts pushed the machine towards the clusters of oak and chestnut trees, conifers and beech huddled together on the side of the mountain about 300 metres below the summit. The Puss Moth rocked and bucked as it fought back against the wind. Bert felt as if he was back with All-weather Mac fighting for control of the giant Fokker. But he wasn't. He was descending towards the Casentino Valley surrounded by desolate mountains that some of the locals said were haunted by demons. Bert felt all alone in the fog so far from home. Only the great iron cross on the mountain nearby reminded him that God was near if Bert felt like praying. A chill ran right through his body as Bert felt the Moth sinking further and faster, down, down, down. His left wing was fluttering like a humming bird's, and he was losing control.

The giant cross stood tall and proud as Bert fell out of the sky. His left wing was twisted and wrenched by the violent weather, and there was a splintering, shearing noise as it tore loose. The sharp crack would have been terrifying had anyone been in the mountains to hear it. Bert's suitcase flew out of the gaping hole in the cabin as if trying to flee. Bert fought with every ounce of life he had left, but there was nothing he could do. The machine plummeted straight to the ground. The propeller crashed into the earth, gouging a hole, and the engine made a huge dent in the earth.

Bert was hurled about the crumpled cabin, and the jagged metal ripped his lower back like a thousand knives. His head smashed against the instrument panel, fracturing his skull. His whole body felt as if it was broken. After the terrifying crash an eerie quiet descended over Bert and his wrecked plane. Somehow, though, he was still alive. Somehow he'd survived another close call. Wizard Stone would have approved. His senses were all blurred, but he thought he could hear a dripping noise. Bert could smell petrol leaking from the torn fuel tanks. He had to get away before the whole thing blew up. He was cut and battered all over, but he dragged himself from the twisted, torn wreckage and tumbled out onto the hard, cold earth. His left shoe had been wrenched off in the crash and his helmet torn loose, but he didn't notice the coldness of his foot. Blood gushed down his back. Dazed, he looked around for a moment and tried to focus his foggy brain on the whirling, spinning world around him. Bert could feel blood seeping down his face.

He crawled and dragged himself for 80 metres and collapsed beside a small bush, the blood from the deep cuts on his back staining the ground around him red. He rolled onto his side, crossing his shoeless left foot over the right. He thought he could hear voices down the mountain. A small fire broke out in the wreckage as the hot metal ignited the spilled petrol. Bert lay there in the cold and quiet and pulled his coat around him. He felt himself starting to lose consciousness. Somewhere down the ravine a hungry wolf was startled by the violence and the noise of the crash, and its nostrils flared at the smell of blood. The animal's hot breath escaped from its mouth as it began to pant with excitement.

Chapter 26

*While other pilots of smaller but more raucous
calibre trumpeted to the world their plans, hopes and
accomplishments, Bert Hinkler moved in silence, and
nobody was ever aware of what he intended until he was
actually on the way. So it was with his last strange flight.*

The *Sydney Morning Herald*, Monday, 20 February 1933

*The Reserve Personnel of the Regia Aeronautica and
all members of the Aero Club salute the body of the
glorious aviator Herbert John Hinkler, flyer of the
Atlantic, who fell whilst attempting to carry out a
sublime task in the service of civilisation and progress.*

**Placard from the Aero Club of Florence that adorned
the city during Bert's funeral procession, 1 May 1933**

A sense of foreboding spread immediately it was realised
that Bert had failed to turn up at Brindisi or Athens. Two
days after he'd left Heath Row, there'd been no news of him,
although Benito Mussolini ordered that a special watch
be kept at every aerodrome fringing the Mediterranean.
Friends and family took heart from speculation that Bert

might have gone all out while his petrol lasted, and come down in some remote spot beyond Brindisi or in North Africa. The same plane had carried Bert for twenty-two hours across the Atlantic so he could have made it all the way to the African coast.

As she frantically waited for news of Bert, Katherine kept herself hidden from the press spotlight as it focused on Frances and Nance and their public prayers for him. Katherine knew the situation was desperate, however, as Bert had promised to send her a telegram if there was any trouble on the journey, and there had been only deathly silence since he'd telephoned her the night before his departure.

Two and a half days after Bert disappeared his old air-race rival Frank Courtney remained upbeat, saying that he wouldn't be surprised if Bert suddenly turned up in Bushehr or Jask. Jim Mollison reckoned that Bert was probably on a Greek island while C.W.A. Scott, whose record Bert was trying to break, said that worry was unnecessary as Bert was the kind of pilot who always went steadily and quietly.[1]

Nance and Maida were still in New Zealand and, when interviewed at the Hotel Cargen in Auckland, Nance tried to put on a brave face. 'I have had long periods of anxious waiting when my husband has been on previous long flights,' she said stoically.

> I have become more or less accustomed to them, and now any feeling of anxiety is always modified by faith in my husband. When Bert is on a long-distance flight he always likes to make the first hop a good one.
> No news does not necessarily mean bad news. I am

> proud of my husband's flying, and have implicit faith
> in his ability.

Nance's real fears, however, were betrayed by her red eyes and nervous manner.[2] In Bundaberg, Frances said while she had the utmost confidence in Bert, the absence of any information since her son had left England was beginning to cause worry. Ron Hinkler, who was twelve at the time, remembers the terrible time; his grandmother trying to cope with not knowing but becoming sadder and quieter as each day went by.

Bert had been so secretive about his plans and the route he would take that authorities had few ideas about where to begin a search but, three and a half days after he'd disappeared, General Balbo's Italian Air Ministry issued instructions to all its air stations to look for Bert in cooperation with the French.

Jim Mollison's new wife, Amy Johnson, and fellow aviatrix Lady Mary Bailey offered to help in the search of the Alps being organised by Wally Hope, the three-time winner of the King's Cup. Hope made his headquarters in Switzerland after a tourist reported seeing a plane like Bert's flying over Morgins. Other sightings were reported in the Rhone Valley of southern France, and the British Broadcasting Corporation appealed directly to thirteen European countries to make urgent wireless broadcasts urging citizens to aid in the quest.

Then there were false sightings and erroneous reports that Bert's body had been found, that he had flown to Russia and was now working for Stalin or that he was on a secret British Government mission to China. Others were prepared to swear that they had seen the little pilot striding merrily through the streets of London, safe and sound, rugged up against the winter chill.

As Wally Hope began his search around the Matterhorn, a postman delivering mail to the empty Mon Repos house noted a smashed window and state of disorder in the dining room. He peered through the windows to see that every room had been ransacked. Thieves had done Bert over, upending drawers and furniture. Police said the robbery was particularly callous as Bert had now been missing for eleven days and his relatives had grave fears for his life. The contents of drawers and cupboards were thrown about on the floor and a photograph of Frances had been knocked off the wall and the face ground in with the heel of a shoe. Neighbours said a boomerang they'd seen on the wall inscribed 'Hope you soon return, Bert', a gift from a relative in Australia, was missing, and police believed that plans for the Ibis had also been taken. The only other things stolen, however, were four two-gallon tins of petrol from a back shed where the Ibis was housed. The plane itself was left undamaged. News of the robbery only pushed the arrow deeper into Nance's heart as she prepared to journey from Auckland to Sydney on the *Marama* then press on to meet Frances in Brisbane.[3]

Maida sailed home to England on the *Rangitata* from Wellington, back to her lodgings at the Sacred Heart Convent in Gloucester Road, Regents Park, to wait for news, and on 24 January Nance arrived in Sydney. With tears in her eyes she told waiting reporters: 'I still hope that he is alive somewhere, and will be found. I am only hoping that he is not injured and suffering. That is the uncertainty of it.'[4]

Two days later, Frances was on the Brisbane River wharf to meet Nance as she arrived from Sydney on the *Ormiston*.

George Hinkler, Bert's old 'hand-me-up-a spanner man', had come down from Tully where he was working as a cane-cutter and starting a taxi business, and accompanied his mother from Bundaberg. Lores Bonney and a few family friends of the Hinklers were there also offering support.

Nance and Frances embraced for a long time on the wharf, and there were more tears as reporters told the pair that Wally Hope had abandoned the search after five days, saying that with all the snow across the Alps he might have flown over Bert's plane a dozen times and never seen it. He told the British papers that any money left over from funds raised for the search would go to a memorial in Bert's honour. That only made the weeping louder among the Hinkler women.

George Hinkler had never seen his mother so stressed. 'We all were optimistic with the probable exception of mother,' George said. 'Bert had come through so often that despite natural concern at his being missing so long, we believed that he would turn up, smiling, in the long run. But mother was different this time. Previously she never worried greatly. Now she had a feeling that something had gone wrong. We tried to restore her old confidence but to no avail. Bert was always his mother's boy.'[5]

Nance began to suffer insomnia, which gave way to nightmares. Six weeks after Bert disappeared *The Sketch* newspaper mounted another aerial search around Avalon in France and, although their plane flew so low it almost touched the tree tops, they could find no trace of wreckage. Frances raised the prospect that Bert's plane might have been tampered with.

In London, at his Cannon Street office near St Paul's Cathedral, solicitor Leslie Pearkes, Bert's old comrade from the war was inundated with letters from clairvoyants, soothsayers and astrologers claiming that Bert's body would be found where nobody could have guessed. In official correspondence with the Italian authorities Pearkes said he was working on behalf of Bert's wife, but only a few people in the world knew that person was not the woman being quoted around the globe as Mrs Hinkler.

For nearly two months Nance stayed in Bundaberg with Frances then travelled down to Brisbane from Bundaberg by car to stay with the Grüter family, who had relocated. Nance told the *Brisbane Courier* on 28 March: 'I cannot believe that he is lost until I have absolute proof. I still hope and believe that, when the snows of the Alps melt after the winter, it will be found that he has been safe in some snowbound place in the mountains.' The crisis and weeks of heartache had not dented her own affection for aviation and, recalling that she had flown many thousands of miles with Bert, she said she still might try to qualify for her own pilot's licence when she returned home so that she could fly Bert around. Lores Bonney was planning her own flight to England in the Gipsy Moth, and Nance had even considered going with her.[6]

On 10 April, Frances joined Nance in Brisbane and, together with about 150 other relatives and aviation dignitaries, including Qantas boss Hudson Fysh, they farewelled Lores Bonney from Archerfield aerodrome, bound for London. Everyone, especially Lores' husband Harry, prayed for her safety. A day later Bill Lancaster, desperate to regain the public favour and earn some much-needed cash, took off from Lympne hoping to break Amy Johnson's record for the flight to Cape Town. He was flying an Avian named *Southern Cross Minor* that his father had bought for him from Kingsford Smith. Only Lancaster's parents, Chubbie and one journalist were there to see him off.

The following week Leslie Pearkes announced in London that he was applying to the courts to have Bert presumed dead in an effort to clear his estate. Bert's relatives in Queensland wondered what the hell Pearkes was jabbering about as Nance was still telling reporters she believed Bert was alive and waiting for the snow to melt. Nance decided it was no good waiting in Queensland for news. She would go back to England to see Maida and care for her mother. She boarded the P&O liner *Strathaird* in Brisbane, and when it berthed in Melbourne on Anzac Day, 25 April, she placed a wreath at the Cenotaph. The next day, when the *Strathaird* reached Adelaide's Outer Harbour, Nance told the press she was going home to England to find her husband.

Instead someone found Bert for her just a few hours later. On the morning of Thursday, 27 April 1933, Gino Tocchioni, a 25-year-old charcoal burner, trying to eke out a living from the forests of the Apennines, left his home in the small Tuscan town of Castelfranco di Sopra and was fossicking around with his dog on the side of Pratomagno. The place was so foreboding and the stories of the demons so vivid that only charcoal burners ever ventured up that high. The area was deadly for aeroplanes, too, and a French airliner with eight passengers had crashed nearby only a few days earlier, killing five people. But spring had brought new life to the slopes after a particularly fierce winter, and Tocchioni found himself on Pratomagno just before 10 a.m. in an area called Piana delle Vacche (Plain of the Cows).

The cold was still biting but, while there was snow a metre deep near the summit of Pratomagno, it had melted away from the mountainside. Tocchioni was working his way down a spur of the mountain between the summit and the Hill of the Wolf when a silvery white flash caught his eye from higher up. It was the smashed remains of an aeroplane. Near a tree was the battered remnant of a wing and some torn saplings; there was rubbish strewn about as though blown by a hurricane and in the midst of it a large suitcase. There was evidence of a small fire in the wreckage, but Tocchioni guessed that rain and fierce winds would have quickly extinguished it. As Tocchioni's dog sniffed about, the young Italian saw something else. The sight seared into his brain with such force that he could never forget it.

About 80 metres from the main part of the wreckage, resting against a bush, was the body of a man dressed in a dark suit, lying on his back, his left arm resting on his thorax and his right arm extended. The body was turned slightly to the right, as though he'd arranged himself to sleep. But this had not been a peaceful slumber. Most of the face was missing. Tocchioni recoiled in horror. He almost retched when he saw that the right hand was shrunken and the left hand was missing, as though it had been chewed off. Next to the gnawed left wrist were some small bones and a gold watch that had stopped at three o'clock.

Tocchioni wanted to get away from there as quickly as possible and alert the police. He and his dog headed home towards Castelfranco di Sopra as fast as they could go on the treacherous mountainside but, just a short way into his journey, Tocchioni met another charcoal burner named Raffaello Cari. He explained what he'd seen, and Cari persuaded him to show him the wreckage and Bert's body. Then together the two men trudged back to Castelfranco di Sopra and reported the find to the *carabinieri*. Before long police and militiamen began arriving during the evening to mount a search. A campfire could be seen on the summit in the night as word spread about what the two men had uncovered. At daybreak, a group led by police chief Marshal Romeo Aureli began the four-hour climb from the village of Cetica to the wreckage, using torch flares to illuminate the way in the dull morning mist. Among the searchers were Dr Giuseppe Ghedini, a chemist and air force reserve lieutenant; Donatello Cosci, a photographer; and a reporter from the Florentine newspaper *La Nazione*. At 7.30 a.m. Aureli's party found another group on the site with one waving a handkerchief to alert them of their presence. Pieces of the crumpled Puss Moth were scattered about in a small cleared area devoid of foliage except for a couple of stunted juniper bushes, although the whole area was surrounded by tall tress. Cosci began photographing the wreckage and Bert's mutilated body. About 350 metres from the main wreckage higher up the slope was the left wing.

Marshal Aureli reached inside Bert's suit pocket and extracted a passport with the number 23416 issued on 18 March 1932 in Ottawa, Canada. The first name was clearly Herbert, but it looked as if the weather had obliterated the surname, although the place of birth was clearly Bundaberg, Queensland, Australia, and the date of birth 8 December 1892. Inside Bert's coat there were also ten small photographs of Katherine standing next to a Puss Moth and seven negatives of the same photos, some gold cufflinks and some paper covered in calculations. A wallet contained thirteen Bank of England five pound notes, two one-pound notes, a Dublin lottery ticket, 75 *lire* and some coins. Two and a half kilometres away three farmers found Bert's logbook in its protective leather pouch.

All about was the detritus of disaster, an inflatable boat, two oars, an empty oil cylinder and one left shoe. Close to the plane were maps marked with red and blue ink showing the route between London and Bundaberg. A petrol tank was found further down the mountain past Bert's body, and higher up the mountain were pieces of canvas from the left wing, which had probably been blown there by the wind. Later, another £55 was found.

A health officer, Dr Domenico Vettori, examined Bert's body and reported that the cranium had been fractured and was completely open, revealing all the bones in the face except the jawbone and parts of the cranial bone at the base of the skull. There was a depression next to the body about 10 centimetres deep and 40 centimetres wide, indicating that Bert might have fallen hard on the ground cracking his skull and breaking his back, although Dr Vettori in his official report theorised that 'during those last few moments of life and spasms of agony, the wounded man may have summoned the strength to turn himself before dying'. Later there was evidence that Bert had survived the crash and crawled 80 metres to his point of collapse, buttoned up his coat and arranged himself for sleep. Sometime after death his body had been attacked by a wolf.

Dr Ghedini, examining the wreckage and the site, speculated in his report that 'the unexpected demise of the flight could have been caused by the plane having clipped some high oak tree because of the very poor visibility, or by one of those thunderstorms in the Pratomagno which, especially in January, can generate without warning winds of immense violence. Thus damaged, the gliding plane could not have continued its progress and would have fallen vertically with the result that the propeller and the motor were thrust into the ground.' The propeller, a Sport Type Hamilton Ground-Adjustable Air Screw, was buried deep in the earth, and the engine had gouged out a hole 10 centimetres deep. One of the party, Aladino Fabbrini, later commented that he saw a tall beech tree with the tip cut off, which could have cut the left wing and torn it from the fuselage.

Marshal Aureli gave orders for the wreckage and the body to be guarded, pending official word to remove them. The news was conveyed to the British Embassy in Rome and quickly went around the world.

On Saturday, 29 April, the *Strathaird* was sailing towards Fremantle, the last port of call in Australia before heading back to England, when the captain began to receive radio messages confirming Bert's death. The details about the state of his body and Bert's horrific injuries were so gruesome that he thought it an act of kindness to keep them to himself and break the news to Nance gently at a later time. Nance was having tea in the lounge with other passengers, however, when a radio telegram from a West Australian newspaper was handed to her.

Nance's eyes widened in horror before she dropped her cup, sending tea and broken china splattering as she dashed off to her cabin to weep alone. Frances was travelling by train across the Nullarbor to farewell Nance at Fremantle when her worst fears were confirmed. When the train reached the railway stop at Cook, the scene of Bert's record cross-country flight in 1928, she was handed a telegram from George breaking the bad news. The old woman cried all the way to Kalgoorlie almost a thousand kilometres away but, by the time the train pulled in, she had composed herself enough to say that it was better to know the truth than to remain in suspense indefinitely.[7]

Immediately he heard the news in Toronto, attorney Alfred Bicknell drafted a letter to Mrs Bert Hinkler of Mon Repos, Thornhill Park, Southampton, offering his condolences and informing her that on 19 October 1931 Bert had prepared his will naming Nance as his executrix and sole beneficiary.

On that Saturday at Eagle Farm racetrack in Brisbane where Bert had landed in 1928, all the jockeys wore black armbands as Will Yet won the Hinkler Handicap. In Bundaberg flags flew at half mast. On Pratomagno the order was given to bring Bert off the mountain, and in Rome Benito Mussolini decreed that Bert was to be given a state funeral worthy of one of the greatest aviators in history. Il Duce sent a telegram to Sir Ronald Graham, the British Ambassador in Rome, expressing his sorrow. General Balbo immediately sent an air force captain and a representative of Italy's Air Ministry from Rome 290 kilometres to Pratomagno to ensure that Bert's remains were treated with the utmost honour.

In Fremantle Frances boarded the *Strathaird* to console the woman she'd regarded as a daughter-in-law for sixteen years. Nance remembered that the last time she was in Fremantle, Bert had jumped from the dock onto the ship to greet her and that her cabin had been alive with flowers and congratulatory telegrams. Now there were only tears and condolences. 'I never gave up hope that Bert would turn up till I got that wire,' she exclaimed. 'Oh, why did he go in such weather?'[8]

On the mountainside where he had lain for nearly four months, Bert was wrapped in a sheet and placed in a zinc case, which was put on the back of a donkey for the precarious trek down the steep mountain path all the way to Cetica. There, Bert's body was taken by car down a winding narrow road to the village of Pagliericcio almost five kilometres away where a local carpenter named Lambreto Broggi had prepared a walnut coffin. One of the search party told the local press: 'There is a strange grandeur about the spot where Mr Hinkler lay. It is habitually sombre and rainy and is lashed by constant storms. Even the trees seem stunted. It was as though Mr Hinkler were offered as a human sacrifice to the demon of the mountain. But with the sun shining, the body looked strangely peaceful. Mountain torrents due to melting snow had washed over him.'[9]

In Pagliericcio, Bert's remains were met by a troop representing the Young Fascists of the Upper Centino and a group of soldiers who formed a guard of honour. Local nuns gathered his helmet and gloves and the aircraft's clock to be presented to Frances. A car then took Bert another five kilometres to Strada-in-Casentino, the biggest village in the municipality of Castel san Niccolo, which had a population of about 2000 living among the hills. There at 8.30 p.m. the coffin was carried into the Casa del Fascio, the House of the Fascists. It was placed upon a specially built catafalque and surrounded by flowers as well as altar candles and lamps veiled by mourning cloth. A guard of honour stood by as the local governor, the mayor of Castel san Niccolo, a local nobleman, the Duke of Aosta, and various police, political and military chiefs led a sombre procession past the coffin to pay their respects. Throughout Strada and all the villages nearby flags draped in black were displayed as a sign of mourning. The women of Strada stayed up all night sewing a Union Jack from strips of coloured sheets. Although they were very much part of Fascist Italy, local bandsmen spent two days learning to play 'God Save the King' and 'Rule Britannia'.

In London the British press lauded Bert. *The Times* lamented that, although he was a great pilot, he could never make real money out of his achievements. 'His fertile mind was always throwing up ideas,' it said, 'but he had been virtually unemployed for the last four years. If he had possessed as good a business sense as he had an air mechanical sense he would not have been risking record-breaking flights at forty years of age. Because the world found no steady employment for him, Hinkler undertook an exploit that might well have been left to younger men.' The *Daily Mail* described Bert as 'a great aviator and thorough gentleman' who 'did great things modestly and endeared himself to everyone' while the *Daily Herald* rated Bert 'one of the great heroes of our time ... second to none in courage, ability and achievement — yet in life he never won the distinction and recognition due to him'.[10] Across the Atlantic the *New York Times* headlined its report with 'Great Flier Gone'.

Throughout Australia the push began to bring Bert's body home and give him every accolade the nation could provide. Billy Hughes said it was only fitting that one of Australia's greatest heroes should be given a State funeral and that Canberra's Capitol Hill would be the appropriate place for the grave and national monument.

Nance sent a telegram from the *Strathaird* saying it was her wish that Bert be buried in Australia and that the Hinkler family felt it would be appropriate for him to lie forever next to his father in Bundaberg cemetery. George Hinkler backed her up, saying it was always Bert's wish to end his days in the country of his birth.

High above Pratomagno, Mussolini's friend, the Florentine aviator Vasco Magrini, dropped a wreath on the crash site, and in Canberra Joseph Lyons, now Prime Minister, announced that the Commonwealth Government would meet all expenses incurred in bringing Bert's body home in accordance with the wishes of his widow, Nance. A State funeral would be arranged, something that Kingsford Smith said was only fitting for a true Australian hero.

But all those plans did not allow for the fact that, under Italian law, Bert's burial could not be delayed. If Bert was to be reburied in Australia, an exhumation could not take place until October as Italian law prohibited that procedure during the warmer months.

On Sunday, 30 April, at 6 p.m. members of the Regia Aeronautica lifted Bert's coffin onto their shoulders and carried him proudly through the streets of Strada as all the villagers came out to pay their respects. A deputation arrived to take Bert's body to Florence. With them was a representative of the British Embassy and General Balbo's finest officer, who would ensure that Mussolini's wishes for a grand farewell were carried out. Heavy rain pelted the hearse as it bore Bert's body 50 kilometres to Florence, but Bert was used to bad weather. Black flags of mourning were flown in every home the hearse passed. When the funeral car and its escort finally reached Florence after a long, solemn drive, Lieutenant General Ivan Doro was waiting there with a detachment of Black Shirts to march beside Bert's coffin as it was taken to the Aero Club late in the evening. There a guard of honour in dress uniform was assigned to stand watch. Many of the wreaths surrounding the casket, including a wreath from General Balbo, were so big that it took two men to carry them. Bert's coffin was draped in the Italian and British flags with a small Australian flag on top, and altar candles flickered like yellow tulips.

The following day, Monday, 1 May, as many as 100,000 mourners filed past Bert's coffin until 6 p.m. when the funeral was due to begin. Leslie Pearkes travelled to Florence to represent Katherine, who was too distraught to attend, although Pearkes said only that he was representing the Hinkler family. Katherine had the same aversion to publicity as her husband of seven months.

Two Anglican priests were in Florence ministering to the city's large British population, and Pearkes asked them to officiate. The Revd J.R. Vincent, vicar of Eye, was assigned to the ceremony and arrived at the makeshift chapel at the Aero Club at 5.30 p.m. in cassock and surplice. Then, in the warm glow of a Tuscan spring twilight, the funeral procession began its journey through the ancient streets. General Balbo had ordered two companies of infantry, a company of the Regio Aeronautica and a company of the Fascist Militia to escort the funeral procession. General Aurelio Liotta, representing Balbo, was one of the pall bearers, along with General Gino Poggesi and the Prefect of Florence. For three kilometres the mourners walked slowly with the army band in front playing funeral marches followed by the men carrying their enormous wreaths. The hearse was drawn by horses covered with black velvet and plumes, and was surrounded by as many as 20,000 mourners. Immediately behind the hearse marched the British Consul of Florence, Major C.W. Maclean, and Pearkes. Behind them were the two clergymen. People leaned from windows and tossed flowers on top of the hearse or stood silently to attention on the footpaths giving Bert the Roman salute. Beside the Italian generals and the local government officials was Colonel Harold Stevens, the military attaché from the British Embassy in Rome, dressed in a vivid red tunic that was in stark contrast to the more sombre black of the Fascist elite.

Pilot Vasco Magrini circled the city from above dropping flowers. Placards from the Aero Club adorning the walls of buildings proclaimed Bert an aviation martyr. When the funeral cortege reached Piazza San Felice, the procession halted and the troops presented arms. The name Herbert Hinkler was called out and the troops responded: 'Present.' A volley of shots was fired into the air, and the ensuing long silence was finally broken when the Fascist band struck up 'Rule Britannia' and 'God Save the King'. The procession moved on for a few hundred metres to the ancient Porta Romana (Roman Gate), where a fleet of cars waited. The Italian mourners withdrew, leaving the British and Australian contingent to proceed by car the three-kilometre journey up and down a steep hill to the Cimitero Evangelico Agli Allori (Evangelical Cemetery of the Laurel).

Its groves of cypress trees and rose bushes made for a serene resting place. Bert was lowered into the ground a long way from the cane fields around Gavin Street but warm in the embrace of friends. A small Australian flag was placed on his coffin amid the wreaths, and some of the mourners gathered blossoms from the cemetery to send to Bert's mother in Australia.

Some of the mourners looked up into the clear, blue, cloudless Italian sky and saw swallows larking about, chasing each other, diving here and there and looping the loop. As night began to fall over Bert's grave the birds were revelling in the sheer joy of flight.

Epilogue

I haven't met anyone who knew Bert who would discredit him in any way — he was quiet, very determined. When you look at the chapters of his life, day to day, month to month there was only one thing that he was ever interested in — and that was flying. He had some social activities but basically it was all flying. Even at home it was all flying or tinkering with aeroplane pieces in the backyard.

**J.A. 'Lex' Rowland, president of Bundaberg's
Hinkler House Memorial Museum**

My uncle achieved fame by performing incredible feats of courage and endurance and establishing many world records in his short life. He flew his tiny little aircraft over every continent. He sought no publicity for himself in all these adventures. Indeed he was shy, unassuming and retiring. His only concern was his deep and abiding love for aviation, the future it could hold for the world, and the opportunity to accept and overcome new challenges.

Bert Hinkler Jr, Bert's nephew

Bert was gone but not forgotten, certainly not by the women who adored him. After her worst fears had been realised, Frances decided to stay with relatives in Western Australia for another five months because the reminders of Bert were everywhere in Gavin Street. At sixty-seven she didn't know how her heart would cope back in Bundaberg. Nance returned to England alone on the *Strathaird* on 2 June, but now her country idyll was lonely and dark. Many of Bert's cups and souvenirs from a truncated lifetime in aviation still adorned their home and were constant reminders of their sixteen years together. The forlorn Ibis in their back shed recalled all of Bert's stalled ambitions and frustrations.

Katherine divided her time between her brother-in-law's home and the village of Castletown in the Scottish Highlands where she could get away from civilisation and be alone with her thoughts beside the ocean that her man had once traversed so bravely.

Despite the tragedy, others followed Bert to challenge fate. Bill Lancaster had disappeared just a day into his flight to Cape Town and hadn't been heard of for nearly two months when news came that Lores Bonney had also disappeared flying to London from Brisbane. Thankfully the plucky Brisbane housewife finally arrived at Croydon on 21 June, sunburnt but otherwise hale and hearty after a flight lasting sixty-seven days. She had crashed her 'little ship' off Siam, run out of petrol in Bulgaria, was mistaken for a spy in Czechoslovakia and almost collided with a mountain in Hungary.

Leslie Pearkes informed Nance that following Bert's marriage to Katherine, the Canadian will naming Nance as the heir was invalid. Nance had known for a long time the role Katherine had in Bert's heart, so it wasn't a complete shock even if the news of the marriage took her by surprise. After all she and Bert had been through, she was just grateful for the sixteen years they'd spent together. She would keep the name Nance Hinkler for the rest of her life. Katherine received Bert's English estate of £906/10/10, but Nance still had Mon Repos and their house on Havelock Road.

Even with the perils encountered by aviation adventurers, air travel was becoming more and more popular. Some of the pioneers couldn't keep up with the changing times, however, and twenty-one years after Bert saw his very first aircraft, Wizard Stone's Blériot copy, Louis Blériot's factory closed its doors in the depths of the Great Depression. On that same day Mussolini's government announced that it would erect a grand monument to Bert overlooking the place where he fell. The monument was sculpted from a block of Travertine marble, stood 210 centimetres high and 120 centimetres wide, and featured an eagle with a broken wing.

There was speculation throughout Australia that Bert's burial in Florence would only be temporary and that by the end of the year his remains would be brought home for a State funeral in Australia. The Prime Minister's Department announced that it would meet all the costs involved but, when Frances finally returned to Queensland after her five months in the west, she put an end to the notion. Leslie Pearkes had told her about Bert's marriage to Katherine and Katherine's wishes that Bert should rest in peace. 'To bring Bert's body to Australia would only cause unnecessary worry and expense,' Frances told the press, 'and it would be terribly harrowing for us. Nothing at all can be gained by bringing him here. Australia can erect some monument to his memory without bringing his body from its quiet resting place in Italy.'[1]

Four and a half months after Bert's funeral, Pearkes was back in Italy on top of Pratomagno representing Katherine at the unveiling of Bert's monument on 17 September. Joining him in the four-hour climb up the mountain was Colonel Harold Stevens from the British Embassy, representatives of Mussolini and Balbo, and several hundred young Fascists, members of the Italian Youth Organisation, who marched from adjacent towns and local villages. Gino Tocchioni and Raffaello Cari, who found Bert's body, joined the procession en route. Two wreaths were laid at the base of the monument, one from the Italian Government and the other from Katherine, who wrote on her card: 'In affectionate memory of my beloved husband, who sleeps in Italy, whose people have my eternal gratitude for their wonderful kindness.'

All the guests at the ceremony descended the mountainside for 300 metres to where a cross made from the Puss Moth's struts marked the spot where Bert had crashed. The wreckage had been removed on the backs of donkeys the day after Bert's funeral though some locals souvenired pieces of the machine. Everyone stood at attention as two aeroplanes flying overhead dipped three times in salute to Bert's memory. The monument was paid for by the Arezzo Aero Club from donations from local villagers.

Katherine emerged from her cocoon of privacy to write to the Australian Government on 2 October, finally putting an end to requests for bringing Bert home to Australia. 'Some time before my husband's body was found, but when it was no longer possible to hope for other than a tragic finding, I decided that wherever he was eventually discovered was to be the scene of his burial. If his name is to be remembered by future generations of Australians, I hope that remembrance will rest on whatever he achieved rather than on the place of his burial.'

In Australia, a national campaign was started for schoolchildren to plant trees in Bert's honour, and Prime Minister Joseph Lyons granted Frances a pension of £2 a week for life in recognition of Bert's contribution to the development of international aviation.

Solicitors in Brisbane revealed that although Bert had been without steady work for years, he had been a hard saver and left a sizeable estate of £12,181, made up almost entirely of bank deposits and war bonds in Queensland. Bert had died without a valid will and, under English intestacy law, Katherine was to receive £1000 free of death duties with the bulk of the residuary estate going to Frances in the event of Katherine's death. There was also the block of land in Perth.[2]

In December 1933, eleven months after the crash, Katherine gave formal permission for the twisted wreckage of Bert's Puss Moth, which had been held at the military airfield in Pisa, to be destroyed.[3] Six months, later in June 1934, she left Glasgow on a ship called *California* and returned to the house her father had bought on 37th Street, Astoria.

C.W.A. Scott's England-to-Australia record, which Bert had been trying to break, was obliterated by Scott himself in October 1934 when he and Tom Campbell Black, in a specially designed de Havilland DH.88 Comet Racer, took just two days, four hours and thirty-three minutes to fly from Mildenhall in East Anglia to Darwin en route to Melbourne in a race sponsored by MacRobertson's confectionery company to publicise their new chocolate treat called the Freddo Frog. Scott, who trumped a stellar field of twenty, including the husband and wife Mollisons, said he owed an enormous debt to Bert Hinkler, who had inspired him and so many other aviators.[4]

Nance had every reason to celebrate at the same time with the birth of her first grandchild, Maida's daughter Patricia 'Paddy' Canavan, on 31 October in Southampton. The following month Frances was invited to the Blue Mountains resort town of Katoomba for the opening of Hinkler Park, and in Australia and England, parks, roads and hotels were named in his honour, including the Hinkler pub in Southampton, near Gavan Street off Hinkler Road.

Frances still had four living children and a growing brood of grandchildren, and her daughter Queenie, born on Bert's twelfth birthday, had a similar adventurous spirit. She once advertised for pen pals, describing herself as having 'grey eyes, brown hair, fair complexion and a little over five feet tall'. 'I am very fond of having a good time,' she wrote, 'and believe me, I sure have it. Bert gave me a Kodak folding camera and I develop all my own snaps. We have a Ford Sedan car and I have won several medals and shields for my driving abilities. All I want are long letters with plenty of pep in them.'[5] In 1935 Queenie married a Bundaberg man named Lou Palm, and in later years they owned a motel near Hinkler Park.

Frances was nearly seventy in 1936 when an Italian shipping company gave her and George free passage on the *Esquilino* to visit Bert's grave. She carried with her a large number of wreaths from friends and relatives. She and George spent a long time sitting beside Bert's grave and were well pleased with the setting of his resting place. On 20 April they were guests at a civic reception hosted by the Mayor of Florence, Count Paolo Pesciolini, who told the audience: 'I am pleased to receive the mother of a hero.' The heroes of all countries were as dear as ever to Italians, he said, and the present political conditions in Europe had not altered that. Frances gave the Count thirty varieties of seeds from Queensland, which were planted in public parks and gardens in Florence in Bert's memory.

Even at her age Frances wanted to climb Pratomagno to see where the life that had started in Gavin Street, with the help of Dr May and the midwife Mrs Pashley, had ended, but the long climb was blocked by snow. Instead she spent her time in Italy thanking the villagers for what they had done for her son. They gave her a piece of Bert's clothing and a registration plate, marked 'D.H. Aeroplane Type Puss Moth 2049', taken off the smashed aircraft. Frances met Gino Tocchioni, the charcoal burner who found Bert's body, and he told her that Bert probably lived for some time after the crash and died peacefully in his sleep.[6]

The Hinklers left Italy for England where they said a final goodbye to Nance and where Frances was honoured with a tour of the Houses of Parliament in Westminster, escorted by Lord Clydesdale, an aviator who was the first man to fly over Mount Everest. He made an old woman's eyes well up when he told her that Bert Hinkler was always his hero.[7]

George and Frances also finally met Katherine in a tearful get-together. She was visiting her sister in Glasgow but felt that she had been welcomed into a whole new family from the other side of the world. For years later she would remind Frances of their first meeting, how George was so 'brotherly' to her, how he looked so much like her very own 'dear Bert' and how Frances had been such a 'gentle, kindly lady' who had taken this 'strange daughter-in-law' into her arms. Katherine said from that moment she would always remember Frances with 'deep love and gratitude'.

While that was happening in Britain, the Governor-General of Australia, Lord Gowrie, travelled to Bundaberg's Buss Park to unveil another memorial to Bert, saying: 'What we owe to these intrepid aviators can never be estimated and the memorial will be a reminder to the present generation and to those who are to follow of what civilisation owes to these courageous and skilful men.' The following year, 1937, the Royal Automobile Club of Queensland unveiled a memorial on Hummock Lookout, Bundaberg's highest point, overlooking Mon Repos beach.

Nance's daughter Maida eventually moved with her family to Cape Town, South Africa, and asked Nance to move there, too. Nance still had many friends in England and her mother to look after, but she began to make plans and sold No. 4 Havelock Road to Southampton Council for £1600 in 1938. In later years the site became a carpark. In 1941 Nance gave Bert's *Times Atlas*, which he had used to navigate the world, to the Ordnance Survey, the national mapping agency in England.

After World War II Nance eventually joined Maida and her family in Cape Town. Maida had called her house 'Rangitata' after the ship on which they had sailed together to Auckland in 1932 as Bert readied the Puss Moth. Nance rented out Mon Repos to a caravan builder for some years. She tried to donate the Ibis to a museum but there were no takers, so she left it in the shed and the caravan builder hoisted the plane into its ceiling to give him room to run his business. In 1952 when Nance eventually sold Mon Repos to the caravan builder for £2500 he turfed Bert's dream out into the yard. It was about to be dumped when it came into possession of Henry Stisted, managing director of the Hampshire Aeroplane Club, who took it to Eastleigh Aerodrome to be rebuilt. When engineer Bill Dunning was inspecting the derelict plane he found tucked under a wing stub one of the great treasures of aviation history: Bert's logbook from the 1928 flight to Australia, as well as patents for the Avian's undercarriage and its certificate of airworthiness.[8]

Stisted displayed the Ibis at the Royal Aeronautical Society's Hatfield Aerodrome Show on 14 June 1953 and announced plans to manufacture the plane as the ideal private tourer that Bert had envisaged. Despite Nance's efforts to retrieve the Ibis, it remained in Stisted's possession at his shipyard on the Solent. Bert's log book, however, arrived in Australia on 15 June for the National Library of Australia in Canberra, making the journey on a Qantas Constellation appropriately named *Bert Hinkler*, which was also carrying film of Queen Elizabeth's recent coronation. The Coronation had all of Bundaberg buzzing, especially with the news that the young Queen would visit their city in March 1954. Frances celebrated her eighty-seventh birthday at Gavin Street on 28 August 1953, over the moon at the promise that she would get to shake the Queen's hand in six months. It was one piece of good news for her after she had lost her driver's licence at eighty-five. She always assumed she had right of way. A few days after her birthday, however, Frances was taken ill and was taken to Bundaberg General Hospital where she died on

5 September 1953. She was buried beside her father and husband in Bundaberg's General Cemetery.

Nance was still trying to retrieve Bert's Ibis when she died on 28 July 1958, aged eighty-one. Maida buried her in Cape Town under a headstone inscribed: 'In loving memory of my darling mother, Nance Hinkler'.

In Southampton, Henry Stisted slumped into financial difficulties and was declared bankrupt. The hangar at his shipyard where he stored the Ibis was cleaned out by the new owners to make room, and the wooden plane was left to rot outdoors. It eventually fell apart. Children eventually used Bert's pride and joy for an enormous bonfire on Guy Fawkes' night, 5 November 1959.

The same fate almost befell two other aeroplanes crucial to Bert's story. In 1970 Ted Wixted, from the Queensland Museum, retrieved Bert's Avro Baby from its last own Jim Suitor after he discovered that it had been kept under a house in Melbourne and all but forgotten for thirty-four years. It was restored by the Queensland Aero Club at Archerfield and since then has been on display next to the Avian at the Queensland Museum. In 1973 while 69 Gavin Street was being renovated, the wings and other pieces of Bert's glider were found under the house where they'd been for more than half a century.

The Mon Repos house would probably have vanished if not for the efforts of Bert's ardent supporters Wixted, Kevin Lindeberg, a Maryborough man then living in London, and Lex Rowland, a Bundaberg engineer and lifelong friend of Bert's nephew, Ron Hinkler. Lindeberg affixed a plaque from the Royal Queensland Aero Club to the side of Mon Repos in 1974, declaring it the former residence of the record-breaking Australian aviator. The house was then in the possession of Southampton Council. In 1979 the council planned to tear it down to build flats for aged care. Bert's new generation of friends fought to save it with the same tenacity he showed flying into storms.

Rowland, the son of a World War I digger, was not about to let a piece of Australian history suffer the fate of the Ibis. 'To understand the achievements of Bert,' Rowland said, 'you have to understand the world he was born into':

> He built a glider in the backyard of a little country house at a time when it was like rocket science and when no one in his world had any money. He sourced his materials from the dump, from the kid up the road who had a couple of wheels, from someone who had some old timber lying around — he scrounged everything he could and did the best he could with what was available to him. He spent his whole life scrounging to do his best.[9]

Rowland submitted a proposal to the Bundaberg Bicentennial Community Committee that Mon Repos be taken apart and rebuilt in Bundaberg. He and two other Bundaberg men, Stan Lohse and Merv Purkis, flew to Southampton in May 1983 to supervise the dismantling of the home, and for the next four weeks they chipped away the Bursledon bricks and removed the timber frames and timber staircase. They even found Bert's original kitchen sink dumped in a well in the backyard next to the site of the old shed.

The house was shipped to Australia in two 20-tonne containers and reconstructed near the centre of Bundaberg on the site of the new Botanic Gardens, by members of the Rotary Club of East Bundaberg and assorted volunteers including Bert Bent, Ray Townsend, John Wientjens and Bert's nephew Bryce Palm. The house now overlooks the lagoon where Bert watched the ibises as a boy in knickerbockers. On 16 June 1984, Mon Repos was officially opened in its new location by Queensland Premier Joh Bjelke-Petersen and the former Mayor of Southampton, Councillor Dorothy Brown. The same year the federal electorate around Bundaberg was renamed Hinkler. Queenie, the last survivor of Bert's siblings, visited the reconstruction site many times and was delighted to see Bert's English home for the first time, although she had received many letters written from there more than half a century earlier.

Queenie was eighty years old when she gave one of her last interviews. Her memory was fading but she still had plenty of pep, as she remembered her brother being 'quiet and very clever with an imagination that was quite wonderful'.[10]

Thanks to renewed interest in Bert's achievements, Bundaberg began to host the Hinkler Memorial Lectures, which brought some of the great minds of aviation to the city, one of them being NASA astronaut Don Lind, who had logged 168 hours in space. Bundaberg council presented Dr Lind with a small piece of wood, taken from Bert's glider, as a souvenir of his visit. Lind gave the memento to Lieutenant Colonel Dick Scobee, commander of the final Space Shuttle *Challenger* mission. Scobee took the wood with him on board the *Challenger* and placed it in a small plastic bag inside his locker. Tragically, Scobee and all six of his crew members were killed when the

Challenger exploded during lift-off from Cape Canaveral on 28 January 1986.

While the *Challenger* disintegrated, the piece of Bert's glider was found intact inside the locker on the seabed off the Florida coast and returned to Hinkler House. Bert's transplanted English house became the centrepiece of Bundaberg's gardens, but in 1988 Bert's childhood home, Woodbine Cottage, built at 69 Gavin Street by John Hinkler a hundred years earlier only to descend into disrepair, burnt down.

With the march of time the world Bert Hinkler knew changed remarkably. Avro's experimental works and airfield at Hamble were overtaken by houses, and Avro itself was swallowed up by British Aerospace. The journey from London to Australia that had taken Bert fifteen days was now a daily occurrence. In April 2011 the Qantas A380 named Bert Hinkler started flying London to Sydney in 21 hours. But it took the pioneering aviators to make modern air travel, safe, reliable and economical. They all made sacrifices, some small and some great.

As Bert's nephew Bert Jr once pointed out: 'Imagine if you will, the determination of [my uncle] who alone flew these aircraft over vast distances and wide oceans. He had to remain awake and alert in conditions of incredible loneliness, no one to talk to, no radio, entertainment or communication in an open cockpit through rain, hail, snow, sun and wind day after day. Airfields were few and far between and at most places little more than unlit grassy fields or sand.' Hinkler House, as it became known, gradually began to fill with Bert's personal items: letters, photographs, documents, artefacts and furniture, the Ibis throttle control rescued from the ruins, even the Salonola from Tattersalls

Club, donated by Nance's granddaughter Paddy Canavan, who became a leading South African actress.

As the Botanic Gardens grew around the Mon Repos house it was given a new neighbour in 2008 with the opening of the $7.5 million Hinkler Hall of Aviation, an interactive museum celebrating Bert's achievements. With 4000 items on display, including the *Times Atlas* that Nance had given the Ordnance Survey in 1941, it quickly became a leading tourist attraction in Queensland, showcasing Bert's rebuilt glider, a copy of the Ibis and replicas of the Baby, Avian and Puss Moth.

In the years since Bert's death legends and rumours mushroomed. The official cause of the crash was put down to a well-documented design fault in the Puss Moth's airframe, which under turbulent conditions could cause a wing to break away in mid-air. But there were many theories about what caused the crash other than the official explanation, and the Queensland Museum's Ted Wixted spent decades trying to interest a sceptical Scotland Yard in investigating his conviction that Bert had been the victim of sabotage. He claimed that Bert's propeller had been tampered with, that it came apart in mid-flight and that Bert was trying to make an emergency landing when he came down on the mountain.

Australian adventurer Lang Kidby, who recreated Bert's England-to-Australia flight in 1998 flying an Avian that Bert had tested in Manchester, investigated the crash. He says there is no mystery at all around Bert's death, that he simply was caught in atrocious weather and perished like so many other great pilots in similar conditions.

Certainly Katherine seemed to feel Bert's loss more than anyone. She never spoke about him publicly and died in

1976 still known as Katherine Hinkler and still mourning the death of her husband of just seven months. On 18 June 1939, six and a half years after she and Bert's mother had both lost their soul mate, Katherine sat down in her father's home at 21/35 37th Street, Long Island, Astoria, New York, and wrote to Frances. Calling the resolute old lady 'my dearest mater', she filled Frances in on some personal details, on her mother's illness, the struggles of her new job at an advertising agency, which had just lost a big account, on her nephew Billy doing well at school and looking forward to university, on her sister Jean taking a business course to busy her mind after the sudden death of her husband and of the visit to the New York's World Fair by King George VI and his radiant Queen Elizabeth.

> I had a note the other day from old Sr Becuccin, the custodian of the cemetery at Florence telling me that he's taking proper care of the grave, for which of course, I pay him every year [Katherine wrote]. He is a decent old soul, but I feel it necessary to prod him every now and then. If work continues at all, I hope to try to manage to go there next year but at the moment it is only a hope.

Katherine then opened her heart about the love of her life.

> I was a little bit taken aback at you asking me whether I was thinking of remarrying. I realise that my letters are not very informative, but it is difficult for me to make clear how quiet is the life I lead. I have lost all desire for entertainment or company and seldom leave the house except to go to the

office. As time goes on one doesn't cry, but nothing can take away the bitter sense of loss. If [Bert] had been spared, I think we could have made a good life together, as he was taken the best I can do is to keep busy.

Bert is still as dear to me as when I saw him last and no one can ever take his place. To me he was the best of husbands and the best of companions.[11]

At Woodbine Cottage, where she had raised her family and lost her own husband, Frances read the letter carefully and shared Katherine's grief. Time had not eased her pain. She took off her glasses and folded Katherine's letter carefully and put it back in its envelope.

Frances closed her eyes and thought of Bert lying beside the bush up there in the snow on that forbidding Italian mountain, how he pulled his thick coat around him and shivered against the icy wind. What must have been going through his mind as he waited for help to come? Did he fall asleep hearing the echoing voices of children on the beach as he felt himself becoming weightless? 'Go higher, Bert, go higher, mate,' Charlie Laffan and Joe Marks and May had called out to him all those years ago as the waves rolled in on Mon Repos beach and Bert took flight in the glider. As Bert fought against the cold and pain, did his thoughts drift back to Bundaberg and how he looped the loop in the Baby and flew under the spans of the longest steel traffic bridge in Australia?

Frances thought about Bert waving to her from his open cockpit on that magical day in 1921, so full of life and so happy to be flying, ready to taxi his tiny biplane up Gavin Street right to her front door as he'd promised.

'Cheerio, Mum,' he had yelled to her as he circled the old weatherboard house then came back again with a whoosh of the plane, waving with unbridled joy. 'Cheerio Mum. Cheerio.'

Frances wiped away a tear as she thought about Bert closing his eyes for the last time and the snow covering his face and body like a shroud. Bert had made her so proud, and his daring had helped change the world for the better. She remembered how she had waved back to her son from the front yard of Woodbine Cottage as he thrilled the Bundaberg crowd with his aerobatics. Now she realised that she was waving goodbye. 'Cheerio, Bert,' Frances said softly. 'Cheerio.'

Appendix I

Orville Wright took over the Wright aviation business after Wilbur's death but sold the company in 1915. He piloted an aircraft for the last time in 1918. His sister, Katharine, renewed an old college friendship with Henry Haskell, a newspaperman and widower. Despite Orville's protests, the pair married in 1926. Orville was devastated, refused to attend her wedding and cut off all ties only agreeing to visit her on her deathbed when she contracted pneumonia three years later.

Orville suffered a fatal heart attack on 30 January 1948. He was seventy-six and had seen the aeroplane progress from an idea in a bike shop to supersonic flight. The *Wright Flyer I* is on display at the Smithsonian Institution in Washington.

During the 1930s Sir Alliott Verdon-Roe (he added the hyphen later in life) became a high-profile supporter of British Fascist Oswald Mosley. In the Second World War, two of his sons were killed in action while serving with the Royal Air Force. He died in 1958, aged eighty.

Roy Chadwick, Avro's chief designer and Bert's great friend, went on to build the mighty Lancaster bomber in World War II. After the war he began developing Avro's first jets but was killed in a crash of the sixty-seat piston-engine airliner, the Avro Tudor 2, at Woodford Aerodrome in Manchester on 23 August 1947. He was fifty-four.

George Augustine Taylor, the epileptic who founded the Aerial League of Australia, joined the 7th Light Horse in October 1914 aged forty-two. He died aged fifty-five at his home in Sydney when he slipped in the bath, struck his head and drowned.

John Duigan, who built and flew the first Australian-made aircraft with the assistance of younger brother Reg, gained Aviator's Certificate No. 211 at Brooklands, Surrey, in April 1912 using a tractor biplane built by A.V. Roe. He enlisted in the Australian Flying Corps and received the Military Cross for gallantry. He ran his garage, Old Bridge Motors, at Yarrawonga in northern Victoria from 1928 until 1941. He died on 11 June 1951 aged sixty-nine. His aircraft is on display at Museum Victoria, Melbourne.

Following his Australia tour of 1910, Harry Houdini packed the Voisin into storage in England and never found time to fly again. He remained the world's greatest magician and escape artist until 31 October 1926, when he died in Detroit of peritonitis from a ruptured appendix. He was fifty-two. Today the site of Australia's first officially recognised powered flight is directly under the flight path of Melbourne's Tullamarine Airport nearby, and on

Holden Road, Diggers Rest, a stone marker competes with long grass to identify the place where Harry Houdini flew in 1910.

William Hart, the flying dentist and the first registered pilot in Australia, never flew again after his accident in 1912. In January 1916 he enlisted in the Australian Imperial Force, then became a lieutenant in the Australian Flying Corps No. 1 Squadron and went to Egypt and Britain as an instructor, although he was declared medically unfit with epilepsy. For a time Hart owned Bert's Avro Baby after Bert sold it to Harry Broadsmith who was running the Australian Aircraft and Engineering Co. Ltd. In 1943 Hart dropped dead in Sydney's central business district.

After his spate of crashes in Australia, Wizard Stone returned to America with his wife Irene and daughters Edna and Yvonne in 1917. He entered the aviation section of the Army Signal Corps as a civilian and served in the experimental section at McCook Field, near the Wright brothers' hometown of Dayton, Ohio. In 1923 he packed up his family and moved to Santa Monica, California, where he rented a house on Pacific Street for $40 a month just a short walk from the Douglas plant for the Army Air Forces. He was the inspector-in-charge there until 1935. He died suddenly on 8 June 1943 aged sixty-three.

Tommy Sopwith was knighted in 1953 and lived to the age of 101. He recovered from his financial crisis after World War I and challenged for the America's Cup with his yachts *Endeavour* in 1934 and *Endeavour II* in 1937.

Noel Pemberton Billing, Supermarine's founder, retired from politics in 1923 and concentrated on the movie business, writing the script for the play High Treason, which was filmed in 1929 as one of Britain's first talkies. In the 1930s he ran a casino in Mexico with boxing great Jack Dempsey. He died in 1948 aged sixty-six.

After his mail run from Melbourne to Sydney, Maurice Guillaux continued to give aerial demonstrations until his Blériot was badly damaged at Sydney's Ascot Racecourse on 3 August 1914. He spent six weeks in hospital. After war began in Europe, Guillaux returned to France and was attached as an instructor in 1917 to No. 5 Squadron, Australian Flying Corps, in Shawbury, England. In 1917 Australian newspapers reported that Guillaux had actually been spying for the Germans and was executed by a firing squad. The following year the papers reported that Guillaux was in fact a war hero who had died in a crash on 22 May 1917 at Villacoublay, France.

Guillaux's Blériot XI Looper was used for some years at Ballarat Flying School and is on display at Sydney's Powerhouse Museum.

Russian pilot Evgeniy Gvaita, who flew a Baby from Hamble to Moscow, was arrested during Stalin's purges but later released. He served in the Russian army during World War II, repairing tanks, and died in 1946 aged fifty.

Latvian colonel Janis Indans, who befriended Bert after the 1900-kilometre flight to Riga, recovered from serious injuries in an aircraft crash in 1928 to participate in goodwill flights around Europe in 1930 and 1936. He was promoted to the rank of general at the outbreak of World War II but was arrested by the Soviets in February 1941 and executed by firing squad in Moscow's Butyrka prison.

Horace Brinsmead, Australia's Controller of Civil Aviation, was badly injured in an air crash at Alor Setar in Malaysia when one of Kingsford Smith's ANA Avro X machines, the Southern Sun, crashed on take-off in 1931. He recovered and decided to continue his trip on a KLM flight. It crashed on take-off on 7 December 1931 in Bangkok. Brinsmead was an invalid until his death in Melbourne on 11 March 1934.

While three of the conspirators in the assassination of Archduke Franz Ferdinand and his wife Sophie were hanged, Gavrilo Princip, who fired the fatal shots, was, at nineteen, too young for the death penalty and instead was sentenced to twenty years' jail. He served just three and a half. One of his arms was amputated as a result of his tuberculosis, and he died on 28 April 1918 at Terezín prison near Prague.

Following his brother's death, Sir Keith Smith became the Australian agent for Vickers and the elder statesman of Australian aviation. He died in Sydney on 19 December 1955 aged sixtyfour and is buried near his brother and parents in Adelaide's North Road Anglican cemetery. His Vickers Vimy is on display at Adelaide Airport.

Ray Parer took a break from aviation after ending up in hospital following a crash at Boulder, Western Australia, in 1921. He competed in the 1934 MacRobertson England–

Australia Air Race but only for an hour — his Fairey Fox biplane started misfiring over the English Channel and he made an emergency landing in a French field.

He joined the RAAF in World War II but became an engineer aboard a small boat used for supply and reconnaissance along the northern coast of New Guinea. He spent the last years of his life running two small farms at Mount Nebo on Brisbane's outskirts.

He died in 1967, aged seventy-three. His cousin was the World War II photographer Damien Parer.

Actors Spencer Tracy and Alec Baldwin portrayed Jimmy Doolittle in film versions of the daring bomber raid he led over Japan on 2 January 1942, a month after the Japanese had devastated the American fleet at Pearl Harbor. He died in 1993, aged ninety-six and he is buried in Arlington National Cemetery among America's most revered heroes.

Alan Cobham's Flying Circus was an enormous success touring England, giving exhibitions and joy rides in the 1930s. Cobham was also instrumental in the development of aerial refuelling and died in Poole, Dorset, in 1973, aged seventy-nine.

C.W.A. Scott took over Cobham's Flying Circus in 1936 and continued to win air races. He served as an air-raid ambulance driver, then as a Royal Naval Reserve pilot in World War II before acting as a test pilot and flying instructor for de Havilland in Canada. He killed himself with his service revolver during a fit of depression in 1946. He was forty-three.

On Saturday, 2 September 1933, while the Arezzo Aero Club was getting ready to unveil Bert's monument high on Pratomagno, across the Atlantic at Floyd Bennett Field, Brooklyn, Mussolini's Lord of the Distances, General Francesco de Pinedo, crashed and burned to death while taking off on a flight to Baghdad.

Amelia Earhart became the first woman to fly solo across the Atlantic in 1932 but disappeared aged thirty-nine in 1937 between Lae in New Guinea and Howland Island 4000 kilometres away during a planned round-the-world flight.

On 29 July 1932, Amy Johnson and Jim Mollison married and continued to break aviation records around the world. His drinking and womanising took their toll, however, and the marriage ended in 1938. During World War II she flew for the Air Transport Auxiliary and in 1940 bailed out over the Thames Estuary and drowned. She was thirty-seven. In 1953, Mollison's pilot's licence was revoked because of his drinking. He died of pneumonia in 1959, aged fifty-four.

Lores Bonney followed her Australia-to-England feat by making the first ever flight from Australia to South Africa in 1937. She was ninety years old in 1988, when along with Charles Lindbergh's nephew, the acting US Consul David Seal, she launched the Hinkler Australian Bicentennial Air Race at the Queensland Museum. In her last few years she watched hang gliders from the balcony of her home at Miami on Queensland's Gold Coast. She died there in 1994, aged ninety-six.

After the kidnapping and death of his son, Charles Lindbergh moved with his wife Anne to Europe in 1932, and they eventually had five more children. A German immigrant carpenter, Bruno Richard Hauptmann, went to the electric chair for the crime in 1936 still protesting his innocence.

In his autobiography, Lindbergh attacked the morals of womanising aviators. Following his death in Hawaii in 1974 aged seventy-two, it emerged that in addition to his American family he had three secret families in Europe and had fathered as many as seven other children with a pair of sisters in Germany and with his European private secretary. The *Spirit of St Louis* is on display at the Smithsonian Institution.

Charles Kingsford Smith's Australian National Airways was ruined by the Great Depression and the 1931 crash in the Snowy Mountains of one of his aircraft, the *Southern Cloud*. He was attempting another record-breaking flight from England to Australia in the *Lady Southern Cross* when he and co-pilot Tommy Pethybridge disappeared on the night of 8 November 1935 off the coast of Burma.

A year earlier, Smithy's long-time co-pilot Charles Ulm disappeared off the coast of Hawaii.

The *Southern Cross* is on display at Brisbane airport.

Bert's monument on Pratomagno was destroyed by vandals toward the end of World War II as Fascism was in its death throes, but authorities erected a new memorial to his memory without the political symbolism.

General Italo Balbo, Mussolini's right-hand man and the only prominent Fascist to oppose Italy's alliance with

Hitler, died when he was shot down over Tobruk by friendly fire from Italian antiaircraft guns in 1940. Balbo's friends believed it was a political assassination orchestrated by Mussolini.

Il Duce's decision to plunge Italy into war alongside the Nazis quickly backfired. Mussolini and his mistress Clara Petacci were executed by Communist partisans in 1945 and their bodies hung from meat hooks at an Esso garage in Milan.

Bert's compatriot on the bombing raids over Germany, Sidney Cotton, invented the Sidcot flying suit, a specially designed thickly padded overall, and it became standard kit for British pilots from the end of World War I until the 1950s. His World War II spying missions over Germany inspired Cotton's friend, Ian Fleming, the author of the James Bond novels. Despite many business successes throughout his adventurous life Cotton died penniless and largely forgotten in 1969. He is buried in the small Tallegalla Cemetery near Ipswich, Queensland.

Chubbie Miller became Mrs Jessie Pugh when she married a commercial pilot in England in 1936. She lived a quiet life out of the spotlight until her death in 1972 in Hammersmith, aged seventy-one.

She would be forever linked with Bill Lancaster who, on the night of 13 April 1933, took off in Kingsford Smith's old blue-andsilver Avian from the Moroccan outpost of Reggan intending to make a 1200-kilometre crossing of the Sahara on his way to Cape Town. After less than an hour in the air his engine failed and he crash-landed in the desert.

Lancaster spent eight days sheltering under the plane's wing, dying of thirst, thinking of Chubbie, lighting rescue flares and waiting for help. Chubbie did her best to organise a search, but help finally arrived twenty-nine years too late. Lancaster's mummified remains were found by a detachment of the French Foreign Legion in 1962. The Legionnaires found Lancaster's remains under one of the Avian's wings. (The remains of Lancaster's plane are now with Bert's Baby and Avian at the Queensland Museum.) Inside his wallet were two photos of Chubbie, and beside him a diary in which he jotted his final words of love for her as he waited to die.

There was no confession, no mention, in fact of Haden Clarke. Perhaps old Bill was innocent after all.

Appendix II
Pre-World War II Aviation Awards

Fédération Aéronautique Internationale Gold Medal

This medal was established in 1924 and was first awarded in 1925. It is reserved for those who have contributed greatly to the development of aeronautics by their activities, work, achievements, initiative or devotion to the cause of aviation.

Year	Recipient
1925	General Francesco de Pinedo (Italy)
1926	Sir Alan J. Cobham (UK)
1927	Charles A. Lindbergh (USA)
1928	Bert Hinkler (Australia)
1929	Captain D. Costes (France)
1930	Maréchal Italo Balbo (Italy)
1931	Dr Hugo Eckener (Germany)
1932	Sr D. Juan La Cierva (Spain)
1933	Wiley Post (USA)
1934	C.W.A. Scott (UK)
1935	Not awarded
1936	Jean Mermoz (France)
1937	Miss Jean Batten (UK)

Britannia Trophy

For the British aviator or aviators accomplishing the most meritorious performance in aviation during the previous year.

1913   Captain C.A.H. Longcroft, RFC

1914   Squadron Commander J.W. Sedden, RNAS

1915–18   No award due to World War I

1919   Captain Sir John Alcock

1920   H.J.L. Hinkler for a non-stop flight Croydon–Turin 1046 kilometres (650 miles) in nine hours thirty-five minutes in an Avro Baby

1921   No award

1922   F.P. Raynham

1923   A.J. Cobham

1924   Wing Commander S.J. Goble & Flight Lieutenant I.E. McIntyre

1925   A.J. Cobham

1926   Sir Alan Cobham

1927   Lieutenant R.R. Bentley

1928   Squadron Leader H.J.L. Hinkler for the first flight to Australia in a light aircraft. London to Darwin 17,710 kilometres (11,005 miles) in 15 days solo in an Avro 581E Avian.

1929   Hon. Lady Mary Bailey

1930   Squadron Leader C. Kingsford Smith

1931   Squadron Leader H.J.L. Hinkler for a flight from New York to London via South America and the South Atlantic, 17,000 kilometres in forty-one days in a DH 80A Puss Moth

1932   Captain C.F. Uwins

1933   J.A. Mollison

1934   C.W.A. Scott & T. Campbell Black

1935	Jean Batten
1936	Jean Batten
1937	Flying Officer A.E. Clouston
1938	Squadron Leader R. Kellett
1939	Alex Henshaw

Segrave Trophy

Awarded to the British national who accomplishes the most outstanding demonstration of the possibilities of transport by land, sea, air or water.

1930	Charles Kingsford Smith
1931	Bert Hinkler
1932	Amy Johnson
1933	Malcolm Campbell
1934	Ken Waller
1935	George Eyston
1936	Jean Batten
1937	A.E. Clouston
1938	A.T. Goldie Gardner
1939	Sir Malcolm Donald Campbell

Notes

CHAPTER 1

1 Benito Mussolini, *My Diary 1915–17*, Small, Maynard & Co., 1925.
2 R.J.B. Bosworth, *Mussolini's Italy: Life Under the Fascist Dictatorship, 1915–1945*, Penguin Books, 2007.
3 Bosworth, *Mussolini's Italy*.
4 Aaron Gillette, *Racial Theories in Fascist Italy*, Routledge, 2002.

CHAPTER 2

1 From *The Air Up There* by Dave English, McGraw-Hill Professional, 2003.
2 Charles Meyer, *A History of Germans in Australia 1839–1945*, 1990.
3 *Brisbane Courier*, 25 December 1865, p. 2.
4 Isaac Noake's brewery was sketched by the colonial artist John Glover.
5 *Brisbane Courier*, 23 August 1864, p. 2.

CHAPTER 3

1 *Brisbane Courier*, 24 February 1928, p. 19.
2 Giancarlo Maiorino, *Leonardo da Vinci: The Daedalian Mythmaker*, Pennsylvania State University, 1992.
3 *Independent* (London), 27 April 2005.
4 *Morning Bulletin* (Rockhampton), 22 July 1933, p. 14.
5 Bundaberg in Print, Bundaberg Newspaper Company, 2009.
6 *Brisbane Courier*, 21 September 1901, p. 13.
7 Patek Philippe actually designed the first wristwatch for a woman in 1868, but it was a one-off.

CHAPTER 4

1   *Queenslander* (Brisbane), 14 May 1904, p. 28.
2   John Evangelist Walsh, *One Day at Kitty Hawk: The Untold Story of the Wright Brothers and the Airplane*, Crowell, 1975.
3   Fred Howard, *Wilbur and Orville: A Biography of the Wright Brothers*, Dover Publications, 1987.
4   *Bundaberg in Print*, Bundaberg Newspaper Company, 2009.
5   *Bundaberg in Print*, Bundaberg Newspaper Company, 2009.
6   Gleanings in Bee Culture, January 1, 1905, pp 36 to 39.
7   *Brisbane Courier*, 24 February 1928, p. 19.
8   *Bundaberg in Print*, Bundaberg Newspaper Company, 2009.
9   Paul Hoffman, *Wings of Madness: Alberto Santos-Dumont and the Invention of Flight*, Hyperion Press, 2003.
10 *Morning Bulletin* (Rockhampton), 22 July 1933.
11 Bert Hinkler's unfinished memoirs.

CHAPTER 5

1   *Weekly Times*, 19 March 1910.
2   Phil Scott, *The Wrong Stuff? Attempts at Flight Before (and After) the Wright Brothers*, Hylas Publishing, 2003.
3   *Time*, 27 April 1936.
4   Simonetta Falasca-Zamponi, *Fascist Spectacle: The Aesthetics of Power in Mussolini's Italy* (Studies on the History of Society and Culture), University of California Press, 2000.
5   Charles Harvard Gibbs-Smith, *The Invention of the Aeroplane, 1799–1909*, Taplinger, 1966.
6   Bosworth, *Mussolini's Italy*.
7   *Advertiser* (Adelaide), 19 July 1910, p. 9.
8   *Brisbane Courier*, 25 July 1910, p. 5.
9   *Argus* (Melbourne), 19 March 1910, p. 18.
10 *Queenslander* (Brisbane), 12 March 1910, p. 13.
11 *Brisbane Courier*, 12 October 1910, p. 19.
12 *Brisbane Courier*, 18 June 1910, p. 5.
13 *Brisbane Courier*, 19 March 1928.
14 *Brisbane Courier*, 24 December 1910.
15 *Morning Bulletin* (Rockhampton), 25 February 1928, p. 9.
16 *Bundaberg Mail*, 25 March 1912.

CHAPTER 6

1   *Brisbane Courier*, 25 February 1928, p. 15.
2   *Bangor Daily Commercial* (Bangor, Maine), 18 August 1913.

3   Rodgers' first transcontinental flight on a Wright biplane, the *Vin Fiz*, took fifty days and included sixty-nine stops. His plane was damaged and repaired so many times en route that nothing remained of the original at the finish but the drip pan and vertical rudder.

4   Bundaberg Mail, 29 May 1912.

5   *Morning Bulletin* (Rockhampton), 7 July 1936, p. 6.

6   *Morning Bulletin* (Rockhampton), 7 July 1936, p. 6.

7   *Sydney Morning Herald*, 8 June 1912, p. 9.

8   A. Scott Berg, *Lindbergh*, G.P. Putnam's Sons, 1998.

9   Later to become part of Sydney Airport.

10   *Brisbane Courier*, 8 July 1912, p. 7.

11   Bettiens, *Hinkler: Hyperbole, Hypocrisy and Humbug versus Authenticity and Accuracy in Australian History*, self-published, 1985.

12   Bettiens, *Hinkler*.

13   Bettiens, *Hinkler*.

14   *Flight*, 12 September 1912.

15   *Advertiser* (Adelaide), 21 October 1912, p. 10.

16   Bert Hinkler's unfinished memoirs.

17   Bettiens, *Hinkler*.

18   Bert Hinkler, letter to his mother, from Auckland 24 April 1913.

19   Bert Hinkler unfinished memoirs.

20   Bert Hinkler, letter to his mother from Sydney, 15 June.

21   Bettiens, *Hinkler*.

CHAPTER 7

1   William J. Claxton, *The Mastery of the Air*, Echo Library, 2007.

2   *Bundaberg News and Mail*, 2 March 1928, p. 2.

3   *Flight*, 1 March 1928.

4   Mary Soames, *Clementine Churchill: The Biography of a Marriage*, Mariner Books, 2003.

5   *Flight*, 19 June 1914, p. 647.

6   The Vickers gun was based on the machine gun designed by Hiram Maxin, who had failed to get off the ground with his giant bat.

7   Bert Hinkler in letter to his mother from Liverpool England, 29 March 1914.

8   Bert Hinkler in letter to his mother from Liverpool England, 29 March 1914.

9   Knights of the air: the life and times of the extraordinary
     pioneers who first built British aeroplanes by Peter King,
     University of Iowa Press, 1989.
10   *New York Times*, 26 December 1913.
11   *Advertiser* (Adelaide), 10 November 1913, p. 16.
12   *Camperdown Chronicle* (Victoria), 23 April 1914, p. 4.
13   *Sydney Morning Herald*, 27 April 1914, p. 9.
14   *Sydney Morning Herald*, 8 May 1914, p. 9.
15   *Sydney Morning Herald*, 13 May 1914, p. 13.
16   *Brisbane Courier*, 2 June 1914, p. 7.
17   *Sydney Morning Herald*, 17 July 1914, p. 9.
18   *Advertiser* (Adelaide), 20 July 1914, p. 15.
19   *Flight*, 12 June 1914.
20   *Flight*, 3 July 1914, p. 711.
21   Rich Stowell, *The Light Airplane Pilot's Guide to Stall/Spin
     Awareness*, Rich Stowell Consulting, 2007.
22   Bert Hinkler's unfinished memoirs, 1933.

CHAPTER 8
1   Don Berliner, *Aviation: Reaching for the Sky*, Oliver Press,
     1997.
2   *Sydney Morning Herald*, 22 May 1893, p. 6.
3   Frederic Morton, *Thunder at Twilight: Vienna 1913–1914*,
     Collier Books, 1990.
4   Luigi Albertini, *The Origins of the War of 1914*, vol. 2.,
     Oxford University Press 1953.
5   Morton, *Thunder at Twilight*.
6   J.A. Mangan, *A Sport-Loving Society: Victorian and
     Edwardian Middle-Class England at Play*, Routledge, 2006, p.
     275.
7   *Flight*, 10 July 1914.
8   Janusz Piekalkiewicz, *The Air War, 1939–1945*, Blandford
     Press, 1985.
9   Bert Hinkler's memoirs.
10   Bryan Cooper & John H. Batchelor, *Fighter: A History of
     Fighter Aircraft*, Macdonald & Co., 1973.
11   Ray Bonds, *The story of aviation: a concise history of flight*,
     Barnes & Noble Books, 1997, p. 71.
12   Justin D. Murphy, *Military Aircraft, Origins to 1918: An
     Illustrated History of Their Impact*, ABC-CLIO, p. 112.
13   *Australians at War: A Pictorial History by Anthony
     MacDougall. The Five Mile Press. 1995.*

14 Bert Hinkler in a letter to his sister Queenie from Newcastle on Tyne, 19 December 1914.

15 Bryan Cooper, *The Story of the Bomber, 1914–1945*, Cathay Books, 1974.

16 *New York Times*, 15 April 1915, and *Poverty Bay Herald*, 16 April 1915, p. 3.

17 The L9, built in March 1915, made four raids on England before exploding in flames along with L6 while being refuelled in its hangar on 16 September 1916.

18 Bert Hinkler in a letter to his mother from Whitley Bay, Northumberland 5 May, 1915.

19 Charlie Laffan suffered wounds to his back and chest in the Dardanelles on 12 April 1915 two weeks before the Anzacs stormed Gallipoli. Taken back to England to convalesce, he married Amy Dodd that year before returning to Bundaberg in December. His commanding officer, Hugh Quinn, was shot by Turkish snipers on 29 April and buried in Shrapnel Valley cemetery. Lieutenant Colonel Hubert Harris, who helped Bert get his first job in Brisbane, died at Gallipoli on 31 July 1915.

20 Group Captain Keith Isaacs, RAAF (Ret.), 'Wings over Gallipoli', *Defence Force Journal*, Gallipoli, 75th Anniversary 1915–90.

21 *Sydney Morning Herald*, 7 July 1915, p. 12.

CHAPTER 9

1 Albert Bushnell Hart, *Harper's Pictorial Library of the World War*, Vol. 10, 1920.

2 http://jarrowlife.co.uk.

3 The L10 built in May 1915, also attacked London on 17–18 August 1915 causing ten deaths and injuring forty-eight people. It exploded during a thunderstorm on 3 September 1915 near Cuxhaven, Germany.

4 Edward V. Coggins, *Wings That Stay On*, Turner Publishing Co., 2000.

5 E.F. Cheesman (ed.), *Reconnaissance and Bomber Aircraft of the 1914–1918 War*, Harleyford Publications, 1962, p. 9.

6 Ian Castle & Christa Hook, *London 1914–17: The Zeppelin Menace*, Osprey Publishing, 2008, p. 36.

7 Bert Hinkler in a letter to his mother from Shepherds Bush, London 11 March, 1916.

8 Letter from C.G. Grey to Bert's de facto wife Nance Hinkler 4 December 1931.

9   Bert Hinkler in a letter to his mother from London 1 April 1916.
10 Bert Hinkler in a letter to his mother from London 1 April 1916.
11 Bert Hinkler letter to his sister Queenie from France 30
    September 1916.
12 *New York Times*, 9 August 1916.
13 It finally appeared on 13 March 1917.
14 Eric Lawson &, Jane Lawson, *The First Air Campaign:
    August 1914–November 1918*, Da Capo Press, 1996, p. 98.

CHAPTER 10

1   Manfred Richthofen (Freiherr von), *The Red Baron*, Doubleday,
    1969, p. 120.
2   Hayden McAllister (ed.), *Flying Stories*, Octopus Books, 1982.
3   The 'Red Baron' nickname became popular only after World
    War I. During the war the Germans called von Richthofen
    Der Rote Kampfflieger (the 'Red Battle Flyer'), which was the
    name of his autobiography. The French called him *le Diable
    Rouge* (the 'Red Devil').
4   Bert Hinkler in a letter to his parents from 'The Front', May
    (no day) 1917.
5   James McCudden, *Flying Fury: Five Years in the Royal Flying
    Corps*, Casemate, 2009.
6   Stephens survived the amputation and returned to RNAS
    service in late 1917.
7   Bert Hinkler in a letter to his sister Queenie from France, 29
    May 1917.
8   Bert Hinkler in a letter to his parents from 'The Front', May
    (no day) 1917.
9   Bert Hinkler in a letter to his parents from 'The Front', May
    (no day) 1917.
10 Bert Hinkler in a letter to his parents from 'The Front', May
    (no day) 1917.
11 Bert Hinkler in a letter to his parents from 'The Front', May
    (no day) 1917.
12 Peter Kilduff, *Red Baron: The Life and Death of an Ace*,
    David & Charles, 2007.
13 Theresa M. Towner & James B. Carothers, *Reading Faulkner:
    Glossary and Commentary. Collected Stories*, University Press
    of Mississippi, 2006, p. 282.
14 Jonathan Nicholls, *Cheerful Sacrifice: The Battle of Arras
    1917*, Pen and Sword Books, 2005.
15 *New York Times*, 28 March 1917.

16 In July 1918, Rathborne led a mass breakout through a tunnel from the Holzminden POW camp near Hanover and made it back to safety.

17 Bert Hinkler in a letter to his mother from France, 27 August 1917.

18 Bert Hinkler in a letter to his mother from France, 27 August 1917.

19 Ronald Dodds, *The Brave Young Wings*, Canada's Wings, Stittsville, Ontario, 1980.

20 Bert Hinkler in a letter to his mother from France, 27 August 1917.

21 Bert Hinkler in a letter to his sister Queenie from France, 8 December 1917.

CHAPTER 11

1   He had a little list by Julian Mitchell, *Spectator*, 5 July 1997.

2   Ted Smout died in 2004 aged 106, strongly opposed to Australian involvement in foreign wars.

3   Adrian Hellwig, *Australian Hawk Over the Western Front: A Biography of Major R. S. Dallas*, Grub Street, 2005.

4   Wayne Ralph, *William Barker, VC: The Life, Death and Legend of Canada's Most Decorated War Hero*, John Wiley & Sons Canada, 2007.

5   Flying the Camel in 1918 by Ronald Sykes, DFC, *Flight International*, 2 May 1968.

6   Bert Hinkler in a letter to his parents from Eastbourne, 11 May 1918.

7   Norman Macmillan, *Offensive Patrol: The Story of the RNAS, RFC and RAF in Italy 1917–18*, Jarrolds London, 1973.

8   Gaetano V. Cavallaro, *The Beginning of Futility*, Xlibris, 2009.

9   John R. Schindler, *Isonzo: The Forgotten Sacrifice of the Great War*, Praeger Publishers, 2001.

10 Mussolini, *My Diary 1915–17*.

11 Some 5490 Sopwith Camels were built. They were responsible for shooting down 1294 enemy aircraft.

12 Bert Hinkler in a letter to his sister May from Italy, 2 October 1918.

13 Schindler, *Isonzo*.

14 Bert Hinkler in a postcard to his sister May from Italy, October (no day) 1918.

15 David Edgerton, *England and the Aeroplane: An Essay on a Militant and Technological Nation*, Macmillan & Centre for the History of Science, Technology and Medicine, University of Manchester, 1991.

16 Alan Bramson, *Pure Luck: The Authorised Biography of Sir Thomas Sopwith*, Crecy Publishing, 2005.

17 Guilfoyle had been awarded the Military Cross in 1917, served again during World War II, became an air commodore and was awarded the OBE. After a life of military heroism he was killed in 1948 by an exploding spirit stove while camping in bushland at Belgrave in the Dandenong Ranges near Melbourne. He was 57.

CHAPTER 12

1 *Barrier Miner* (Broken Hill, NSW), 5 March 1919, p. 4.

2 *Barrier Miner* (Broken Hill, NSW), 24 March 1919, p. 1.

3 *Sydney Morning Herald*, 4 April 1919, p. 7.

4 The site now houses the Atlantic Cool Climate Crop Research Centre and the offices of Agriculture Newfoundland and Labrador.

5 *West Australian* (Perth), 17 April 1919, p. 7.

6 *West Australian* (Perth), 18 April 1919, p. 5.

7 *New York Times*, 16 April 1919, p. 3.

8 *Argus* (Melbourne), 29 May 1919, p. 7.

9 *Sydney Morning Herald*, 30 May 1919, p. 7.

10 *West Australian* (Perth), 10 June 1919, p. 5.

11 *Examiner* (Launceston), 20 March 1928, p. 7.

12 *Advertiser* (Adelaide), 16 December 1919, p. 7.

13 H.G. Castle, *The First to Australia*, an article in *Wonders of World Aviation*, Vol. 1, ed. Clarence Winchester, Amalgamated Press, London, 1938.

CHAPTER 13

1 *Flight*, 26 June 1919.

2 Aubrey Joseph Jackson & Roger T. Jackson, *Avro Aircraft Since 1908*, Putnam Aeronautical, 1990.

3 Edward P. Wixted, *The Last Flight of Bert Hinkler*, Vantage Press, 1992.

4 Wixted, *The Last Flight of Bert Hinkler*.

5 Information supplied to Hinkler Hall of Aviation in 1987 by Fred Doland, longtime resident of Southampton.

6 Examiner (Launceston), 20 March 1928, p. 7.

7   Margaret Dove & Rosemary Lapham, *Roy Chadwick: Aircraft Designer 1893–1947*, Thirlby Publicity, Cheshire. (Dove and Lapham were the daughters of Roy Chadwick.)(it was a brochure – with no date of publication).
8   *Bundaberg Mail*, Tuesday 12 April 1921.
9   Examiner (Launceston), 20 March 1928, p. 7.
10 Bert Hinkler and the Avro Baby, by E.P. (Ted) Wixted, Queensland Museum, 1991.
11 Bert Hinkler in a letter to his parents from Turin, 1 June 1920.
12 Bert Hinkler in a letter to his parents from Turin, 1 June 1920.
13 Bert Hinkler in a letter to his parents from Turin, 1 June 1920.
14 Bert Hinkler in a letter to his parents from Turin, 1 June 1920.
15 *Flight*, 10 June 1920.
16 Stanley Brogden, *The History of Australian Aviation*, Hawthorne Press, 1960.
17 C.G. Grey in a letter to Frances Hinkler, 3 June 1920.
18 *Flight*, 17 June 1920.
19 Falasca-Zamponi, *Fascist Spectacle*.
20 Roy Mackenzie, *Solo: The Bert Hinkler Story*, Ure Smith, 1962.
21 *Flight*, 29 July 1920.
22 British aviation company AT&T went out of business in 1921 in the face of competition from government-subsidised French airlines operating the London–Paris route.
23 Sebastian Ritchie, *Industry and Air Power: The Expansion of British Aircraft Production, 1935–41*, Frank Cass & Co., 1997.
24 Tully and Lieutenant James Medcalf disappeared without trace attempting to fly a Stinson monoplane with a Wright Whirlwind engine from London, Ontario, to London, England, in 1927.
25 From a tribute given by Roy Chadwick following Bert Hinkler's death.

CHAPTER 14
1   Alliott Verdon-Roe, *The World of Wings and Things*, Arno Press, 1979, p. 116.
2   General Yusuf al-Azmah was killed at the Battle of Maysalun 20 kilometres west of Damascus on 23 July 1920.
3   Bert Hinkler in a letter to his partner Nance, from SS Ascanius, 2 March 1921.
4   Bert Hinkler in a letter to his partner Nance, from 'Somewhere at Sea', 5 March 1921.

5   Bert Hinkler in a letter to his partner Nance, from 'Somewhere at Sea', 5 March 1921.
6   Bert Hinkler in a letter to his partner Nance, from SS Ascanius, 2 March 1921.
7   *Western Mail* (Perth, WA), 28 April 1921, p. 30.
8   *Sydney Morning Herald*, 15 April 1921.
9   *Sydney Morning Herald*, 6 April 1921, p. 12.
10 *Brisbane Courier*, 12 April 1921, p. 7.
11 *Bundaberg Mail*, 12 April 1921.
12 *Bundaberg Mail*, 12 April 1921.
13 Bert Hinkler in a letter to Nance from Bundaberg, 12 April 1921.

CHAPTER 15
1   *Bundaberg Mail*, 12 April 1921.
2   The building was given a roof in 1955 and is now known as the Moncrieff Theatre.
3   C.G. Grey, Editor of *The Aeroplane* in a letter to Nance Hinkler, 18 April 1921.
4   *Bundaberg Mail*, 25 April 1921.
5   *Brisbane Courier*, 26 April 1921, p. 6.
6   *Bundaberg Mail*, 28 April 1921.
7   Bert Hinkler in a letter to Nance, 28 April 1921.
8   The hotel closed in 1971 and was knocked down to make way for the MLC Centre.
9   *Sydney Morning Herald*, 28 April 1921, p. 7.
10 *Sydney Morning Herald*, 2 May 1921, p. 8.

CHAPTER 16
1   *New York Times*, 13 July 1921.
2   *Sydney Morning Herald*, 23 May 1921, p. 8.
3   *New York Times*, 17 July 1921.
4   Mike Covello & James M. Flammang, *Standard Catalogue of Imported Cars 1946–2002*, Krause Publications, 2001.
5   *New York Times*, 13 July 1921.
6   *Flight*, 21 July 1921.
7   Wixted, *The Last Flight of Bert Hinkler*.
8   *Argus* (Melbourne), 17 April 1922, p. 9.
9   *West Australian* (Perth), 2 June 1922.
10 Bert Hinkler writing in *Aeronautical Engineering* (a supplement to *The Aeroplane*) 30 September 1922.
11 *Flight*, 14 September 1922.

12 John Gooch, *Mussolini and His Generals: The Armed Forces and Fascist Foreign Policy, 1922–1940*, Cambridge University Press, 2007.
13 Wixted, *The Last Flight of Bert Hinkler*.
14 From a tribute given by Roy Chadwick following Bert Hinkler's death
15 *Flight*, 28 June 1923.
16 'Flying in Australia', Paper by Bert Hinkler, read by aviation writer Major F.A. de Vere Robertson at the Engineers Club, Coventry Street, London, 6 February 1924.
17 *Sydney Morning Herald*, 2 June 1925, p. 8.
18 *Flight*, 9 July 1925.

CHAPTER 17
1   *Flight*, 22 April 1926.
2   *Mercury* (Hobart), 8 July 1926, p. 7.
3   *Time*, 16 August 1926.
4   *Brisbane Courier*, 16 August 1926, p. 7.
5   *Flight*, 26 August 1926.
6   *Folkestone, Hythe, Sandgate and Cheriton Herald*, 18 September 1926.
7   *Brisbane Courier*, 23 September 1926, p. 10.
8   John Fishwick Leeming, *Airdays*, G.G. Harrap, 1936.
9   Leeming, *Airdays*.
10 Leeming, *Airdays*.

CHAPTER 18
1   *West Australian* (Perth), 26 February 1927, p. 11.
2   *Cairns Post*, 14 March 1927.
3   *Brisbane Courier*, 15 March 1927.
4   *Brisbane Courier*, 21 March 1927, p. 15.
5   *Brisbane Courier*, 30 March 1927, p. 21.
6   *Singapore Free Press and Mercantile Advertiser*, 11 June 1927, p. 11.
7   Time, 25 April 1927.
8   From a tribute given by Roy Chadwick following Bert Hinkler's death.
9   *Time*, 30 May 1927.
10 *Flight*, 2 June 1927.
11 Bert Hinkler in a letter to his parents from Manchester, 14 July 1927.

12 From the collection of the Hinkler Hall of Aviation, Bundaberg.

13 Bert Hinkler, 'Twelve hundred miles non-stop', *Airways*, October 1927.

14 *Bundaberg Daily News and Mail*, 2 March 1928, p. 2.

CHAPTER 19

1 As quoted in the *Mercury* (Hobart), 17 November 1927, p. 7.

2 *Bundaberg News and Mail*, 14 October 1927.

3 Ralph Barker *Verdict on a lost flyer: the story of Bill Lancaster* G.G. Harrap, 1969.

4 *Brisbane Courier*, 17 October 1927, p. 15.

5 *Examiner* (Launceston), 21 October 1927, p. 7.

6 *Brisbane Courier*, 19 September 1927, p. 15.

7 *Argus* (Melbourne), 5 November 1927.

8 *Argus* (Melbourne), 18 November 1927, p. 15.

9 'Bert Hinkler's nightmare flight', *Everybody's* (magazine), 21 September 1966.

10 *Argus* (Melbourne), 21 November 1927, p. 17.

11 *Register* (Adelaide), 21 November 1927, p. 9.

12 *Examiner* (Launceston), 21 March 1928, p. 7.

13 *Examiner* (Launceston), 21 March 1928, p. 7.

14 *Examiner* (Launceston), 21 March 1928, p. 7.

15 *Examiner* (Launceston), 21 March 1928, p. 7.

16 *Examiner* (Launceston), 21 March 1928, p. 7.

17 *Examiner* (Launceston), 21 March 1928, p. 7.

18 *Examiner* (Launceston), 21 March 1928, p. 7.

CHAPTER 20

1 *Examiner* (Launceston), 21 March 1928, p. 7.

2 *Examiner* (Launceston), 26 March 1928, p. 9.

3 *Airways*, March 1928.

4 *Bundaberg Daily News and Mail*, 9 February 1928, p. 5.

5 *Aircraft*, 31 March 1928 p.431; *Aircraft* April-May 1928 p. 518; *Examiner* (Launceston) 22 March 1928, p. 7.

6 *Herald* (Melbourne), 17 February 1928.

7 'Love is in the air', *Sunday Times*, 29 February 2004.

8 There are actually 105 islands in the chain.

9 *Daily Telegraph Pictorial*, Sydney, 23 February 1928.

CHAPTER 21

1   *Advertiser* (Adelaide), 22 May 1930, p. 15.
2   *Bundaberg News and Mail*, 24 February 1928, p. 5.
3   *Canberra Times* 24 February 1928 p.1
4   *Queenslander* (Brisbane), 1 March 1928, p. 17.
5   *Morning Bulletin* (Rockhampton), 6 February 1928, p. 9.
6   *Northern Territory Times* (Darwin), 24 February 1928, p. 2.
7   *Bundaberg News and Mail*, 27 February 1928, p. 2.
8   Forde became Prime Minister of Australia on 6 July 1945 following the death of John Curtin and was replaced in the office by Ben Chifley seven days later.
9   *Northern Standard* (Darwin), 24 February 1928.
10 *Daily Telegraph Pictorial*, 24 February 1928, p. 2.
11 *Daily Telegraph Pictorial*, 25 February 1928, p. 2.
12 *Register* (Adelaide), 25 February 1928, p. 11.
13 The organisation was initially known as the Aerial Medical Service.
14 Bettiens, *Hinkler.*
15 *Argus* (Melbourne), 27 February 1928, p. 15.
16 *Brisbane Courier*, 27 February 1928, p. 18.
17 Ron Hinkler, interview with author, Hinkler Hall of Aviation, 25 August 2010.
18 *Daily Express*, 25 February 1928, p. 8.

CHAPTER 22

1   Mackenzie, *Solo.*
2   *Bundaberg News and Mail*, 2 March 1928, p. 2.
3   *Flight*, 23 February 1928.
4   *Lethbridge Herald*, 24 February 1928.
5   *Brisbane Courier*, 5 March 1928, p. 15.
6   Ron Hinkler, interview with author, Hinkler Hall of Aviation, 25 August 2010.
7   *Brisbane Courier*, 2 March 1928, p. 13.
8   Terry Gwynn-Jones, 'Lores Bonney: Australian Female Pilot', *Aviation History*, May 2000.
9   *Courier-Mail* (Brisbane), 2 February 1991.
10 *Brisbane Courier*, 10 March 1928, p. 21.
11 *Sydney Morning Herald*, 12 March 1928, p. 12.
12 *Barrier Miner* (Broken Hill, NSW), 13 March 1928.
13 *Canberra Times*, 17 March 1928, p. 1.
14 *Brisbane Courier*, 15 March 1928, p. 13.
15 *Mail* (Adelaide), 24 March 1928, p. 8.

16 *West Australian* (Perth), 2 April 1928, p. 17.

17 *Advertiser* (Adelaide), 4 April 1928, p. 14.

18 *Mercury* (Hobart), 5 April 1928.

19 Mackenzie, *Solo*.

20 Mackenzie, *Solo*.

21 *Advertiser* (Adelaide), 9 December 1931, p. 15.

22 *Sydney Morning Herald*, 8 June 1928, p. 12.

23 Brenda Haugen *Amelia Earhart: Legendary Aviator*. Compass Point Books, 2007

24 *Bundaberg News and Mail*, 25 June 1928.

25 The Register (Adelaide) 27 August 1928, p.8.

26 Western Argus (Kalgoorlie) 25 September 1928, p. 32.

CHAPTER 23

1 R.H. McIntosh & J.S.S. Spry-Leverton, *All-weather Mac*, Macdonald & Co., 1963.

2 *Register News-Pictorial* (Adelaide), 14 January 1929, p. 12.

3 *Sydney Morning Herald*, 5 December 1928, p. 22.

4 *Sydney Morning Herald*, 30 October 1928, p. 11.

5 *Sydney Morning Herald*, 30 October 1928, p. 11.

6 *Argus* (Melbourne), 30 November 1928, p. 7.

7 Bert Hinkler in a letter to his mother from *Mon Repos,* Thornhill Park, Southampton, 10 December 1928

8 *Canberra Times*, 20 December 1928, p. 1.

9 *Mercury* (Hobart), 22 February 1929, p. 7.

10 *Northern Standard* (Darwin), 14 May 1929, p. 2.

11 *New York Times*, 21 June 1929.

12 *Morning Bulletin* (Rockhampton), 20 July 1929, p. 8.

13 Bert Hinkler in a letter to his mother from *Mon Repos*, 28 August 1929

14 The Gympie-born Sunderland was three years older than Bert and a leading sports administrator and journalist. He was secretary of the Queensland Rugby League, Queensland Cricket Association, Queensland Amateur Boxing Association and Queensland Wrestling Union. He was also a Queensland league selector and coach, a member of the Australian Rugby League Board of Control, manager on three Kangaroo tours of England and manager of the Wigan Rugby League Club. He covered rugby league for radio and newspapers in Australia and England.

15 Brisbane Courier 4 March 1930, p. 5.

16 *Register News-Pictorial* (Adelaide), 15 July 1930, p. 3.

17 *Hampshire Advertiser and Southampton Times*, 20 September 1930.

18 Dorothy Hook remarried only a few months after Eric's death, to Reginald Hopper, a retired dentist, who had written a letter of sympathy to her.

19 *Townsville Daily Bulletin*, 19 July 1930, p 4.

20 Bert Hinkler to his business partner Rowland Bound from Hotel Fort Shelby, Detroit, September 18, 1930.

21 *New York Times*, 20 October 1930.

22 *Queenslander* (Brisbane), 30 October 1930, p. 22.

CHAPTER 24

1 *Daily News* (Huntingdon, Pennsylvania), 12 February 1931, p. 1.

2 *Townsville Daily Bulletin*, 23 February 1931, p. 5.

3 *Sydney Morning Herald*, 1 May 1931, p. 12.

4 *Advertiser and Register* (Adelaide), 8 May 1931, p. 22.

5 *Morning Bulletin* (Rockhampton), 11 May 1931, p. 7.

6 Bettiens, *Hinkler.*

7 Bert Hinkler in a letter to Nance from New York, 25 October 1931.

8 *Time*, 9 November 1931.

9 *Trinidad Guardian*, 11 November 1931.

10 *Mercury* (Hobart), 30 November 1931, p. 7.

11 As quoted in *Mercury* (Hobart) 10 December 1931, p.9

12 *Brisbane Courier*, 9 December 1931, p. 13.

13 *Flight*, 25 December 1931.

14 *Sydney Morning Herald*, 19 December 1931.

15 *Sydney Morning Herald*, 21 December 1931.

16 *Barrier Miner* (Broken Hill), 27 January 1932, p. 1.

17 *Advertiser* (Adelaide), 10 August 1932, p. 9.

18 *Sydney Morning Herald*, 19 August 1932, p. 9.

19 *Barrier Miner* (Broken Hill), 5 November 1932, p. 3.

CHAPTER 25

1 *Cairns Post* (Queensland), 16 February 1933, p. 7.

CHAPTER 26

1 *Morning Bulletin* (Rockhampton), 10 January 1933, p. 7.

2 *Sydney Morning Herald*, 11 January 1933, p. 13.

3 *Morning Bulletin* (Rockhampton), 19 January 1933, p. 7.

4 *Brisbane Courier*, 25 January 1933, p. 11.

5   Wixted, *The Last Flight of Bert Hinkler*.
6   *Brisbane Courier*, 29 March 1933, p. 17.
7   *Western Argus* (Kalgoorlie), 9 May 1933, p. 27.
8   *Townsville Daily Bulletin*, 2 May 1933, p. 4.
9   *Sydney Morning Herald*, 1 May 1933, p. 9.
10 *Morning Bulletin* (Rockhampton), 1 May 1933, p. 7.

CHAPTER 27

1   *Courier-Mail* (Brisbane), 9 September 1933, p. 12.
2   *Cairns Post*, 19 December 1933, p. 7.
3   The Gipsy engine was salvaged and used in a Genairco aircraft for some time before being sold in Brisbane in 1948 for £25 for use in a Gipsy Moth.
4   *Advertiser* (Adelaide), 16 November 1934, p. 21.
5   From the collection of the Hinkler Hall of Aviation, Bundaberg.
6   *Queenslander* (Brisbane), 28 May 1936, p. 20.
7   *Courier-Mail* (Brisbane), 18 June 1936, p. 13.
8   *Courier-Mail* (Brisbane), 16 March 1953, p. 2.
9   Lex Rowland, interview with author, Hinkler Hall of Aviation, 25 August 2010.
10 *Courier-Mail (Brisbane)*, 1 February 1985, p.15
11 Katherine Hinkler in a letter to Frances Hinkler, from Long Island, New York, 18 June, 1939.

ACKNOWLEDGMENTS

The life of Bert Hinkler has intrigued me since the early 1970s when I was a small boy on a school trip to the old Queensland Museum, then situated in the Brisbane suburb of Bowen Hills. I was terrified of heights back then and the sight of a tiny silver biplane hanging from the lofty roof of that cavernous building sent a shiver down my spine. When I was told that a man had flown in that little machine all the way from England, alone and unassisted, through storms and over mountains and deserts, jungles and oceans, I realised that Queensland had produced a hero to rival the most daring in the world.

Bert Hinkler was an enigma, a man who lived much of his adult life in the international spotlight but who always kept his private secrets very close to his chest. I travelled the world researching his life and times — from Bundaberg, where he was born, to Southampton and London where he lived, to the Pratomagno Mountains where he died, and to Florence where he was awarded a State funeral by Benito Mussolini as one of the great aviators of history.

Along the way so many people gave of their time and resources to help me and I am eternally grateful. This book would not have been possible without the unstinting generosity of the Hinkler Hall of Aviation in Bundaberg and to the team leader there, Colleen Foglia. Colleen provided so much assistance in shining a light on all areas of the public and private life of an extraordinary adventurer.

Thanks also to Lex Rowland, the president of the Hinkler House Memorial Museum and probably the best friend Bert Hinkler ever had. Lex has spent much of life preserving the personal effects and memories of Bundaberg's favourite son and national treasure.

Thank you also to Carolyn Mitchell from the Hinkler Museum and to Bundaberg mayor Lorraine Pyefinch, who realised the importance of Bert Hinkler's story and to Lang and Bev Kidby, Australia's intrepid husband and wife adventurers who recreated Bert's 1928 England to Australia flight seventy years later.

I would also like to thank Bert Hinkler's nephew Ron Hinkler and Ron's sister-in-law Margaret Hinkler for their recollections and insights. At 90, Ron was still able to provide first hand accounts of Bert's many adventures in Bundaberg in 1928. Thanks also to Nance Hinkler's granddaughter Paddy Canavan for providing so much of Bert's correspondence and personal effects to the Hinkler Museum.

Tom Laffan, the grandson of Charlie Laffan and Carolynn Lingard, the granddaughter of Bert's great friend Dr Otto 'Joe' Grüter also gave their recollections and Mayva Burckley, the greatniece of Katherine Hinkler, remembered her Aunt Kathy as a quiet, shy and gracious old lady living quietly in New York.

Kevin Lindeberg, who did so much to preserve the memory of Bert Hinkler, generously provided advice on Bert's final flight. Kevin helped ensure Bert's Southampton home, Mon Repos, was saved from demolition and in 1974 was instrumental in presenting medals to the Italian men who had found Bert's body and treated him with such respect. All contributed greatly to Bert's memory as did Robyn Henry, a descendant by marriage of Bert Hinkler's German grandmother Anna Volk. I am indebted to Kathy Buckley and Meg Lloyd at the Queensland Museum, Marjorie Bennett and Josie Huang at Brisbane's Oxley Library, Lucy Nuttall from the National Library of Australia, the staff of the State Library of New South Wales, the Oakey Army Air Base, the RAAF Museum at Point Cook, the RAAF Museum at Williamtown, the Smithsonian Institution in Washington DC and the Science Museum in London.

Thanks also to Doug Ring for his fact-finding mission in Florence and to editor Michael Crutcher, David Hele, Selina Steele and Gwen McLachlan from the *Courier-Mail*.

Mike Colman, one of Australia's finest writers, provided invaluable assistance in preparing my manuscript and my colleagues Arthur Stanley, Kevin McDonald and Ray Wheatley were always there with advice and encouragement. Thanks especially to Karen Penning from HarperCollins whose enthusiasm for the project saw this biography take wing, to Amruta Slee for seeing it safely through to its final destination and to editors Rochelle Fernandez and Cathryn Game for the outstanding job they did with the text. I also owe a great debt of thanks to other authors who previously wrote about Bert — Ted Wixted, Roy Mackenzie and Wing Commander Roy Bettiens.

And finally I owe the biggest debt of gratitude to Squadron Leader Herbert John Louis Hinkler AFC, DSM and the intrepid men and women like him whose passion for aviation saw them realise a shared dream. Through their daring and tenacity they made air travel cheap, reliable and as commonplace as the motorcar.